FLORENTINE CODEX

Florentine Codex

General History of the Things of New Spain

FRAY BERNARDINO DE SAHAGUN

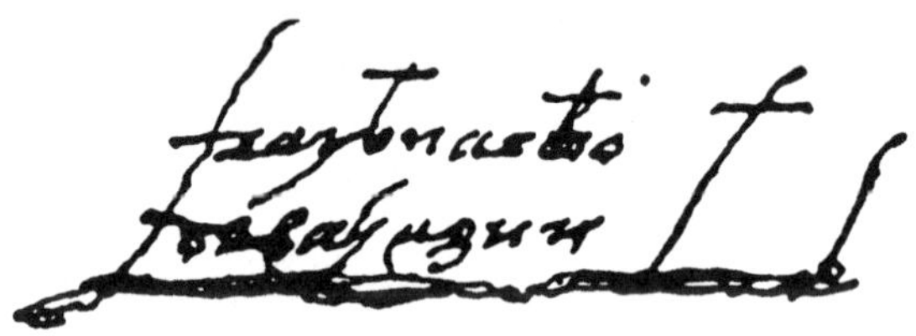

Book 4 – The Soothsayers
and
Book 5 – The Omens

Translated from the Aztec into English, with notes and illustrations

By

Charles E. Dibble
University of Utah

Arthur J. O. Anderson
School of American Research

IN THIRTEEN PARTS

PARTS V AND VI

*Chapter heading designs are from the Codex
except a few in Book IV taken from the Real Palacio MS*

Published by
The School of American Research and The University of Utah

Monographs of The School of American Research and Museum of New Mexico
Santa Fe, New Mexico

Number 14, Parts V and VI 1979

Second edition, revised

First paperback edition 2012

ISBN: 978-1-60781-160-2 (BOOKS 4 & 5)
ISBN: 978-1-60781-192-3 (SET)

Published and distributed by
The University of Utah Press
Salt Lake City, Utah

CONTENTS

FOURTH BOOK, WHICH TELLETH OF THE BOOK OF DAYS WHICH THE MEXICANS HANDED DOWN

CONTENTS

FIFTH BOOK, IN WHICH ARE TOLD THE OMENS IN WHICH THE MEXICANS BELIEVED

LIST OF ILLUSTRATIONS

BOOK IV

following page 126

LIST OF ILLUSTRATIONS

BOOK V

BOOK FOUR--THE SOOTHSAYERS

Comiença el libro
quarto, de la astro
logia Judicia
ria, o arte adi
ujnatoria
Indiana.

De la Arte Adivinatoria

FOURTH BOOK, WHICH TELLETH OF THE BOOK OF DAYS WHICH THE MEXICANS HANDED DOWN. THIS WAS IN ORDER THAT THE READERS OF THE DAY SIGNS[1] MIGHT STUDY THE GOOD AND EVIL DAYS. IN IT WERE SET FORTH THE DAY SIGNS HERE RECOUNTED, AND HOW THOSE WOULD FARE WHO WERE BORN ON THEM. AND THIS BOOK OF DAYS IS MORE CORRECTLY CALLED SORCERY, FOR IT BELONGED TO THE SORCERERS.

INJC NAVI AMUXTLI: YTECHPA TLATOA, IN TONALAMATL, IN QUJTITLANJA MEXICA: IEHOATL INJC QUJTTAIA TONALPOUHQUE, IN QUALLI CEMJLHUJTL, IOAN AMO QUALLI: YN JPAN MONEZCAIOTITIUH TONALLI, IN NJCAN MOTENEOA: AUH IN QUENAMJQUE IEZQUE IN JPAN TLACATIA. AUH IN, Y, TONALAMATL OC CENCA IE MELAOAC, IC MOTOCAIOTIZ, NAOALLOTL, CA NAOALTI INTECH POVIA.

First Chapter, which telleth of the first sign, which was named One Crocodile, and of the good fortune which they merited who were born then — men or women. These same destroyed and ruined it because of their negligence.[2]

Injc ce capitulo, itechpa tlatoa, injc centetl machiotl: in jtoca ce cipactli, ioan in qualli tonalli in qujmâceoaia, in vncan tlacatia, in toqujchti, in cioa: çan iehoantin qujpoloaia, qujmotlacalhujaia, yn jpampa in jntlatziviliz.

Here beginneth the count of each day. Just as each week was reckoned, so each of the thirteen-day periods went taking its place until one year had passed. Once more at its start began the count of each day.

The first day count was named One Crocodile.[3] It was the very beginning and precise starting point of all the day counts, whereby began, continued, and came to an end the year [of 260 days].[4]

Nican peoa in cecemjlhujtlapoalli in iuhquj cecentetl semana ic mopoaia, matlatlaqujlhujtl omeey motlalitiuh, injc otlatocatiuh ce xivitl: Oc ceppa itzintlan oalpeoa in cecemjlhujtl tlapoalli.

Achto tonalpoalli ytoca ce cipactli: vel ipeuhca, vel itzin in cemjlhujtlapoalli, ynic vmpeuhtiuh, ôtlatocatiuh: ioan injc ontlantiuh ce xivitl.

---

1. Cf. Bernardino de Sahagún: *Historia general de las cosas de Nueva España* (Angel María Garibay K., ed.; México: Editorial Porrúa, S. A., 1956; hereafter referred to as Garibay ed.), Vol. IV, p. 359 (*Tonalpouhqui*); also Horacio Carochi: *Arte de la lengua mexicana* (México: Imprenta del Museo Nacional, 1892), pp. 423 ff., where in conjugation of the verb *poa,* the preferred meaning is "to read." Alonso de Molina: *Vocabulario de la lengua mexicana* (Julio Platzmann, ed.; Leipzig: B. G. Teubner, 1880), and Rémi Siméon: *Dictionnaire de la langue nahuatl ou mexicaine* (Paris: Imprimerie Nationale, 1885), give the meanings "to read," "to relate," etc., besides "to count." See also Miguel León Portilla: *La filosofía náhuatl estudiada en sus fuentes* (México: Instituto Indigenista Interamericano, 1956), p. 205; on pp. 204 ff. there is a discussion of the readers and reading of day signs.

2. In Bernardino de Sahagún: *Historia de las cosas de Nueva España* (Francisco del Paso y Troncoso, ed.; Madrid: Hauser y Menet, 1906), Vol. VII (hereafter referred to as *Real Palacio MS*), pp. 280 ff., the text has been divided into the chapters which appear in the *Florentine Codex,* and each one given a descriptive heading, in Spanish and in Sahagún's handwriting. The Aztec heading appears to be a rendition in Nahuatl of Sahagún's Spanish. It will be noted that some of the chapter divisions to be found below appear to be arbitrary.

3. In the "Primeros Memoriales" of the *Real Palacio MS* (Vol. VI of the Paso y Troncoso ed.), pp. 73-74, 107, Sahagún begins the day count with One Dog (*ce itzcuintli*). *Cipactli* is usually translated as crocodile; alligator would perhaps be more correct.

4. *Xiuitl.* Though the term means a year of 365 days, a 260-day ceremonial year is meant.

It became as the leader of this group of thirteen days which belonged with it: Two [Wind],[5] Three House, Four Lizard, Five Serpent, Six Death, Seven Deer, Eight Rabbit, Nine Water, Ten Dog, Eleven Monkey, Twelve Grass, and Thirteen Reed.

Injn matlactetl vmei in tonalli, in iuhquj itlavilanoan muchioa, yn jtech povi: iehoatl in vme acatl, ey calli, navi cuetzpali, macujlli coatl, chiquacen mjqujztli, chicome maçatl, chicuei tochtli, chicunavi atl, matlactli itzcujntli, matlactli oce oçomatli, matlactli vmome malinalli, matlactli omej acatl.

These various days, as it was said, all were good. He who was then born a nobleman, it was stated, would be a lord, a ruler; he would prosper; he would be rich and wealthy. And if a commoner were then born, he would be a brave warrior — a valiant chief, esteemed, honored, and great. He would always eat. And if a woman were then born, she would also prosper and be rich. She would have drink and food available. She would have food for others to eat; she would invite others to feast. She would be respectful. She would be visited by others; she would await them with drink and food, with which to revive and refresh the spirits and bodies of those who lived in misery on earth, who, as they slept so they awoke — the destitute old men and women, and orphans; the forsaken; and all would be realized and come to pass that was undertaken; nothing would fail; of her fatigue and effort, nothing would be in vain. Successful would be her dealings around the market place, in the place of business; it was as if it would sprinkle, shower, and rain her wares upon her.

In jzqujtetl in tonalli: iuh mjtoaia, muchi qualli: in aqujn ipan tlacatia pilli; mjtoaia tecutiz, tlatocatiz, motlacamatiz, mocujltonoz, motlamachtiz: Auh intla maceoalli ipan tlacatia, oqujchtiz, tiacauhtiz, maviztiz, panvetziz, motleiotiz, onca qujquanj iez: auh intla çioatl ipan tlacati, no motlacamatiz, mocujltonoz, oniez in qujz, in qujquaz, tetlaqualtiz, tecoanotzaz, tetlacamatiz, ipan calacoaz, qujtechieltiz in atl, in tlaqualli: ypal ihiiocujoaz, ypal ceviz in jiollo, in jnacaio, in tlaihiiovitinemj tlalticpac, in iuhquj cochi, in iuhquj meoa, in jcnoveve, yn jcnoilama, in jcnopiltzintli, in tlacnocaoalli: yoan muchi neltiz, muchi onieoatiz, in tlein maailia, atle nenqujçaz, in jçiaviz, yn jtlapaliviz, atle nenvetziz, vel motitianqujz in tianquiznaoac, in nentlamachoian: iuhqujn pipixaviz, ipan tepeviz, ipan tzetzeliviz in jtiamjc.

And furthermore they said that even though favorable was the day sign on which he had been born, if he did not strictly perform his penances, if he took not good thought, if he did not accept the reprimands and punishment meted out to him, the punishment with which he was punished and the correction with which he was corrected, the exhortations of the old men and the old women; if he became bad and perverse and followed not the way of righteousness, succeeded in nothing, and entirely by his own acts brought himself to ruin, despised himself, brought harm to himself, failed, lost through his own neglect, gave up, and endangered that which might be his good fortune, — his reward, and his lot: then he tarnished, polluted, and ruined with debauchery his birthright. Thus he found and merited affliction. As was the sleep, so was the awakening.[6] Nowhere was he content, nowhere

Auh no yoã quitoaia: ma nel ivi in qualli itonal ipan otlacat, intlacamo vellamaceoa, intlacamo vel monotza, intlacamo qujcuj, intlacamo itech qujpachoa, in atl cecec, in tzitzicaztli, yn inonotzaloca, in izcaliloca, in veuetlatolli, yn jlamatlatolli, in çan tlaueliloti, tlavelilocati, in çan âie vtli qujtoca, atle onqujça, çan ynevian mopopoloa, motelchioa, mjxpopoiomjctia, mĵiecoa, conmjxcaoaltia conmocavilia, qujmjtlacalhuja, yn jmâceoal iezquja, yn itonal, yn jnemac, qujteuhiotia, qujtlaçollotia, qujtlaçolmjctia yn itlacatiliz: ic cococ, teupouhquj qujmottitia, qujmomaçevia, in iuhquj cochcaiotl, iuhquj neuhcaiotl, acan avia, acan vellamati, ompa onqujça in qujtzaqua tlalticpac netolinjliztli: ca nel omoneviiavi, yn jpampa yn jtlauelilocaio, inj atle ipan tlattaliz, yn iaquentlattaliz, yn jtlaaujlmachiliz, aiac oconcaujli, ca ixcoian ynevian oqujmochichivili in toneviztli, in chichinaqujztli, ic telchioalo, aoc tle ipan itto, aoc ac

5. *Ome acatl* has been corrected to read *ome ecatl* in the *Real Palacio MS*, p. 280.

6. *In iuhquj cochcaiotl, iuhquj neuhcaiotl*: Carochi, *op. cit.*, pp. 451, 456, favors the meaning of a general sustenance (*nocochca noneuhca*; *cochcayotl, neuhcayotl*), though his examples do not parallel the phrasing here found. Possibly the rendering should be: "As for sustenance, nowhere was he content."

happy. He was destitute; on earth misery engulfed him. For verily he brought it on himself — because of his wickedness, disregard, shamelessness, and neglect. No one bequeathed it to him, for by his own will and of his own fault he brought unto himself injury, torment, and pain. Hence he was despised and disregarded. No one any longer obeyed him; no one became his friend; he stood by himself. No one took account of his personality. Everywhere he was hated; nowhere was he liked; nowhere did he give pleasure. But he was regarded as a thing, and looked at, for now he was a vagabond, proscribed, completely outlawed; he was on the outside, lingering on the outskirts; impudent and shameless. He went about haughty[7] and drunk. For truly he was abandoned to evil and feared. His side was sore; his head ached — it was in pain — so that he was incorrigible, suffering, and dejected. For he was full of evil — so perverse was he.

And of anyone who had gained merit and reward being then born, his fathers and mothers said: "Upon a good day sign hath he been born and created and come forth on earth; he hath arrived upon the earth on [the day sign] One Crocodile. Let him be bathed." [8]

Whereupon they gave him a name. They called him Cipac. Or else, they gave him the name of another one of his grandparents. Etc.

And, on the other hand, if it were the wish [of the parents], perchance they passed over the days; perchance they settled upon still another day for him to be bathed. For One Crocodile bore with it all favorable day signs.

And if it were a man who was born, when they bathed him they adorned for him a small shield, upon which they put four small arrows. And to it they bound his umbilical cord. They entrusted it to and sent it in the charge of brave chieftains, who left it at the battlefield. Right there where they fought, where there was fierce battle, at the crossing of the waters, they buried it.

And if it were a woman, when they bathed her, they put into the vessel in which she was bathed, the large earthen bathing vessel, her spindle, her cotton,

qujtlacamati, aiac icnjuh qujchioa, yioca quetzalo, aoc ac iiel qujtta, novian tlaelitto, âcan velitolo, âcan tlapaqujltia, ça tlatto, ça itto, ca ie tlaztlacolli, ie tlaîtolli, ie centlaîtolli, ie tetenco câca, ie tetenco pipilcac, ie tepan onoc: injc âquen tlatta, injc moquatlaztinemj, mjvintitinemj, ca nel otlauelcaoaloc, otlaellelaxiti, otlaxillãquauhtili, otlatzonteconquauhtili, otlatzonquauhtili inic auel monotza, ca iiolaçic, iiellelaçic, qujmaxilti, ynjc tlaueliloc.

Auh in aca vel mâceoale, ilhujle, ipan otlacat: njman qujtoaia in jtahoan, in jnaoan, ca qualli tonalli in jpan otlacat, oiecoc, otlalticpacqujz, omotlalticpacqujxti, ce cipactli: ma njman malti,

ic qujtocamacaia, ic qujnotzaia, cipac: anoço itla oc centlamantli, icolhoan intoca in qujmacaia, etc.:

auh tel çan teiollotlama; in açoc concholoItizque, açoc contlalizque oc centetl tonalli, ipan maltiz: ca ie qujcenvica in ce cipactli, ca muchi qualli tonalli.

Auh intla oqujchtli otlacat: in jquac caltiaia, chimaltontli qujchichiviliaia, ipã temj navi mjtotonti: auh itech qujlpiaia in jxic, intech qujcaoaia, intech qujpiloaia in tiacaoan, iaopan concaoaia: vel oncan in necalioa, in tlaiecolo, yn japaniocan contocaia.

Auh intla çioatl otlacat: ynjc caltiaia imalac, ichcauh, itzaoalcax, ioan ipopouh, iochpanoaz ipan contemaia yn jnealtilcax, in jnealtilapaz: yc qujnextiaia,

7. Cf. Angel María Garibay K.: "Paralipómenos de Sahagún," *Tlalocan,* II, 3 (1947), pp. 239 and 247 (n. 61), where *timoquatlaztinemi* is translated *tienes la cabeza destornillada.*

8. The corresponding Spanish text usually uses "baptize" for *maltia,* etc.; see however, Ch. 37, *infra* (*tlaquaatequia,* etc.).

her spinning bowl, her sweeper, and her broom. Thus they showed that the girl was one who went nowhere; only the house was her abode. Hence, near the grinding stone, at the edge of the hearth, they buried her umbilical cord.

in âcampa ianj cioatzintli, çan cali ichan: ic çan metlatitlan, tlecujlnacazco contocaia yn jxic.

And this count of days — so was it claimed — was an invention of the two called and named Oxomoco and Cipactonal, who gave it to the people. Oxomoco they painted as a woman, and Cipactonal [as] a man. They who were readers of day signs embellished their book of days with their representations, which they placed in the middle when they painted them. For it was so said that there they became lords of all the day count.

Auh inin tonalpoalli, iuh mjtoaia: iehoan intlanextil, iehoan qujtemacaque, in vmentin teneoalo, intoca Oxomoco, ioan cipactonal: in Oxomoco cioatl inic qujcujloaia: auh in Cipactonal oqujchtli: in tonalpouhque catca yn jntonalamauh qujiollotiaia, yn jmjxiptla ynepantla qujntlaliaia, injc qujcujcujloaia: ca iuh mjtoaia: vncan tlatoque muchioa yn jpan ixqujch tonalpoalli.

Second Chapter, which telleth of the second [day] sign, which was named One Ocelot, and which was not a good day sign for those who were born on it — men and women — to obtain reward; but, nevertheless, he who showed prudence might well be saved through forethought; and of those born on [this day sign] almost all became slaves.

The second day sign which set in was named One Ocelot. When it set in, it was said to be an evil day sign, one of fierce beasts.

It bore with it and presided over all its series[1] of thirteen, which belonged to it: Two Eagle, Three Vulture, Four Motion, Five Flint Knife, Six Rain, Seven Flower, Eight Crocodile, Nine Wind, Ten House, Eleven Lizard, Twelve Serpent, and Thirteen Death.

And those who were then born, whether nobleman or commoner, so it was said, would die in war, be taken away, abandoned, imprisoned, seized. And all bad was his lot; misery befell him. He only wallowed in evil and he was covered with filth. Nowhere had he good repute. He committed adultery, was an adulterer, adulterous, one who seized other skirts and blouses, one who remained on female navels.

And even though one such became a valiant chieftain, brave, a taker of captives, indeed he sold and yielded himself to slavery; he became someone's digging stick and tump line; he yielded to the digging stick and tump line. So it was said: "Thus was his day sign; thus was his life. On such a day was he born; thus was his birthright."

But [if] he emerged great, some brave chieftain, he was not sold [but] lived on earth in tranquillity: one who was not lazy; diligent and careful, vigilant, a receiver of [ritual] benefits, a doer of penances, one who fasted and bled himself; who swept, shook out clothing, gathered up rubbish, laid fires, and at night held vigil, rose in vigor, and was circumspect; who

Injc vme capitulo: itechpa tlatoa, injc vntetl machivtl, in jtoca ce ocelutl: ioan in amo qualli tonalli, in qujmomâceviaia in aqujque ipan tlacatia, in toqujchti, in cioa: auh tel in jca innezcaliliz, in vel nenotzalizpatia: auh in aqujque in jpan tlacatia, y, achi muchintin tlatlacoti muchioaia.

Injc ome moquetza tonalli: ytoca ce oçelutl. In jquac in moquetza, mjtoaia amo qualli tonalli, tequantonalli,

qujcenvica, qujcentlaça, yn itlavilan matlactli vmei, in jtech povi, iehoantin, y, vme quauhtli, ei cozcaquauhtli, navi olin, macujlli tecpatl, chiquaçen qujavitl, chicome xochitl, chicuey cipactli, chicunavi hecatl, matlactli calli, matlactli oce, cuetzpali, matlactli vmome coatl, matlactli vmei mjqujztli:

auh in aqujque ipan tlacatia, y, in aço pilli, anoço maceoalli: iuh mjtoa iaomjquja, vicoia, caoaloia, calaqujloia, axioaia, ioan muchi amo qualli in jmâceoal, in jcnopil muchioaia, çan teuhtli, tlaçolli, ic mjlacatzotinemj, teuhtli tlaçolli cololotinemj: acan tlacaitolo, tetlaxima, tepan iauh, tetlan aaquj, cueitl, vipilli tepan cana, icioaxic ietinemj.

Auh intlanel aca tiacauh, oquichtli, tlamanj muchioaia, vel monamacaia, motlacocaoaia, tevic, temecapal muchioaia, victli, mecapalli qujmottitiaia, iuh mjtoaia: ca iuhquj itonal, iuhquj iol, iuhquj ipan tlacat, iuhquj itlacatiliz:

auh çã vei qujçaia in aca tiacauh, amo monamacaia, in jvian oalnemja tlalticpac: iehoatl in amo tlatziuhquj, in jeel, in tlamocujtlavianj, in cochiçanj, in tlâcelianj, in tlamaceoanj, in moçaoanj, in mjçonj, in tlachpananj, in tlatzetzeloanj, in tlacujcujnj, in tletlalianj, in ioalli qujtztoc, in popoxiuhteoa, in mocujtivetzi, in amo moteteca, in amo moxiccaoa, in

1. The linguistic concept illustrated in this sentence by the use of *quicenvica* and *itlavilan* presents a semantic problem difficult to put into English. Therefore in this Book we generally translate *vica* as "bear with it," and *itlavilan,* or *itlavilanoan,* as "its series," or companions, or group.

was chaste and conscientious; who was audacious, who saved all, who sought his sustenance; who planned, sought, and watched for that which might alleviate, for that which he might lay hand on in the near future, and for what he might offer his children; for what might be obtained, and what he could quickly seize if sickness and misfortune came.

Thus, everywhere he watched for, considered, and sought whatsoever he might use as merchandise, whatsoever his manner of wares might be; whatsoever he might live by, by which he might increase and augment his goods and his gains.

And this one emerged, and rose to honor, if he deliberated well, and was attentive, not resentful of criticism, nor lazy. The counsel with which he was counseled and the rearing with which he was reared took effect; he seized and held fast to it. And if he was made fun of, he took no revenge; he made no reprisals. He returned nothing in kind.

And if a woman were then born, it likewise befell her as hath been said and told above. If a noblewoman was an adulteress, her head was crushed between two stones so that she died. And only in misery and affliction was she given to dwell. She encountered misery and want. Nowhere on earth was her face radiant; nowhere on earth was she [of any account]; nowhere was she regarded; nowhere did she hold a husband. Thus was it stated: "Just so is her nature; so is her life; so her birthright; and so her day sign. Thus, on such [a day], was she bathed; at such a time was she born. Monstrous was her day sign; a wild beast was she; hers was the day of the wild beast, etc."

And they venerated Four Motion as a day sign. Thus did they say, that it was the day sign of the sun. Moctezuma paid great honor to it. When it was this day, when Four Motion set in, they slew quail and offered incense before the image of the sun; they placed on it what was known as the spreading red arara feather device. And at noon captives died and were slain [as sacrifices].

And for him who was then born, no [true sign] appeared. In two ways might it fall. They said that if it were a man, he might either take captives or die in war. As they said, "With this the sun is nourished." Hence everyone did penances when it was this sign. At this time all came together from all parts; none remained or did otherwise. Verily, everyone — men, women, children — cut their ears and

vmpilcatoc, in jxqujch caana, in qujtemoa in jcochca, yn jneuhca, in qujlnamjquj, in conjttilia, in contlachielia, tle itech vmpatiz, tle itech ontlaanaz in macujl, in matlac, tlê qujmonmacaz in jpilhoan, çan onmaçoaz, tlê concujtivetziz in ooalla cocoliztli icnoiotl:

ic noviiampa mjxtia tlanemjlia, qujtemoa, in tlein qujmonanauhtiz, in catleoatl inanauh vmmuchioaz, in tlein vel ic onnemjz, ic onmacoquetzaz, ic ontlapiujaz itlatquj icnopillouh.

Ioan iehoatl qujçaia, panvetzia, in vel monotza, in tlacacquj, in amo qujquammati, qujtemati in onotzaloca, izcaliloca, içan itech qujpachoa, içan qujmacuj, qujmapiquj: auh intla ica necacaiaoalo, amo qujtecuepiliaia, amo qujcuepcaiotia, atle ic qujlochtia.

Auh intla çioatl ipan otlacat: no iuhquj ipan muchioaia, in tlacpac omjto, omoteneuh: intla cioapilli tetlãximaia, quatepipitzinjloia injc mjquja: auh çan icnoiotica, cococaiotica, in monenemjtiaia, icnoiotl, netolinjliztli qujtztinemj, âcan ixtona in tlalticpac, âcan tlalticpac ca, âcan motztica, âcan vel oqujchpia: ic mjtoaia, ca njman iuh qujz, iuhquj iioliliz, iuhquj itlacatiliz, iuhquj itonal, iuhquj ipan malti, iuhcan tlacat, âtlacacemelle in jtonal, ca tequanj, tequantonale. Etc.

Auh in naolin qujtonaltiaia: iuh qujtoaia, itonal in tonatiuh, cenca qujmaviztiliaia in Motecuçuma: yn jquac, y, moquetzaia naolin, tlacotonaia, tlenamacaia, yn ixpan ixiptla tonatiuh, qujtlaliaia itoca cueçaltonameiotl: auh in nepantla tonatiuh, mjquja, mjctiloia, in mamalti:

auh in aqujn ipan tlacatia, atle vel inezca, vme vitz qujtoa. Yntla oqujchtli aço tlamaz, anoço iaomjqujz: in iuh qujtoaia, ca ica mozcaltia in tonatiuh, ic muchi tlacatl tlamaceoaia. yn jquac, y in vncã, y, cenvetzi, ipanoca, aiac mocaoa, aiac ixcavi, vel mochi tlacatl in oqujchtli, in çioatl, im piltzintli, monacaztequia, mjçoia, mjtoaia: ic izcaltilo in tonatiuh.

drew blood. It was said: "Thus was the sun nourished."

And Seven Flower was said [to be] good and bad. As a good [sign], in certain places the scribes paid it honor and were devoted to it. They set up its image and made offerings to it. Also those women who were embroiderers and cotton thread workers first fasted for eighty days; some fasted for forty or twenty days, when penance was done. Thus they requested of it that what they undertook might be well done; [that] their embroidery or design might be a work of art well fabricated and well painted. All therefore offered incense and slew quail; and all bathed and sprinkled themselves with water, when [the fasting] had been lifted. Then the feast of the day sign, Seven Flower, was celebrated.

And they said when it was not a good [day sign], that if some embroiderer broke her fasting — it was said — then she merited for herself infamy and an ill name. Thus she could only live in vice and become a harlot. For it was said the embroiderers lived in great vice and became terrible whores.

It was said the one who was their goddess, named Xochiquetzal, made sport of and mocked her. And she gave and thus scourged her with piles and infections.

But she who did well her penances, who took heed, and so then attained success, was esteemed, and gained honor for herself. In [all] places she was looked to; by the grace of the people, she lived well on earth.

Also it was said of this [day sign] that he who was born on it would perform all crafts well: he would be a good craftsman; he would plan well great works; he would constantly be prudent, if he took good heed. But if he did not take good heed, nothing resulted; he deserved nothing. He only merited the infamy with which he was defamed and the mockery with which he was mocked.

And Nine Wind was said to be wholly and entirely evil. As to him who was then born, nothing could be made of his life; so nothing would be retained; he could hold nothing; nothing would be kept; nothing would appear; he could do nothing; he was incapable on earth. He was as one driven by the winds, wandering here and there. He might wish to be something, to be someone: he became only nothing. For truly so was his day sign. He might wish for public esteem — to become a mer-

Auh in chicome xochitl: mjtoaia qualli, ioã âqualli: ynjc qualli ceccan vncã tlamaviztiliaia, motemachiaia, in tlacujloque, qujtlaliaia yxiptla, qujtlamanjliaia: no iehoan in cioa tlâmachchiuhque, icpachiuhque, achtopa qujneçaviliaia, nappoaltica, aca vmpoaltica, cempoaltica in moçaoaia: ic qujtlaitlanjliaia, injc itla vel aizque mĵmatizque, toltecatizque, vellalalizque, vellacujlozque: in jpan intlamach, intlacuilol: ic mochintin tlenamacaia, tlacotonaia: auh mochintin mâaltiaia, maujujxoaia, yn jquac neoalco, in vncan ilhujqujxtililoia, chicome xochitl:

auh injc amo qualli, mitoaia, iquac intla aca tlâmachchiuhquj, yneçaoaliz qujtlacoaia, mjtoa: vncã qujmomacevia avilquizcaiotl, aviltocaitl: injc çã âavilnemjz, âavienjtiz, ca mjtoa, tlaquauh avilnemja, mâaviltiaia in tlamachchiuhque,

qujlmach iehoatl inca mocaiaoaia, qujquequeloaia in inteouh catca, itoca xochiquetzal, ioan qujtemacaia, ic temotlaia, xochiciujztli, palanjliztli:

auh in aqujn vel ontlamaceoa in vel monotza, ca oncã qujçaia, maviztia, momavizçotiaia, cana motztica, vel moietztica tepaltzinco in tp̃c:

no iuhquj ipan mitoaia in aqujn ipan tlacati, ca moch vel qujchioaz in toltecaiotl, vel tôtoltecatiz, tlatlanemjliz, iôiolizmatquj iez, intla uel monotzaz: auh intlacamo vel monotza, atle onqujçaia, atle icnopil, çan iaujlqujzca, iquequeloloca in qujmomaceviaia.

Auh in chicunavi hecatl: mjtoaia, motqujtica, moch centlantica amo qualli: in aqujn ipan tlacati, atle vel muchioa yn jnemjliz, atle vel ic tlaçaloia, atle vel ic tlaana, atle vel ic tlatzicoa, atle ivelnezca, atle veli, atle veliti in tlaticpac, çan iuhqujn ecatocotinemj, avic iatinemj, conmonectia in ma itlati, in ma acati, çan atleti: ca nel iuhquj itonal, conjxtoca, ipan onmjxpoa, in ma pupuchtecati, in manoce cujcujcanjti, teaachti, tetlâtlavicalti, tecâcamanalhuj. Etc. atle veliti, çan tlaqualania, çan nẽia motlatlamotla, mone-

chant, or even a singer, or a page, or a bearer of burdens, or a jester, etc. He was capable of nothing; he only quarrelled. To no purpose did he struggle; in vain did he travail. Even though he became a brave warrior, nowhere was he considered, nowhere admitted. It was said: "No one [needed] the sweat of his brow; no one paid attention to him or sought him out." And although it appeared that thus he gained a livelihood, and something he put aside for himself, he was a failure; like the wind, like the water were his results. Nothing could he retain, nothing could he keep. Unfortunate were his efforts.

nencoa, moquauhtlaça in manel tiacauhti: anocan ompouhquj, âcan onaqujlo, mjtoa: aiac itztzocujtl, aiac ica, aiac qujtemoa: auh intlanel neçi ic motlaiecultia, intlanel itla ic motlâtlamachia aonieoati, çan iuhqujn ehecatl, iuhqujn atl onqujça, atle qujtlaçaloltia, atle qujtlatzicoltia, çan nen vetzi yn jtlapaliviz.

Third Chapter, which telleth of the third sign, named One Deer; and the good fortune which those then born — men or women — merited. And if it were not realized, these lost it through laziness.

In third place set in a day sign, the one [named] One Deer, and it also bore with it thirteen [days]. These are Two Rabbit, and Three Water, Four Dog, Five Monkey, Six Grass, Seven Reed, Eight Ocelot, Nine Eagle, Ten Vulture, Eleven Motion, Twelve Flint Knife, and Thirteen Rain.

Many of these day signs, it was said, were good and of a propitious time. Nevertheless, some mixed and mingled with them, so that they corrupted, as will be told. Here are told their qualities as they went in order.

He who was then born a nobleman, who was of noble lineage,[1] became a ruler and gained fame. Because of him there was drink and food; he rewarded others and bestowed upon and laid before them capes, breech clouts, head bands, lip pendants, and ear plugs.

And if it were only a commoner who was then born, the same likewise befell him. He attained his ends; he succeeded. He lived. He became a brave warrior, a valiant chieftain. He surpassed others; he left them overcome. He did not wish to lose stature. Nowhere did he hang on at the end. Nowhere was he inferior, the younger brother, the child, the blighted one. Proceeding everywhere mature, [like] something well-developed; going first and foremost, at the head, he brought his life to successful fruition. Nowhere did he deal in shameful things; he was ashamed of nothing and ashamed of no one. Nothing deterred him; he did not live in humiliation; nowhere did he turn tail in battle. In nothing did they consider him a woman.

Injc ei capitulo, itechpa tlatoa: injc etetl machiotl, in jtoca ce maçatl: yoan in qualli tonalli, in qujmomaceviaia yn ipan tlacatia, in toqujchti, in cioa: auh intlacamo inpan neltiaia, çan iehoantin in tlatziviliztica qujpoloaia.

Injc expa moquetza tonalli: iehoatl in ce maçatl, no matlactlomej qujvica, iehoatl in vme tochtli, ey atl, navi itzcujntli, macujlli oçomatli, chiquacen malinalli, chicome acatl, chicuei ocelotl, chicunavi quauhtli, matlactli cozcaquauhtli, matlactli oce olin, matlactlomome tecpatl, matlactlomei qujavitl.

In jzqujtetl in tonalli, mjtoaia: qualli, ieccan: auh tel cequj iitla actiuh, itzalan actiuh, injc itlacauhtiuh, in iuh moteneoaz: vncan mjtoa inneneixcaujltoca, injc tecpantivi:

in aqujn ipan tlacati pilli, in tetzon, in teizti, in tetzicueuhca, in tetzicueoallo, in tetlapanca, in techpa qujz, iol, in teujtztzo, in teaoaio, in tetentzon, in teixquamol, in teezço, in tetlapallo, tlatocaiotia, oalmoteniotiaia, ipal atlioaia, ipallaqualoia, tetlauhtiaia, qujtemacaia, tetech qujtlaliaia in tilmatli, in maxtlatl, in tlalpilonj, in teçacatl, in nacochtli:

auh intla çan maceoalli ipan tlacatia, no iuhquj ypan muchioaia, oallacnopilhuiaia, oalqujçaia, oalnemja, oqujchtia, tiacauhtia, tecâcaoaia, teihicaoaia: amo mopatzaoallanj, âcan tlatzimpiloa, âcan tetzacuja, âcan teiccauhti, xocoioti, amo patzactzintli, noviian mochamauhtiuh, tlachamauhtiuh, tachcauh icatiuh, tlaiacatitiuh, panj îcatiuh, conqujxtilitiuh yn jnemjliz, âcan pinaviztlamati, atle qujmamati, aiac qujmamati, atle quitzicololtia, amo pipinonemj, âcan tzinqujzcatlaiecoa, atle qujcioatlamachtia.

1. Andrés de Olmos, in *Grammaire de la langue nahuatl ou mexicaine* (Paris: Imprimerie Nationale, 1875), p. 212, groups most of these terms as synonymous with *"Parientes de algunos que salen de un tronco"*; Sahagún, in "Memoriales con escolios," *Academia de la Historia MS* (Vol. VI of the Paso y Troncoso ed.), cap iv, pp. 206, 208, defines the terms figuratively as *persona que tiene sucesores.* Siméon, *op. cit.*, as well as Sahagún, *loc. cit.*, gives literal meanings of most of them. See also Sahagún, *Florentine Codex,* Book VI, cap. xliii, and X, caps. v and xiii.

And if it were a noblewoman, or only a common [woman], who was then born, so likewise it was her lot. She was considered as a man, esteemed as if a man; a comforter. Hence she caused others no apprehension, was not negligent, and did not dishearten others.

And also it was said that one who was born upon this [day sign], One Deer — it was told that he was exceedingly timorous; he lived thinking only of his fears; he walked with his terrors, and only lived afraid, indeed frightened to death. When he witnessed a thunder clap, or a bolt of lightning, or lightning flash — a flash of lightning — then he could not endure it. Indeed the lightning and thundering frightened him and caused him to be in terror and dread.

And so they said that sometimes, on some occasions, it happened to him; for his fear followed him and persisted with him; his fears came upon him as a judgment. For his dread came upon him. Verily, he was struck by lightning; that befell him which he feared and of which he lived in anxiety. And even if it was summer, he was still smitten by a summer flash. Also, when he bathed in the water, there he died, drowned; his eyes were torn out;[2] his finger nails were removed and torn out.

Hence was it said: "Verily, so was his lot; so was he born. Even as the deer is a great coward, just so was he, whose day sign this is, a great coward; fearful." So seldom did his kin, his parents, trouble themselves; they did nothing for him.

And also it was told that then, too, was one of the times when those known as the Goddesses descended. They made offerings to them, and then they clothed [their images] in their paper vestments and their paper adornments.

Auh intla çioapilli: anoço çã maceoalli ipan tlacatia, no iuh mâceoale catca, teoqujchtlamachti: iuhqujn oqujchpovi, teacotlaz, atle ic tenentlamachti, amo tenmachonj, amo tecuetlaxo.

Auh no ioan mjtoa: in aqujn ipan tlacati ce maçatl: qujlmach cẽca momauhtiaia, çan jmaviz in qujmattinenca, çan imauhcac in nemja, çan mamauhcanenca, vel iolmjquja, in jquac qujcaquja tlatlatzinjliztli, anoço tlavitequjliztli, tlapetlanaliztli, tlapetlanjllotl: njman âconiecoaia, vel qujçaviaia, qujcujcujtiuetziltia, qujmavizcujtia in onotlapetlan, onotlatlatzin.

Auh iuh qujtoa, in quẽman, in quenmanjan ça ipan neltiaia, ca imaviz contocaia, ipã ontlamelaoa, ça imaviz qujtlamachiliaia, ca inemauhtil ipan oniauh, vel vitecoia, ipan muchioaia in qujmacaci, in qujmamattinemj. Auh intlacanelmo xopantla, çan tonalhujteco: no ioan in jquac atlan maltia, vncan mjquja, ilaqujlo, ixtelolococopinalo, iztitlatlaxo, izticocopinalo,

ic mjtoa, ca nel iuhquj itonal, iuhquj ipan motlacatili: in iuhquj maçatl, cenca momauhtianj: çan no iuhquj in aqujn itonal catca, vel mauhca tlacatl, mavitzoco: ic çan yca mellaquaoa, in joaniolque, in jtaoan, aquẽ commatia.

Auh ioan mjtoa: no vncan ceppa ipan temoia, in moteneoa çioateteu: vncan qujntlamanjliaia, ioan vncan ic qujntlaquentiaia yn jmamatlaquen, in jmamanechichioal

2. Cf. Spanish text.

Fourth Chapter, which telleth of the second house, when it was the time of this sign, named Two Rabbit; and those then born in it did nothing but drink wine.

Injc navi capitulo: itechpa tlatoa, injc ontetl calli, in jpan, y, machiotl, in jtoca vme tochtli: auh in vncan tlacatia, iehoan in çan qujxcavia tlatlaoana.

And of Two Rabbit, which followed, it was said that he who was then born was a great drunkard. Indeed, he required, lusted for, and used wine like a pig, he gorged himself and was a glutton with wine. Only to it did he dedicate himself; he depended upon it, consumed it to excess, and overindulged himself in it. He took it to himself inhumanly and needed it immoderately. Only his drinking did he consider. With it he awoke, with it he arose; never did he arouse himself, take notice, or sober up.[1]

Auh in qujoaltoqujlia vme tochtli: mjtoa, in aqujn ipan tlacatia, cenca tlaoananj, vel qujtolina qujztlaquj, qujpitzonequj in vctli, vel ocpoça, ocxixicuj: çan iee in qujmotequjuhtia, ipã mjxpoa, qujmotequjmaca, qujmotlaelmaca, âqujmotlacamaca, qujtlaelnequj, çan jauh povi, ipan oaliiça, ipan oalmeoa, aic mozcalia, aic tlachia, aic ix qujcuj:

In truth, sometimes he no longer took food. At such a time he only became a slave to it. No longer did he take to his bed. Night after night, when he arose, he visited various wine makers' houses begging wine. Never did he come to his right mind. He was not well even when he drank nothing. And he did not bother about it, nor abhor it, nor become distressed nor nauseated by it even though it were only the dregs, which indeed were like spoiled clots, with dirt, or full of gnats — full of filth and rubbish. So he swallowed it, sucked it in, and gulped it. Like a dog he licked his lips.

in nel quenman, aoc qujtlaquallotia, ça iuhcapan in conmomaca, aocmo qujpepechtia, ioiooac in moquetza, tlachicque inchã cacalaquj, tlatlapevia, aquenmã tlapohuj in jiollo, âvel ca in maca tle conj: auh aoc quen qujmati, amo qujtlatzilhuja, amo yvic eoa, amo qujtlaeltia, in manel ça xaiocujtlatl, in çan iuhquj tetzacpol, chapantica, anoce moca çaioli, çaiollo, moca tlaçolli, tlâtlaçollo, ça iuhquj qujtoloa, iuhquj qujçolotza, qujlteqùj: iuhqujn chichi motempapaloa.

If he did not find wherewith he could become drunk, in order to buy wine he hurriedly seized his cape, or his breech clout, thereby finding for himself poverty. He could not abstain or steel himself.

Intlaca oc tle qujtta, qujtlaoanaz, ic moccoviz, qujcujtivetzi in jtilma, yn jmaxtli: icnoiotl ipampa qujmottitia, aocmo vel motlacaoaltia, moiollotechioa:

Nevermore thereafter did he live in bliss and contentment. Still, when indeed he passed a calm day, once again he was quite drunk, very drunk, lying stupefied, filthily drunk. No longer did he take heed. He pitched forward upon his face; he fell head first. He went wallowing in ordure,[2] with blanched or reddened face, debauched, with hair tangled, uncombed, twisted, and matted; no more did he tend

njman aoqujc vellacaconemj, tlacaco tlamati, in ma oc ivian oncemjlhujti, onocuel ivintic, tequjxocomjc, onocuellapolo, tlaelivintic, aocmo qujmati, ça mjxicquetza, motzonjcquetza, cujtlanexiuhtinemj, ixtenexiuhtinemj, ixchichilivi, ixchichilpul, quapôpoliuhtinemj, quatzomaiuhtinemj, quapôpolpol, quatzômapol, aoc onmomatoca, aoc onmopepetla, aoc onmoquapepetla, intlanel cana momaiavi, mjx-

1. *Ix qujcuj.* See *ixniccui* in Molina, *op. cit.,* and Siméon, *op. cit.*

2. Cf. Olmos, *op. cit.,* p. 236; *yça tzompachpul, yça cuitlanexpul monemitia.*

it with his hands, or comb and arrange it. If somewhere he threw himself down, and fell on his face, or his nose, or his knees — if he fell and skinned his knees; or he broke a hand or a foot, etc., — no longer did he heed or note the pain. Nowhere was there peace or virtue in his face.

toxaoa, moiacatoxaoa, motlanquatoxaoa, motlanquaxipeoa, momapoztequj, mocxipuztequj. Etc. aocmo qujmati, aocmo qujtecococamati, aoccan tlacacemelle, aoccan tlacaiectli yn jxaiac:

And his hands only quaked, quivered, and shook. And his speech was no longer prudent; it only quavered. He only spoke as a drunkard; intemperate words emerged from his lips, which he should not have said. Continually he shouted at others, harangued them, affronted them, and quarreled with them. All that he said was not fit to be repeated. He went howling and shouting, boasting that he was a brave man. He danced in a circle, opening wide his mouth as he sang. He was disrespectful and impudent. He seized everything to brandish and raise as a threat — the beast, the stone, the club.[3] He went carrying his stone or his piece of wood with him, constantly troubling and threatening people, and blocking the way.

auh in jma ça cuecuechca, ça viviioca, papatlaca, ioan in jtlatol aocmo mĵmati, ça cuecuechca, çan tlatlaoancatlatoa, ça much tlacaçollatolli in jcamacpa qujça, in qujcacamacaoa, çan jc nemj in tetzatzilia, in tetlacaqujtia, in tepinauhtia in teaoa: much qujtoa in aitolonj oiouhtinemj, tzatzitinemj, moqujchitotinemj, momamantinemj, mocamatzaiana in cujca, atle qujmauhcaitta, atle qujmamati, much qujcujtivetzi, cacocuj, cacoleoa in tequanj, in tetl, in quavitl: iteuh iquauh ietinemj, tlacatl qujcocomonja, tlacatl qujcuecuetlanja, vtli qujtzatzacutinemj:

He brought poverty to his children — always causing them fear, constantly terrifying them, scattering them.

icnoiotl qujmjttitia in ipilhoan, muchipa qujnmamauhtia, qujmjiçavia, qujncecenmana,

Never did he sleep or rest easily. In time he fell exhausted, consumed by pain and affliction. No more did he say: "Wherewith will my home appear attractive?" — [for] he thought of nothing but his wine. Only rubbish prevailed and ashes were strewn throughout. In his home, no one swept; no fire burned. It remained in darkness. Misery reigned.

aic tlacacochi, motlacateca: qujnjquac quauhtenvetzi, in jellel onacic in onmellelaxiti, aocmo qujtoa, in tlein ic ontlavelneciz nochan: ça mache in jvc qujmati, ça tlaçolli qujztoc, tequjxqujtl coxontoc, in jchan, aiac tlachpana, amo tlatla, tlaioaticac, icnoiotl qujztoc,

It mattered not where with others he slept and lay down to sleep. [For] his heart was only there in the taverns, the wine shops. When he found no wine, he seemed anguished of heart, as if he hung high, or tumbled into a pitfall, like a vagabond.

ça canjn tetlan cocochi, tetlan mocochteca, ça vmpan ca iiollo tlachiccan, vctlaliloia, in atle qujtta vctli, iuhqujn nentlamati yiollo, iuhqujn aco pilcac, iuhqujn âactiuetzi, iuhqujn avic iauh.

And if somewhere he found a drinking place, there he satisfied his longing, quieted his anguish, as if gladdened and calmed.[4] There he sat firmly and fast, dedicated to sitting, seated happily. No more did he think to depart.

Auh intlacana otlaipantili tlaoanoia: iuhqujn vncan motlatlalia yiollo, iuhqujn iioiolipan, iuhqujn iiollo yiztaia, yiollo cecelia. vncan moteteuhtlalia, motepitztlalia, mocentlalia, mopaccatlalia, aoc tlacaoaliztlamati.

And if he were bidden to drink somewhere, as never before did he spring up to run and take pains to enter. As if spontaneously,[5] he suddenly ran,

Auh intlacana tlaoancanotzalo: iuhqujn aoc ie choloteoa, ie çomocacaquj, iuhqujn ce inacaz, iuhqujn onviçinj onmotlaloa, mjçiuhcatlaloa, momama-

3. Cf. Siméon, *op. cit.* (*tequani*) and Olmos, *op. cit.*, pp. 240, 242, and elsewhere (*tetl, quauitl*), where the terms *tequani, tetl,* and *quauitl* are used metaphorically for "chastisement." Sahagún, however, renders them literally.

4. Cf. Sahagún, *Florentine Codex,* Book VI, cap. xli, fol. 193*v*.

5. Cf. Sahagún, "Memoriales con escolios," p. 204 (gloss 8).

dashed, and went hurling himself along. He had no shame; no one now abashed or embarrassed him.

iauhtiuh, aoc tle ipinaviz, aocac qujmamati, aocac qujpinaoa.

And yet they reviled him. No one gave him the name of a man of consequence; nowhere had he the name of a man. Everywhere he was simply detested and hated. Nowhere could he approach people; everywhere he made confusion. If somewhere there was a reunion, he dispersed them — he scattered and disbanded them. They let him alone; he was avoided. There was silence [when he came]; a bristling antagonism and withdrawing of friends.

Auh tel aocac no tle ipan qujtta, aocac qujtlacatoca, aoccan itlacatocaia, çan noviian tlaelitto, tlaqualanja, aoccan vel tetlan motlalia: novian tlapaçoloa: Intlacana cenielovac: tececenmana, texixitinja, temomoiaoa: ipan macavi, tlalcavilo, ipan cactiuetzi, ycnjppaçulli, icnjmmoiactli.

Hence was it said: "Verily, thus was his day sign. What is to be done?" And seldom was there courage or hope in his behalf. It was said that he would go to fall down somewhere; to meet destruction, to die, to collapse somewhere. Perhaps he would fall from some cliff; or down into a chasm, or into the water; he would cast himself into the river and drown. Or somewhere he would fall into the hands of evil men and die at their hands.[6] They would rob, plunder, and despoil him, leaving him quite bare.

Ic ytolo: ca nel yuhquj ytonal, quennel chioaloz: auh ça ica neellaquaoalo, yca netlapalolo, ytolo: ça can vetzitiuh, ça can popoliviz, ça can mjqujz, ça can quauhtenvetziz: aço cana motepexiviz, motlaxapuchhujz, matlanviz, matoiaviz, atlan mjqujz, anoço cana inmac vetziz in tlaveliloque, inmac mjqujz, qujtlacujcujlizque, qujtlacencujlizque, qujtlanamoializque, qujpetztoccaoazque:

And more: not only could all this happen, but he embraced vice and evil. Sometimes he committed adultery; he stole; he scaled walls to tempt and seduce [women]. His drunkenness caused him to do it. Wine showed and was apparent on his face. And when it dawned, his eyes were inflamed, his eyelids drooped, ached, and watered: a decrepit drunkard's face. Nowhere was he regarded as a man. Continually his lips moved from side to side.

yoan amo çan quexqujch in jpan iauh, in qujmonamjctia yavilqujzca, yn jtoloca: in quenman tetlan aquj, ichtequj, tepan tepantemo, tecamanalhuja, tetzitzquja: ytlaoancaio maitia, vctli qujmoxaiacatia, yvcxaiac ietinemj: in oallathuj yxpupuçaoa, ixtenmjmjlivi, ixquatoleeoa, ichchichitintinemj, yxovcpul, aoccan motlacaitta: achcan cochcamachaloa.

And if one was not a great drinker, when it dawned it made him very sick, sickened and affected by the wine. Also, his eyelids burned and his eyes ached; it made him sick in the head and made it sore. He wished not to arise from bed; rather, he lay wrapped in blankets, and slept all day. Neither could he eat; he was nauseated and wished to vomit. With difficulty could he dispel and overcome it.

Auh in amo cenca tlaoanjnj in oallathuj cenca qujcocoa, muccôcôa, mucvia: no ixquatoleeoa, ixeeoa, itzontecon qujcocoa, qujtzonteconeoa, aiel meuhtoc: çan qujmjliuhtoc, cemjlhujcochi, ano yellaquaz: çan motomaoa, motlaeltia: aiaxcan in qujcaoa in qujmopopololtia.

6. *Maquiz* in the *Real Palacio MS.*

Fifth Chapter, which telleth how many kinds of drunkards there were.

And it was said that the wine was known as Four Hundred Rabbits.

One drinker might not harm or belittle his day sign. The wine did not irritate him; it did not cause him irritation or make a fool of him. He only went to sleep, and continued to sleep. He became pale and remained pale, sitting with drooping head—remaining with head bowed; he sat rolled up like a ball, and remained coiled; he sat embracing himself, hugging himself; he rested on his shins, and remained on his shins; he squatted on his heels and remained on his heels. He was only by himself, and calmly went off by himself. Peacefully he stretched out; quietly he fell down exhausted. In no way did he offend one. He stretched out, rumbling as he slept, groaning, snoring, as if he had torn off his nose, as if he enjoyed the sleep.

And one of them only wept. He loosed tears as if bringing good to himself, sobbing as he pressed them out. Like hail stones they showered down, a great course of water simply streaming down. His tears buried him. He could not stop. Verily, that which the wine made him remember ate his heart out.

And for one of them his only joy and pleasure was in song, in singing. He wished not to talk; he neglected listening to jests, to counsel, to stories. As if it unleashed his song, when he drank the wine, he so recalled his song, as if it engulfed him. So the wine worked on him.

And another did not sing; he did nothing but talk. Uncontrolled he talked; he spoke much. He chattered, jabbered, gibbered, and mumbled. With ill-will he eavesdropped and betrayed others. He blustered, vaunted, and sang praises of himself; he esteemed and made himself out as great. He belittled what others said, speaking deceitfully and constantly shaking his head. He pretended to be rich and reprimanded the poor; he pretended to be superior, to be

Injc macujlli capitulo, itechpa tlatoa: in quenjn tlatlamantiticate tlaoanque.

Ioan mjtoa, in vctli ic moteneoa centzontotochti:

in aca tlaoanquj, amo qujtlaveliaia, amo ica mocaiaoa, in jtonal, amo qujçuma in vctli, amo ipan tlaneçomaltia, amo qujtlavelilotilia: çan cochtimotlalia, cochtica, mjctimotlalia, mjctica, tolotimotlalia, tolotica, motapaiollalia, tapaiolca, momalcochotimotlalia, monaoatectimotlalia, çan mocototztlalia, cototzca, moxoxolotlalia, xoxoloca, çan mocauhtica, çan jviian tetlalcavia, iviian moteca, iviian quauhtenvetzi, atle ic teixco nemj, quaqualacatoc in cochi, cotalotoc, icotocatoc, iuhqujn moiacatzaiana, iuhqujn qujtlamachtia cochiztli.

Auh in aca çan ie choca, qujxaiovitoma, iuhqujn mocnelia, iuhqujn tzitzicunoa, iuhqujn mopatzca, iuhqujn tecivitl pixavi, iuhqujn açã cempantli qujtoca ixaio, auel motlacaoaltia, vel iiollo conqua in tlein qujlnamjctia vctli.

Auh in aca çan ie ipac, çan ie ivelmach, in cujcatl, in cujqujztli: amo tlatlatoznequj, aiel qujcaqujz in camanalli, in nenonotzalli, in tlatolli: iuhqujn ie qujtlapolhuja ycujc, in onoconjc vctli, iuhqujn qujtlalnamjctia, iuhqujnma conapotzavia ycujc, iuhqujn conanjlia vctli.

Auh in aca amo cujca, çan mache tlatoa: çan ie vnmanantlatoa, çan ie tlatlatoa, tlatetoa, tequjtlatlatoa, popolocatjca, qujqujnacatica, mjtleuhtica, tecacaca, techicoitoa, mochachamaoa, motlatlanjtztia, moçiçinoa, moieoaitoa, moveveilia, moveinectica, tepapatzauhtica, xixictlatotica, moquaquacuecuechotica, mocujltonocanectica, teicnotlacaaoatica, motachcauhnectica, machicanectica: iuhqujn ac çan momattica, âmopatzaoallanj, âmotempanavillanj, âmoten-

one in authority. Haughtily, he thought well of himself. He did not deflate himself; he did not overcome nor chastise his tongue. No one could force him to recant. He thought himself superior, better than others.

Indistinct was his speech. What did he say? He was as if stirred, and his words bubbled up and burst forth. It was as if he argued, harangued, enforced silence, and drove all people away, put them to flight, numbed them with terror, visited them with afflictions, made them shrink with fright, and assailed them with his words.

It seemed that he disgusted others, and did not inquire what they said. Wherever they may have spoken, or undertaken something, he seemed to make little of it and kick it aside. But when he had drunk nothing, he seemed to be dumb, one who whispered, fearful of people, quite frightened.

For all this he excused himself by saying: "It is because I no longer knew what I said; for I was drunk. The wine had taken effect upon me; I was overwrought."

And another drunkard was very suspicious. He misunderstood; not as things were did he hear them. Often he blamed his wife. If anyone only looked at her, he then said to him: "Why dost thou make eyes at my wife?" Then he gave rise to hatred, fury, and murder, etc. And all that which was spoken he took as applying to him. He suspected that when there was occasion for mirth, he was thereby being defamed, the object of ridicule. Without reason he belabored the people. The wine and drinking cursed him.

And if it were a woman, she simply went to her knees; she remained on her knees. No longer was she rational. She sat with legs outstretched; she remained with legs outstretched. And if she were much besotted, if she were much affected, her hair simply formed a mantle over her. She tumbled there, with hair streaming out, etc.

All of these kinds [of drunkenness] here mentioned, each one, showed upon and were the doing of the drunkard. It was said: "So is his rabbit. Thus was his day sign; in this way did the wine gods manifest themselves on him." And if a drunkard fell over a precipice, or else fell somewhere [else], it was said: "He was affected by the wine gods." Because in many ways the wine showed its power,

aqujllanj, aiac vel qujtlatolilochtia: vel moieoatoca, motepanaviltoca,

aixnezqujn itlatol, tlein mach qujtoa, iuhqujn momoloca, iuhqujn qujmomolotza ytlatol, iuhqujn qujcuecuepotza itlatol, iuhqujn môolhuja, iuhqujn motititza, iuhqujn cactoc qujteteca, iuhqujn tececentlaça, iuhqujn tetotocaticalac, iuhqujn tepôpouhtitlaz, iuhqujn tetotoliuhtitlali, iuhqujn tecocototztlali, iuhqujn tecujcujtiuetz, itlatol:

iuhqujn tequacêcepouh, iuhqujn acontetemoa, tlein qujtoa: canjn mach ontlatoa, canjn mach ontlaana, iuhquj̃ tlatlacxotla, iuhqujn tlaquêqueça: auh in ie atle conj, iuhqujn nontli iuhqujn anaoatl, vel teimacazquj, vel mauhquj,

ça ixqujch injc mopâtia, in qujteilhuja: ca aocmo njcma, in tlein njqujto, ca njvintic, ca notech motlali, njtlaneçomalti.

Auh in aca tlaoãquj vel ipan chicotlamati, chîchicotlacaquj, amo iuh tlâtlacaquj: mjiecpa tetech qujtlamja yn jcioauh: in açaca çan conjtta, ie cuel qujlhuja: tle ic tiqujxnotza in nonamjc: vncan qujpeoaltia in qualantli, in tlauelli, in nemjctiliztli. Etc. Ioan moch qujmocujtia, in tlein tlatolli mjtoa: ioã in tlein vetzqujlilo, in momatica iehoatl in ica nenonotzalo in vetzqujlilo, çan jliviz in teaaoa, qujveuexcatlachieltia in vctli, in tlailli.

Auh intla çioatl: ça papachiuhtimotlalia, ça pâpachca, aocmo qujmati, momemelauhtimotlalia, momemelauhtica: auh intla cenca vel oivintic, in vel oiellelacic, ça itzon qujquentica; vncan quauhtenvetzi, itzon patlaoatoc. Etc.

In jzqujtlamantli in: njcã omoteneuh, iceceiaca itech neci, iceceiaca itlachioal tlaoanquj, mjtoa: ca iuhquj itoch, iuhquj itonal, iuhquj ic ipan mjxeoa, in totochtin: ioan intla omotepexivi tlaoanquj, in anoço cana ovetz, mjtoa: omotochvi: iehica in mjeccã qujça itlachioal vctli, ic mjtoa: centzontotochti: ipanpa ca amo çan quexqujch in jtech qujça âqualli.

it was called the Four Hundred Rabbits; for very few did it affect favorably.

And when, it was said, the day Two Rabbit set in, then was celebrated the feast day of the principal wine god, who was called Izquitecatl. And although only he alone was named, yet at that time they remembered all the wine gods, who became the wine. Thus was Izquitecatl greatly revered. They set up his image in his temple. There they laid gifts before him; for him they sang and provided music with gourd tubes. And before him stood a stone basin, called two-rabbit basin — full, to the brim. Into the wine dipped the drinking tubes, extending from it so that those who sampled the wine stood drinking it: but only those who could drink, the old men, the old women, the intrepid warriors, the bold, the foolish, who paid the debt with their heads and their breasts. That is, they would be captured sometime when war was declared; or else on issuing forth [to battle] they would capture others and take prisoners. So [by drinking] they went about mocking death.

Ioan in jquac mjtoaia, moquetza tonalli, vme tochtli: vncan ilhujqujxtililoia, in jmachcauh totochti: in moteneoa Izqujtecatl: auh macivin çan jcel moteneoa, ca oncan qujncemjlnamjquia, in totochti, ovcti, ic cenca maviztililoia in izqujtecatl, qujtlaliaia ixiptla in jteupan: vncan qujtlamanjlia, quicujcatia, qujtlapichilia acocotica: yoan ixpan icaca tecomjtl, itoca vmetochtecomatl, tentimanj, pexontimanj, in vctli: ipã manj piaztli, piazçotimanj, mamazço ic conjtimanj in aqujque vmpa ontlatlapaloa: tel çan iehoan in ie tlaoananj, in veuetque, in jlamatque ioan in iaotlaueliloque, in mjivintia: in aquen tlatta, in qujpopoa, yn intzontecon, yn jmelchiqujuh, qujtoznequj: ca onvicozque in quenmã, in ooalmjto iaoiotl: auh no ce onqujçativi, oaltecalaqujzque ontlamatiuj: ic momjqujzquequelotinenca:

And the wine which they drank never came to an end; [the basin] never stood empty. The wine makers, the wine making officials, continued pouring it into [the basin]. All came assembling there where they cut the maguey, when everywhere it was the time and season for breaking into the maguey. This was because then they offered new wine. If someone for the first time broke into the maguey, he first poured the extracted material there. Thus they said he poured out wine and offered the wine-pouring to Izquitecatl; they gave him wine to drink.

auh in vctli quja, aquenman tlamja, âquēman cactoc, in contecatimanj tlachicque, tecutlachique: ixqujch oalacitimanj in tetlâchic, yn noviian tlachicpan, tlachicoaian, ca vncan vitzmana intla aca iãcujcan otlatlapan, vncã achto qujteca in jtlachic: ic qujtoaia tlatoiaoa, qujmanjlia itlatoiaoal in Izqujtecatl, qujtlatoiavilia:

But not only at this time did they pour wine; rather, always were offerings so made in his temple.

auh amo çanjio iquac, y, in tlatoiaoaia: ca çan muchipa iuh tlamanca, in iteupan.

Sixth Chapter, which telleth of still another house on the sign [One Deer], called Three Water. It was in part good, in part adverse, in part only in between.

On the day sign Three Water, there was said to be good and ill.

For he who was born on it, so it was said, would prosper. All his wealth would come easily. He would be successful in gaining a living.

But, on the other hand, quickly would vanish that which had come to him. Like water it would pass away — as if carried off by the river, as if engulfed by the water. Never was he content; never happy. In vain did he cast and hurl himself against obstacles. Nowhere could he feel tranquil. Indeed, in all the things which he undertook, though he went on elbow, shank, and knee, vain and fruitless were his efforts and fatigue. He only frustrated himself.

The day sign Four Dog: whosoever was then born — so it was said — would prosper. Swiftly would appear that which he required — his drink, his food. Even if he did nothing all day, it was not apparent whence or through whom his heart was calmed, whence he gained strength, whence he took sustenance, there where he whiled away the whole day. But somewhere by the intercession of others, he secured that which his children needed to eat. Without his forethought came what they were to eat. He did not know whence his sustenance, his [provision for] journeying, came. Though he did and worked at little, forthwith appeared his consolation and he achieved something.

And thus they said: if he bred dogs, he whose day sign was the dog, all would mate. His dogs would grow; none would die of sickness. As he trafficked in them, so they became as [numerous as] the sands, and so they barked.

It was said: "How can it be otherwise? The dogs share a day sign with him. Thus the breeding of dogs resulted well for him."

He sold them all. And all which were born, all came to be capes [for him]. Also owners and breeders of dogs became rich, and the price of dogs

Injc chiquacen capitulo: itechpa tlatoa, in oc ce calli, in jpan jn machiotl: in jtoca ei atl, cequj qualli, cequj tetolinj, cequj çan tlanepantla ca.

In jpan ei atl tonalli: mjtoa qualli, ioan amo qualli:

ipampa in aqujn ipan tlacatia, iuh mjtoaia motlacamatiz, in ixqujch itlatquj, aiovi necia, vel motlaiecoltianj:

auh iece çan jciuhca, vmpoliuhtiuetzi in tlein qujmonextiliaia, iuhqujn atl onquiça, iuhqujn atoco, iuhqujn amoiaoa, aic avia, aic vellamati, çan nenia motlatlamotla, çan nenia moquauhtlaça, âcan tlacaco tlamati, nelli mach in jxqujch câana, yn jmolicpi, itetepon, itlãqua ic moquequetza, çan atleti, çan nen vetzi yn jçiaujz, in itlapaliviz çan monenencoa.

Navi itzcujntli, cemjlhujtonalli: in aquĩ ipan tlacatia, iuh mjtoaia motlacamatiz, iciuhca neciz, in jtech monequj in jauh, yn itlaqual, in maca nelle ai cemjlhujtl: aneztica in campa tepal cevi iiollo, in vmpa pâti, vmpa ihiiocuj, vmpa qujtlaça cemjlhujtl: auh ça vmpa cana tepal qujcnopilhuja, in jntech monequj ipilhoan, injc ihiiocujzque, ainemachpan in neçi qujqua: amo quimati in campa oallauh inenca ivtlatocaia: intlanel çan tepiton, itla onai, itla contequjpanoa, njman neçi in jneiollaliliz, itla qujcnopilhuja:

yoan iuh qujtoaia intla itzcujnnemjti, in itzcujntli itonal, mvch vel moquetzazque: oapaoazque in jtzcujoa, aiac cocolmjqujz, iuhqujn tlanecujlivi, iuhqujn tlatexaliuj, iuhqujn tlapipitzca,

mjtoaia: quenel noço itonalecapooa in itzcujnti, injc vel itech mochioa itzcujnnemjtiliztli,

ixqujch qujnnamaca, auh ixqujch tlacati, moch quachqujçaia no ic mocujltonoaia, no ic vncatca in itzcujnpatiiouh, itzcujne, in jtzcujnnemjtianj: iehica

was so high, because they were eaten and needed by the people in days of old. They were in the market place — they arranged them[1] in their respective places. When dogs were sold, they seemed to have great jowls and mouths; they were judged, sought after, and coveted; whatever kind would be taken, whether short haired or long haired. Since they barked and whined, they bound, tied, and wrapped the muzzles of each of them; they were there frothing at the mouth.

ca qualoia, tetech monequja, in ie vecauh, vnmanca in tianqujzco, qujnaoaltemaia in chichinamacoia, in itzcujnnamacoia, iuhqujn tlatenmetlapilivi, iuhqujn tlatentomaoa netlâtlâttililo, netlatlanectilo, neiicoltilo, in catle onanoz: in aço tetzictic, anoço paçoltic, iuhqujn tlananalca, iuhqujn tlanenecivi, mochintin teteñaoaletoque, tlatetenjlpilti, têtenjlpitoque, in tetenpopoçoquillo ietoc:

And when they killed them, they dug a hole; they plunged and pressed their heads down in it with their hands, thus simply suffocating them in the mud. And the owner of a dog which had died put a cotton cord about its neck, stroked and caressed it with his hand, and said to it: "Stand guard for me there! Thou shalt pass me over the place of the nine rivers."

auh injc qujnmjctiaia, qujtlatataquja in jntzontecon, vncan qujmonpolactia, qujnteteppachoa, injc çan qujmjhiiomjctia çoqujatitlan: auh in itzcujne, in ie onmjquj itzcujn, icpatl concozcatia, conpepetla, conmapepetla, qujlhuja: Xinechalmochieli, tinechalmopanaviliz in chicunaoapan:

And some slew them only when they stole the dogs. They just fell upon and caught them in nooses; they were pounced upon and lassoed about the necks.

auh in cequjnti ic qujnmjctiaia, in jquac çan qujmjchtequja, chichime, çã qujnvitonja, qujntzonvia, movitonja, moquechtzonvia.

Five Monkey was said to be a good day. He who was then born was like the workings and qualities of the day: the telling of tales, and jesting; the amusement and entertainment of others. Neither did he thereby cause anger. That which was his joke or his story thus brought forth smiles and laughter. Everything amused and brought joy to the people; everything gave them contentment and consolation; everything was pleasing to hear. No one did he disgust. But if in something he offended someone, sometimes letting slip an evil word, so misstating what he repeated in haste without reflection, he himself made it good so that the humiliation was not noticed. So he corrected and made good his words. Thus there was no anger.

Macujl oçomatli, mjtoa, qualton tonalli: in aqujn ipan tlacatia, çan vel iê itequjuh ilhujl, ynemac catca, in tlatlaquetzaliztli, in cacamanalli, in teellelqujxtiliztli, tececemeltiliztli, amo no ic tlaqualanja, in tlein icacamanal, in jtlatlaquetzal, injc queoa vetzqujztli, injc tlauetzquitia, moch tececemelti, moch tlapactia, moch tepac, moch teiolipan, moch mouelcaquj, aiac qujiolitlacoa: auh intla noço itla teiolitlaco quēman qujcamacaoa, ic motenpatilia, in ainemachpan tlein qujtotiuetzi, çan no ie compatia, âneztica in tleinton ic convellalia, ic contlamachia itlatol: ic amo tlaqualanja,

For so was it said that such was his day sign; so was he born on the day of the monkey; for he gave people pleasure; was friendly to all — everyman's friend, a desirable person.

ipampa iuh mjtoa ca nel iuhquj itonal, iuhquj ipan tlacat, in oçomatli ca teaavilia, mochi tlacatl icnjuh, tececemjcnjuh, nenequjztontli.

Six Grass, so they said, was evil, a day sign of wild beasts. For he who was then born lived only in torment on earth, suffered pain and trouble, and found afflictions. And of his children, not one survived, nor became strong, nor matured; all simply

Chiquacen malinalli iuh mjtoa: amo qualli, tequanj tonalli: ipampa in aqujn ipan tlacatia, çan tlaihiiovitinemjz tlalticpac, toneoatinemj, chichinacatinemj, cococ teopouhquj, qujtztinemj: auh in jpilhoan amo ceme moquetza, avel oapauj, amo vel mo-

1. *Qujnaoaltemaia*: *quinualtemaia* in the *Real Palacio MS*. Reference to the *Florentine Codex*, Book XI, cap. i, ff. 16*v*-17*r*, suggests that the terms *chichi, itzcuintli*, etc., were not strongly differentiated; *xoloitzcuintli* is described as the glabrous variety (*chichi çan njmã hatle in jtomio*).

died. And sometimes they became slaves and sold themselves.

Seven Reed was said to be good. Whosoever was then born, man or woman, was one who merited, deserved, received, and found that which he required. He would have his property, goods, and wealth. And that which was done, all endured; all prospered. Nothing failed; nothing perished in vain. Through his pains and fatigue, without struggle, he achieved his effort.

Eight Ocelot and Nine Eagle, Ten Vulture, Eleven Motion, Twelve Flint Knife — all of these were days in no way good. So it was said that he who was then born was without merit, deserts, or blessings. He was quite purposeless on earth.

And Thirteen Rain, so they said, was good, because it was the last day. He who was then born, man or woman, was fortunate. He would have all he required to eat and drink. His home needed nothing. And also it was said that he would become an old man, [or she] an old woman. He would grow old, bent with age, because this day sign on which he was born ended the series.

oapaoa, çan moch onmjctivi: auh in quēman vellacutli mocuepaia, monamacaia.

Chicome acatl: mjtoaia qualli, in aqujn ipan tlacatia in oqujchtli, in cioatl, mâceoale, ilhujle, nemaque, necinj in jtech monequj: onca in jaxca, in jtlatquj, in jioca: auh in tlein maailia, moch tlaçaloa, moch oniehoati, atle nenqujça, atle nenpolivi, in jnecocol, yn jçiaviz, in aitlaaxcanvil, in jtlapaliviztica qujtta.

Chicuei ocelotl, ioan chicunavi quauhtli, matlactli cozcaquauhtli, matlactloce olin, matlactlomome tecpatl. Yn jzqujtetl in, atle qualli in tonalli, iuh mjtoaia: in aqujn ipan tlacati, atle imaceoal, atle ilhujlti, inemacti, çan oalnenenqujçan tlalticpac:

auh in matlactlomey qujavitl, iuh mjtoa qualli: ipampa iça tonaltzontli, in aqujn ipan tlacatia, in oqujchtli, in cioatl, tlacnopilhujanj, moch onca in jtech monequj, in qujqua, in quj, atle monectoc in jchan: auh ioan mjtoaia vevetiz, ylamatiz, tlachicalhujz, coliviz: ipampa ca qujtlamja in tonalli ipan otlacat.

Seventh Chapter, which telleth of the fourth sign, named One Flower. And the man born upon it, they said, and it was averred, would be happy, quite able, and much given to song and joy: a jester, an entertainer. And it was said that the women were great embroiderers. It was said that this sign was indifferent; that is to say, a little bad and a little good.

One Flower and all of its various companions set in, so forming [a set of] thirteen days. Two Crocodile followed it, and Three Reed,[1] Four House, Five Lizard, Six Serpent, Seven Death, Eight Deer, Nine Rabbit, Ten Water, Eleven Dog, Twelve Monkey, and Thirteen Grass.

These various ones, it was said, were evil; but also it was said that they were somewhat good.

In this manner was considered the one then born, nobleman or only commoner. He would become a singer, a bearer of joy, a teller of tales, an artisan. And he found and merited his consolation, his riches. He lived content and happy when he was devoted to his day sign; that is, when he reflected and did his penance well.

And [as for] him who was not devoted to it, who disregarded it, who only disdained his day sign, then, so was it said, when one such was a singer, or some artisan or skilled craftsman, if there was food on hand and wealth was there, he became presumptuous, superior, ungrateful, proud, haughty, disrespectful, filled with pride. So he acted superior in mind and heart, in his songs, and in his wisdom, as a poet, a designer, a composer, a master of song.

And if somewhere there were an invitation to a feast and to song, to discussion and the forgivenness of differences, he disregarded and ignored the sweetness of the protector of all,[2] the flowers, tobacco, suste-

Inic chicome capitulo, itechpa tlatoa: injc nauhtetl machiotl, yn jtoca ce xuchitl: auh in toqujchti ipan tlacatia, qujtoaia: qujlmach papaqujnj iez, vel mozcalianj: ioan vel qujmocujtlavia in cujcatl, ioan in paqujliztli, ioan câcamanaltinj, câcamanale: auh qujl in cioa, vevey tlamachiuhque: qujlmach çan tlanepantla ca injn machiotl, qujtoznequj achi tetolinj, ioan achi qualli.

Moquetza ce suchitl, ioan yn jzquitetl ytlavilanoan: injc matlactetl omei tonalli muchiuhtica in yehoatl contoqujlia vme cipactli, yoan ey acatl, navi calli, macujlli cuetzpali, chiquacen coatl, chicome mjqujztli, chicuei maçatl, chicunavi tochtli, matlactli atl, matlactli oce ytzcujntli, matlactlomome oçomatli, matlactlomey malinalli:

in jzqujtetl in, mjtoaia amo qualli: auh yoan mjtoaia, achi qualli.

Injc motta in aqujn ipan tlacatia pilli, in anoço çan maceoalli cujcanj, papaqujnj, tlatlaquetzanj, totoltecatl muchioaia: auh qujttaia, qujmaceoaia in jneiollaliliz, in jnetlamachtil, pactinenca, vellamatia: in jquac ipan mjmatia ytonal, qujtoznequj: in jquac vel monotzaia, in vel ontlamaceoa.

Auh in aqujn amo ipan mjmatia, in atle ipan qujttaia: çan qujtlavelia yn jtonal: ca iuh mjtoa: in jquac aqujn cujcanj, anoço aca toltecatl, tlachichiuhquj: intla ie vnca qujquanj, ye vnca ynccujltonol: auh ie conpopoa, ijxco, ijcpac, ie qujmana, contepopoaltia, yz ic moquetza, iz ic moqujxtia, ic teijxco, teicpac nemj, ic atlamattinemj, ic cuecuenoti, injx, injiollo, in jcujcanjo, in inemach, injc tlatlatianj, injc tlaiolhujanj, injc cujcapiqujnj, inic cujcatoltecatl:

auh intla cana coanotzalo, cuicatlalhujlo, tlacaqujtilo, molcaoaltilo, aocmo vmpa conjtta, aoc tle ipan qujtta, in javiaca, in jtzopelica in tloque, in naoaque, in xochitl in jetl, in atl, in tlaqualli: auh in ne tilma-

1. The *Real Palacio MS* gives the correct day, *ecatl.*

2. Tezcatlipoca. Cf. *Florentine Codex,* Book VI, fol. 203*r* (*tzopelic, avijac*).

nance, and even the cape. For verily there was everything in his home. Nothing was required; he had an abundance, so he thought.

And the mothers and fathers, the lord, the captain of the guard,[3] the seasoned warrior[4] he despised; he no longer respected nor regarded one. He no longer addressed one with solicitude. When some poor old men and women, or a youth, met and greeted him, he despised them. He only talked through his nose; addressed one through clenched teeth; and growled and snuffled at him.

So it was said that truly his wealth had made him proud, for he by whom we live no longer esteemed him. However, he by whom we live, who had endowed him, took from and deprived him of his deserts. Not without result were his pride and presumption.

Then sickness came upon him. Perchance he became blind, or had a malady of the groin or decaying of the genitals; or paralysis, or the gout; or he became dumb, speechless; or deaf, hard of hearing; or he lost his teeth; he had haemorrhoids, or a cancer. Sores came upon him. Our lord consigned him to oblivion, and abandoned him. He went about shaking and tossing his head, which ached and was inflamed. He went about exhausted and in agony. At this time he wished death to free him from his torment and suffering. No longer was it a time for pride; he could endure no more; he asked for death. O that there might be an end! No longer was anyone concerned with him; no one recognized him as superior. He was only glanced at.

Indeed he came upon and lived in great misery. Dissipated, even as water flowed away, were his possessions which had brought superiority, thrown away like rubbish. Sickness left him divested to the same degree that he had lived in pride when nothing was needed in his home.

And when he died, he only aroused pity. Nothing was laid over him; he was only cast out naked; there was nothing at hand to be used as wrappings for the dead. He went in pain and affliction. Misery lay ahead of him. Just as he had lived, just so he perished, because he had neglected his deserts. For he had lived in deceit in the rituals of song and dance.

tli, ipampa ca nel ie muchi vnca in jchan, ca aoc tle monectoc, aoc tle quitemachia, in iuh momati,

ioan in tenan, in teta, in tecutli, in achcauhtli, yiaotequjoa, aoc tle ipan qujtta, aoc ac tle conpoa, aoc ac quixtilia, aoc no iellatoa, in aca qujnamjquj, in qujmotlapalhuia, in icnoveve, yn jcnoilama, in tlapaltzintli: aocmo vmpa conjtta, ça iiacacpan tlatoa, ça onqujqujnaca, ça conqujqujnatza, ça iacaqujqujntlatoa,

ic mjtoa ca nel ie ca tlamachtia in jnecuiltonol, ca aoc tle ipan qujtlattilia, in jpalnemoanj: auh in tel ie oqujmanjli, in jpalnemoanj, in oqujmotzitzqujli, conmocaoaltilia in jmâceoal, amo nenqujça yn jatlamachiliz, ymatlamatiliz:

njmã cocoliztli itech motlalia, aço ixpopoioti, quexilivi anoço tlapalanaltia, cocototzavi, cooaçivi, anoço nonti, nonõti, nacatzatzati, nacaztzatzaivi, anoço tlanquaalaviliztli, xuchiçiviztli, qualocatl, qualoc itech motlalia, xomolli, caltechtli conjttitia in totecujo, caltechtli contocatimoteca, motzontlaujtzotinemj, moquatlaujtzotinemj, iquatla mantinemj, mjpitztinemj, mociauhpouhtinemj, mociauhquetztinemj; ie vncan in momjqujtlanj, itoneuhcopa, itoneuhcacopa, aoc iatlamatian, acontlaiecoa, in qujmjtlanjtoc mjqujztli, in ma cuele popolivi, aoc ac no ica, aoc ac qujmocujtia, aoc ac qujmjximatcatoca, ça tlatlâtto:

vel conjtta vmpa onqujça in jcnotlacaiotl, tlatlatlamj, iuhqujn atl onqujça in jxqujch ocatlamachtiaia ytlatquj, vellanaoac tlavica, qujpetztoccaoa in cocoliztli, izqujmpan atlamattinemj, in atle monectoc ichan:

auh injc onmjquj, ça tetlaoculti, aoc tle itech vetztotiuh, ça petlauhtiuh, aoc neçinj in tlein iqujmjliuhca, vel totoneoatiuh, chichichinacatiuh in jiollo, vel iiacacpa qujqujztiuh in netolinjliztli, ça iuhquj oniauh, iuhquj onpôpolivi ipampa ca ueli no concauh ymâceoal, injc oiztlacattinen vevetitlan, aiacachtitlan:

3. Juan de Torquemada: *Segunda parte de los viente i un libros rituales i monarchia indiana* (Madrid: Nicolas Rodriguez Franco, 1723), pp. 544-545.

4. Arthur J. O. Anderson and Charles E. Dibble: *Florentine Codex,* Book II, "The Ceremonies" (Santa Fe: School of American Research and University of Utah, 1951), p. 102.

For, so was it said, he had fallen into great sin.[5] There rags and tatters lay strung out; there misery and orphanhood were the reward. And there was the great flood, the great crag, the pit, where there was a falling into the flood, or from the crag, or into the pit.[6] And there lay the snare, where one was snared.

ca iuh mjtoa, tlaalavi, tlapetzcavi, âtlacacemellecan vncan vilantoc in tzotzomatli, in tatapatli, vncã mâceoalo in jcnoiotl, in jcnotlacaiotl: auh vncan icac, in vei atoiatl, in vei tepexitl, in tlaxapuchtli, vncã neatoiavilo, netepexivilo, netlaxapuchvilo: ioan vncan manj in tzonoaztli, vncan netzonoazvilo:

So was it said of him to whom it so befell that his fate and merits had been good; only of his own will and by his own act he had harmed, destroyed, and ruined it, etc.

ic mjtoa, in aqujn iuhquj ipan muchioaia, y, qualli ocatca: in jtonal, in jmâceoal, ça inêviian, ça onmonevianvi, in oconmjtlacalhuj, in oconmopôpolhuj, yn oconmotlaçolmjctili. Etc.

And if a woman were born upon the day One Flower, it was said that she would be an able embroiderer. But nevertheless, in order to gain her deserts, and to achieve skill in embroidering, she should do great penances, and fast, and draw blood when the day sign One Flower set in. But if she did not do penances, if she took not good heed, if her upbringing and training were not good, she herself harmed her day sign.

Auh intla aca cioatl, ipan tlacatia ce suchitl: mjtoaia, vuellamachchiuhquj iez: auh iece injc vel quicnopilhujz imâceoal, injc vel qujttaz tlâmachtli, cēca tlamaceoaia, moçaoaia, mjçoia in jquac moquetzaia ce suchitl tonalli: auh intlacamo tlamaceoa, intlacamo vel monotza, intlacamo vellaoapaoalli, vellazcaltilli mochioa, çan no qujtlaueliaia yn jtonal:

Likewise it befell her (as was told here) that her labors were in vain; she merited complete poverty and misery. Thus her deserts only came to an end, to naught; they became corruption. She became a harlot, a courtesan. She sold herself; she became a paramour. For it was said that just so was her day sign, One Flower; for it fell two ways. They said it was good and evil.

no iuhquj ipan muchioaia (in iuh omjto njcan) atle onqujçaia, çan moch icnoiotl, netoliniliztli in qujmomaceviac auh injc ça ontlatzontia, ontlatzonqujxtia, ça aujlqujzcaiotl, in jnemac mochioa, aavienjti, maaujltia, monanamaca, motzitzinnamaca: ic mjtoa, ca nel iuhquj itonal in ce suchitl, ca vme vitz qujtoa, qualli, ioã âqualli.

Also it was said that when One Flower set in, then began, continued, and was always held, a dance, a procession. But only Moctezuma in his own heart knew — [for] no one [else] determined — for how many days he established his dance. Perchance for forty days there would be dancing.

No yoan mjtoa, in jquac moquetzaia ce suchitl: vncan oncempeoa, vncan vnmocemana, in muchipa maceoalo, netotilo, çan iee qujmati in Motecuçuma yiollotlâma aiac qujiocoia, in quezqujlhujtl, qujtlaliz ymaceoaliz in aço vmpoalilhujtl manjz mâceoaliztli:

And that it might be known that a dance had been arranged, two poles with flowers were set up; they remained at the palace of the ruler. Thus was made known the day of the flowers: there would be enjoyment of and rejoicing over the day of flowers.

auh injc necia, ynjc temaceoaliztlalhujloia, vme suchiquavitl oalmoquetzaia, oalmomanaia tecpan, tlatocan: yc monextia in suchilhujtl, suchipacoa, nexuchitlamachtilo:

At that time the ruler determined and requested the kinds of song to be intoned — perhaps after the manner of those of Cuextlan,[7] the drunkards of Cuextlan;[8] or of Huexotzinco or Anahuac; or the merchants; or those of Nonoalco, or Cozcatlan; or of

vncã tlatlâtlamj, tlanenequj in tlatoanj, in catle cujcatl coneoaz, in anoço cuextecaiotl, tlaoancacuextecaiotl, vexotzincaiotl, anaoacaiotl, oztomecaiotl, nonoalcaiotl, cozcatecaiotl, tenjcaiotl, tepetlacaiotl, chichimecaiotl, metztitlancalcaiotl, otoncujcatl, quata-

5. *Florentine Codex*, Book VI, fol. 191*v*: *tlaalauj, tlapetzcauj in tlalticpac*. See also fol. 210*v*.

6. Cf. also *loc. cit.* The passage is metaphorical.

7. Probably Huaxteca. See, however, Sahagún (Garibay ed.), X, 29, 78-82 (cf. Vol. I, p. 9, for reference system, to be used hereafter except in special cases).

8. Cf. *ibid.*, IV, 7, 5.

the Tenime;[9] or those of Tepetlan; or the Chichimeca; or those of Metztitlan; or the Otomí warriors or of the Quaquata; or the rabbit songs; or songs with two-toned drums, etc.; or women's songs; or those of the girls with the lock of hair at the side of the head. Or perchance only songs of debauchery, or of bragging; or of the sick, or of the cripples; or of the shorn ones; or of vice, etc.

cujcatl, tochcujcatl, teponazcujcatl. Etc. çioacujcatl, atzotzocolcujcatl, auh in anoço çan aujlcujcatl, ixcuecuechcujcatl, cococujcatl, quappitzcujcatl, quateçoqujcujcatl, aujlcujcatl. Etc.

So it was said that verily the [day sign of the] flower was in place.

yc mjtoaia ca nel onjcac in suchitl.

And then the majordomos gathered together all the ruler's dancing array which he requested, and which he might exhibit; whatever he might desire to dance in, in which he would show himself to the people.

Ioan vncã qujcenqujxtiaia, in cacalpixque in jxqujch imâceollatquj tlatoanj, qujtlanenectia, qujtlâtlattitia, in catle coneleujz, ipan onmjtotiz, ipan ontetlattitiz:

And then he gave devices to the chieftains, the insignia-bearers, the Otomí, the shorn ones, the commanding generals, the generals, those who struck, encircled, overtook, hemmed in, and spied on the people.

ioan vncan qujntlavizmacaia, in tiacaoan, in tetlaujcecaoa, in otomj, in quaquachicti, in tlatlacatecca, in tlatlacochcalca, in tevitequjnj, in temalacachoanj, in teviltequjnj, in tetzacujianj, in tetlallanvianj:

And at that time, in truth, favors were accorded and distributed. He singled out, by means of gifts, all the singers, the singers from the common folk, the song-writers, the composers, the beaters of drums — the ground drums, the two-toned drums; two-toned drum players, those who started the singing, those who led, those who gave the pitch, and those who whistled with their fingers; and the leaders and conductors of the dance, the dancers, those who urged the dancers on, those who distributed them, those with trembling voices, those who made noises like a weasel;[10] the circle dancers, and all who belonged and worked with those mentioned.

yoan vel oncan mocnaviaia, mopixqujaia, tlatemachiaia, netlauhtiltica, in jxquich cujcani, mâceoalcujcanj, in cujcatlalianj, in cujcapiqujnj: auh in tlatzotzonquj, in vevetzonquj, teponaço, teponaçoanj cujcaito, cujcaanquj, cujcatlazquj, yoan in mapipitzoanj: auh in teiacanquj, in teiacananj, mjtotianj, motlaqujtotianj, tlamoiauhquj, tozcacuecuechoanj, tocujlechoanj, tlacocoloanj: moch iehoan intech povia, intech açia, in mjtoa:

Before them came their food, the prepared foods: — tamales with beans forming a sea-shell on top; fruit tamales; tamales of a dough of maize treated with lime; hard tamales with maize grains thrown in; tamal-stones; large tortillas; coarse, white tortillas; rolled tortillas; doubled tortillas, tortilla pies; tortillas shredded, or wrapped about turkey; tamales formed in rolls; tamales of maize; ground-up tamales; crumbled tortillas; folded tortillas; meat with grains of maize.

ixpampa vitz, itlaqualtzin, in tlaqualtectli, in quatecujcujlli, xocotamalli, tenextamalli, tetamalli, tlatzincujtl, tamaltetl, vei tlaqualli, quauhtlaqualli, tlaxcalmjmjlli, tlacuelpacholli, tlaçiiocuepalli, tlaxcalcototztli, totolqujmjlli, tamalmjmjlli, tamalatl, tamalcuecuechtli, papaiaxtlaxcalli, papaiantlaxcalpacholli, nacatlaoio.

And when they had tired and were wearied of dancing, then they took and burned the two flowered poles. And then they fashioned and adorned still

Auh in jquac otlatziuh, in ocontlatzilhuj mâceoaliztli, njman qujcalaqujaia, qujtlatiaia, in vme suchiquavitl: auh iquac oc centlamãtli, ic qujxiptlaiotiaia,

9. Cf. *ibid.*, X, 29, 94-95; *gente bárbara* was a term generally understood by *tenime*.

10. In describing the sound made by the weasel Sahagún, Book V, chap. vi, reads *auh injc tlatoa pipitzca, iuhquin mapipitzoa: tocujleoa tocujlechoa. . . .* See also, Olmos, *op. cit.*, p. 235 (*tocuileua*). See also p. 165, below.

another flowered pole. This they ignited, set fire to, and burned. And so silence reigned and it was still; it remained calm in the city; no one stirred or made a noise. For the flowers had burned; they had been destroyed by fire.

But none the less, in the home of each nobleman and lord there was much singing and rejoicing. Only and alone at the palace was the dancing ended. All the people rejoiced completely.

qujchichioaia, çan no suchiquavitl: iehoatl tlatlaia, qujtlatiaia, qujtecaviaia: ic cactimomanaia, cactiuetzia tlamattimomana in altepetl, aoc ac tlaolinja, tlachalanja: ipampa ca omotlati otlatlac in suchitl:

auh tel in ceceiaca inchan pipilti, tlatoque, vel cujcoia pacoaia, çaniio, çaniiocan in tecpan mocaoaia in mâceoaliztli, in mochi tlacatl in cempaquja.

Eighth Chapter, which telleth of the fifth sign, named One Reed. And it was not a good day, [nor] those with it. It was said that those born then, if they were born in the ninth house, named Nine Crocodile — they said and it was averred that one would be a slanderer and bearer of false witness. And it was thought that this sign was the day of Quetzalcoatl. Therefore the lords and noblemen then paid their devotions and made offerings.

The day sign One Reed set in. With it were reckoned the evil days, those of an unfavorable time.

Following it came Two Ocelot, and Three Eagle, Four Vulture, Five Motion, and Six Flint Knife. These various days were said to be evil, of an unfavorable time.

It was held that One Reed was the day sign, the time, of Quetzalcoatl. For Quetzalcoatl represented the wind, and was therefore thought a god. And when the day One Reed set in, the lords and noblemen paid him great honors. They made offerings at the *calmecac,* the place called Mexico [calmecac].[1] For there was kept the image of Quetzalcoatl. Before him they arranged and spread offerings. Everything they then prepared for him. They placed on him his various array and paper vestments. And before him they laid out flowers, tobacco, [vessels] full of incense, and drink and food. So they said that then they dedicated and assigned the day sign to Quetzalcoatl.

And so they said it was an unfortunate time. He who was then born, whether nobleman or commoner, was of scant merit or deserts. Just as worthless as the wind was his life. It was swept away by the wind. As nothing were his lineage and origin. For in the time of Quetzalcoatl the wind [god] had he been born; for such was his nature. The same befell her if it was a woman.

Injc chicuei capitulo: itechpa tlatoa, injc macujltetl machiotl, in jtoca ce acatl: auh amo qualli tonalli in jtech ca, qujlmach in aqujque vncan tlacatia, intla vncan tlacatia, injc chicunauhtetl calli, in jtoca chicunavi cipactli: qujtoaia qujlmach cenca techicoitoanj, ioan teteixpanvianj: auh qujlmach injn machiotl, iehoatl itonal in quetzalcoatl: ipampa in tlatoque, in pipilti, vncan muxtlaoaia ioan tlamanaia.

Moquetza ce acatl tonalli, ic mocempoa in amo qualli, in amo ieccan izqujlhujtl,

qujtoqujlitica yn jpan vme ocelutl, ioan ei quauhtli, navi cozcaquauhtli, macujlli olin, chiquacen tecpatl: in jzqujtetl in tonalli mjtoaia amo qualli, amo ieccan,

qujlmach itonal catca itonalpan in quetzalcoatl. Iehica in quetzalcoatl, i ehecatl ipan mjxeoaia, injc tevtocoia: auh in jquac in moquetzaia ce acatl tonalli, cenca tlamaviztiliaia in tlatoque, in pipilti, tlamanaia in calmecac, yn jtocaiocan mexico, ca vncan pialoia in jxiptla Quetzalcoatl, ixpan qujtlatequjliaia, qujtlamâmacaia much iquac qujcencaviliaia, itech qujtlaliliaia, in jzqujtlamantli inechichioal, yn iamatlatquj, ioan ixpan qujtequjliaia suchitl, yetl, qujcopaltemjliaia atl, tlaqualli, qujmanjlia, iuh qujtoaia vncan qujtonaltia, qujtonalquechia in Quetzalcoatl.

Auh injc mjtoa: amo ieccan, in aqujn ipan tlacatia pilli, anoço maceoalli, atle cenca imâceoal, ilhujl catca, çan iuhqujn ehecatl ipã povia inemiliz, êcatocoia, atle itlaanca, inelhoaio mochioaia: ipampa in jtonalpan quetzalcoatl, êecatl otlacat, ca njman iuhcan oquiz, no iuhquj ipan muchioaia, intla çioatl,

1. The *calmecac,* house of priestly learning, is defined as "*'lugar de linaje de la casa' y escuela de nobles*" by Arturo Monzón in *El calpulli en la organización social de los tenochca* (México: Instituto de Historia, 1949), p. 77. There were six, in the nobler *calpulli* (pp. 47-52). See Mexico calmecac in *Florentine Codex,* Book II, appendix on temple buildings.

And in this way did the readers of the day signs remedy it: if someone were born on these several days, they passed over them and waited for Seven Rain. At that time they bathed him, that they might give him a name. For in that way they remedied his fate; then they brought him out at a good time and it resulted at a propitious moment. They made it partly good. Thus they expected that perchance his fate and deserts might become something — if he lived, were well reared, and played his part well; because later, there, they had set in Seven Rain;[2] they put their trust in Seven Rain.

They said it was a good day. Merciful, pitying, and compassionate was the one born precisely upon it. He became fortunate. It was as if his fortune, his deserts, his good luck rained down upon him: as if it sprinkled on or swirled about him. It was said that verily so was his day sign, Seven Rain.

And he who was born on it was forthwith bathed, and they gave him a name. No longer did they pass over it, or delay or postpone it.

Nevertheless, the morrow, Eight Flower, which came next and following, was also the same. It, so they said, was also good. If someone were born on it, they also at once bathed him and gave him a name. For this reason they did so: they feared the one which followed in order — Nine Crocodile.

This, so they said, was in no way good; it was perverse, full of vice. It accorded one rags and tatters. Nothing could become a remedy or cure for the day sign which had followed.

Only and exclusively immersed in and dedicated to evil was the one then born. He was given only to talking; he went wrapped in discussion. Words were his hair. He was hot-tempered.[3] He twisted words. Great was his glee if somewhere there was a shout; there he ran and listened to what was said. If somewhere there was discussion and something was said, he went among the people sowing discord; he went causing disagreements and dissension; he confounded and disunited them.

He disregarded and showed no regret for insinuations, spreading rumors, and continued lying. Falsehood and deceit he went about sowing here and there among the people. He interrupted conversa-

auh injc qujpatiaia tonalpouhque, intla aca ipan otlacat izqujlhujtl oc conchololtiaia, qujchieltiaia in chiconqujavitl qujnjquac caltiaia inic qujtocamacazque, ipampa ic qujpatia in jtonal, vncan qujieccaquixtia, ieccan qujça, chicoqualtia, ic conjttilia, in aço ça itla ilhujl, imâceoal, muchioatiuh intla nemiz, intla uel oapaoaz, intla uel moquetzaz ipampa oc vncan in chicomatl qujtlaliaia, vel qujtemachiaia in chiconqujavitl.

qujtoaia ca qualli tonalli, icnooa, teicnoittanj, tetlaocolianj, in aqujn vel ipan tlacatia, tlacnopilhujanj muchioaia, iuhqujn ipan tzetzelivi, iuhqujn ipan pipixauj, iuhqujn momoloca ilhujl, imâceoal, icnopil, mjtoa ca nel iuhquj itonal in chiconqujavitl.

Auh in aqujn ipan tlacatia, çan niman iquac maltia, qujtocamaca, aocmo conchololtia, aocmo qujtlatviltia, aocmo connechcatlaça:

auh tel no iuhquj in imoztlaioc qujtztica, in qujtoqujlitica. Chicuey suchitl: iuh qujtoaia no qualli, intla aca ipan tlacatia: çan njman no iquac caltiaia, qujtocamacaia, ipampa iuh qujchioaia, y, iehoatl qujmacaçia in oallatoqujlia, chicunavi cipactli:

iuh qujtoaia njman amo qualli, amo tlacacemelle, motqujtica teuhtli, tlaçolli, tzotzomatli, tatapatli, qujteilhujltia, aoc tle ipatica, aoc tle ipaio mochioa, in qujoaltoqujlia tonalli,

çaniioca tetlaactica mjxcaujtica, injc amo qualli in aquĩ ipan tlacatia, çan tlatolli cololotinemj, tlâtolli cololhujtinemj, tlâtoltzon, tlâtolli, itlaqual tlâtolnecujl, cenca ivelmach intla cana neaio, vmpa motlaloa, tecacaquj, intla cana nenonotzalo, itla itolo, tetzalan, tenepantla, motecatinemj, techalanjtinemj, tenetecheuhtinemj, tetlatolçaçaca teiollocôcoltia:

atle ipan qujtta, amo qujtequanmati in ovitlatolli, in tetzauhtlatolli, ihiztlacati, iztlactli, tenqualactli, tetlaqujquanjtinemj, motlatolcujcujtlavia, qujtlatlâtlalilia in tlatolli, tlâtolpiqujnj, tlatolcampax, tlatolcacam-

2. We have read *chicomatl* as *chicome atl,* possibly a miswriting of *Chicome quiauitl.*

3. *Tlatolli itlaqual.* See *Florentine Codex,* Book VI, cap. xli; Sahagún (Garibay ed.), VI, 41, 10: "Salta como granizo de albarda. *Este refrán se dice de aquellos que tocándolos un poco con alguna palabra áspera luego saltan en cólera y riñen y echan ponzoña por la boca, y cuando oyen hablar mal de otro luego ayudan.*"

tions, deceived, and distorted and twisted the words in his mouth. He spoke incoherently and let fall rumors; he listened secretly. He loitered among people and raised questions among them. He kept his own counsel. He never guarded a secret nor held a trust. He would straightway divulge and make known one's sins, one's words. In public disgrace, he thus went from house to house.

pax, tlatolchochopoc, tenênexotla, motepâpachivia, teca nênemj, teca tlâtlâtlanj, mononotza, atle vel itic tlalilo, atle vel ixpan mjtoa: njman tepan qujcenmana, tepan qujmoiaoa in tetlatlacol, in tetlatol, tetenco qujtlaztinemj, ic tepan cacalaquj,

He was ignorant and uninformed as to his livelihood. Always he faced and continued to be with misery. He wore an old cape and threadbare breech clout. He owned no miserable rags, had nothing to cover his hips or spread over his shoulders. He lived in poverty, in his house, exposed to inclement weather. Never was it warm; old, worn mats and seats were strewn about. No one swept. Rubbish was all about and surrounded him.

an iê qujmati, an iê qujlhuja, in tlein inenca, ic muchipa icnoiotl, qujtztinemj, itech eoatinemj, itilmaçol, imaxtlaçol ietinemj, aonmonamjquj in jtatapa, âoalnecinj yn jquezpan onoz, in jquechtlan pilcaz, aoneoatinemj, in jcalitic calceceoazco, aic tlatotonja, petlaçolli icpalçolli, ueuetztoc, aiac tlachpana, tlaçolli moteujlacachoa, tlaçolli imoteujlacachoaian,

And he only lived in sorrow and anger, emerging in wrath, groaning. He sought for something that might give him joy, or solace his heart, or bring him contentment. But what could he do? For verily, at such a time was he born; his alms were misery. For so was his day sign — one of vice.

auh çan moxixicotinemj, moçôçomatinemj, mjhitleuhtinemj, qujqujnacatinemj, qujtemoa in ma itla ic ompaquj, in ma itla ic oncevi in jiolo, in ma ic onvellamati, quen çan nel conchioaz: ca nel iuhcan otlacat, in icnoiotl iieoaia, ca iuhquj itonal, in tlaçolli, teuhtli.

And Ten Wind, as hath been said, was a good day sign, as well as the three following it — Eleven House, and Twelve Lizard, and Thirteen Serpent. All were favorable. Ten Wind bore them all along and influenced them.

Auh in matlactli hecatl: iuh mjtoaia, qualli tonalli: ioan in oc etetl qujtoqujltica in matlactloce calli, ioan matlactlomome cuetzpali, matlactlomei coatl: muchi qualli, qujncenvica, quj̃centlatalhuja, in matlactli hecatl:

So it was said that he who was then born had as all his gifts fame, honor, valor, riches, and wealth. As was said, strong was the day sign. None could mock, chide, or belittle him, because he had been born in a "time of ten."[4] So it befell man and woman.

iuh mjtoaia: in aqujn ipan tlacatia, muchi inemac in teniotl in maviçotl, in oqujchiotl, in necujltonolli, netlacamachiliztli, iuh mjtoaia: cenca tonalchicaoac, aiac vel qujquequeloa, aiac vel ica mocacaiaoa, aiac vel qujmoxixictia: ipampa ca tlamatlactian in otlacat, iuhquj ipan muchioaia, in oqujchtli, in çioatl.

4. The term *tlamatlactian* can be translated only imperfectly, because of the unique features of the system of reading the day signs. The numbers ten to thirteen all include the term *matlactli* (ten); and, generally, to days including and following ten, good, or at least similar, qualities were attributed.

Ninth Chapter, which telleth of the sixth sign, called One Death, and of the good fortune belonging to it. It was said to be the day sign of Tezcatlipoca. And many were the offerings and blood sacrifices with which they did him honor. And each person provided much pleasure to the slaves.

One Death set in. This was said to be a good day sign, but also somewhat bad, as will here appear in its discussion. For it was said that when this occurred, then they honored Tezcatlipoca. The lords greatly venerated [the day sign]. Each one made offerings and beheaded quail at his personal [altar] in his house and in each of the *calpulcos* in the temples called *teocalli.*

Thus did they speak: "This one is he by whom we live, Titlacauan, master of the earth, master of the lords of the earth, who now hath his blessed day."

For everyone then showed devotion, was humbled, and sorrowed, in order that he would show them favor. And not alone did the lords thus act, but also the brave warriors, the seasoned warriors, and the wealthy, the rich, and he who was wise; for the day sign of Titlacauan had set in. They also observed the day sign and made offerings in his dwelling place in his *calpulco.* For this reason they showed great devotion, for this was the time to pray for favors.

And as for its not being accounted a good and favorable time: there then was fear and dread lest this same one be wrathful and wilful. For thus did they say: "He whom he had favored and honored, and to whom he had revealed his sweetness, fragrance, and mercy, from this same one he might withdraw and remove it." Yet it was not without reason; when [the man] became vain and haughty, he disregarded and neglected what was his birthright. Still [the god] showed compassion and gave it as a gift to the one who sought him diligently and who went about weeping and sighing for his sake. So was it said that everywhere he was awaited; everywhere there was humility and sorrow before him. Nowhere was the dwelling place of the war [god]

Injc chicunavi capitulo: itechpa tlatoa, injc chiquacentetl machiotl, in jtoca ce mjqujztli: ioan in qualli tonalli itech ca, qujlmach itonal in Tezcatlipuca: auh mjec in ventli, in nextlaoalli injc qujmaviztiliaia, ioan cenca qujnpapaqujltiaia in tlatlacoti.

Moquetza ce mjqujztli: ynjn mjtoaia, qualli tonalli: auh ioan achi amo qualli, in iuh neçiz nican, ipan itlatollo, ca mjtoa in jquac, y, vncan qujtonal tiaia in Tezcatlipuca, cenca tlamaviztiliaia, in tlatoque, tlamanaia, tlacotonaia, ceceniaca yn jncalitic, in jmjxcoian in cacalpulco, in moteneoa in teucalli, in teucalco:

iuh qujtoaia, ca iehoatl in jpal tinemj, in titlacaoan, in tlalticpaque, in tlaltecue, in axcan itonalpantzinco,

ic muchi tlacatl vncan tlatemachiaia, nentlamatia, tlaocuiaia, injc qujcneliz: auh amo çanioque in tlatoque, iuh qujchioaia, y, no iehoan in tiacaoã, in tequjoaque, yoan in mocujltonoa, in motlacamati, ioan in aqujn qujmatia, ca itonal moquetza in titlacahoã, no tlatonaltiaia, tlamanaia, in jchã, in jcalpulco: ypampa injc cenca tlatemachiaia, ca vncan tlaitlanjliloia, injc teicneliz:

auh injc amo qualcan, ieccan, ipan machoia, ca vncan nemauhtiloia, ymacaxoia, injc amo çan no iê moçomaz, monenequjz, ca iuh qujtoaia, in aqujn qujcnelia, in oconmaviçolti, in oixpan conqujxti, in jtzopelica, in javiiaca, in jtetlaocoliliz: çan no iê conjnailia, conjquanjlia, tel amo çan nen iquac in ie atlamati, in ie cuecuenoti in aoc tle ipan tlatta, conmjxcaoaltia, in jmâceoal, ocatca, oc iê qujcnoitta, connemactia, in qujtlamatataqujlia, in jca chocatinemj, elciciuhtinemj, ic mjtoaia: noviian chialo, noviian ivicpa nentlamacho, tlaocoialo, âcan vel ichan in iaotl Tezcatlipuca: çan jtlan conantinemj in jpetl, jcpal.

Tezcatlipoca; he only went withdrawing rule and power from others.

And of him who was born on the day sign One Death it was said that he would prosper and be rich, whether a nobleman or only a poor vassal. Many were his gifts. Honor came his way and rested on him when he performed well his penances and humbled himself. But if he did not do well the penances, purely by his own act he forsook and harmed his day sign.

Auh in aqujn ipã tlacatia itonal ce mjqujztli: mjtoaia mocujltonoz, motlamachtiz, intla pilli, anoço çan maceoaltzintli, muchi inemactia, itech açia, itech pachivia, in maviçotl: iquac in tlauellamaceoa, mocnomati: auh intlacamo uellamaceoa, ca çan yneujian conmocaujlia, qujmjtlacalhuja yn jtonal.

If, at this time, someone were born, then they bathed him and gave him a name. Small children performed the naming ceremony.[1] If a boy had been born, they therefore called forth [as his name] Miquiz, or Yaotl, Cenyaotl, Necoc yaotl, Chicoyaotl, or Yaomauitl. So they placed on him a name of Tezcatlipoca. Of this one it was said: "None may wish him harm: none may wish him to die." If anyone should wish or desire his death, he would simply sicken and suddenly die.

yn jquac, y, tla aca otlacat, njman caltiaia, qujtocamaca, qujxicvenquaqualia in pipiltotonti, intla oqujchtli otlacat, ic qujnotza mjqujz, anoço iaotl, ceniaotl, necoc iaotl, chicoiaotl, iaomavitl, ic qujtocamamaia in Tezcatlipuca: injn mjtoaia, aiac vel qujcocoliz, aiac vel qujmjqujtlanjz, intla aca qujmjqujtlanj, qujmjqujztemachia, çan iê in mococolia onmjctiuetzi.

At this time it was the day sign of the slaves, the wretched slaves, whose dwelling places were by the hones for sharpening and the grinding stones. None of the slave-owners could scold them, or abuse them with vile words, or call angrily or indignantly to them when they learned that the morrow would be the day sign of Tezcatlipoca. They then, first, took from them, struck off, and removed from them the wooden collars, the curved ones in which they were held and with which they went about restrained lest they flee. Then they soaped them and bathed them, and made much of and flattered them. They showed them great esteem, because, so they thought, they were his likenesses and representatives:[2] his beloved sons. It was said that they were like the blue cotingas, the trupials, the precious birds of Tezcatlipoca. And those who owned slaves warned and on threat of death[3] ordered their children, youths, and growing sons, commanding them sternly and rigorously, not to chide, deal vainly with, nor strike the slaves.

Auh in jquac in catca ipan tonalli: in tlatlacoti, in tlatlacotzitzinti, in teatexatitlan, temetlatitlan innemjan: aiac vel qujmaoaia, aiac vel qujntenquanviaia, qujntlauelnotzaia, qujnqualancanotzaia, in tlacaoaque, in oqujmatque, ca muztla itonalpan iez in Tezcatlipuca: njman achto qujntomaia, qujtequjlia, qujntlaxilia in quauhcozcatl, in coliuhquj, injc pieloia, inic ilpitinenca, injc amo cholozque: njman ic qujmamoviaia, qujmaltiaia, cenca qujntlaçotlaia, qujnxoxocoiomatia, vel qujnmavizmatia, ipampa iuh qujmatia, ca ixiptlaoa, ipatillooa, ytlaçopilhoan, mjtoa iuhqujn iquecholhoan, içaquantotooa, itlaçototoan in Tezcatlipuca: auh in tlacaoaque, vel qujnnemachtiaia, qujnmjqujznaoatiaia, qujntlaquauhnaoatiaia, qujntepitznaoatiaiaia, in impilhoan, in jntlazcaltilhoan, yn intlaoapaoalhoan: injc amo qujmaoazque qujncuecuenochichioazque, anoço qujnvitequjzque in tlacaoã:

---

1. Of this ceremony, the Spanish text reads: *"combidauan a los njñ os, y les dauan de comer: para q̃ supiessen el nombre, del que auja nacido: y le diuulgassen a bozes, por las calles."* Eduard Seler, in *Einige Kapitel aus dem Geschichtswerk des Fray Bernardino de Sahagun* (Stuttgart: Strecker and Schröder, 1927), p. 315, translates an explanatory passage from the *Academia de la Historia MS*: *niman ye ic quimonnotza in oquichpipiltotonti In iquac ouallaque niman ye ic quimmamaca in ixicuen ontlatlani*[*a*] *in tlein ytoca auh quinilhuia in aço yaotl anoço uitzitl auh niman ye ic tzatzitiui quihtona xiualhuia tocniuane xicxicuenquaquaqui i yaotl yquac quicaquiztilia in itoca inic mochi tlacatl ic quinotzaz — dann ruft er die Knaben. Nachdem sie gekommen sind, gibt er ihnen die Nabelschnur-Opfergabe und fragt* (*die Angehörigen*), *wie es heisst, und er nennt ihnen* (*die Namen*) *Yaotl oder Uitzitl* (*Krieger oder Kolibri*). *Und darnach fangen sie an zu schreien und sprechen: "Kommt her, Freunde, das Nabelschnuropfer Yaotls essen." Dann melden sie seinen Namen* (*des Kindes*), *mit dem alle es nennen sollen.*

2. See *Florentine Codex,* Book VI, fol. 203*v*.

3. *Qujntepitznaoatiaiaia*: the term so appears in the Nahuatl column.

And if any chid them, so it was said, thereby he brought upon and burdened and visited upon himself misery and affliction. It was as if pustulate sores had covered and been fastened on him; it seemed that, as a gift, it has been transferred to and left with him. At that time were given him his deserts, for he had brought upon himself great sin and wrong.[4] Furthermore, he had put on the wooden collar. Even so would he be, even so would he attain, as had become the lot of the beloved son of Tezcatlipoca. He would be struck and beaten; he would be pursued from one place to another. Never would he be settled on the land, nor let alone, nor found in repose. He would not rest. Thus was it said: never would the cooking pot rest filled; never would he work with security.

auh intla aca oqujmaoac, iuh mjtoaia, iehoatl ica oalmjlacatzoa, conmomamaltia, ic movitequj in victli, in mecapalli, iuhqujn tzotzoviztli itech oalmotlalia, itech oalmoçaloa, iuhqujn manoçe mactli, itech oaltzopi, itech oalmocaoa, vncan conmocaujlia, in jmâceoal ic matoiavia, motepexiuja, oc iehoatl onmaquja in quauhcozcatl, oc iehoatl oniez, iuhquj conjttaz, y, in iuhquj ittitilo, itlaçopiltzin Tezcatlipuca, vitecoz, tzotzonaloz, avic chololtiloz, aquenman tlaltechpa choloz, aonjxcaoaloz, aquēman tlaliloz, aiac moceujz, iuh mjtoa: aquenman caxtenmanaloz, aic tlacaco quichioaz:

And as it had been said that he had brought upon himself great sin and wrong, so was looked upon with great terror that which he might do. In this way did Tezcatlipoca ridicule, make sport of, mock, and curse him. Perchance somewhere he would be ceremonially bathed; he would die in sacrifice as a bathed victim. And it was said: "He will die sacrificed as a war captive. They will cook him in an olla and eat him." Because at one time the wretched slave was beaten, [the god] transferred his sins upon him. So he feared this, for it befell one that although he became rich, swiftly misery came to him, poverty frayed him. [Of the god], thus was it said: "He only maketh sport of one. Of no one can he be a friend, to no one true." They said Tezcatlipoca enriched one, and thereby visited him with pain and affliction.

auh injc mjtoa: matoiavia, motepexivia, ynjc cenca tlamauhcaittililoia, in nel qujchioaz, injc ica mocaiaoa Tezcatlipuca: injc qujquequeloa, injc ica maviltia, injc qujtelchioa, aço cana altiloz, tlaaltilmjqujz: ioan mjtoaia teumjqujz, qujpaoacizque, qujquazque: ipampa ca ica omoquavitec, in tlacotzintli, ytech oqujcauh in jtlatlacol, injc qujmacacia, y, ca tepan mochioaia, in manel mocujltonoa, ca içiuhca ytech pachiujtiuh in icnoiotl: itech eoatiuh in netolinjliztli: iehoatl injc mjtoa: çan teca maujltia, aiac vel icnjuh, aiac nellin qujlhuja Tezcatlipuca, tecujltonoa, ioan ic temotla in cococ, in teopouhquj,

Then if someone out of his torment cursed him as a sodomite, it was no longer his time of pride when he said to him: "O Titlacauan, thou sodomite! Thou wretched sodomite! Thou hast made fun of and mocked me!" So also did he speak if someone had let his captive flee: "Thou sodomite, O Titlacauan! O that this had likewise befallen thee! Be accursed, that thou hast given me a captive only to make sport of me!" When he said this, which was only his word of torment, what good was it? For so had he been mocked, it was said. Those whom this had befallen were the foolish, who disregarded, destroyed, and dissipated that which was their riches and merit.

ic vncan in aca qujcujlonaoa, itoneuhcacopa, aoc iatlamatian in quilhuja: Titlacaoane, cujlonpole, cujlontepole, otonmotlamachti, otonmoquequelo: no iuh qujtoaia, intla aca oqujchololti imal, cujlonpole, titlacaoane, ma ça njman iê iuh tienj, ma motelchioanj, in tinechmaca malli, ca çan notech otonmoquequelo: in iuh qujtoaia, y, ca ça itoneuhcatlatol, iê tle ça ne, ca ica oneaujltiloc, mjtoa: iehoan in iuh inpam mochioaia, y, in aquj mamatcaoaque, in atle ipan tlatta, in oconpopouhque, yn jmjxco, yn jcpac oqujmanque, in jnnecujltonol, yn jnmâceoal ocatca, in ocacica, injc oteneoaloia, itoloia in tlalticpac oqujchtli, tlalticpac tiacaoan, ca mjtoa: in iuhquj

4. Cf. *Florentine Codex*, Book VI, fol. 210: *otimatoiavi, otimotepexiuj*: *qujtoznequj*: *otimovitili, aiac omjtzovitili;* in the Garibay ed., VI, 43, 37, this is translated as *"Tú mismo te has despeñado. Se dice por el que por su culpa cayó en algún gran crimen o peligro."*

Those who attained [captives] were hence known as and called "earth warrior" or "earth chieftain." For, it was said, just as in battle the chieftain was a captor, just so he was rich and attained worldly goods. Hence was it said, "earth warrior," "earth chieftain."

And in this manner poor slaves achieved glory and honor. For it came to pass that if some poor slave, mocked, beaten, and made to suffer, still escaped, he became rich and wealthy. This same one bought slaves and prospered, governed, and was ruler of all. His kin were attentive of him. When this had happened, perhaps when all was abandoned and desolate, those who had been householders were perchance not there — had gone, — for perchance all was destroyed and wasted. But this same is he who set up the house; he set up the light and torch and brought fame to the slave-buyer's house, where the slave-owners were. Thus was it said: in truth the master of the earth, he through whom we live, causeth no one to lose by negligence; he hath wasted and destroyed the house of those who bought slaves, and to him who was only a poor slave, our lord gave honor and favor. Thus he honored him. Perhaps now often he entertained guests and gave them food. He assembled and gathered people together. He had them dance. He gave them gifts — this [slave] who thus appeared, who was born upon such a day sign, One Death. Hence it was called good and somewhat evil.

iaoc tiacauh tlamanj, no iuhquj in mocujltonoa, câçi in tlalticpacaiotl, ic moteneoa: tlalticpac oqujchtli, tlalticpac tiacauh:

auh injc moteniotia, momaujzçotia, tlacotzitzinti, ca muchioaia, intla aca tlacotzintli, ica onecaiaoaloc, oujtecoc, otlamaceoaltiloc, oc ie qujça mocujltonoa, motlacamati, ie ne tecoa, ie nê onca, ie nê ivic mocemjtquj, ipan moceniacatia, ie nê qujcemjtta in teoaniolque, in jquac, y, aço ipan tlacacaoaltic, aço ipan cactiuetz, acaço caque, aço centlanque in chaneque ocatca, aço tlalpoliuh, aço tlaliooac, auh ie nê calli qujmantica, ie nê tlaujlli ocotl qujquetztica, ie ne tlateniotitica, in jchan tecoanj in tlacaoaque ocatca, ic mjtoa: ca nel aiac qujmoxiccavilia in tlalticpaque, in jpalnemoanj, ontlaliooac, otlalpopoliuh in jnchan ocatca tecoanjme auh ça tlacotzintli inic ontlateniotia moqujmocnelili totecujo: injc qujmaviçoaia, y, aço ie quezqujpa, tecoanotza, tetlaqualtia, tenechicoa, tecentlalia teitotia, tetlauhtia, iehoatl in ic neçi, in iuhquj tonalli ipan tlacatioaia, ce mjqujztli, injc mjtoa qualli, ioan achi amo qualli.

Tenth Chapter, which telleth of still other houses, which were called in part good, and in part evil and miserable.

That which followed, which came second and took second place, was named Two Deer. As was said, so they ascertained and proved it to be an evil day. Only misery did it yield one. Of him who was then born, nothing became his reward: he would only ever live in woe. And he was much afraid and cowardly — an arrant coward. In fear he dashed into the crowds; he came full of fear, dissolved in timidity, faint-hearted. Everywhere he hid himself — he lived in hiding. He concealed himself from others and lived apart.[1] He took sudden frights, and trembled as with chills and fever. When he heard some unusual and terrifying talk, he was alarmed. If someone shouted, or if someone banged or stamped his feet, he blenched and turned white with fear, as if he had no more blood; just like white paper. His heart thumped and fluttered as if shaken like a rattle. His lips quivered and trembled. No longer as usual could his speech come forth, if he pondered or had something in mind, or if something occurred to him.

And Three Rabbit, so it was said, was good. For him then born, that which he ate appeared. It was not apparent nor understandable whence he obtained his reward. So it was said that he was like a rabbit. Without its being apparent, grass, herbs, and maize straw served him as food. Vegetation burst forth over the land, spreading green, fresh, tender, germinating, sending forth shoots, growing green — very green, extending a rich green; a twisted tangle of plants, deep green, matted, growing together, everlasting. Only in grassy fields and swards were the rabbit's dwelling place, burrow, and grazing place. He lapped and sucked up the dew; with nodding head and nipping tooth he nibbled up his food. Just so was the vassal or the man when the time of his day sign was Three Rabbit. It was not apparent how

Injc matlactli capitulo, itechpa tlatoa, in oc cequj calli, in omoteneuh cequj qualli, cequj amo qualli tetolinj.

In contoqujlia, in cononcaiotia, in tlaoncaiotia, itoca vme maçatl: iuh mjtoaia, iuh qujpantiaia, iuh qujneltiliaia amo qualli tonalli, çan icnoiotl qujtemaca: in aqujn ipan tlacatia, atle imâçeoal muchioaia, çan muchipa motolinjtinenca: auh cenca momauhtianj, vcl mauhquj, mâmauhquj, mauhcatepetla, mavitzoco, mauhcaçonequjnj, mauhcaiollo, mjinaia, mjinaxtinemj, motenetlatilia, teueuecapavitinemj, mocujcujtivetzi, iuhqujn âatonavi, viviioca, yn jtla ovi tlatolli, mauhca tlatolli qujcaquj, mjçavia in aca tlaquauhtlatoa, anoço aca tlacocomotza, tlatiticujtza, çiiocopinj, iztaia, iuhqujn aoc ezço, ça iuhqujn amaztalli, yiollo chôcholoa, yiollo papatlaca, iuhqujn tlacacalatztiuetzi iiollo, iten papatlaca, iten viviioca, aocmo iuhquj quiqujça in jtlatol, intla ça itla iiollo conmati, intla itla yiolipan, intla itla iiollo contoca.

Auh in ey tochtli: iuh mjtoaia qualli, in aqujn ipan tlacatia, neçi in qujquanj. âneztica, âmachiztli, in campa qujcnopilhuja, in jmâçeoal, iuh mjtoa in iuhquj tochin, âneztica in jtlaqual, çacatl, xiuhtzintli, eloçacatl, in qujmoquaqualtia, popoçocatoc, cececliztoc, cecelia, cecelpatic, itzmolinj, oalitzmolintiuh, xoxoujxtoc, xoxopaleoatoc, xixinmaltic, xixinmaliuhtoc, xixiuhcaltic, popotzauhtoc, pepettoc, âpoliviztlanquj, çã çacatla, çacatitlan, in jnemjan, in jqujçaian in jtlaquaquaian tochin, âoachquâqua, aoachchichina, qujioiomeuhtica, qujn tlatlaniomeuhtica, in jtlaqual. No iuhquj in maceoalli in tlacatl, in jtonalpan ei tochtli, amo neztica, in quenjn neci itlaqual, âneztica in quenjn ipan oallauh ineuhca, ycemjlhujtiaia.

1. The *Real Palacio MS* includes the word *tetlatlayavalhuitinemi* (*rodear por no topar con otro,* according to Molina, *op. cit.*), after *teueuecapavitinemj.*

his food appeared, nor known how came his sustenance, his daily ration.

And Four Water, so it was said, was an evil day sign. It offered one only misery. He who was then born nowhere was content. He lived only harassed and struggling for the necessities of life. And if perchance something were his reward, just like water it passed by, carried away and scattered by the current.

Likewise Five Dog was evil, as was said. Then they celebrated the day sign of Mictlan tecutli; it was his day sign. Similarly, neither was Six Monkey good, so it was said. Thereafter, all the different days in the time of Seven Grass became good. He who was born upon the various day signs mentioned, they did not yet bathe nor give a name. Later all were bathed together on Seven Grass, because, as it was said, it was claimed always to be a favorable time on the seventh day sign, the one which then became seventh and took seventh place. This was a time of one's merit and reward. And he who was then born they then at that very time bathed and gave a name.

And Eight Reed and Nine Ocelot, as was said, were by no means good day signs but days of wild beasts. He who was born upon them merited only misery. Not yet did they bathe him; later they considered it on Ten Eagle. Till then[2] they waited for it, in order to cause his day sign to result favorably, so that perchance something might come as his merit, if he lived. But nevertheless he might not weaken; still, painfully he could acquire and in torment seek it.[3]

And when well established and apparent, Ten Eagle, so it was said, was a good day sign. Of him who was then born, favorable were the deserts. It was a time of manliness, valor, grandeur, and bravery. It was a day sign of strength and courage. He urged people on; he was spirited toward others; he instilled courage and valor; he was fearless of death. He hurled himself against the foe; he joined in the fray; he shook others off scornfully, drove them into corners, broke into enemy ranks, took after those who fled, and threw himself upon them, was most intent upon the foe, and aroused complete terror. No one would give him occasion to quarrel; no one would dare him,[4] nor contain him, nor sur-

Auh in nauj atl: iuh mjtoa, amo qualli tonalli, çan icnoiotl qujtemaca, in aqujn ipan tlacatia, acan aviaia in jiollo, çan tlaçiiauhtinēca, qujhiiovitinenca: auh intlaçanoço itla ymâceoal, çan iuhqujn atl onqujça, onatoco, onamoiaoa.

No iuhquj in macujlli itzcujntli: amo no qualli, iuh mjtoa: vncan qujtonaltiaia, in mjctlan tecutli, itonalpan catca. No iuhquj in chiquacen oçomatli, amo no qualli, iuh mjtoa: qujn cen vncã qualtiaia, in izqujtetl in tonalli, yn jpan chicome malinalli: yn aqujn ipan tlacatia, in jzqujlhujtl in omoteneuh aiamo caltiaia, aiamo qujtocamacaia, qujn cen jpan maltiaia, in chicome malinalli: ipampa iuh mjtoa, qujlmach muchipa qualcan, yn jpan chicome tonalli, in vncan tlachicometi, chicometioaia: vncan ca teilhujl, temâceoal: auh in aqujn ipan otlacat, njmã vel iquac caltiaia, qujtocamacaia.

Auh in chicuei acatl, ioan chicunavi ocelotl, iuh mjtoa: njman amo qualli tonalli, tequantonalli, in aqujn ipan tlacatia, çan netolinjliztli in qujmaceoaia: auh aiamo caltiaia, qujn jpan qujmattiuja, in matlactli quauhtli, vm contlachieltia, injc qujieccanqujxtia, itonal, in aço ça itla imâceoaltitiuh intla nemjz: auh iece camo caxaujz, oc ivivi in qujcujz, in qujttaz, toneujztica.

Auh in vel icatia, ixcoia, matlactli quauhtli, iuh mjtoa: qualli tonalli, in aqujn ipan tlacatia, vel mâceoale catca, in jpan oqujchiotl, tiacauhiotl, quauhiotl, oçeloiotl, tonalchicaoac, tonallapalivi, vel teujuj, teujc mjxtlapaloanj, tetlaquauhtlamachti, teoqujchtlamachti, âmjqujzmauhquj, teca momotlanj, tevic mopetlatiuh, texoxocoa, texoxomolaquja, tepetlaticalaquj, tetocaticalaquj, teitqujtiuetzi, vel moteixcaujanj, centlamauhtia, aiac vel qujpeoaltia, aiac vel ixco ieoa, aiac vel qujiacaolinja, aiac vel qujiacapeionja, aiac uel qujquequeloa: njman temotzoloa, temotzolqujtzquja, teujc moçoneoa, tepan moxittomonja: ipampa ca iuhquj itonal in tecoçauhquj, icxicoçauhquj, vei quauhtli:

2. *Vm*: *vmpa* in the *Real Palacio MS.*

3. The *Real Palacio MS* continues with the words *chichinaquiztica tlamacevaliztica.*

4. *Eua* in *ibid.*

round him, nor ridicule him. He would then seize one, grip him firmly,[5] and rise up against and burst forth upon him. This was because so was the day sign of the valiant, courageous, great warrior.

Then was the time when the one who had been born was bathed, [whether] man or woman.

And Eleven Vulture, so it was said, was also a good day sign. He who was then born, they said, would grow old; he would become bent with age. The sun would fulfill him and take him into his house. Because the vulture was aged, he who was then born would share [the attribute].

Likewise Twelve Motion and Thirteen Flint Knife, which ended the series, were each good. Ten Eagle bore and favored all these, and made them all good, so that they fell together as favorable day signs. For so was it said the different day signs in the tenth place were always a favorable time.[6] He who was then born was very well regarded. They said that there were three more day signs until the series in which he was born ended; three more days to arrange one's life and favorable aspects of one's life.

njman iquac maltia, in aqujn ipã tlacatia, in oqujchtli, in cioatl.

Auh in matlactloce cozcaquauhtli: iuh mjtoa, no qualli tonalli, in aqujn ipan tlacatia, qujtoaia veuetiz, coliujz, qujtlamjz, qujcalaqujz in tonatiuh: ypampa ca veve, in cozcaquauhtli ipan otlacat vevetioaia.

No iuhquj in matlactlomome olin, ioan in tlatzonqujxtia, matlactlomej tecpatl: izqujtetl qualli, muchi qujncenvica, qujncentlatalhuja, qujncenqualtilia, in matlactli quauhtli, injc cenvetzi qualtin tonaltin: ca iuh mjtoa in izqujcan matlactioaian: in aqujn ipan tlacatia cēca qualittoia, qujtoaia: ca oc Etetl tonalli, in qujtzacuja, ipan omotlacatili, oc etetl tonalli, injc vnnemjz, in qujmoqualtitinemjz.

5. *Temotzoltzitzquia* in *ibid.*

6. Following *matlactioaian,* the additional phrase *ypan tonalli muchipa qualcã* in the *Real Palacio MS,* makes this rendition possible.

Eleventh Chapter, which telleth of the seventh sign, named One Rain, and of the evil day signs which belonged with it. They said that those then born were sorcerers and soothsayers and demons. — And *tlacatecolotl* meaneth demon. — Almost all the houses belonging to this [sign] were evil and unfavorable. Only the thirteenth was good.[1]

Injc matlactli oce capitulo: itechpa tlatoa, injc chicontetl machiotl, in jtoca ce qujavitl: ioan in amo qualli tonalli, in jtech catca: quilmach in aqujque vncan tlacatia, nanaoalti catca, ioan tetlachivianj, tlatlacatecolo: auh in tlacatecolotl, ca iehoatl qujtoznequj in Diablo, achi muchi in calli itech pouhquj, in amo qualli, in amo iectli: çanjio inic matlactetl vmey qualli.

One Rain set in, of which it was said that it was in no way a good day sign. It was full of evil, vice, misery, orphanhood, affliction, suffering, anguish, misfortune, and indigence.

This was because during the time of this day sign, so it was said, then descended those known as the Goddesses, inhuman ones, mockers of the people. Hence most sternly [parents] commanded their children not to go out; not to travel along the roads. They should only remain at home. Thus did they speak to them: "Go not forth. You will encounter the Princesses, for they descend and arrive upon earth." Hence the fathers regarded them with fear, lest one of [the children] might develop misshapen lips, or crossed eyes, or a hare lip, or be possessed.

When this [day came], everywhere in the Goddesses' sanctuaries and temples — everywhere offerings were made. For in every single place stood a temple of Goddesses, in each neighborhood,[2] there at crossroads. They covered with white streamers each of the images which were there — five [figures] of stone, placed in a row, their faces rubbed and painted with liquid rubber. He who made a vow to them covered them at the time of their descent, at the time of their day count, on the day sign of their descent. As many of them as there were he covered with white paper streamers.

Moquetza ce qujaujtl: injn mjtoaia, njman amo qualli tonalli, motqujtica teuhtli, tlaçolli, icnoiotl, icnotlacaiotl, tlaciaujliztli, tlacococaviliztli, teopouhcaiotl, atle onqujçaliztli, atle oneoatinemjliztli:

ipampa in jpan, y, tonalli, iuh mjtoa: ca vncan temoia, in moteneoa cioateteo, âtlacacemelleque, teca mocaiaoanj: ic cenca qujntlaquauhnaoatiaia, in tepilhoan, in aiac qujçaz, aiac vtli qujtocaz: çan cali onozque: iuh qujmjlhujaia maca xonqujçaca, anmotenamjctizque, ca temo, ca tlalpan açi in çioapipilti: ic qujntlamauhcaittiliaia in tetaoan: injc amo aca tennecujliviz, ixnecujliujz, tenpatziujz, itech qujneuaz:

in jquac in, in noviian çioateupan, çioateucalli, noujian tlamanaloia, ca noviian cecentetl mãca, in çioateucalli, cecentlaxilacalpã vncan in omaxac, teteujtl qujmonquequentia, in vmpa catca, ymjxiptlaoan, macujlteme in teme, tecpantoca, tlaolxaoalti, moolxauhque in aqujn ivicpa monetoltiaia, qujntlaquentia yn jquac in intemoia, yn jntlapoalpan, in jpan tonalli temoia, izqujteme amateteujtl qujnquentia.

---

1. The Spanish text reads, in part: *"los que en este signo nacen, son nigromanticos, bruxos, hechizeros, enbaydores. Es de notar, que este vocablo tlacateculotl, propiamente qujere dezir, nigromantico, o bruxo: inpropiamẽte se usa, por diablo: casi todas las cosas deste signo: eran de mala digestion. Pero la decima casa, y la tercia decima casa, uniuersalmente ẽ todos los signos: eran felices."* See Anderson and Dibble, *op. cit.*, Book XII, "The Conquest of Mexico," p. 21, nn. 1, 2, 3, on *naualli, tlacatecolotl,* and *tetlachiuiani.* Depending upon the context, we have at times translated *tlacatecolotl* as demon.

2. *Ibid.*, Book VIII, "Kings and Lords," p. 58, n. 13.

And then also at that time died those who were in jail, who were there for something which demanded the supreme penalty: perhaps an adulterer, or a thief, or a fire priest of whom something had been found out — perchance he had had a paramour — and who was known as an evildoer; or whatsoever sin he had committed. Also of the captives some then died.

Auh yoan no iquac vncã mjquja in quauhcalco onoca, in jtla ic cate, in vei qujtzacuticatca, aço tetlanxinquj, anoço ichtecquj, in anoço tlenamacac, itla oittililoc, aço momecati, in moteneoa tlaçolchiuhque in çaço catle in ovi oqujtlaco: no iehoan in mamaltin, cequjntin vncan mjquja,

It was said that through these Moctezuma received life. By them his fate was strengthened; by them he was exalted, and on them he placed the burden. So it was said that it was as if through them once more he were rejuvenated, so that he might live many years. Through them he became famous, achieved honor, and became brave, thereby making himself terrifying.

mjtoa: ca iehoan inca mozcaltiaia in motecuçoma, inca motonalchicaoaia, inca moquetzaia, inca moqujxtiaia, iuh mjtoa: iuhqujn oc ceppa inca mopilqujxtiaia, ynjc vecaoaz, inca motleiotia, momaujzçotia, motequantlalia, ic motlamauhtilia.

And when someone was then born,[3] they feared that the [Goddesses] might at that time descend. But later, on Three Crocodile, he was bathed; then they made his fate somewhat better, for, so it was said, Three Crocodile was a good time.

Auh in aqujn ipan tlacatia, qujmacacia injc vncan temoa: auh qujn jpan in ei cipactli, maltiaia, vncan achi qujqualtilia in jtonal, iuh mjtoa: ca qualcan in jpan ey cipactli.

And also it was said that he who was then born a nobleman became a sorcerer, an astrologer.[4] That is to say, he was inhuman. He changed himself into something [else]; because of it he turned himself into something [else]. Perchance he had as a disguise a wild beast,[5] etc.

No yoan mjtoaia: in aqujn ipan tlacatia pilli, naoalli mochioaia tlâciuhquj, qujtoznequj: amo tlacatl, itla qujmonaoaltiaia, itla ic mocuepaia, aço tequannaoale. Etc.

And if [he were] a commoner, likewise it was his work to turn himself into perhaps a turkey, or a weasel, or a dog. Whatsoever was his guise became his magic form. All his task was to assume and accumulate all manner of evil. He influenced women; he bewitched and was clever with women;

auh intla maceoalli, no iuhquj itequjuh catca, aço totoli, aço coçamatl, anoço chichi, ipan moqujxtiaia, in çaço tlein inecuepaliz, ynaoal mochioaia, muchi itequjuh, qujcenmama, qujcemololoa, in jxqujch tlauelilocaiotl, cioanotzquj, xochioa, cjoatlatole, tempachioace, tetlatlacuepili, teiolmalacacho, teioiolmala-

3. An additional phrase in the *Real Palacio MS* will change the meaning somewhat: *ayamo maltiaya, ypampa — and when someone was then born, not then was he bathed for they feared. . . .*

4. Angel María Garibay K.: "Paralipómenos de Sahagún," *Tlalocan*, II, 2 (1946), p. 171.

5. *Ibid.*, pp. 170-172: *"en primer término significó . . . algo así como un 'demonio familiar,' o un 'doble' del alma, a manera del egipcio* [citing a passage in *La leyenda de los soles*]. . . . *De esta primaria significación pasó a la de la 'duplicación de la persona,' o el 'desdoblamiento.' . . . Se concibe el brujo capaz de tomar las formas que él quiera, de aparecer en diversos modos y lugares, de ejecutar obras que no son del hombre común: hay en él algo más que hombre: hay un* nahualli *poderoso y multiplicado."* Derivation of the word may be from *nahuali, nahuala, "verbo arcaico, que encontramos en muchos compuestos. Su sentido es en general 'engañar, disimular' y conviene muy bien al prestidigitador, como al mago, que con embustes, fundados o sólo subjetivos, embauca a las gentes. En Molina hallamos, entre otros, los verbos*: nahualcaqui, *entrar disimulado, con cautela, secretamente;* nahualcuilia, *tomar algo a otro con cautela o disimulación;* nahuallachia, *asechar mirando, etc. Cabe dudar, sin embargo, si este verbo es el primitivo de* nahualli *o un derivado suyo."*

In Hernando Ruiz de Alarcón, Pedro Sánchez de Aguilar, and Gonzalo de Balsalobre: *Tratado de las idolatrías, supersticiones, dioses, ritos, hechicerías y otras costumbres gentílicas de las razas aborígenes de México* (México: Ediciones Fuente Cultural, 1953), pp. 24 ff., it is said that *"se dedicaban al animal que el demonio les señalaba para que fuessen lo que llaman* nahualli. . . .

". . . quando el niño nasce, el demonio por el pacto expresso o tacito que sus padres tienen con el, le dedica o sujeta al animal, que el dicho niño ha de tener por nahual, *que es como dezir por dueño de su natividad y señor de sus acciones o lo que los gentiles llamaban hado, y en virtud deste pacto queda el niño sujeto a todos los peligros y trabajos que padeciere el animal hasta la muerte.*

". . . advierto la denominacion y significacion del nombre nahualli, *que puede deribarse de una de tres raizes que significan: la primera, mandar; la segunda, hablar con imperio; la tercera, ocultarse o reboçarse, y aunque ay conveniencias para que se acomoden las dos primeras significaciones, me quadra mas la tercera, que es del verbo* nahualtia *que es esconderse cubriendose con algo, que viene a ser lo mesmo que reboçarse, y assi,* nahualli *dira reboçado, o disfreçado debajo de la appariencia del tal animal, como ellos conmunmente lo creen."*

See also Chap. 31, n. 1, *infra.*

he knew their secrets. He recovered things for people. He provoked and incited people, and caused them to believe diverse things. And [he was] a demon; he caused demons to enter one; he destroyed people and brought them to ruin. He swept people's paths for them [indicating sins which they must confess];[6] he set up ceremonial wooden figures of those killed in war, and caused them to burn for people.[7] He was a magician, one who removed his leg.[8] These were only the works of this person.

cacho, teiollapan, teioiollapan, tetlatlaneltoqujti, ioan tlacatecolotl, tetlatlacatecolovia, tepoloa, tlâtlalpoloa, tecacalochpana, teevillotlatia, tetlatlatoqujlia, tlauj-puchtli, mometzcopina, çan vel iê itequjuh,

He hired and lent himself to others in order to make his living. When at night he went forth somewhere to ruin people, he changed himself into, perhaps, a turkey, or a weasel, or a dog. He who hated someone hired him to destroy his enemy, when he wished and willed death upon him. Four times, on four nights, he performed his task when he destroyed people.

ic tlaqueoalo, ic motetlaqueoaltia, ic motlaiecoltia, in cana iooaltica tepolotiuh, aço totoli, aço coçamatl, anoço chichi, ipã mocuepa, in aqujn tecocolianj quj-tlaqueoa, injc qujpolotiuh itlacocolil, in qujmjquj-tlanj, qujmjqujztemachia, nappa nauhiooal in onte-poloa, in qujchioa itequjuh:

This same one sought out an evil day sign; then was the time to destroy someone. When he had done his task well on one, when already four times he had returned to the victim's home, it was said: "He hath drawn him forth." But sometimes [the evil-doer] fell into [his victim's] hands; he fell and was taken into the hands of others, and was seized and quickly captured. The brave one who was to be destroyed, who was hated, vigilantly stalked him in order to catch him. He seized his hair; from the top, the crown, he pulled hair from his head. He jerked off his hair; he seized, wrenched, and tore it off; he removed his hair. No more did he escape. Forth-with he died; he could only reach his home to die.

çan no iê qujtztiuh, in aqualli tonalli, in vncan ite-poloaia, in aca ouel qujchiuh, in ie nappa oilo ichan, mjtoa: ocontlaqujxtili, auh in quenman temac vetzi, temac aquj, temac maquja, axioa, cujtiuecho, in aqujn iolchicaoac pololonj, cocolilonj, uel qujmo-pachiuia injc caci, qujtzoncuj, iquanepantla, yquaiol-loco qujmomotzalhuja in jtzon, qujquatemotzol-tzitzquia qujquavivitla, qujtzoncopina, aocmo qujça, njman iquac mjquj, ça onmjctaci in jchan:

And if in vain he tried to remedy, or, indirectly, to palliate [the situation], so that he might not die, still seeking to follow his work and control and estab-lish his fate, in vain he contrived to take or borrow something — perchance water or fire, or a bowl, which he borrowed from the house of the one he had gone forth to destroy, who had there seized him. But if the one to be destroyed were indeed wise, prudent,[9] and well advised, he gave nothing at all to anyone. All during the day, until [the next] dawn came, he lent nothing to anyone. On the morrow,

auh in oc nen, ic mopatiznequj, ic mopaiaoaloch-tiznequj, injc amo mjqujz, oc motlaiecoltia, motonal-anaznequj, motonallaliliznequj, oc nen itla qujmo-cujcujcachioa, qujmotlatlanevia, aço atl, aço tletl, aço caxitl, in conmotlaneuja ichan in oqujpoloto, in vmpa ocacique: auh in vel qujmati, in tlaueuemach-tilli, in tlanonotzalli in pololonj: njman aoc tle quj-temaca, in iuh cemjlhujtl in oallatvic, aoc tle qujte-tlaneuhtia, yn jmoztlaioc: ic vncan vel tematlac ma-quja, in tlacatecolotl, onmjquj, ca nel ie oncan ca itequjuh, ca iê in qujtetemoa, ca ie vncan ca ipoliujz:

6. Cf. Leonhard Schultze Jena: *Wahrsagerei, Himmelskunde una Kalender der alten Azteken* (Stuttgart: W. Kohlhammer, 1950), p. 350: *"Das Fest des Wegefegens wurde zu Ehren der Göttermutter* teteoinnan *gefeiert, deren Priester die Beichte derer entgegennahmen, die sich geschlecht-lich versündigt hatten. Das Wort besagt also: Er fegt den Leuten den Zugangsweg zu den Häusern wieder sauber; in übertragenem Sinn: Er be-wirkt dass die Leute geschlechtliche Sünden zu beichten haben und dadurch ihrer ledig werden."*

7. Cf. *infra*, Chap. 19, where a full description appears.

8. Cf. variant translation in Jena, *op. cit.*, p. 141: *"Und hinter ihm kommt eine Hexe her, eine vom Monde, die genau so gut jenes Arbeit tut."*

9. *Tlanehmachtilli* in the *Real Palacio MS.*

then, indeed, the demon was enclosed in one's net. He died. For in truth this was his destiny, for they sought him continually, and it then was the time of his ruin. For he knew in his heart, while yet he lived, that perchance somewhere he might be seized. For so had he been born only to die.[10] Never was he content nor happy; he went about in rags, poorly clothed. And he lived only in suffering. He raged over drink and food. Everywhere was he feared; nowhere could he enter among people. No one was his friend.

ca njmã iuh iiollo qujmatia in oc nemj, in aço cana axioaz: ca njman iuh ipan tlacat içan miquiz: njman aic avia, aic vellamati, itzotzoma, itatapa ietinemj auh çan moxixicotinemj, maçoma, motlaqualçoma, noviian imacaxo, acan vel tepan calaquj, aiac icnjuh:

But although he were seized and taken, he was not frightened, nor did he therefore cease. He paid no heed. If he had children, always he lived the same, never wishing to mend his ways. There he went to his end, and they punished him. Thus all went; thus all was destroyed.

auh in manel ie oanoc, oaxioac, amo ic momauhtia, amo ic motzaqua, amo ic qujcaquj, intla oncate ipilhoã, çan mochipa iuh nemj, amo qujcaoaliztlamati, vncan activi quitzacutiuj, much iuh vi, much iuh polivi,

Just so if it were a woman, all evil were her works. She lived in great misery. Nowhere was her home. Even though she were a noblewoman, nowhere was she favored or noticed. Just as if dead, she lived in affliction. It was said that just so was her day sign one of misery.

çan no iuhquj itequjuh catca intla çioatl, muchi amo qualli in jtequjuh catca, cenca motolinjtinenca, âcan ichan, in manel cioapilli, âcan ixtona, âcan motztica, can iuhquj onmjquj, totoneoatiuh in jiollo, mjtoa ca nel iuhquj itonal in jcnoiotl.

10. *Yn çan can miquiz* in *ibid.*

Twelfth Chapter, which telleth of still other houses. Some were only indifferent and some were in no way good.

The time of the day sign Four Wind was said to be good and bad. For then were slain those called doers of evil, the adulterers. They placed their heads in a noose and choked, strangled, or hanged them, or struck them on the back of the head, or crushed their skulls under a rock. Only at night were they killed: when it dawned, and they were already bloated, they cast them each into the water. Likewise then died some of the captives. Through them, so it was said, Moctezuma received new life (as hath been told) on [the day sign] One Rain, when [the Goddesses] descended. And this was also the time that the [aforementioned] demons and sorcerers destroyed people. And since there was fear on this day sign, Four Wind, everywhere they put cardoon[1] into the smoke openings [of the houses]. They stuffed and crammed it in. Thereby, so it was said, they frightened them away.

But the merchants,[2] those known as distinguished traders[3] and vanguard merchants,[4] who were rich, greatly esteemed and honored this [day sign]. For then they laid out in the sun[5] all the precious things which they had hidden away—the green stone, the objects made of [ordinary] green stone and resplendent green stone; the round ones, round like

Injc matlactlomome capitulo: itechpa tlatoa, in oc cequj calli, cequj çan tlanepantla ca, cequj vel njman amo qualli.

In jpan nauhecatl tonalli, mjtoa qualli, ioan amo qualli, ca vncan mjctiloia, qujnquechmecanjaia, qujnquechtzonviaia, qujnmecanjaia, qujnpiloa, qujncuexcochvivitequj, qujnquatepipitzinja, in moteneoa tlaçolchiuhque, in tetlanxinque, çan iooan in mjctiloia, in oallatvi ie tlacujtlapoçaoa, atlan qujmonmamaiavi. No ioan cequjn vncan mjquja in mamalti, iuh mjtoa: ca iehoan inca mozcaltiaia in Motecuçoma (in iuh omoteneuh) ipan ce qujauitl in vncan temoa: auh ie no vncan tepopoloaia, in omoteneuhque tlatlacateculo, in nanaoalti, auh injc imacaxoia, in ipan in tonalli nauecatl in tlecalco noujian caaqujaia, in tlacateculoxocovitztli, qujpopotzaqujaia, qujcacacatztzaia: iuh mjtoa ca ic qujnpeviaia.

Auh in iehoantin pochteca, in moteneoa: acxoteca, in oztomeca, in motlacamati, iê qujveimatia, qujmaviztiliaia, ca vncan qujtotonjaia, in ixquich tlaçotli qujtlatiaia, in chalchiujtl, in chalchiuhtli, in quetzalchalchiuhtli, in ololiuhquj, in tomatic, in acatic, in ie ixqujch cozcatl, in cozcapetlatl, in patlaoac, in pitzaoac, xiujtl: auh in jxqujch nepapan ivitl, in quetzalli

1. *Xocouitztli.*—Francisco J. Santamaría: *Diccionario general de americanismos* (Méjico: Editorial Pedro Robredo, 1942), Vol. II, p. 154: *jocuiste—Bromelia pingüin L. "En Méjico, nombre vulgar de una planta de las regiones tropicales, que crece como un metro de altura y echa hojas semejantes a las de la piña. . . . propiedad antiescorbútica."*

2. Translatable also as "men of Pochtlan," a *barrio* of Tenochtitlan occupied by merchants, whose gods were Tiçaua, Macuilocelotl, Xihui, Tlati, Xilo, Tepoztecatl, Coyotlinahual, Chicome xochitl, Xochiquetzal, Yiacatecutli (Arturo Monzón, *op. cit.*, p. 50). See also Alfonso Caso: *Instituciones indígenas precortesianas* (México: Instituto Nacional Indigenista, 1954), pp. 23-24, for a résumé of the social and economic importance of the *pochteca.*

3. *Acxotécatl* or *pochtecatlailotlac, "mayor o principal entre los mercaderes . . . tanto como si dijésemos que es gobernador de los mercaderes, y estos dos nombres . . . se atribuyen al que es mayor principal, gobernador, o señor, o que es casi padre y madre de todos los mercaderes"* (Sahagún, Garibay ed., X, 16, 5).

Jena, *op. cit.*, p. 248 (citing Seler, *Ges. Ab.*, II, 60): *"alter chichimekischer Volksstamm in der südöstlich des Sees von Mexiko gelegenen Landschaft Chalco."* Acxotlan was a merchant's *barrio* in Tenochtitlan; gods were Naui Ehecatl, Chiconquiauitl, Xomocuil, Cochimetl, Yacapitzauac, Nacxitl, Chalmecaciuatl (Monzón, *loc. cit.*).

4. Cf. Anderson and Dibble, *op. cit.*, Book I, "The Gods," p. 18 and n. 5. Jena, *op. cit.*, p. 328, citing Seler, *Ges. Ab.*, II, 1070: *"Mann aus dem Orte Oztoman . . . , der auf Wanderschaft gehende Klein und Markthändler sowohl als der auf weite Reisen gehende Grosskaufmann, auch Kaufmann i. A."*

5. *Ibid.*, p. 145.

tomatoes, the cylindrical ones;[6] and all the neck bands, and the matted neck bands; and large and small pieces of turquoise; and all the different kinds of feathers — quetzal tail feathers: the well-pointed ones, the well-curved ones, the wide ones, the long ones, which, they said, indeed extended a fathom. And these were just the tail feathers. And those they called down feathers,[7] the very small ones, the chili-green ones and the crest feathers of the quetzal;[8] and feathers of the red spoonbill[9] [*teoquechol*], which is now called *tlauhquechol;* and the blue cotinga, the amethyst-colored ones,[10] the yellow parrot,[11] the multicolored parrot, the troupial,[12] the red and yellow parrot,[13] the scarlet parrot,[14] the blue parrot,[15] the dove; and aquamarine feathers, etc. And skins of wild animals, and mats of wild animal [skins]; and wooden chocolate-beaters; and gourd stoppers.[16]

in vel iaque in vel vitoliuj, in patlaoac, in viiac, in qujlhuja cezciacatl içan moteca: auh in çan totocujtlapiltic, ioan in qujlhuja quetzaliacatl, in çan tepitoton, in chilchotic, ioan in tzinjtzcan, in teoquechol: in axcan mjtoa tlauhquechol, ioan in xiuhtototl, in aiopal, in toztli, in tozcujcujl, in çaquan, in cochoivitl, in chamolin, in cujtlatexotli, in coçôtli, in xiuhapalli. Etc. yoan in tequaneoatl, in tequanpetlatl, auh in aquaujtl, in atzaccaiotl:

Verily, all their goods, which lay strewn [and scattered in the tribal quarter] temples[17] they arranged in order and in rows upon precious capes. They sorted, ordered, and disposed them. Then they offered incense and beheaded quail. Of this it was thus said: "They place things in the sun." And when they had placed them in the sun, and when they had offered incense during the day, later,[18]

in ie mochi intlatquj in teintoc, [ỹ pixauhtoc. yn calpulco] in teucali, tlaçotilmapan qujcentecaia, qujcuecuentiliaia, qujtlatlamantiliaia, qujviujpanaia, qujtetecpanaia, vncan tlenamacaia, tlacotonaia, iehoatl injc mjtoa: tlatotonja, auh in jquac otlatotonjque, in otlenamacaque, cemjlhujtl, catepan tlatlaqualo, aatlioa, mopixtoque, in pochteca veuetque, nepielotoc, tlachichinalotoc, tlanecutoc, tlaaujaxtoc, puctleoatoc,

---

6. Cf. *Florentine Codex,* Book XI, cap. viii, fol. 205: *injc tlatlalili, ololtic, acatic xictic, tomatic, chiquinalca, tlachiquinaltectli, tlachiquinallili, tlacanaoalli, tlaxãtlaxcalteuhtlalili,* for which the corresponding Spanish text reads: *"Labranse estas piedras unas redondas y agujeradas, otras largas y rollizas, y agujeradas, otras trianguladas, otras cortadas al sesgo, otras cuadradas."*

7. Quetzal nose plug, in Jena, *loc. cit.*

8. *Tzinitzcan.* Sahagún (Garibay ed.), XI, 2, 2 and 4, describes both the crest of the quetzal and a bird of the same name: *Trogonorus mexicanus, T. ambiguus* (*ibid.,* Vol. IV, p. 366). In Seler, *Collected Works* (J. Eric S. Thompson and Francis B. Richardson, eds.; Cambridge: Carnegie Institution of Washington, 1939), Vol. V, p. 2, it is quetzal tail and shoulder feathers of dark green with metallic sheen; in *ibid.,* Vol. II, Pt. 3-4, p. 137, a bird with black and green feathers.

9. *Tlauhquechol.* In *ibid.,* Vol. IV, p. 62, white and red spoonbill; Vol. II, Pt. 3-4, p. 63, red heron; p. 124, red spoonbill; p. 137, rose-colored heron. Cf. also Sahagún (Garibay ed.), XI, 2, 5; *Ajaja ajaja* (*ibid.,* Vol. IV, p. 356).

10. Sahagún (*op. cit.,* XI, 2, 9) mentions an *ayoquan* found in mountains about Cueztlan and Michoacan — of painted, black beak and black feathers except those of the tail, which are half-white; another bird of the same name is a waterfowl of yellow beak; feathers at joint of wing are green; long wing and tail feathers are brassy, with white and green; body feathers are red. *Agamia agami* (*ibid.,* Vol. IV, p. 324).

In "L'orfèvrerie des anciens mexicains et leur art de travailler la pierre et de faire des ornements en plumes," Congrès International des Américanistes, *Compte-Rendu* da la Huitième Session Tenue à Paris en 1890 (Paris: Ernest Leroux, 1892), note to § 68, Eduard Seler translates *ayopal* as *topaze enfumée,* referring to Molina, *op. cit., christal amarillo — ayopalteuilotl.*

11. Seler, *Collected Works,* Vol. IV, p. 33. Cf also Sahagún (Garibay ed.), XI, 2, 16; Santamaría, *op. cit.,* Vol. III, p. 210.

12. Seler, *op. cit.,* Vol. II, Pt. 3-4, p. 114. *Gymnostinops Montezumae* (Sahagún, Garibay ed., Vol. IV, p. 372).

13. Seler, *op. cit.,* Vol. IV, p. 33. Santamaría, *op. cit.,* Vol. I, p. 371: *"especie de loro, del género* Chrysotis." *Cocho* or *cochotl — "Papagayo rojo y morado." Amazona albifrons albifrons* (Sahagún, *op. cit.,* Vol. IV, p. 328).

14. *Ibid.,* IX, 1, 2. Cf. also, however, *chamolin* (*chamol*) in Santamaría, *op. cit.,* Vol. I, p. 461: *"Nombre vulgar que en el Estado de Guerrero, en Méjico, se da al tabachín o chacalsúchitl." Chamolsúchitl*: Azt., *chamolli* (*penacho*) — *"tabachín o flor del camarón* (Poinciana pulcherrima)."

15. Cf. Sahagún, *loc. cit.*

16. Corresponding Spanish text: *atapadores de galapagos para tecomates.*

17. An omission in the *Florentine Codex,* to be noted in comparing the passage with the text of the *Real Palacio MS,* placed in brackets, brings the Nahuatl closer to Sahagún's corresponding Spanish.

18. *Catepan*: the cedilla is missing in the original.

everyone ate and drank. The old merchants lay guarding and watching, smoking, inhaling the fragrance, and taking their pleasure. Smoke drifted upward and was overspread. Food was spread out in abundance; nothing was lacking. Of this it was thus said: the merchants heated things; they placed them in the sun.

puctli mantoc, tlaqualli qujqujztoc, atle monectoc, iehoatl injc mjtoa, ca tlatonaltia, tlatotonja, in puchteca.

And when it grew dark, there was drinking. All of the old merchant men and women assembled. When they became drunk, then they vaunted, boasted, and blustered over their wealth, their achievements, their valor, and especially wheresoever they had set foot; that is to say, wheresoever they had gone to arrive; the things which they had discovered, the manner of their return, their coming back. So they had gone to perform their labors and to circle about the surrounding provinces, to encounter the waste lands, to descend into the gorges — everywhere entering places of danger and drawing into fields of battle. And verily in some places they were besieged and ambushed. Perhaps only one or two escaped the hands of the enemy, coming to leave word with and inform the people that they had first broken and scattered the rampart and enclosure of eagle and ocelot warriors.

Auh in oiooac tlatlaoano, mocecentlalia in puchteca veuetque, in puchteca ilamatque, intla otlaiujntic, vncan qujmopopoaltia, qujmeeoaltia, ic mjxmotlatoque, yn innecujltonol, yn intlaiecoliz, yn jmoqujchtiliz, oc cenca iehoatl: in canjn icac imjcxi, qujtoznequj: in canjn acitinemj, in quexqujch ic conmati, in quexqujch imjloch, innecuepal, ic quichiuhtinemj, injc qujlacatzotinemj anaoatl, injc ixtlaoatl qujnamjctinemj, injc atlauhtli quitemovitinemj, in noviian calactinemj, in ovica, in iaotitlan qujztinemj: auh in nel cana impan oalmotzaqua, qujnpoiomjctia, aço ça ce, vme, in tematitlampa qujça, in qujoalcaoa tlatolli, in oalteitoa, iehoan achtopa qujpetla, qujxitinja, in quauhtenamjtl, quauhtlatzacujlli, ocelotenamjtl, ocelotlatzacujlli,

So there they made light of, scoffed at, exposed, revealed, abused, and tortured those who knew no places, who had gone nowhere, who nowhere in any degree had set foot anywhere; who only at the ashes of his fire called himself a warrior[19] and lived prudently[20] and impudently only here in the market place. Only here, the market place, did he frequent, buying, selling, and deceiving. And this was when, because of their suffering, these cast into the fire — or it fell by the wayside — their rearing, because they were troubled and moved by the counsel of their fathers and mothers. So there at the place of congregating there was dispute, discussion, abuse, faultfinding, and belittling. They sat jostling and besmearing one another, disputing and quarreling among themselves, contending, refuting, and bragging. They paid no heed to others' answers; they did not consider others to be superior.[21] They chattered.[22] Likewise, they were often arrogant; each one had his own opinion; they made little of and

ic vncan qujquequeloa, ica maujltia, qujtlatlacaqujtia, qujcocoa, qujtotoneoa, qujcocolhuja, qujchichinachilia yn jiollo, in acan onmati, in acampa ianj in acan quentel, in acan icac icxi, in çan njcam inextitlan mooqujchitoa, çan njcan tianqujzco in mjmantinemj, tlaxtlapalotinemj, çan njcan in motitianquja, tlatlanecujloa, tlatlaxiccuj, auh ie vncan in ĩtoneuhcacopa, motlecomaiavi vevetzteoa, yn intlazcaltilhoan, in jntlaoapaoalhoã, injc vel imjtic oaaçic intecoco, in teitic aaçic intlatol, in jntahoan, yn jnnaoan, injc vncan in necentlaliaia maaoa, mononotza, moquequeloa, mopâpatla, mopapatzaoa, moquezicçatoque, moçoqujmotlatoque, motlatzoujlitoque, moquâquatoque, mjxquâquatoque, motlatolxopeuhtoque, moiehoatocatoque, âmotenaqujlmatque amo motenpanavillanj, chachalacatoque, no çac in jz moquixtia: muchi tlacatl cecentetl itlatol, atle ipan qujmotztilitoque, amo commopovilitoque in jnnecujltonol, yn jnnetlamachtil: huel nononqua mutachcauhnequj, mocecentecpoa, cecentecuti, cecenme mo-

19. *Mooquiquichitoa* in the *Real Palacio MS. Nicam*: *nican* is meant.

20. *Mimâtinemi* in *loc. cit.*

21. Possibly *amotenanquilmatque* and *amo motepanavillanj* are intended.

22. *Chachalacatoque* in the *Real Palacio MS.*

held in no esteem the riches and prosperity of others. Indeed, each one alone wished to be best; each one thought himself a lord, a superior person; each one thought of himself as the only one, the best. Each spoke for himself; none would talk to them or say a word in their behalf, unless he were a vanguard merchant, one who knew distant lands; unless he were very rich, dealt in goods in his house, or were a buyer of slaves,[23] a ceremonial bather of captives to be sacrificed; unless in his house were carrying frames stuffed and creaking; unless in his house one drank from black jars, gourd vessels, etc.

This was because each one of the merchants himself placed things in the sun at his own house on the day sign Four Wind.

mati, mocecocamati, nononqua motlatalhuja, aiac vel inoan tlatoa, aiac vel inpal onmocencamavia: intlacamo oztomecatl, intlacamo veca matinj: ioan intlacamo cenca mocujltonoa, intlacamo ontlaaaquj ichan, intlacamo tecoanj, intlacamo tealtianj, intlacamo câcatzcatoc, nânatzcatoc ichan cacaxtli: intlacamo poctecontica, aiotectica atlioa ichan et.[a].

Ipampa injc ceceniaca tlatonaltiaia, puchteca in jncacalitic: in jpan jn tonalli navecatl.

23. Or "one who summoned guests."

Thirteenth Chapter. Here is told and mentioned what was an evil manifestation for him who stumbled or fell at this time; and the evil which befell those born at this time, in the eighth house, called Eight Death. Here are told all the various kinds of evil which belonged with [the day signs].

Likewise was it said: no one [on the day sign Four Wind] might quarrel, nor fall, nor trip, nor stumble, nor sprain an ankle, nor break nor twist a foot. So there was apprehension. It was said: "O that this may not always be! He is affected by Four Wind." That is to say, he was hurt on Four Wind.

And also it is told that as to him who was then born, the readers of the day signs made it favorable for him and provided him with merits. He would, so they said, become rich and a chieftain, a brave warrior; he would become terrifying and menacing; he would gain honor; he would be of a strong day sign. And they did not yet bathe him, [they bathed him later][1] on Seven Serpent. So they said that they made the day sign even stronger for him so that he became very rich, provided with merits, gifts, and good deserts. For [the day sign] Seven Serpent represented our sustenance — grains of dried maize, completely edible. And so they said that the days of the seventh place were always a time of good.

But Five House and Six Lizard, which followed, as hath been said, were in no way good day signs. Both were the times of ritual to Macuilxochitl and Mictlan tecutli. For the one born at this time, man or woman, nothing resulted as his deserts. He labored only in vain; his fate, deserts, and gifts were full of misery. And he was only given to talk, completely enveloped in talk. He was hot-tempered.[2] He reprimanded people; he only knew how to agitate them and cause them to riot. So it was said, so was he reprimanded, when he restrained one from doing something, belabored one in something, or besmirched someone: "At least sometimes the brute is human! The vile brute, the mean and vile-tongued one, the fool! What can be done? His is the day

Injc matlactli vmey capitulo, vncan mjtoa: qujlmach amo qualli inezca catca, in aqujn moteputlamjaia, in anoço vetzia, yn ipan jn: ioan in amo qualli inpan muchioaia, in aqujque vncan tlacatia, in jpã ic chicuetetl calli: yn jtoca chicuey mjqujztli: vncan moteneoa in jzqujtlamantli in amo qualli intech ca

No ioan mjtoa: aiac vel maoaia, anoço motlaujtequja, motepotlamja, motecujnja, moxoquechaquja, moxocuetlanja, mocxicueloa: ic tlatenmachililoia, îtoloia, ma qujcencuj, ca omonauecauj, qujtoznequj: ca nauecatl in jpan omococo.

No ioan mjtoa: in aqujn ypan tlacatia, qujpãtiaia, qujnemactiaia, in tonalpouhque, iuh qujtoaia: mocujltonoz, ioan tiacauhtiz, oqujchtiz, tlamauhtiz, tlamamauhtiz, momaujzçotiz, tonalchicaoac iez: auh aiamo caltiaia, in jpan chicome coatl, iuh qujtoaia: oc cenca vel ipan qujtonalchicaoaia, injc cenca mocujltonoz, injc mâceoale, nemaque, ilhujle, mochioaz: ipampa in chicome coatl ca qujxiptlatiaia in tonacaiotl, in tlaolli, motqujtica qualonj: ioan in iuh qujtoa, in chicometioaia ipan tonalli, muchipa qualcan.

Auh in quioaltoqujlia macujlli calli, ioan chiquacen cuetzpalin: iuh mjtoaia: njmã amo qaulli tonalli, in jonteixtin, y, intlatoaian macujlxochitl, ioan mjctlan tecutli: in aqujn ipan tlacatia in oqujchtli, in çioatl, njman atle imâceoal mochioaia, çan oalnenenqujçaia, motqujtica netolinjliztli, in ilhujl, in jmâceoal, ynemac, ioan çan tlatolli cololotinemj, tlatolli cololhujtinemj, tlatolli itlaqual, tlacatl qujcaoatztinemj, çan ic nemj in tlacatl qujcuecuetlanja, tlacatl qujcocomonja, iuh mjtoa injc aio: in iquac on oitla contechioalti, in on oitla conteecaujlti, in on oitla ic onteatlatzicujnj, macel ica ontlacanemj in tlapalpul, iollochicopul, iollopatlachpul, iollotlaueliloca-pul, quennel noço macujltonale, ca ie iuhque in mamacujltonaleque, aquen tlatta, ca nel ic monotz-

1. The words *quin ompa caltiaia* in the *Real Palacio MS* give this phrase.

2. See Note 3, Chapter 8, *supra*.

sign in fifth position." Just so were those who had their day signs in the fifth position mischievous. This is why they considered that not one of them was a decent person. For such was the time of their birth.

And so the readers of the day signs made it good; they told the people that not then, at the time of his birth, should he be bathed, but that they should wait until Seven Serpent. For at this time, it was still vain to do it. Only later they took care of it. If he were to live, it was not hopeless; something would become his lot; with his penance he would reverse his day sign. Because, as they said, the day signs of the seventh place, it was said, were always a time of good. Just then was the time of the ritual of[3] Chicome coatl, which represented our sustenance, which was real wealth. Likewise they said that if one were to have charge of, or to administer something, he would become solicitous and very diligent; for so his day sign would cause him to develop. That is to say, he made good, undid, and destroyed the day sign upon which he had been born and which was regarded with fear. Thus he himself, by his own penances, caused his day sign to result in good; he did it himself through his prudence.

On Eight Death, it was evil; likewise Nine Deer was in no way a good day sign. For, as it was said, the day signs taking ninth place were in no way a time of good. For whosoever was born on it, man or woman, nothing became one's fate or deserts. Born then were those who became evil-tempered on earth — who vented their wrath; the completely perverted and mad, who lived surrounded by vice, sin, given to talk,[4] the dissolute, living in deceit; the prodigals, fearing no one, presumptuous, respecting no one, esteeming no one; treating no one with reserve. They regarded no one with much consideration, cherished no one much, valued no one. They were very presumptuous, immodest, brazen, and impudent; meddlesome,[5] troublesome, and respecters of nothing; discourteous, evil-spoken, great talkers, big-mouthed, great-mouthed, belittling and depreciating others in their speech. They were mockers and liars. Nothing could be said in the presence of one of these. They were inconsiderate, not given to silence; impudent; evil talkers, who guarded no

que, in amo ceme tlacacemelleque, ca iuhcan tlacatque.

Auh injc qujqualtiliaia tonalpouhque, qujteilhuiaia aiamo vel ipan maltiz, in ipan otlacat, ma oc qujchia in chicome coatl: ca vmpa oc nen titlatemachia, ça qujn iê qujmattiuh, intla nemjz, aço ça nen itla imâceoaltitiuh, ca itla maçeoaliztica qujmocuepililitiuh yn jtonal: ipampa in iuh qujtoaia, in jpan chicome tonalli: qujlmach mochipa qualcan, vel vncan in tlatoaia in chicome coatl, in qujxiptlatiaia tonacaiotl, motqujtica necujltonolli. Ioan no qujtoaia intla tlamocujtlaujz, motlacujtlaujz, iel, iêel, mochioaz, ca ic qujzcaltiaia in jtonal, qujtoznequj: ic qujqualtilia: vncan qujmotlaxilia, qujmopopolhuja, injc otlamauhcaittililoc ipan tonalli otlacat, ic ixcoian inôma, itlamaceoaliztica, qujmoieccaqujxtilia in jtonal, qujmonomâvilia inezcaliliztica.

In jpan chicuei mjqujztli: amo qualli, no ioan in chicunavi maçatl: njman amono qualli, tonalli, iuh mjtoaia: ca in chicunavitioaia ipan tonalli njman amo qualcan, in aqujn ipan tlacatia in oqujchtli, in cioatl, njman atle ilhujl, imâceoal mochioa: iehoantin vncan tlacati in çan tlatlaneçomaltia tp̃c tlaneçomaltitinemj, çan tlatlaueliloc, iollotlaueliloc, teuhtli, tlaçolli cololotinemj, tlalli cololotinemj, atlacanemj, iztlacattinemj, tlaavilqujxtitinemj, aiac qujmauhcaitta, aiac ixco tlachia, aiac qujxitta, aiac qujxtilia, aiac qujmamati, aiac tle ipan qujtta, aiac tle cõpoa, aiac compoa, cenca iz moqujxtia, vel ixquaujtl, yixquauhti, acan ixmavi, nônoviia, aquen tlatta, atle ipan tlatta, âtlatlacatlatoa, tetenquauhti, tetennemj, tenxaxacalpul, camaxacalpul, tlatolcampax, tetenpatztlatoa, tetentlamati, yiztlacati, atle vel ixpan mjtoa, amo iollotlaquaoac, amo tetenpachiuhquj, amo motenmamati, iollocamachal, atle uel itic tlalilo, nenepilmaxal, tenenenxotla nenepilixtlapal, tepapantlaça, teixnecujloa, teixtlaça, teueuetlaça, amo patzaoallanj, axicchioaliztli, çan iee ipan mjxpoa, çan iee qujcemmati, çan iee

3. *Real Palacio MS*: *ytlatoaya.*

4. *Real Palacio MS*: *tlatolli.*

5. Cf. *Florentine Codex,* Book VI, fol. 183*v*.

secret. They were sowers of discord, of gossip,[6] who spoke with tongue in cheek; spreaders of tales. They confused, confounded, and rejected the counsel of elders. They wished not to be deflated. They were not people of honor. These same dedicated themselves to and paid strict attention to constant evil. It was their only labor. All [their] acts and efforts were repeated adultery, thievery, absconding with tribute; making off with many things by trickery, coveting, and deceiving. They were trouble-makers, interpreters of dreams, who brought others into sin, sold goods in secret, sold people in secret, spirited people away, and misled them, calling them by trickery.

icentequjuh in tlatlauelilocaiotl, much ichivil, much itequjuh, tetlâtlanxima, yichtequj, tlâtlaixpachoa, tlatlanaoalchioa, tetlâtlaixtoqujlia, tetlâtlaxiqujttilia, teoovicanaquja, tetlatlanamjctia, tetlatlacolnamjctia, tlatlachtacanamaca, teiichtacanamaca, teiichtacaujca, tenanaoalhujca, tenanaoalnotza,

None of his own food did he eat. He lived with other people, going from house to house, entering others' dwellings.

much aitlaqual in qujqua, teca nenemj, tecacalpanoa, tepan cacalactinemj:

As he had been born, so he grew, shameful and deranged. Then at the start of his childhood, as he had grown in years, incorrigible, too lazy to heed the discourse, he answered impudently or blamed someone else. He was one who became wroth, who turned his face aside in rage and tossed his head in anger, who hung his head. Anger was in his face. He was completely full of evil; wickedness was deep in him. He was perverted, rude; of wicked, evil tongue. Everyone dreaded his tongue and his words. None could equal him in conversation nor best him in talking. So it was said of him: "He is perverted; only words are his lot; he is of evil temper." No man's name gave they him. Everywhere he remained aside from people. He was infamous; he remained a burden to people. Hence was he reviled, proscribed, suspected. Everywhere his life and deeds were regarded with dread. For truly, he had been born in a time of vice and sin. That is to say, indeed, only to be reviled was his gift: nothing good, nothing fine.

njman iuh qujça, njman iuh mozcaltia, in aquen tlatta, in atlacacemelle njmã ipan pilpeoa, njman ipan mooapaoa, in auel monotza, aiel qujcaqujz in tlatolli, çan ie tenananqujlia, tepan qujcuepa, tlatlauelchioanj, mjixtlaça, moquaquatlaça, iixcueloa, mjixcueloa, vel qujmaxilti, iiolaçic, tlaueliloc, vel iollocujcujtla, âtentlacatl, tentlaueliloc, muchi tlacatl qujtenjmacaçi, qujtlatolimacaçi, aiac qujtenaci, aiac vel qujtempanavia, iee injc mjtoa: atlacacemelle, çan tlatolli ilhujl, tlatolli itlaqual, aiac itlacatocaia, noviian tetenco caca, tepan onoc, tepan cenmantoc, injc aujlqujzquj, tlaitolli, tlaztlacolli, noviian mauhcaitto in jnemjliz, in jtlachioal, ca nel iuhcan tlacat, in tlaçoltitlan, teuhtitlan, qujtoznequj: ca çan motqujtica aujlqujzcaiotl, in jnemac, atle qualli, atle iectli:

And the readers of the day signs bettered and remedied the nature of the day sign on which the useless one was born. They arranged that later, upon Ten Rabbit, he would be bathed and given a name. They said that if he should live, perhaps something would be his deserts, though not forthwith. Still by pain and suffering of mind and body, by his penances, he would achieve that which was to be his gift. Later, himself and of his own effort, he would achieve and acquire it, as hath already been said in many places.

auh in nen ic qujqualtiaia, qujqualtiliaia tonalpouhque, in iuhquj itonal ipan otlacat, qujn ipan quitlatlaliliaia, in matlactetl tochtli: injc ipan maltiz, qujtocamacazque, qujtoaia: intla nemjz aço ça itla imâceoaltiz, iece camo caxcanviz, oc totoneoaz, chichichinacaz in jiollo, in jnacaio, itla maceoaliztica qujcnopilhujz, in jnemac mochioaz, qujn inoma, qujn ixcoian qujmjxnextiliz, qujn qujnomaviz, qujn qujmonomaviliz: in iuh ie mjieccan omoteneuh.

6. *Tenenexxotla* in the *Real Palacio MS.*

Fourteenth Chapter, which telleth of the good day signs which correspond to the four houses in this sign; and it was said that the day signs of those then born were good.

And the one day sign, the one day count Ten Rabbit, so it was said, was a very good time. Whoever was then born, whether man or woman, was of great deserts, great gifts, and riches. For just so was it said of the tenth position, when [the day sign] became the tenth. On the tenth day sign, it was always a favorable time, of gifts and recompense, as in its separate accounts[1] hath already been told. But not then, at that time, did they bathe him, on the day sign on which he had been born. They always directed their attention there to the closing day sign, later, when they bathed him and gave him a name, on [Thirteen][2] Monkey; because thereby they greatly strengthened the day sign; they improved his day sign. For, so it was said, a very good time was the closing day sign, the ending and concluding day sign, as will be told in its account.

And the following Eleven Water, and Twelve Dog, and the concluding Thirteen Monkey, as many as these were favorable. Ten Rabbit drew, dragged, amplified, and helped all of them, so that all four were good. It was said that anyone who was born upon these various day signs became a highly favored person; he succeeded and endured on earth.

That is to say, he was not deflated; not one of the least nor the last; nor a man without recognition. He was well respected and recognized; he was famed and honored; hence he was one who prospered, enjoyed glory, was compassionate, and served others. As a chieftain, he was strong, daring in battle, esteemed, intrepid, able, sharp-witted, quick-acting[3] prudent, sage, learned, and discreet; an able talker, and attentive. It seemed as if he set forth his dis-

Injc matlactli on navi capitulo: itechpa tlatoa, in qualli, tonalli: in jntech ca in nauhtetl calli: in ipan in machiotl, ioan qujl qualli intonal catca, in aqujque vncan tlacati.

Auh in jpan in cemjlhujtonalli cemjlhujtlapoalli, in matlactli tochtli: iuh mjtoa, cenca qualcan in aqujn vncan tlacatia, in oqujchtli, in çioatl, cenca mâceoale, ilhujle, mocujltonoanj: ipampa no iuh mjtoa, in matlactioaia, in vncã tlamatlacti, in jpan matlactli tonalli, muchipa qualcan, vncan ca ilhujlli, mâceoalli, in iuh ca itlatlatollo, in ie mjeccan omoteneuh: auh aiamo njman caltiaia, in jpan in tonalli otlacat, qujn cen ompa contlachialtiaia in tonaltzonco, ipan caltiaia, qujtocamacaia: in jpan matlactlonnauj oçomatli ipampa injc cenca qujtonalchicaoaia, qujuecapanoaia itonal, ca iuh mjtoa: cenca qualcan in tonaltzonco, in jca tlantica tonalli, in qujtlamjtica tonalli, in iuh ipan moteneoaz itlatollo.

Auh in qujtoqujlia matlactloce atl, ioan matlactlomome itzcujntli, ioan in tlatzonqujxtia, matlactli vmej oçomatli, izqujtetl qualli, muchi qujcentilinja, qujcenvilana, qujncenteteoana, qujncentlatalhuja in matlactli tochtli, ic nauhteixtin qualtin. Mitoa: in aqujn vncan ipan tlacatia in jzqujtetl in tonalli: cenca tlacnopilhujanj muchioaia, oalqujçaia, oalnemja in tlalticpac,

qujtoznequj: amo patzactzintli, amo çan tetzacuja, amo tlatzinpiloa, amo çan can nenemj, vel iximacho teixpan icac, moteniotia momaujzçotia, injc mocujltonoanj, injc maujztli, injc tetlaocolianj, injc teca muchioanj: auh injc tiacauh injc chicaoac, injc iaotlaueliloc, injc amo tetlaçaltoca, amo ixmauhquj, ioan injc mozcalianj, ixe, iollo, iollotecujcujl, ioliz-matquj, ioliztlamatquj, tlanemjlianj, toltecatl, mĵmatinj: ioan vellatoa, vellacaquj, iuhqujn mjtic qujte

1. *Itlatlatollo.* The Nahuatl text could also read *itlatlacollo.*

2. Read *matlactli omei.*

3. Cf. *yollocuicuitla* in "Memoriales con escolios," pp. 204, 211.

course in meditation,[4] full of sorrow and compassion: one who understood others well, who animated and consoled them, and was understanding. To everyone he brought happiness, as much as to comfort the afflicted and provide succor. So of him it was said that he was a deserver of merit, one of good fortune; that all then resulted as his various gifts here mentioned.

itlatol, choqujzço tlaocollo, vel teitic açic, teiollapan, teiollali, vel mocaquj, muchi tlacatl qujpaqujltia, iuhqujn teaacotlaz, teiizcali: iehoatl injc mjtoa, ca mâceoale, tlacnopilhujanj, ca much oncan qujçaia, in iuhquj inemactia in jzqujtlamantli, njcan moteneoa.

Likewise so became the desert of the woman; she became wealthy and achieved honor; she prospered at the market places as a seller of merchandise; as one who served and showed pity for others, etc.

No iuhquj imâceoal muchioaia in cioatl, mocujltonoaia, momaujzçotiaia, vel motitianqujanj, tiamjcaqujnj, teca muchioanj, tepan tlaocoianj. Etc.

And if such did not befall one, it was said that he himself, by his own doing, neglected and destroyed his day sign through vice, because perchance he took not good heed, perhaps did not perform the penances well, as hath already been told in many different places.

auh intla aca amo iuhquj ipan mochioaia, mjtoa: ca ça ixcoian, inêviiã conmocaujlia, qujmotlaçolmjctilia in jtonal: ipampa acaço uel omonotz, acaçomo uel otlamâceuh, in iuh ie mjieccan omjto.

And hence was it said that it was a very favorable time on the closing day sign, on Thirteen Monkey (and the other closing day signs); hence then was when they bathed the one born on the various day signs mentioned which Ten Rabbit influenced. This was said because it was averred that four governed at this time. These [each] tarried for a day and made favorable the concluding day signs. Their names were Tlauizcalpan tecutli, and Citlalli icue, and then Tonatiuh, and Tonacatecutli. The readers of the day signs hence considered it favorable and said that precisely at this time were fortune and favor. And likewise they said that the one then born would become aged; they said that he would finish his work, endure on earth, and be admired.

Auh injc mjtoa: cenca qualcan in tonaltzonco, in jpan matlactlomej oçomatli (ioan in oc cequj ipan tonaltzontli) injc vmpa qujnjquac qujmaltiaia in tlacatia in jpan in izqujtetl tonalli omoteneuh in qujncenteteoana, matlactli tochtli ipampa mjtoa, qujlmach muchipa navintin vncan tlatoa: iehoan tlacemjlhujtiltia, qujtlatalhuja in tonaltzontli itoca Tlauizcalpan tecutli, ioan citlalli icue, njman ic tonatiuh, ioan Tonacatecutli: iehoatl injc qujquallittaia tonalpouhque, in qujtoaia: ca uel vncan ca ilhujlli, nemactli, ioan no qujtoaia, veuetioaia, in aqujn vncan tlacatia, qujtoaia, qujtlamjz, monemjtiz in tlalticpac, tlamaujçoz

4. *Quiteca* in the *Real Palacio MS.*

Fifteenth Chapter, which telleth of the eighth sign, called One Grass, and the evil day signs with it. But it was said that the second house was good. And all the others, of ninth place, and all the others which started with the ninth — the tenth, the eleventh, the twelfth, and the thirteenth[1] — were said all to be good.[2]

One Grass set in. This was said to be in no wise a good day sign: a day of wild beasts, dreadful. The one then born lived only in misery. Though he found his consolation, yet it only disappeared and faded away.

And he begat children. All his children grew, like dense hair, as if in abundance. They were like trees, like rocks; the earth swelled up. But when he had already begotten, soon he experienced how his children were torn away, faded away, quickly fled, and suddenly died, en masse; all scraped clean, going along their way, buried, receding, cleared away. None remained. Death, mortality, claimed still another.

Like a wide road he gave support to his parents.[3] He was as if struck by lightning. Father and mother, each one by himself, arose, sat meditating, and loosed tears for the loss of his children, only afflicted, always preoccupied, deprived of everything. Gone were those who had made them proud and esteemed, those received in payment, as offerings; those who had lived together, assembled, gathered, united, esteemed, appropriated. Behold, in truth he had begotten children; in truth he had beheld them. Hence this was said to be an evil day; one only of wild beasts, full of misery.

And he who was then born, they did not then bathe; later, on the day sign Three Ocelot, they bathed him. The readers of the day signs so said that the third position was always a favorable time. It

Injc caxtolli capitulo: itechpa tlatoa, injc chicuetetl machiotl, in jtoca ce malinalli: ioan in amo qualli tonalli in jtech ca, auh qujl injc ontetl calli qualli: ioan in jxqujch oc cequj chicunauhtetl in jxqujch oc cequj, in jtech vmpeoa injc chicunauhtetl calli, ie injc matlactetl, ioan injc oce, injc omome, inic vmei, qujlmach qualli catca.

Moquetza ce malinalli, injn mjtoa: njman amo qualli tonalli, tequanj, imacaxonj, in aqujn ipã tlacatia, çan motolinjtinenca, tel qujttaia in jneiollaliliz: auh çan ompoli, çan onqujztiqujça,

ioan mopilhoatiaia, muchintin moquetzaia, in jpilhoan, iuhqujn tlaquauhtzonqujça, iuhqujn tlaneujuja, iuhqujn quavitl manj, tetemmanj, tlalli cuecuetlaca: auh in ie oqujchiuh çan jc qujmati, in iuhquj motlâpevia ypilhoan, onmototocatiuetzi, onmototocatiqujça, muchintin, onmjctiuetzi, ololiuhtiuj, mocemĵchictivi, oncemoti, onmotoca, onmototocatiuj, onjchictiuj, aocac mocaoa, in oc ce conpeoalti mjqujztli, mjquiliztli,

iuhqujn otli patlaoac qujmonquechilia, yoampooan, icetcaiooan, itlapancaiooa, itzicueoallooa, ycotoncaoa, icotoncaioa, iezçoan, itlapalloa iuhqujn ipan tlatlatzinj in teta, in tenan, iioca moquetztiqujça, motztimotlalia, mjxaioujtoma, injc oqujmonpolo ypilhoan, ça itolol, ymalcoch qujchiuhtica, centlamjc qujmattica, qujcentlamjtica, oiaque in intech oatlamatia, in jntech ocuecuenotia, in oqujmonpopoaia, in jxco oqujnmanaia, in oqujtepeujtinenca, in ocololhujtinenca, in oqujtetepeujaia, ocoololhujaia, oqujmomactocac, omonelchiuh, ie on ma nelli omopilhoati, ie on ma nelli oqujmjttac: iehoatl injc mjtoa, amo qualli tonalli, çan tequanj, motqujtica icnoiotl:

auh in aqujn ipan tlacatia, aiamo caltiaia, qujn jpan caltiaia, in ey oçelotl, cemilhujtonalli, iuh qujtoaia, in tonalpouhque, ca muchipa qualcã in eitioaia, amo netenmachoia, iehoatl injc qujoallatotoquj-

1. *Matlactli* is understood in the last three numbers.

2. Corresponding Spanish text: "*Capitulo qujnze, del octauo signo: llamado ce malinalli, y de su aduersa fortuna. La segunda casa deste signo: tenjanla por buena, y vnjversalmente todas las casas, de nueue arriba, s 10. 11. 12. 13: las tenjan por buenas.*"

3. Cf. Olmos, *op. cit.*, p. 212.

was not hopeless. This one the readers of the day signs thus sought out so that they might then somewhat better the day sign of the one born on One Grass.

liaia tonalpouhque, injc achi vncan qujqualtiliaia itonal, in jpan tlacatia ce malinalli.

And the day sign Two Reed, which followed, they said was a very good day sign; because also at that time they honored Tezcatlipoca Titlacauan by placing the image of [a god] called Omacatl. In the same manner [as Tezcatlipoca][4] was the face painted; they ornamented it when they placed it.

Auh in qujtoqujlia, vme acatl tonalli qujtoaia vel qualli in tonalli: ipampa ca no vncan qujtonaltiaia yn Tezcatlipuca, titlacaoa, injc qujtlaliaia ixiptla itoca Omacatl: çan no ivi in mjchioaia, ic qujchichioaia, injc qujtlaliaia:

And whosoever wished to place the image of Omacatl guarded it in his home for two hundred [days]. He placed it on the day sign Two Reed. And if he who placed it did something well, that is, if now his goods and possessions increased and appeared, no more did he wish to relinquish it. He just placed and introduced it permanently into his home, and guarded it for a long time.

auh in aqujn qujnequja, qujtlaliaia in jxiptla Omacatl, matlacpoaltica in qujpiaia ychan, ipan in qujtlaliaia, vme acatl tonalli, auh intla ie itla vel maailia, in aqujn oqujtlali, qujtoznequj: intla ie tlapiuja, ixneçi, iaxca itlatquj, aocmo qujcaoaliztlamatia, çan qujcentlaliaia, qujcencalaqujaia in jchan, vecauhtica qujpiaia:

And if now he wished to abandon it, and no longer to guard it, he likewise abandoned it on the day sign Two Reed. This same one chose his day sign; on [the day sign] in which he had placed it, on it likewise he abandoned it. He left it there at his temple in the *calpulco* of Omacatl, and went offering it incense. And there, to take it, would go he who earlier had wished to guard it in his home. The old men of the tribal district accompanied it with song; the [new] householder served food to the people; there was feasting and drinking in his home. And when it grew dark there was drunkenness. In the same way was the placing and termination. Then was the breaking off and the finishing; then they observed the two hundred days of guarding it in one's home when [the image] entered as well as when it left.

auh intla ie oqujnec in qujcaoaz, in aocmo qujpiaz: çan no ipan in qujcaoaia vme acatl tonalli, çan iee qujmattiuja in jtonal, ipan in qujtlaliaia, no ipan in qujcaoaia: vmpa concaoaia in jteupan, in jcalpulco omacatl, qujtlenamaqujlitiuh: auh vmpa canatiuh, in aqujn oc iê oqujnec, qujpiaz ichan, qujcujcatiaia in calpuleque, ic tetlatlaqualtia in chane, tlatlaqualo, aatlioa, yn jchan: auh in oiooac tlatlaoano, çan ie iuh tlatlalilli, çan ie iuh tlatecolli, çan vncan tectica, çan ie vncan tlantica, çan ie vncan qujmattiaia, in matlacpoaltica pialoia techan iquac calaquja, no iquac qujçaia:

And, it was said, he who was then born, they said, would become rich and wealthy. And well would he gain his livelihood. What he might do would not fail. He would find his consolation.

auh mjtoa: in aqujn ipan tlacatia, qujtoaia mocujltonoz, motlacamatiz, ioan vel muchioaz in jnetlaiecoltiliz, in tlein maailiz, amo nenqujçaz, vel qujttaz in jneiollaliliz.

And on Four Eagle, and Five Vulture, and Six Motion, so it was said, these various day signs were in no way good. They were always as hath been said. For him who was then born, his fate, his gifts, were the same: misery. He lived given to talking; he would bear false witness; accusations were made; there were outcries; among others he lived in vice, corruption, and evil, as hath already in many places

Auh yn jpan nauj quauhtli, yoan macujlli cozcaquauhtli, yoan chiquacen olin, iuh mjtoa: njman amo tle qualli in jzqujtetl yn, tonalli, çan muchipa iuh mjtoa: in aqujn ipan tlacatia, çan yee in jlhujl, inemac in netolinjliztli, yoan tlatolli cololhujtinemj, tetlatolevia, yoan tlatolevilo, oiovilo, tenepantla qujtlalitinemj in xixtli, cujtlatl, in aqualli: in juhquj ye mjieccan omoteneuh. Auh in oc nen ic qujqualtiliaia

4. At this place in the *Real Palacio MS* a marginal note in Sahagún's hand reads: *"de la cerimonia de la ymagẽ de Tezcatlipuca."*

been said. But for him who yet lived, the readers of the day signs made it good. Later, when Seven Flint Knife took its place, they then bathed him, because, as was said, the seventh place was always a favorable time. Nothing thus damaged the day sign; precisely at this time were fortune and gifts, for it was the time of the rituals of [the goddess] Chicome coatl, etc.

And Eight Rain and Nine Flower: already hath it been told and revealed how then was a time of evil. For then was when were born the thieves, the adulterers, etc. — those to be feared and dreaded on earth, who mocked people, the perverted, as many times is mentioned in the separate accounts.

And on Ten Crocodile, so they said, it was a favorable time. Then were born the rich, the wealthy, the satisfied, the content, the happy on earth, men and women. Just so were the following — Eleven Wind, and Twelve House, and Thirteen Lizard. Ten Crocodile bore them all with it, and favored them all. These different concluding four day signs were good. So all went traveling in their course. Those there which achieved the "ten" [5] position were all of a favorable time. Thus came arriving the thirteenth day sign, which concluded [the group of day signs].

tonalpouhque: qujn jpan qujtlaliaia in chicome tecpatl, iquac caltiaia ipampa ca omjto, ca muchipa qualcan in chicometioaia: atle yc itlacauhtica in tonalli, vel vncan ca ilhujlli, nemactli: ca ytlatoaia in chicome coatl. et.[a]

Auh in chicuei qujaujtl, yoan chicunavi suchitl: ie omito, ye omoteittiti in quenjn amo qualcan vncan yn: ca vncan in tlacatia, in qujçaia in jchtequjnj, in tetlatlãxima. Etc. yn imacaxonj, in mauhcaittonj tlalticpac, in teca mocacaiaoa, in atlacacemelleque in iuh mjec tlamantli omoteneuh itlatlatollo.

Auh in jpan matlactli cipactli: iuh qujtoa, qualcan vncan tlacatia, in mocujltonoa, in motlacamati, in avia, in vellamati, in paquj tlalticpac, in oqujchtli, in çioatl, çan ie no iuhquj, in qujtoqujlitica matlactloce hecatl, ioan matlactlomome calli, ioan matlactlomej cuetzpalin, qujncenvica qujncentlatalhuja in matlactli cipactli, izqujteme qualtin in ontlatzonqujxtia, nauhteme tonaltin, çan moch iuh otlatocatiuj, in vncã oaçic matlactioaia ie qualcan, in jxqujch ic onacitica matlactli vmej tonalli, in tlatzonqujxtia.

5. Ten (*matlactli*) is an element in the Nahuatl terms for eleven, twelve, and thirteen.

Sixteenth Chapter, which telleth of the ninth sign, called One Serpent.[1] It was considered a good day sign, if those same ones then born did not harm it. And the merchants expected much of it, because of their way of livelihood.

One Serpent set in. It was said to be a good day sign. Of one born on it, they said his deserts and merits would be to become wealthy. There would be wherewith to eat and drink. And in war, in time of battle, he would become a brave warrior and a chieftain; he would attain renown, honor, glory, and fame. Perchance he would be a ruler or a lord. And if it were a woman, she would be quite rich; she would be a good provider; she would be well-born. She would look to and guard the services and the property of our lord. She would be a guardian and administrator. Much would she gather, collect, save, and justly distribute among her children.

But it was also said that although such became the deserts of one then born (as is already said in many places), if he did not diligently do penance, if he paid not good heed, he indeed failed, and personally brought upon himself that he lost through neglect, and destroyed and ruined what were his deserts. This was because he neglected things, worked unwillingly, was lukewarm, and lacked forethought and diligence. Indolent, he let nothing be done. He was careless, exceedingly careless, slothful, negligent, listless, and slow; a great and heavy sleeper. And he was incorrigible. He would only neglect things through laziness; advice offended and angered him.

So it was said of him: "So he is; he made no provision for food, for there was constant running about." There was no getting to bed, no arising; he stretched his limbs, quite exhausted by fatigue and effort. To no purpose did he give or publicly display wealth and prosperity, and the joys and comforts of wealth.

And it was said that on One Serpent the merchants and vanguard merchants,[2] the exploring

Injc caxtolli oce capitulo: itechpa tlatoa, injc chicunauhtetl machiotl, in jtoca ce coatl: qujlmach qualli tonalli: intlacamo çan iehoantin qujtlacozque in vncan tlacati: auh in puchteca cenca qujmatatacaia, in jpampa in jnnetlaiecoltiliz.

Moquetza ce coatl: injn mjtoaia, qualli tonalli: in aqujn ipã tlacatia, qujtoaia: ilhujle, maceoale iez, mocujltonoz, oniez in qujquaz, in qujz, auh in iaoc, in iaopan, oqujchtiz, tiacauhtiz, momavizçotiz panvetziz, maviçoaz, moteniotiz, aço tlatocatiz, tecutiz, auh intla cioatl, vel motlacamatiz, vel motlaiecoltiz, vel motlacatiz, qujttaz, qujpiaz in jteicneliliz, in jcococauh totecujo, tlaçaloanj, tlapachoanj iez, vel qujntlaçalhujz, qujntlapachilhujz, qujntetzontiz, qujntlatlamachiz in jpilhoan,

auh ioan mjtoa, maçivi in iuhquj in inemac mochioa, in jpan tlacati (ca ie omjto mjieccan) intlacamo iê vellamaceoa, intlacamo vel monotza, catle vnqujça, ca ixcoian conmocaujlia, qujmjxcaoaltia, qujmopolhuja, qujmopopolhuja, in jmaceoal ocatca: ipampa içan tlatlacomati, tlaavilmati, tlaquelchioa, tlatlacanequj, qujtenmati, acontlaeltia, aiel atle conmochichioaltia, vel cujtlatzcopic, cujtlatzcocopic, cujtlananaca, cujtlaçotlac, cujtlatzol, qujtenmatitl, cochpal, cochmjmjl: ioan auel monotza, çan qujtenmati, qujquammati, qujtlauelchioa, in tlatolli,

iehoatl injc mjtoa: ca nel amaxcauja, in qualonj, ca netotoqujlilo, amo neteteco, amo nequequetzalo: vel ixqujch maana, vel ontlamj in ciaujztli, in tlapaliuiztli, amo çan motenenmaca, amo çan teixpanvetzi, in necujltonolli, in netlamachtilli, in netlacamatiliztli, in netlacamachiliztli.

Ioan mjtoa: in jpan in ce coatl, cenca qujqualittaia in puchteca, in oztomeca, in jaque, in nênemjnj, in

1. In the MS, apparently *ce oçelotl* has been corrected to read *ce coatl.*

2. *V. supra,* Chap. 12.

merchants[3] and traveling men, those who entered distant lands, regarded [the day] as very favorable. It was their day sign and time count, when [a merchant] took to the road and set forth to far lands.

And he who was about to set forth, when he had prepared himself and filled and made ready the carrying-frames, then summoned, gathered, assembled together, assembled together,[4] and notified his elders, the old merchants. They were given drink, food, and wine, in order to make it publicly known that this one now wished to depart and go hence; to break away; that he still wished to abandon the people and disappear. And, it was said, he still wished to be extinguished from view for a time. In this way he made it clear to the people; he made it very clear to the people. That is to say, it was well known to those who yet tarried in their homes, to those who went nowhere.

vecacalaqujnj, intonalpan catca, intlapoalpan catca, iehoatl qujtztivia, vncan vmpeoaia in veca:

auh in aqujn ie vmpeoaz in omochichiuh, in otlacacaxten, in otlacacaxchichiuh: njman tetlalhuja, qujncentlalia, qujnnechicoa, qujnnechicoa, qujnmachitia in jveveiovan, in puchteca veuetque, atlioa, tlaqualo, tlaoano, injc teixpan motlalia, in aqujn ie oncholoteoaznequj, ie onmoquetzteoaznequj, ie onueuetzteoaznequj, in oc ontetlalcaujznequj, oc ompoliuhtoznequj, ioan mjtoa: oc onmjxceujznequj, quexqujch caujtl injc teixco ovevetz, omach teixcoveuetz, qujtoznequj cenca ie macho, in jc ie vecaoa ichan, in jc aoccampa iauh.

3. Cf. Sahagún (Garibay ed.), Vol. IV, p. 371.

4. In the MS, *qujnnechicoa* is repeated.

The Seventeenth Chapter telleth of the admonitions of the old merchants when they counseled their sons as they were about to depart and gain their livelihoods in distant places, when for the first time they wished to go and set forth.

Injc caxtolli omome capitulo: itechpa tlatoa, in jntenonotzaliz puchteca, in veuetque, in qujmjlhujaia inpilhoan, in jquac ie oneoazque, in veca motlaiecoltizque, in qujn jiopa iaznequj, vmpeoaznequj.

And then the old men besought each one; they greeted, animated, and encouraged him; they prepared and singled him out; they greeted him with tears, prepared him to receive misery and torment, etc.

Auh njman ic ceceiaca qujtlatlauhtia in veuetque: qujtlapaloa, qujchicaoa, quellaquaoa, qujtetziloa, âco qujlpia, qujchoqujztlapaloa, qujtlaquammaca in netolinjliztli, in tlaihiioviliztli. Et[a].

They said to him: "Thou art here, O my son, my beloved son; O youth, my beloved youth! O noble youth, thou hast sought out, beckoned to, and summoned thy mothers and fathers, the merchants, the vanguard merchants, the exploring merchants. Verily, here thou lookest into their faces; thou knowest them. Ah! They will leave and offer thee a word of advice and counsel. This they have carried and borne; it tutored and trained,[1] so that they benefited in such places as the forest and the deserts.

Qujlhuja ca njcan tonca nopiltze, nopiltzine, telpuchtle, notelputze, telputztze: ca otiqujmontemo, otiqujmontzatzili, otiqujmonnenotzallan, in monaoan, in motahoan, in puchteca, in oztomeca, in iaque: ca njcan imjxco, ymjcpac, titlachia, tiqujmonjximati, â mjtzcavilizque, â mjtzmacazque in cententli, yn cencamatl, in jntlatquja, yn jntlamamaia, in jntlacazcaltiaia, in jntlacaoapaoaia, injc otlamaviçoque, in iuhcan in quauhtla, in çacatla:

"And this is the word of advice and counsel with which I console thee, who art my beloved son. So I become thy mother and father; so thou hast me as protector and comforter. Thou who art poor shalt already set forth from and leave the city, thy home — Mexico, Tlatilulco, or Tenochtitlan. Already thou art about to abandon and forsake thy kinsmen; already thou art about to abandon thy home, the rooms of thy house, thy homeland, the resting-place of thy head, thy child's crib, thy hair-tuft. Already thou comest to One Serpent, the straight way, the wide road;[2] already thou followest along and goest toward the desert and the plain.

auh injn ca njcan cententli, cencamatl, ic njmjtziollalia, ic njmjtzchicaoa in tinopiltzin, inic njmona, njmota, injc timonanmati, injc timotamati: timotolinja, ca ie tonmoquetzaz, ie tocontlalcaviz in altepetl, in mochan in mexico, in tlatilulco, anoço in tenuchtitlan, ie tiqujmoncauhtiaz, ie tiqujmõcauhteoaz, in mooaniolque: ie tontlacauhteoaz in mochan, in mocalitic, in moqujzcan, in moiolcan ỹ moquechtetzon ionocan, in momanaoal, anoço momatetzon, ie toconnamjqujz in ce coatl, in vtli melaoac, in vchpantli, ie tocontocaz, ie toconnamjqujz in jxtlaoatl, in vei tlalli.

"Wretched art thou, O my son, O youth! Exert all thy force. Where, in sooth, shalt thou live? Shalt thou perchance die here? O that somewhere the

Timotolinja nopiltze, telpuchtle, ma ximellaquaoa, can nel timonemjtiz? cuix njcan timomjqujliz? ma cana ixtlauhto, popouhto: in inchoqujz, in jntlaocol,

1. Cf. Angel María Garibay K.: *Llave del náhuatl* (Otumba: Imprenta Mayli, S. A., 1940), p. 109, for use of imperfect; *tlatquja, tlamamaia, tlacazcaltiaia,* and *tlacaoapaoaia* could be rendered as "protection." Cf. Olmos, *op. cit.*, p. 211, and Siméon, *op. cit.*

2. Cf. Sahagún (Garibay ed.), IX, 3, 5: "Ce coatl otli melauac, *que es uno de los veinte caracteres o signos de la arte adivinatoria.*"

tears, the pity of thy elders, the old ones, may go as reward and recompense, to gird and clothe thee. For[3] thus did thy elders go. For they went learning of war, performing the way of life of the road. So with struggle they gained and sought [honors] from the Lord of the near, of the nigh. So they prayed.[4]

"But [as for] this: then to it! Be covered and engulfed by torment. For now shalt thou come to know, take, and deal exclusively with misery, hunger, starvation, thirst, emptiness,[5] fatigue.[6] For verily thy provisions have ended — that with which one hath traveled. Perhaps thou shalt chew dry tortillas — parched tortillas, wretched, tough-cooked things, ill-smelling tamales. Perhaps thou shalt drink sour, bitter water, dirty and foul.

"And verily, thou shalt draw near to, approach, and come against the menacing river, which seemeth a torrent, roaring and crashing as it sweepeth by. It carrieth everything with it and goeth destroying great trees. And there shalt thou wait some days; thou shalt be isolated by the water; thou shalt suffer with thy pangs of hunger and unrest.

"If thou wouldst gain honor by such as this, O my son, be not shameless; do not faint; be not womanish. Give thyself completely to the torment; enter into it; deliver thyself to it with all thy force, so preparing for it, etc. For verily thou seekest and travelest into such places as thy elders, the old men, served. For they thus hurled themselves at and delivered to torment, and exposed themselves to danger and adversity. For not without reason did the merchants take and find leadership and the wisdom of old age, become leaders, and receive their authority in exchange.

"And of this, O poor youth, if something should be thy reward and deserts, if our lord should show esteem by something for thee, thou must first feel and profit by the pain, the afflictions, the privations, the ambushes. Such is exacted from those who go from city to city. Yet there will be times of need. Thou shalt become tired and worn out; thou shalt stand exhausted; thou shalt go wearied by heat, spent by winds. Thy face will become dust-covered and

in motechiuhcaoan, in vevetque: in njcan ic mjtzapana, ic mjtzqujmjloa: a oiuhiaque in motechiuhcaoan, ca inteoauh, intlachinol oqujmattiaque, oqujchiuhtiaque in vtli, in nenemjliztli, injc oqujtlamatataqujlitiaque oqujtlaitlanjlitiaque in tloque in naoaque, injc ixillan, itozcatlan omamaiauhtiaque:

auh injn, macuele timaliuj, ma xocontimalo in tlaihiioviliztli, ca ie toconmatiz, ie toconjxcaujz, ie toconcenmatiz in netolinjliztli, in apjzmjqujliztli, in teociujliztli, in amjquiliztli, in atetzocoaqujliztli, in ciammjqujliztli: auh in nel otlatlan in motacatzin, in motlatocaia: cujx a ticmoqualtiz, in tlaxcalquappitztli, in tlaxcaltotopochtli, in totopuchtzintli, in tamaliiacatzintli: auh cujx a ticmjtiz in xococ atl, in alchichic, in tlaelatl, in atzoatl.

Auh ca itech taçitiuh, itech tipachiujtiuh, itech timotzotzonatiuh in temamauhti atl, in iuhquj çolonj, in iuhquj tetecujcatiuh xaxamacatiuh ic iauh, in moch qujujca qujtzineuhtiuh, vevei quaujtl: auh ca vncan tiquezqujlhujtiz, timatzaquaz, titlaihiioujz in mocujtlaxcoltica, in monetequjliztica:

intla ticmaujçoz, in iuhquj in, nopiltze, ma titlapinauhti, ma titlacuecuetlaxo, ma timocioatlamachti, iê xicmocenmaca, itlan xaquj, xicmotlaquammaca, ic ximotetzilo in tlaihiioujliztli. Et.[a] ca nel ie in tictemoa, ca ie in tictotocac, ca iuhcan otlacotique in motechiuhcaoan, in veuetque, ca ic omomotlaque oqujmomacaque in tlaihiioujliztli: injc amo oqujtlaçotlaque in jntzontecon, yn jmelchiqujuh, ca amo cacujque qujnencujque injc oqujttaque in tachcauhiotl, in veueiotl, injc ie petlati, ie icpalti, injc ie contlanevi in jnpetl, in jmicpal in puchteca.

Auh in y, timotolinja telpuchtle, intla itla mocnopil, momâceoal mochioaz intla itla ipan mjtzpoaz totecujo: ca oc toconjttaz, oc toconmaujçoz in tecoco, in tetolinj, in aiecoliztli, in teiacacpa qujqujz: in iuhquj motzaqua in aoacan, tepeoacan: ca oc vmpa onqujçaz, ticiammjqujz, timociappoaz, timociauhquetztiaz, titonalciauhtiaz, teecaciiauhtiaz, tixtlaltzin timochiuhtiaz, tixtlalteuhpipixcauhtiaz, mjxquatzin tlatlatiaz, mjtonaltzin ticmacujtiaz, vel tima-

3. *Real Palacio MS: ca.*

4. Corresponding Spanish text: *"Y en esto, ganaron la honrra que tuujeron: como la ganan los hombres valientes, en la guerra: con estos trabajos, alcançaron de nuestro señor, las riquezas que dexaron."* Cf. *Florentine Codex*, Book VI, cap. xliii, fol. 203*v* (*texillan, tetozcatlan oqujz*).

5. *Atetzocoaqujliztli*: problematical; *a-te-tzotzocolli-aqui?*

6. Corresponding Spanish text: *"es menester que os esforceis, y tẽgais animo: para sufrir los trabajos, que os estan aparejados: que son, hambre, y sed, y cansancio, y falta de mantenjmjentos."*

deathly white. Thy forehead will burn; thou shalt wipe the sweat off with thy hand; indeed thou shalt be bathed [in it]. In the corner, by the wall, behind the door, thou shalt hang thy head. Thy stomach will stick to thee [from hunger].[7]

"Thou shalt go into, entering, and leaving, city after city. Thou shalt be in danger; it will not be well with thee. That is to say, perchance it will not prosper; perhaps thy stock of goods, thy just deserts, thy dealings, will not result well. Thou shalt be long-suffering; thou shalt shed tears. Thy good deeds will not bear fruit, for fatigue will take thy measure. Indeed, thy breath and courage will end.[8]

"Perhaps somewhere in a gorge, at the mouth of a canyon, on some high place, at the base of a rock, at the foot of a tree, shalt thou sleep. Perchance somewhere thou shalt be destroyed; our lord will end thy existence. And perhaps thou wilt come to make thy way back. For no one knoweth.

"Yet may it be well with thee. Go praying to our lord for mercy. Be not negligent. Think only of and be dedicated to penances. Be diligent in providing water for the washing of the face and hands, and in sweeping and gathering up rubbish.[9]

"No more think of thy life [here], of thy past;[10] no more go directing thy feet to thy past. That is to say, do not go retreating in haste, do not go running to the rear, do not try to retreat, to go by the way; do not go remembering [thy past]. Go realizing completely, knowing, devoting thyself exclusively to suffering. Perhaps the lord of the near, of the nigh, will give thee something as thy merit, as thy desert.

"Perhaps once more thy mothers, thy fathers, and thy kinsmen will look thee in the face. Verily, what thou shalt eat and drink will be the advice we here give thee. For with all this we gird, fortify, and bind thee. We thy mothers and fathers implore thee: pay good attention; look well; take care, O my son. Go in peace, leaving thy aunts and uncles, etc."

In this manner did they animate and encourage the one not yet much experienced — who perhaps

liviz in texomolo, in tecaltech, in tetlatzacujltitlan, timotololtitiez, mocujtlaxcol motech motetecatiez,

timâaquiz, timocacalaqujz, timoqujqujxtiz: in aoacan, tepeoacan, timotzotzonaz, timocacapanjz, qujtoznequj: ac aço can tle uel onmochioaz, ac aço can tle onmaqujtiz in motiamjc, in mocnopillo, in monentlamatia, ca uel icnoioaz in moiollo, mjxaiotzin ticmatentiez: amo ticaxcanviz, in mocneliloca, ca timjhiiotamachioaz, vel ontlamjz in mjhiio in motlapaliujz:

in aço cana atlauhitic, atlauhcamac, tlacopac, tetl itzintlan, quavitl itzintlan timocochitiz, in aço cana timopopoliujtiz, mjtztlatiz totecujo: auh in anoçoc mjloch, monecuepal ticchioaqujuh: caiac vntlamati,

ma oc iê moiolic: xicmotlaocolnonochilitiuh in totecujo, ma timoxiccauh, ma xoconjxcauj, xocõcenmati in tlamaceoaliztli, xicmocujtlauj in tecamapaqujliztli, in temâtequjliztli: auh in tlachpanaliztli, in tlacujcujliztli,

macamo ce mônjca, moteputzco xiqual. et[a] macamo ce mônjca, moteputzco xiqual. Et.[a] macamo cemjcampa, moteputzco xiqualquetztiuh in mocxi, qujtoznequj, macamo xitzintlacçatiuh, macamo xitzinqujztiuh, macamo xitzinqujzcatlaiecotiuh, xioalnacazitztiuh, maca tle xiqualilnamjctiuh: ma çan centlamjc xocommattiuh, ma xoconcenmattiuh, xoconixcaujtiuh, in tlaihiioujliztli, açitla mjtzmâceoaltiz, mjtzilhujltiz in tloque, naoaque:

açoc ceppa mjxco, mocpac tlachiazque in monaoan, in motaoan, in mooaniolque: ca ticquaz, ca tiquiz in njcan ic timjtznonotza, a ixqujch ic timjtzonâpana, timjtzontetziloa, aco timjtzilpia in timonaoan, in timotaoan, timjtztlatlauhtia, tlê ticmati, tle ticmomachitia, tlê ticmatcatzintli nopiltze, ma iiolic ximovicatiuh, xiqujmontlalcauj in maujoã in motlaoan. Et[a].

Ivin in quellaquaoaia, in qujchicaoaia, in aiamo cenca ixtlamati, in aço qujn jiopa tevica, motevicaltia,

7. *Ibid.*: *"tendreys la barriga pegada a las costillas de hambre."*

8. *Ibid.*: *"Y demas desto, os afligira la duda de la venta de vuestras mercadurias: que por ventura no se venderan, y desto tendreys tristeza, y lloro: antes q̃ alcanceis algun caudal, o buena ventura: aueys de ser afligido, y trabajado, hasta lo ultimo de potencia."*

9. *Ibid.*: *"sirujendo humjlmente a los mayores en cosas humildes: como es dar agua a manos, y barrer, et[a]."*

10. Anderson and Dibble, *op. cit.*, Book III, "The Origin of the Gods," p. 40; Seler, *Einige Kapitel*, p. 294 (*die hier, hinter dir* [*zurückgeblieben sind*]; Garibay, *op. cit.*, p. 232 (*supervivientes*). For *xiqual*, read *xiqualcueptiuh* or a similar term. The text is garbled, as is seen in the Aztec column of the MS. The corresponding Spanish text says: *"Mirad que no desmayeis, mirad que no boluays atras de lo començado, mjrad que no os acordeis de las cosas, que aca dexays: continuad, y perseuerad en vuestro camjno, en sufrid* [sic] *los trabaios. . . ."*

for the first time went with and was one of a company of others [going to] places of which he wished to know, and departing for distant lands. Yet everywhere they cared for him, teaching and instructing him with their words. In such places as the forests and deserts he realized the estate of merchant or vanguard merchant.[11]

in canpa ie ontlamatiznequj, injc ie vmpeoa veca, oc noviian qujnemjtia, qujtlâtlattitia, qujtlâtlachieltia in jntlatoltica, in iuhcan quauhtla, çacatla in amaxcanvia in puchtecaiotl, in oztomecaiotl.

11. Corresponding Spanish text: "*Desta manera los mercaderes vieios, a los mancebos: que nueuamente yuã con otros mercaderes, a tierras estrañas a mercadear: los hablauan, y esforçauan: y ponjan delante los trabajos, y dificultades, en que se aujan de ver: ansi en los poblados, como en los desiertos en la prosecucion de su oficio, de mercancia.*"

Eighteenth Chapter. Here are told [what] the talk and discourse were of these same old merchants which they repeated to their sons who already knew distant lands.

And [as for] him who already many times had returned and come back from there and who already had beheld such [distant] places as his frequented and traveled areas, dangerous and ominous places, places of torment, they said little to him; only something well-chosen, measured,[1] approved, complimentary, discreet, agreeable, moderate, pleasing, and commending. No more was it very long and extended; no more on all occasions did they speak, nor annoy him, nor speak lightly, nor harangue inconsiderately.

Only this did they say to him: "Here thou art, O youth. No more art thou a child; no longer art thou like that. Thou art a favored one, for already thou hast regarded and witnessed thy dust-covered places, thy explored places, thy traveled areas which thou hast wished to know.

"In such places as forests, deserts, and cities, there is nothing to bring thee defeat, to frighten, daze, impede, or terrify thee. For already thou hast beheld all places, such as the markets, places where the merchants deal. Behold, we know not whether thy mothers and fathers lose thee forever. Perhaps thou goest for good; perhaps thou goest to be lost; perhaps somewhere into a canyon or a desert thou shalt be forced, and shalt perish; perchance some city thou wilt reach. Perhaps once and for all thou art seen. Yet know and carry in thy heart that thou goest fortified by the tears and compassion of thy mothers and fathers. And if still something may become the reward of us, the old men, perhaps yet thou shalt come back and make thy return, that once more we may know thee.

"And now, take care. Travel the road with caution, lest thou stumble upon something. For desolate,

Injc caxtolli vmei capitulo: vncan moteneoa in tlatolli, in jntenonotzaliz catca, in çan ie no iehoantin, puchteca veuetque, in qujmjlhujaia in inpilhoan in ie onmatia veca.

Auh in aqujn ie mjiecpa iloti, ie mjiecpa mocuepa, in ie onjtztica in iuhcan inentla, inemja, in oujcan, in temamauhtian, in tlaihiioujliztitlan: ça quexqujch in qujlhuja, ca eecauhquj, ca ixieecauhquj, ça tlaiecolli, ça tlauelittalli, ça tamachiuhquj, ça tlaqualittalli, ça ipan qualli, ça ipan tlauelittalli, ça ipan tlaiecolli, aocmo cenca viiac, aocmo cenca vitlatztic, aocmo cenca noviian ontlatoa, aocmo noviian qujnemjtia, aocmo çan ilhujztlatoa, aocmo ça iliviz tlatetoa:

ça ixqujch in qujlhuja. Ca njcan tonca telpuchtle: ca aocmo tipiltontli, aocmo tiuhquj titenmachonj, ca ie tonjtztica, ie tontlachixtica, ie mjxtlalopan, ie mjxnentla, ie mjxonjcac, in vmpa tontlamatiznequj,

in iuhcan in quauhtla, çacatla, in aoacan, in tepeoacã, aocmo tle ic tontlapolotiaz, aoc tle ic tonjxmamauhtiaz, tonjxmjmjctiaz, aoc tle mjtztzicololtiz, aoc tle mjtzixtilquetzaz: ca ic noviian tonjtztica, in iuhcan intlaiecoaian, intlacotia in oztomeca: ca amo ticmati, anoço ie iccen mjtzixcaoa, in monaoan, in motaoan, aço ie iccen tiauh, aço ie cana tonuetzitiuh, aço cana atlauhtli, ixtlaoatl itic timaqujltitoz, timopopoliujtitoz, aço cana tictlantoz in altepetl, aço ie cenmanian mjxco mocpac ontlâtlachia, ca tel iuh qujmattiuh in moiollo, ca moiollo itlan ietiuh, ca ic timellaquauhtiuh, yn jnchoqujz, yn jntlaocol in monaoan, in motaoan: auh intla oqujtla tomâceoal, in tiveuetque, in açoc mjloch, monecuepal ticmochiujliqujuh, ca oc ceppa timjtziximatizque.

Auh in axcan tlê ticmomachitia: ma iiolic xoconmotoqujli in vtli, ma itla toconjcxinamjc: ca amo

1. *Real Palacio MS: ça yeecauhqui, ça ixxehecauhqui.*

ferocious, cruel, and unpeopled, spreadeth the wasteland.[2] Carefully thou shalt go taking by the hand, each of them, gathering in groups, ordering, assembling, and bringing together, they younger brethren. Do not abandon them disdainfully. Advise them as thou goest, that they may take grass and reeds and with them fashion seats [for their elders], there at the places of rest. However, all this we have given — our sighs, our discourses — to such as teachers, forest people, desert people, merchants, travelers, etc. But no longer is it necessary to relate so much to thee. For here we only encourage thee somewhat. Little by little offer thyself to the torment. Use all thy force. Thou knowest what is required, O my beloved son."

When he had been supplicated, then he also returned a few words. Thus he answered and said:

"I thank you for the favor you have shown me, O brave men. You have left me consolation. Who am I? What am I that I deserve this short talk, your encouragement, your motherliness and fatherliness? For you have opened to me [counsel] which was in your bowels, your breasts, which lay resting, guarded, and folded like precious feathers well-curved and well-pointed; like a green stone, round and well-polished; like fine turquoise, well-rubbed and glistening. Shall I perhaps cast you aside? For I go covering myself with your motherliness, your fatherliness, which you do not make mine; it goes entering my throat, it goes with my heart. Etc.

"But this I beg you. What will our lord grant? Perchance I shall yet come to look you in the face. For now I leave you. See to the sweeping and cleaning — the little tasks of sweeping, gathering of rubbish, and laying of fires. Let it not grow dark, nor rubbish stand cast about, in my humble house. Continue to do this. I go leaving only my beloved mother, my beloved great aunt, my beloved elder sister,[3] my beloved aunt, etc. For I go troubled and saddened on their account. Do your duty to them; advise them. Let no one make sport of them. Perchance our lord may somewhere destroy me. So all I thus entrust to you, and my heart is content."

tlacacemelletoc: ca tequaniotoc, motequaniotitoc, amo tlaca onoc in çacatl in tlacotl, ma ivian inmatitech xiquimonantiuh, xiqujmonâantiuh, xiqujmonololotiuh, xiqujmotepeujtiuh, xiqujmoncenqujxtitiuh, xiqujmõnechicotiuh in moteiccaoan: ma tiqujmonnoxiccaujli, ma xiqujmonnotztiuh: injc contecujlizque in çacatzintli, in pepetzintli: ioan injc contetlalilizque, inteicpaltzin, in campa neceujloian, ca tel ixqujch o, in otiqujnmacaque in tihiio, in totlatol, in iuhquj in tlacaoapaoaia, in quauhtlaca, in çacatlaca, in puchteca in jaque et.[a] ca aocmo monequj in quexqujch timjtzcaqujtizque, ca ça njcan achitzin ic timjtzonchicaoa, ma iocuxca itlâ xonmaqujlti in tlaihiioviliztli, ma ixqujch motlapaltzin, tle ticmomachitia nopiltze:

in jquac otlatlauhtiloc, njman no ic cen camatzintli ic tlacuepa, ic tlananqujlia, qujtoa

Oannechmocnelilique in oceloqujchtle: otlacauhquj in amoiollotzin, ac nehoatl, ac njnomati, in njcan cen camatzintli njqujcnopilhuja, yn amotechicaoaliztzin, in amotenaniotzin, amotetaiotzin, ca nocontlapoa in amoxillantzinco, amotozcatlantzinco actica, in cepouhtoc, in cepoatoc, in cuelpachiuhtoc, in iuhquj quetzalli, in vel vitoliuhquj, in vel iaque, auh in iuhquj chalchiujtl, in ololiuhquj, in vel patlaoac, in iuhquj teoxiujtl, in tlamatilolli, in uel cuecueioca, aço cana namechonnotlaxililiz, ca ic nonnapantiuh, noxillan, notozcatlan onactiuh, noiollo itlan onietiuh, in amonaiotzin, in amotaiotzin, in amono anqujmaxcaujlique. Et[a]

Auh inin ca namechonnotlatlauhtilia quẽ tlacaoaz in jiollotzin totecujo, açoc amjtzinco amocpactzinco njtlachiequjuh ca ie namechonnotlalcaujlia, ma ipan anmotlatoltizque in tlachpanaliztli, in tlachpanalli, in tlachpanaltzintli in tlacujcujliztli, in tletlaliliztli: macamo ontlaioaticaz, tlaçolli onqujzticaz, l. onqujztoz, in nocnoxacalco, ma oc conjxcauj in ça iio noconcauhtiuh in nonantzin, in noteçitzin, in nouelticatzin, in naujtzin. Et.[a] ca ica nonnotequjpachotiuh, ica nontlaocoxtiuh, ma ipan anoalmoqujxtizque, ipan anmotlatoltizque, ma caiac ica mocacaiaoaz, in aço cana nechmopopolhujz totecujo: ca ixqujch no ic amotetzinco nonnocauhtiuh, vel onietiuh in noiollo.

---

2. Cf. *Florentine Codex*, Book VI, cap. xliii, fol. 214: *intlacouh inçacapech in vevetque*; the corresponding Spanish text reads: *"Esta es la breña y çacatlatl de los antiguos. Por methaphora qujere dezir. Aquj en este lugar que era de breñas y çacatlales se poblaron primeramente nuestros antepasados, aquj hizieron primeramẽte sus casas de mjmbres y sus casas de çacate o heno."*

Note, however, that in Book IX, cap. iii, Tlacotzontli and Çacatzontli are identified as *dioses del camino.*

3. In "Memoriales con Escolios" (*Academia de la Historia MS*), p. 207, *ueltiuhtli* is translated *vizabuela.*

Then all his household wept over it. There were tearful greetings by all the old merchants, men and women. But he who could not weep only continued to sob behind the others, seeming to weep. And afterwards there was a little rejoicing, consolation, and drinking, to drive away and disperse sorrow. So afterwards all departed and went, and each one entered his own home.

Niman ic nechoqujlilo, in jchantlaca, nechoqujztlapalolo, in ie muchintin puchteca veuetque, puchteca ilamatque: auh in aca auel choca, çan teicampa tzôtzoiontica, mochoqujzcanenequj, auh çatepan achitzin ic papacoa, neiollalilo, tlaoano, injc motlaocolpopoloa, motlaocolcecēmana: ic çatepan netlatlalcaujlo, viuiloa, cacalacoa in techachan.

Nineteenth Chapter. Here are told the offerings which they made for the sake of those who traveled to far places, and how respect was paid for the sake of those who died.

And his household thereupon began the penances. They let themselves become dirty. No longer did they wash their heads with soap, though they could bathe their bodies. Nevertheless, no more did they submerge in water. But every eighty days they arranged the washing of heads with soap. Thus they showed and made it known that they did penance for the sake of their children, their young men, who were still absent. All the time they thus went about doing, however long he was gone.

And if, perchance, he had gone to die, first were notified the old merchants. Their task was to inform and break the news to the people. These introduced a time of mourning into the home of the deceased. Thus they made it known that during four days there would be remembrances; his household would mourn. So they would be visited and consoled, and there would be a burial ritual[1] for their child.

And when four days had gone by, then his household washed their heads with soap. Thus it was said, the deceased was bathed; and thereby they destroyed and banished their grief.

And if somewhere he had died in battle, they set up an image of him made of pine torches bound together.[2] They made and formed his image; they adorned his likeness. This *euillotl* was only a statue of pine logs which they split into sections and afterwards bound together. And they placed upon it all the paper ornaments, the paper array, the paper jacket, the paper neck-band, the paper stole. They piled up, strewed about it, and distributed them so that they would burn all of them with it. When this was done, when they had adorned the statue, when the one dead in battle had been wept, one more day

Injc caxtolli vnnavi capitulo: vncan moteneoa, in ventli in qujchioaia, im impāpa vecanemja ioan injc moxtlaoaia in jpampa in mjquja.

Auh in jchantlaca: njman iquac compeoaltia in tlamaçeoaia, motzoiotia, aocmo mâmovia, tel vel maltia yn jntlac apa, iece, aocmo polaquj: auh nanapoaltica qujmattiuj, in mamovitiuj: injc qujnextia, qujtemachitia, ca ipampa tlamâçeoa in jnconeuh, in jntelpuch, in oqu jxcauhque, ixqujch caujtl iuh qujchiuhtinemj, in jqujn qujçaqujuh:

auh intla noce omjqujto, iehoan achto caqujtilo, in puchteca veuetque, intequjuh in teiolmelaoazque, in teiolpachiujtizque, iehoantin qujcalaquja in choqujztli, in jxaiotl, in jchan omjqujto, ic qujtemachitia, injc naujlhujtl ilnamjcoz, mjccaoatizque in jchantlaca, injc tlapalolozque, ellaquaoalozque, qujmjloloz in inconeuh:

auh in oqujz navilhujtl: iquac mamovia in jchantlaca: ic mjtoa, momjccaaltia injc compopoloa, conjilcaoa intlaocol:

auh intla cana oiaomjc, qujtlaliaia ieujllo, queujllotia, queujllotlalilia, ixiptla qujchichiujlia, injn Evillotl: çan ocoquavitl in qujtzatzaianaia, çatepan qujcujtlalpia: auh ixqujch itech qujtlalia, in amatlatqujtl, in amanechichioalli, in amaxicolli, in amacozcatl, in amaneapantli, qujtlaolololtia, qujtlatepeoaltia qujtlamamaca, injc mochi ioan qujtlatizque: in ie iuhquj in oqujcencauhque evillotl, in jquac ie choqujliloz oiaomjc, oc cemjlhujtica, in jeujllo icalpulco, cemjlhujtl in ca, cemjlhujtl in eoatica: auh qujnjquac in ioalnepantla, qujtlatiaia, vmpa in qujtocaiotiaia, tevitoalco, quauhxicalco, tzompantitlan:

1. *Qujmjloloz*: possibly this refers to wrapping of the dead or clothing of a statue.

2. *Evillotl*: Corresponding Spanish text: *"su estatua de teas, atadas unas, con otras."*

his statue spent in his *calpulco.* One day it was [there]; one day it remained seated. And then, when it was midnight, they burned it there in [the place] which they called the god's courtyard, at the eagle vessel, [or] on the skull rack.

But if the merchant had only died on the ground[3] — that is to say, if he had not died in battle, if perchance he had only taken sick, in the very same way they prepared his statue, but only in his home did it burn — not at midnight: while yet there shone a little sun, when he already was turning on his left side,[4] when the sun hung low, they burned it.

Likewise it was said that at the time of the day sign One Serpent, if it was established precisely at that time, when war was declared and proclaimed among the people, when, it was said, war was announced, at that very time the war began. At that time all the eagle and ocelot warriors set out to battle; all followed, crowded, and filled the road. They arose, they set out, departed, marched, and hastened.

And if one were born upon the day sign One [Serpent],[5] they said, the readers of the day signs corrected it and bestowed gifts upon him. He would become a receiver of favors, worthy of good deserts and merit; he would prosper and have sustenance. But if he did not do his penances well, according to his day sign, his gifts and favors would not come upon him. He himself would harm and destroy it. It was said that by his own act he neglected it and destroyed it by vice, etc.

He who was then born they did not yet bathe; they bathed him later, on Three Deer, and then gave him a name, for the reason already many times told: the day sign of the third place, when they waited for the day, the readers of day signs considered favorable. So they took this following one for him; this time they arranged and postponed it in order to give him a very strong day sign.

And Two Death, which followed, so they said, was evil; at this time there was nothing of merit. But Three Deer, so they said, was a good day sign; this is already related. The third place was always a good time; it was a time of attainment of merit, as the readers of day signs told one. And Four

auh intla çã otlalmjc oztomecatl, qujtoznequj: intlacamo oiaomjc, in aço çan ococolizcujc, çan ie no ivi in qujchichioaia ieujllo, iece çan ichan in tlatlaia, amo ioalnepantla, oc achi tonatiuh, iquac in ie onmotzcaloa, onmopiloa tonatiuh qujtlatiaia.

No ioan mjtoa: in jquac ypan in ce coatl tonalli, intla ipanti, ipan motlalia, in jquac oiaotlatoloc, oteiaotlalhujloc, in omjto, in otecaqujtiloc iaoiotl, vel iqua ipan vnpeoaia in iaoc: vncan iaoqujxoaia, ipan otlatocoia, ipan vnneotemaloia, vnmotema, onmacocuj, onmolinja, eoa, nênemj, icxiconana, in jxqujch quauhtlocelotl:

auh in aqujn ipan otlacat ce oçelotl tonalli, qujtoaia, qujpãtiaia, qujnemactiaia in tonalpouhque, tlacnopilhujanj, ilhujle, mâceoale muchioaz, mocujltonoz, vnca qujquanj iez: auh intlaca mouellamaceoa, in iuhquj itonal in, amo ipan muchioa in jnemac, in jcnopil: çan iehoatl qujmitlacalhuja, qujmopopolhuja, mjtoa: ineviian conmocaujlia, qujmotlâçolmjctilia. Et^a^.

yn aqujn ipã otlacat in, aiamo caltiaia, qujn ipã caltiaia in Ey maçatl: iquac qujtocamaca, ipampa ie mjieccan omjto: in eitioaian tonalli, in jquac tlacemilhujtiltia, qujqualittaia in tonalpouhque: iehoatl ic contlatotoqujliaia, vmpa qujtlatequjniaia, vmpa contlachieltiaia, injc cenca qujtonalchicaoaia.

Auh in qujtoqujlia, vme mjqujztli, iuh qujtoa: amo qualli, atle vncã ca mâceoalli. Auh in ey maçatl: iuh qujtoa qualli tonalli, ie omjto: in eitioaia muchipa qualcan, vncan ca tlacnopilhujliztli in iuh qujteilhujaia tonalpouhque. Auh in navi tochtli, in tlanauhcaiotia tonalli, in nauhcaiopa tlavica, tlacem-

3. *Otlalmic: ibid., "Y si el tal mercader muria, de su enfermedad."*

4. Molina, *op. cit.* (Spanish-Nahuatl), *Lado diestro.*

5. The text reads *ce oçelotl;* it is correct in the *Real Palacio MS.*

Rabbit, the day sign taking fourth place, accompanying the fourth position, they postponed. It also was evil. As they said, each and all of the day signs in the fourth place were evil; there were no good gifts at this time.

Likewise Five Water was also evil. As they said, each and all of the day signs taking the fifth place were bad. Those who were then born were perverted, inhuman, evil. And also they said that at this time, the day sign which took fifth place, was indifferent. Also they said that in this manner was it indifferent: if someone's day sign came as five, if he were well taught and advised, so he grew; it would not befall him as was his day sign — that he might become perverse. Reversed and substituted would be his deserts. By something marvelous[6] he gained fame and honor. It was said that this was during his lifetime. When he was born, a cause of apprehension was his day sign [number] five. They regarded it with fear[7] and apprehension. But as for the present one, it was not inevitable that it would be dangerous. It gained for him merit, fame, honor. Yet it was because he himself, by his penances, had complied and saved himself. For he had taken and heeded the counsel of the elders and the sage advice[8] of his childhood, etc.

jlhujtiltia, amo no qualli, iuh qujtoa: in jzqujcan tlanauhcaiopan tonalli, muchi amo qualli, atle vncan ca qualli nemactli.

No iuhquj in macujlli atl: amo no qualli, iuh qujtoa: in jzqujcan tlamacujltilia tonalli, mochi amo qualli: in aqujque vncan tlacati, amo tlacacemelleque, amo tlaca, tlaueliloque: auh ioan qujtoa, in vncan y, tonalli, macujltioaia, chico qualli no qujtoaia: injc chico qualli intla aca itonal omochiuh macujlli, intla uel mozcaltia, vel monotza ic mooapaoa, amo iuhquj ipan mochioaia, in quenamj itonal itenemac, injc atlacacemelle iezquja, çan jcuepca, çan jc mopatla, in jmâceoal mochioa tlamaujztic ic oalmoteniotia, oalmomaviçotia, itolo in ie nemj, injn iquac tlacat ic tenmachoc in jtonal macujlli: qujtlamauhcaittilique, qujtlatenmachilique: auh in axcan amo oipantic, injc ovitizquja, çan iê teniotl, maviçotl, in oqujmomâcevi, tel ca inôma, itlamaceoaliztica omoqujxti, omocneli, ca oqujtecuili, oqujtecaqujli in veuetlatolli, in jpiltian, ic ooaliztlama. &c.

6. In *ibid.*, the phrase is *ytla maviztic.*

7. In *ibid., quitlaovicanyttilique* (they regarded it as dangerous) precedes *qujtlatlatenmachilique.*

8. *Ovalixtlama* in *ibid.*

Twentieth Chapter, which telleth of the remaining houses belonging to the sign mentioned.

Also the one which followed it, Six Dog, was known as evil. Already related is the nature of those born on all day signs of the sixth position. Nothing at all good became one's gift.

On this one they loaded and heaped up gossip and bad repute. Everything was bequeathed, forced upon, and made a burden to them. They were forced to pay. And these made one embrace, undertake, commit, and seize upon evil. They mistreated, perverted, embroiled, and defamed one; they ignored, confused, confounded, disgraced, and dishonored their elders;[1] they shamed them and sowed confusion. They spotted, ruined, sullied, smudged, and destroyed one's good reputation.[2]

Likewise was it said that he who was born upon this sixth day sign, the readers of day signs also predicted, would be only sickly and weak; or he would soon fall dead. And if he lived, he would live only in suffering; he would wander about, or spend his time in bed, or go about constantly and continuously coughing, pallid, green-faced, white with cold, etc.

And those born upon this irremediable day sign they did not yet bathe; they looked ahead later to Seven Monkey. Thus they somewhat alleviated their day sign. They said: "If they live, perhaps by their penances the evil with which they were born, created, came forth on earth, budded and formed, persisted, and hatched, will reverse and be substituted."

And Seven Monkey they regarded as very good, because, as hath been said in many places, it is a day sign of the seventh place. It was said that it was the time of ritual of Chicome coatl, the likeness of our sustenance, of genuine wealth and prosperity, as the readers of the day signs said.

Injc cempoalli capitulo: itechpa tlatoa, in oc cequj calli, in jtech pouhquj machiotl, omjto.

Auh in contoqujlia, chiquacen itzcujntli: amo no qualli ipan machoia, ie omjto in quenamj inieliz vncan tlacati, in jpan muchi chiquacen tonalli, çan atle qualli in jnemac muchioa,

çan iê qujcenmama qujcemololoa in tlacatlatolli, in aujlqujzcaiotl, muchi iecaujltilo, cujtilo, mamaltilo, intech ontzopi, ioan iehoan qujtecujtia, qujteecaujltia, qujtechioaltia, contematzoltia in aqualli, in teiçolo, in tecatzauh, in tepâçolo, in teaujlqujxti, in teueuetlaz, in teixtlaz, in teixnecujlo, in teixceuj, in teitolotlac, in tetlaitoltili, in tepan tececenma, in teatlatzicujnj, in qujçoqujuja, in qujçoqujmotla, in qujpopoiotilia, in qujxpopoloa in jtlillo, in jtlapallo tenemjliz.

No ioan mjtoa: in aqujn ipan tlacatia, y, chiquacen tonalli, no qujpantiaia in tonalpouhque, çan cocoxcanacaio iez, amo chicaoac, anoçe çan njman onmjctiuetzia: auh intla nemj çan mocococotinemj, iaiatinemj, têtentinemj, tôtolcatinemj, tlâtlaztinemj, pineoatinemj, xoxoujxtinemj, iztaleoatinemj. Et[a].

Auh in aqujque ipan tlacatia in, amo qualtitica tonalli, aiamo qujmaltiaia, qujn jpan qujmattitiviia, in chicome oçomatli: ic achi vmpa, qujqualtiliaia yn jntonal, qujtoaia: intla nemjzque, aço intlamaceoaliztica cuepiz, mopatlaz in aqualli ipan otlacatque, oiecoque, otlalticpac qujzque, oxotlaque, oitzmolinque, otzicueoaque, otlapãque.

Auh in chicome oçomatli: cenca qujqualittaia, ypampa in iuh mjieccan omjto, in chicometioaia tonalli: qujlmach itlatoaia in chicome coatl, in jxiptla tonacaiotl, motqujtica necujltonolli, netlamachtilli, in iuh qujtoaia tonalpouhque:

1. *Teitolotlac*: possibly the negative *a-* or *amo* should be understood.

2. "Memoriales en 3 columnas" (*Academia de la Historia MS*), p. 207. The *Palacio Real MS* gives *teatlatzicuinalhui* for *teatlatzicujnj*. For *tetlatçicuinia* and *teçoquimotla,* Olmos, *op. cit.*, p. 219, gives *destruye el señor, o gouernador el pueblo.*

And to him who was then born she gave all things as gifts — that he would be happy, merry, a great giver of diversion and amusement to others; a witty, well-spoken one who aroused laughter; a true friend, a wholehearted friend of the people, esteemed by all. He could visit everywhere. Everywhere was he heeded, regarded by others.[3] He offended no one. This was because so was the day sign of the Monkey.

And if it were a woman, she would be very rich. She would produce well, make her wares well, and bargain astutely. She would be of good birth, and would arrange and distribute her merchandise and her people. Not failing or diminishing, her dealings, that which she might handle as merchandise, would turn out well. For hers was a day sign of the seventh place; so were her gifts.

And Eight Grass they also regarded as somewhat good, just like all day signs of the eighth position everywhere.

But Nine Reed was in no way good, because, it was said, it was the time of ritual and the day set apart for Tlaçolteotl. Purely vicious was the one then born. This hath already been told. No good at all did one gain as his deserts; only, at this time, his disdain, his abuse, his presumptuous and haughty deeds, etc. Everywhere, this one was like all which became ninth in position, as already hath in many places been told.

And on Ten Ocelot: this was a very good position, as already in many places hath been told in its account. Thus they said, and it was claimed, were the day signs in the tenth [and following] positions, all the day signs which bore [the word] *matlactli*. Then was the time of Tezcatlipoca's ritual, of him who was known as our lord. He who was then born they considered highly favored. They said that his time of birth was the time of the ritual of our noble Lord Tezcatlipoca. If he should live, he would be a person of merit. At once, then, they bathed him.

But if they had their own reasons, they might yet pass over it. Later, then, they looked ahead to the end of the day count when they bathed him, on Thirteen Motion. For all of the end of the day count they considered very favorable. Thus they then very much strengthened for them the day signs in which they bathed them.

auh in aqujn vncan tlacatia, much qujnemactiaia in papaqujnj iez, aaujenj, tecêceltianj, tececemeltianj, camanale, camanaloanj, vetzquiztli queoa, cemjcniuhtli, tecêcemjcnjuh, muchi tlacatl itlaço, novian vel tetlan motlalia, noviian tepal vntlaqua, ontlachia, aiac qujiolitlacoa: ipampa in iuhquj itonal oçomatli:

auh intla cioatl cenca mocujltonoz, itla uel mailiz, uel muchioaz in jtiamjc, vellanecujloz, vel motlacâtiz, qujhimatiz, qujtlâtlamachiz in jtiamjc, in jtlaca, amo actiuetziz, amo caxaoaz, vel mochioaz in jnanauh, in tlein qujmonanauhtiz ipampa in chicometioaia tonale, ca iuh ca inemac.

Auh in chicuei malinalli: no achi qujqualittaia, çan novian iuhquj in ixqujch chichicueey tonalli.

Auh in chicunavi acatl: çan njman amo qualli, ipampa qujlmach itlatoaia, itlacemjlhujtiltiaian Tlaçolteutl, motqujtica tlaçolli: in aqujn vncan tlacati, ie omjto: njman atle qualli qujmâçeoa, çan vncan ca itelchioaloca, iquequeloloca, icuecuenochichioaloca, iaujlqujxtiloca. Et^a^. Noviian iuhcan jn, in jzqujcan chicunavitioaia, in iuh ie mjieccan omjto.

Auh in jpan matlactli oçelotl: ie vel qualcan, in iuh ie mjieccan omjto itlatollo, iuh qujtoa: qujlmach in matlactioaian tonalli, in jzqujtetl tlamatlactetilia tonalli, vncan itlatoaia in Tezcatlipuca: in jpan machoia tt^o^. in aqujn vncan tlacati, cenca qujqualittaia, qujtoaia: ca tematian in otlacat, imatian itlatoaia, in tlacatl totecujo Tezcatlipuca: intla nemjz ca mâceoale iez, ic njman iquac caltiaia:

auh intla qujnequjzque iniolotlama, in oc concholoitizque, qujn cẽ vmpa qujmattivia, in tonaltzonco iquac caltiaia in jpan matlactlomej, olin, ipampa in mochi tonaltzontli, cenca qujqualittaia, ic cenca uel vncan qujntonalchicaoaia, in jpan, qujmaltiaia.

3. This rendition is based on *ōtlacaqui* for *vntlaqua* in the *Real Palacio MS.*

And Eleven Eagle, and Twelve Vulture, so they said, were both only indifferent, not considered only one way; they said they fell both ways. Those who were born on both these day signs they always bathed later, at the end of the day count. At this position they made their day signs favorable.

This one, which is here the end of the day count of the group — Thirteen Motion — this one they regarded as best. For it came concluding, and with it was finished and came to an end, the thirteen day signs. Whatsoever were the deserts of the one then born hath already been told in many places.

Auh in matlactli oce quauhtli, ioan matlactli omome cozcaquauhtli, iuh qujtoa onteixti çan chico qualli, amo çan centettitica, vme vitz qujtoa, in aqujque ipan tlacatia in, onteixti tonalli, qujn cen jpan qujmaltiaia in tonaltzontli, vmpa qujqualtiliaia in jntonal.

Iehoatl in, in njcan cencalpan tonaltzontli, matlactli omej olin: injn oc cenca qujqualittaia, ipampa in qujtlamjtica, yn jca tlantica, ica tzonqujztica matlactli omej tonalli, auh in quenamj imâceoal: vncan tlacatia, ie mjieccan omjto.

Twenty-first Chapter, which telleth of the tenth sign, called One Flint Knife. And it was said that it was of good fortune, and claimed that those then born were brave and became seasoned warriors. And it was said that the women then born were forceful; they were able in all things and made their goods very well. And it was said to be the day sign of Uitzilopochtli, to whom it was dedicated. His domain was war. It was said also to be the day sign of Camaxtli. And when this sign began, they observed the feast [of Uitzilopochtli]. And it was said that all the day signs were good — [all] thirteen.

Injc cempoalli oce capitulo: itechpa tlatoa, injc matlactetl machiotl, in jtoca ce tecpatl: ioan qujl qualli in jtonallo, auh qujl in aqujque vncan tlacatia chicaoaque catca, ioan tequjoacatia: auh qujl in cioa vncan tlacatia oqujchiolloque catca, muchi in veli catca, cenca uel qujnextiaia in jntlatquj: auh qujl itonal catca in Vitzilopuchtli, in jtech pouhquj catca, in jtequjuh catca iiaoiotl, qujl no itonal in Camaxtle: auh in jquac vmpeoaia injn machiotl, qujlhujqujxtiliaia, auh qujl muchi qualli catca in jzqujlhujtl, matlaqujlhujtl vmei.

One Flint Knife set in. On this One Flint Knife, when it tarried for a day, they then made offerings to Uitzilopochtli, whose day sign it was, and to Camaxtli, god of the Uexotzinca.

Thus it is said they made offerings and paid great honor [to Uitzilopochtli] there at his temple, in his tribal district, at the place whose name was Tlacatecco. There was his image guarded, and all his array. They had it all spread out before him and laid in the sun; they offered incense and presented him[1] what were called the quetzal feather cape, the blue cotinga feather cape, the red spoonbill feather cape, the yellow parrot feather cape, and the humming bird feather cape.[2] But only after them came last the no longer very precious feathers, like the white heron feather cape or the reed thrush feather cape.[3] Severally they laid all of them down, offered them separately, arranged them in rows, placed them in order, etc.

Moquetza ce tecpatl: inin ce tecpatl, in jquac tlacemilhujtiltiaia, vncan qujtonaltiaia, ytonalpan catca in Vitzilopuchtli, ioan in camaxtle, vexotzinca inteouh,

injc mjtoa: qujtonaltiaia, cenca quimaviztiliaia, in vncan iteupan icalpulco in jtocaiocan catca tlacatecco, vncan pieloia in jxiptla in jxqujch itlatquj, much ixpan qujtequjliaia, qujtotonjaia, qujtlenamaqujliaia qujtlacotonjliaia, in moteneoa quetzalquemjtl, xiuhtotoquemjtl, tlauhquecholquemjtl, tozquemjtl, vitzitzilquemjtl, auh ça qujtoqujlia, qujtzacuja, in aocmo cenca tlaçoivitl, in iuhquj aztaquemjtl, tzanaquemjtl: muchi nononqua qujtecaia, qujtlatlamantilia, qujcuecuentilia, qujvivipana. Et[a].

And all these precious capes, when they spread them out, remained there a day. By doing this, it was said, they sunned them for Uitzilopochtli. And there offerings were made; there they laid out all the gifts, called fast foods. And all the good, prepared

auh much ie in tlaçotilmatli ipan qujtecaia, vncan cemjlhujtia: iehoatl injc mjtoa qujtlatotonjlia in Vitzilopuchtli, ioan vncan tlamanaloia, vncan qujtecaia in jxqujch ventli, in moteneoa tlacatlaqualli: ioan in jxqujch iectli, in tlachichioalli tlaqualli, in

1. *Qujcotonjliaia* alternatively could mean "they beheaded quail for him."

2. Corresponding Spanish text: *"uno se llamaua quetzalquemjtl, que qujere dezir: capa de quetzales verdes, y resplandeciẽtes: otro se llamaua xiuhtotoquemjtl, que qujere dezir: capa de plumas azules, y resplandecientes: otro se llamaua tozquemjtl, que qujere dezir: capa de plumas amarillas, y resplandecientes: otro se llamaua vitzitzilquemjtl, que qujere dezir: capa hecha de plumas resplandecientes de cinzones."*

3. Cf. Seler, *op. cit.*, p. 233. In *ibid.*, p. 160, n. 2, it is jackdaw.

foods came forth from the palace; and from the houses in the commoners' localities they [also] emerged and came forth.

But only for a little while it was, remained, and rested there. Then the old men of the *calpulli* [of Uitzilopochtli] removed, continued to take and transport, divided, and distributed, what pertained to them. They removed it to a number of places. They consumed all. No one remained alone. Everyone came to it: the devout of the place, those who had fasted for a year; those who had danced and fasted for Uitzilopochtli.

And Moctezuma then offered all manner of precious flowers [before the image] — varied flowers which were sweet-smelling and fragrant: magnolia,[4] maize flowers,[5] cacao flowers,[6] popcorn flowers,[7] and garlands of maize ears,[8] which grew everywhere; basket flowers,[9] raven flowers;[10] yellow and blue tobacco flowers;[11] milky corn silk flowers;[12] and all manner of precious flowers, prepared,—well-formed, well-arranged, made as shields of flowers, circular, radiating, and spreading; and the pleasant-smelling ones. It seemed as if the fragrance, the perfume, spread and blanketed his temple.

And so they burned [tubes of] tobacco — only in bundles. First they bound them about the middle. As they burned them, they filled [the area] before [the image].[13] It was as if the smoke arose, spread a cloud, extended, came to settle, and lay billowing.

Likewise it was said at the time of the day sign One Flint Knife, that the wine-makers showed special concern. At that time they cut and bored

tlatocan oalqujçaia: ioan in çan calla, maceoalpã oaleoaia, oalqujçaia:

auh çan achitonca, in vncan vnmanj, vncan onoc, vncan onmoteca: niman ic qujquanja çan ic concujtimanj, ic conjquanjtimanj, intech povi in calpulveuetque, qujmoxexelhuja, qujmomamaca, quecizqujcan qujmjcuanjlia, vntetlamj, aiac ixcauj, muchi tlacatl itech aci, in vncan tlamaceuhque, in mocexiuhçauhque, in jtech mĵtotinemj, in qujneçaujlia Vitzilopuchtli:

auh in Motecuçoma in jxqujch tlaçoxochitl, in nepapan xochitl, in velic, in aviiac vncan qujmana in iolloxochitl, in eloxochitl, in cacaoaxochitl, in izqujxochitl, ioan cacaoacincozcatl, in izqujcan icac, oacalxochitl, in cacaloxochitl, in coztic iiexochitl, auh in xoxouhquj iiexochitl, in xiloxochitl, ioan in ie ixqujch nepapan tlaçoxochitl, in tlamantli, in vellalalilli, in tlatecujcujlolli, in mĵmati, in chimalxochitl, in ololiuhquj, in momoiaoa, in xexelivi: auh in çaçan tlatlanecutli, iuhqujn tlaujiaxtoc, tlaueuelixtoc, tlaaujiaxtimanj, tlaueuelixtimanj, in jteupan:

auh injc qujtlatiaia iietl, çan cecemmecatl çan iuh cujtlalpitiuh in qujtlatiaia, contenteuj ixpan, iuhqujn puchteoatoc, aiavitl mantoc, aiavitl qujztoc, iuhqujn mômomolocatoc.

No ioan mjtoa in jpan in tonalli ce tecpatl, cenca vncan tlatemachiaia in tlachicque, vncan qujtlapanaia in inmeuh, ic qujtemachiaia injc cenca meiaz,

4. *Iolloxochitl* (*Talauma mexicana* D. C. Don) — Mexican magnolia, a flower reserved solely for the nobility. — Emily Walcott Emmart: *The Badianus Manuscript* (*Codex Barberini, Latin, 241*), *Vatican Library. An Aztec Herbal of 1552* (Baltimore: The Johns Hopkins Press, 1940), p. 310.

5. *Eloxochitl*: probably *Compositae* (?) (Emmart, *op. cit.*, p. 275). In Francisco Hernández, *Historia de las plantas de Nueva España* (México: Imprenta Universitaria, 1942), Vol. III, p. 841, it is classed with *yexochitl*. Santamaría, *op. cit.*, Vol. I, p. 588, identifies it as *Magnolia dealbata* Zucc.; also called *yelosuchil*.

6. *Cacaoaxochitl*: Hernández, *op. cit.*, Vol. III, p. 921, calls it *Quararibea funebris* (Llave) Standl. See also Santamaría. *op. cit.*, Vol. I, p. 250.

7. *Izqujxochitl*: *Bourreria huanita* (La Slave & Lex.) Hemsl. (Emmart, *op. cit.*, p. 275).

8. Cf. Santamaría, *op. cit.*, Vol. I, p. 249.

9. *Uacalxochitl*: *Xanthosoma* sp. (Emmart, *op. cit.*, p. 234); *Phyllodendron affine*, Hemsl., *"Una planta exótica, de las aráceas, cultivada en [Méjico]"* (Santamaría, *op. cit.*, Vol. II, p. 102).

10. *Cacaloxochitl*: *Plumeria rubra* L., attribute of important personages, according to Sahagún (Emmart, *op. cit.*, p. 308). Hernández, *op. cit.*, Vol. III, p. 806, says *Plumeria acutifolia* Poir, *"flor de cuervo."*

11. *Iiexochitl*: *flor de tabaco* (no botanical term given); *"El Yexochitl, que algunos llaman* eloxochitl *o sea flor de* eloti, *y otros* cozauhquixochitl *o* yexochitl *amarillo"* (Hernández, *op. cit.*, Vol. III, pp. 841, 842).

12. *Xiloxochitl*: *Bombax ellipticum* H. B. K., according to Hernández, *op. cit.*, Vol. II, p. 453, and Paul C. Standley, "Trees and Shrubs of Mexico," *Contributions from the United States National Herbarium* (Washington: Government Printing Office, 1923), pp. 793-794; *Callandria anomala* (Kunth) McBride, according to Emmart, *op. cit.*, p. 301.

13. *Real Palacio MS*: *contentimani.*

their maguey plants;[14] so they showed special concern in order that their maguey plants would flow much and produce well. And so they offered gifts in the temple of Uitzilopochtli. There they offered their wine, which had been newly brewed, called *uitztli*; they went pouring it into bowls on which rested sucking tubes. And the ones who there partook of it were the already aged, called *quanueuetque,* who already had the privilege of drinking wine. These drank; they continued drinking with the sucking tubes.

ontlaiez inmeuh: auh injc tlauenchioaia, in jteupan Vitzilopuchtli: vmpa conmanaia in jmoc, in iancujcan tlachictli, in moteneoa vitztli, acatecomac, contecatimanj: vncan ipan icaca ce piaztli: auh in aqujn vmpa vntlatlapaloaia, in ie chicaoaque, in moteneoa quãveuetque: in ie innemac tlaoanaliztli, iehoan conja, ic conjtimanj in piaztli:

And he who was born on this [day], One Flint Knife, they said, would be valiant, a chieftain; he would gain honor and riches.

auh in aqujn ipan tlacatia, y, ce tecpatl qujtoaia, oqujchtiz tiacauhtiz, maujztiz, mocujltonoz:

Likewise, if it were a woman, she would be of merit, gifted, and deserving. Her labors would be good; there would be wherewith to eat and drink; there would be sustenance. She would become rich and wealthy; courageous, strong, reckoned as a man, and hardy. She would give honor as a man. And, [among] all her gifts, she would speak well, be eloquent, give good counsel, and arrange her conversation and manner of speaking well in her home. She would be observant, of good memory, discreet, etc.

no iuhquj intla çioatl, maçeoale iez, nemaque, ilhujle, vel itla mailiz, oniez in qujquaz, in qujz, vnca qujquanj iez, mocujltonoz, motlacamatiz, ioan oqujchnacaio, chicaoac, oqujchtlamatiz, moqujchpoaz, oqujcheoaz, teoqujchtlamachti iez: ioan much inemac vellatoz, motlatoljmatiz, vel tenonotzaz, vellatoltecpanaz, yieieian, icacatian, in qujtlaliz, tlatolli, vel ixe, iollo, mozcalianj iez. Et[a].

And Two Rain, and Three Flower, Four Crocodile, Five Wind, Six House, Seven Lizard, Eight Serpent, Nine Death, Ten Deer, Eleven Rabbit, Twelve Water, Thirteen Dog—all, in truth all, were as hath been told in their account. All went to be considered and were observed as of, and they followed, the same pattern. They were only one, regarded as only one in their relation and account, as they went in order there day by day, each one of the days in its proper place, so proceeding in order, one, two, three, henceforth[15] until they reached and completed the end of the day count, thirteen.

Auh in vme qujavitl, ioan ei xochitl, nauj cipactli, macujlli êcatl, chiquacen calli, chicome cuetzpalin, chicuei coatl, chicunavi mjqujztli, matlactli maçatl, matlactloce tochtli, matlactli omome atl, matlactlomej itzcujntli: in jxqujch in çan moch iuhquj in jtlatollo omjto: çã much umpa itztiuh, çan much vmpa tlachia, çan much vmpa tlaujca, cã ie centetl, çan centettitiuh in jtlatlatollo, in jtoloca, in iuh tecpantiuh, in vncan tlacecemjlhujtiltitiuj, cecenteme tonaltin, in jnieieian ic tecpantiuj in ce, in vme, in ei: ixqujchica, injc onacitiuh, injc ontlatlantiuh tonaltzontli matlatlactlomcci.

14. Corresponding Spanish text: "*Los señores de los magueyes, o taberneros que vendian el pulcre, cortauan, y agujerauan los magueyes: para que manassen mjel en este signo: tenjan que por agujerarlos en este signo, no manaua mucho.*"

15. Bernardino Biondelli: *Glossarium Azteco-Latinum et Latino-Aztecum* (Mediolani: Valentiner et Mues, 1869), has *usquedum* and *hinc* (henceforth, from here on), for *ixquichica.*

Twenty-second Chapter, which telleth of the eleventh sign, called One Monkey, and of its fortune. It was said of those then born that one was a man of good standing, friendly, amiable, and happy, given to music and the other arts. And it was said that at this time descended to earth those who were the "Goddesses"; and that those whom they met on the road or in paths between houses they injured and visited with sickness. And for this reason, when it was this day sign, no one could fare forth. And one who then sickened the physicians forthwith abandoned.

Injc cempoalli vmome capitulo, itechpa tlatoa, injc matlactetl oce machiotl, in jtoca ce oçomatli: ioan in jtonallo, qujlmach in aqujque vncan tlacatia qualli iiollo catca, teicnjoan, tlaçotlalonj, papaqujnj, qujmocujtlaviaia in cujcatl, ioan in oc cequj tolteca-iotl: auh qujl in jquac oaltemoia, in aqujque cioateteu in tlalticpac: auh qujl in aqujque qujnnamjquja, in vtlica, in anoço caltzala qujtlaueliaia cocoliztli itech qujtlalia: auh ipampa in jpan in tonalli catca, aiac vel qujçaia: auh in aqujn iquac mococoaia, çan njman qujxnaoatiaia in titici.

One Monkey set in. This Monkey [day sign] they regarded as favorable.

Moquetza ce oçomatli: inin oçomatli, qujqualittaia:

But also they said that at that time the so-called "Princesses" or "Goddesses" descended. It was the time when they were expected, the time of their arrival. At this time they looked upon the children with much apprehension. They simply shut them in the houses; they did not wish them to appear at the entrances or on the road, so that [the Goddesses] would not come upon or harm them. Perhaps one of them would have twisted lips, or a shrunken mouth; or be cross-eyed or of weak vision; or his lips would quiver or quake; or he would be maddened — a devil would possess him and he would foam at the mouth; or he would have withered, twisted arms; or be lame, etc.

auh ioan qujtoa, no uncan temoaia inchielpan, imaçia, in moteneoaia cioapipilti, cioateteu, cenca vncã qujntlamauhcaittiliaia in tepilhoan, çã qujntzatzaquaia calitic, amo qujmonqujxtitlanja, in qujaoac, in vtlica, injc amo motenamjctizque, qujmjtlacozque, aço aca tennecujliviz, tempatziviz, ixnecujliujz, ixvitzaliviz, iten papatlacaz, iten viujiocaz, iollotlauelilotiz, itech qujneoaz, tenqualacqujçaz, matzicoliujz, macopichaujz, icxi qujujlanaz. Et[a].

And if someone began to sicken, the physicians told him that he would become dangerously sick; he would not recover. For he had come upon the Princesses, and they had set upon him; it was the time of their descent and arrival when [this sickness] began. For it was [so] willed.

auh intla aca ipan opeuh mococoa, qujtcilhujaia in titici, ca tlanauiz, aocmo qujçaz, ca omotenamjcti, ipan oqujzque in cioapipilti, ca intemoian, imêcoian in opeuh, ca oeleujloc:

And likewise it was said that if someone were of good standing, of a good day sign, and able, if at this time they injured him, they said that the Princesses had indeed willed it upon him and that he had contended with them.[1]

auh no ioan mjtoa, intla aca qualli yiollo, in qualli itonal, ioan qualli itlachieliz: vncan qujtlacalhujaia, qujtoaia: ca çan oqueleujque, oqujnmonamjcti in cioapipilti.

1. Corresponding Spanish text: *"Y si alguno que era biẽ dispuesto, enfermaua en estos dias, dezian: que las diosas le aujan desseado la hermosura, y se la aujan quitado."*

And he who was then born they regarded favorably. They said that if it were a man who was then born, he would entertain others and give them solace. Nowhere would he be hated; everyone would be his friend. And [he would be], perchance, a singer, a dancer, or a scribe; he would produce some work of art. For such, then, was his day sign, One Monkey. So they said that indeed thus it came to pass on each of the different Monkey [day signs], as hath been told in many places of the gifts of those then born.

Auh in aqujn ipan tlacatia, ie qujqualittaia, qujtoaia: intla oqujchtli ipan otlacat, ca moteaaujltiliz, motececemeltiliz, acan tlaelittoz, muchi tlacatl icnjuh iez, ioan aço cujcanj, mjtotianj, anoço tlacujlo, itla ic totoltecatiz: ipampa ca njman iuhquj, in jtonal ce oçomatli, iuh qujtoa: çan ie much iuhquj, in jzqujtetl oçomatli in ie mjieccan omjto, in quenamj innemac, ipan tlacati.

And Two Grass was in no way good. They said it was a wild beast. He who was then born would beget very many sons; they would stand like stones; like spawned fish would his sons be. Nevertheless not one would grow, but all merely died, etc. (So hath it been told.)

Auh in vme malinalli: njman amo qualli, qujtoa tequanj: in aqujn vncã tlacati, cenca vel mopilhoatia, iuhqujn tetl icaque, iuhqujn mjchaiatza ipilhoan, çan iê amo ce moquetza, çan much vnmjctiuj. Et[a]. (in iuh omjto).

And Three Reed, and Four Ocelot, Five Eagle, Six Vulture, Seven Motion, Eight Flint Knife, Nine Rain, Ten Flower, Eleven Crocodile, Twelve Wind, Thirteen House: these were all the group of day signs. However, all were as their account told elsewhere. But they were so regarded as they went arranged in their order as [is told] in their separate accounts. There the third place was mentioned as good, and [others] evil.[2]

Auh in ei acatl, ioan nauj ocelutl, macujlli quauhtli, chiquacen cozcaquauhtli, chicome olin, chicuei tecpatl, chicunavi qujaujtl, matlactli suchitl, matlactloce cipactli, matlactlomome hecatl, matlactli vmei calli: in jxqujch in cencalpan tonalli, çan ie much iuhquj in jtoloca in oc cequj omoteneuh, çan iê ic motztiuh, in iuh tecpantiuj, in iuhca ca imjtoloca, vncan inieian in moteneoa qualli, ioan amo qualli.

2. *Ibid.*: *"Todas las otras casas, deste signo: tienen las condiciones de los numeros, en que cayen: como ya esta dicho arriba: Que las terceras casas, son buenas: las cuartas y quintas, y sextas, malas: y las septimas, buenas: y las octauas, y nonas, malas: y las decimas, y undecimas, y tercia decimas, buenas."*

Twenty-third Chapter, which telleth of the twelfth sign, called One Lizard. It was said that those then born were as if agile. Very strong were they of body and spirit. The fourth house, and the fifth, and the sixth, it was said, were unfavorable. And the second and eighth, it was stated, came to be only indifferent.

Injc cempoalli vmei capitulo: itechpa tlatoa, injc matlactetl omvme machiotl, in jtoca ce cuetzpalli: qujl in aqujque vncan tlacatia, iuhqujn tlatlaloapopul catca, cenca chicaoac catca in innacaio in iêel: injc nauhtetl calli, ioã injc macujltetl, ioan injc chiquacentetl, qujl amo qualli catca: auh injc vntetl, ioan inic chicuetetl, qujlmach ça tlanepantla qujça.

One Lizard set in. This they regarded as favorable. They said that he who was born upon it was very strong — of powerful body. He never sickened much. And if, somewhere, he fell down, it had no effect; he quickly got up and arose with vigor. So they regarded him as favored, like his day sign of the lizard. If, somewhere, it hurled itself down from the top of a wall, and suddenly slapped the ground and stirred up the dust, it took no effect; quickly it ran, reached the wall, and scrambled up. Here ended the account. So was it cried out when some became wroth; perhaps death was wished for one. They said: "O friend, there to the earth I shall hurl thee. Thou wilt stir up the dust;[1] thou wilt suddenly be enclosed in the jaws of the lizard!"

Moquetza ce cuetzpalli: inin qujqualittaia, qujtoaia: in aquj̃ ipan tlacatia, cenca chicaoac, chicaoacanacaio aic cenca mococoa: auh intla cana oalhuetzi âquen conmati, meuhtiuetzi, popoxiuhteoa: ic ipan qujuelittaia, in iuhquj itonal cuetzpalli, intla cana tepanticpac oalmomaiauj, oalcapantiuetzi, tlalli qujpototztiuetzi, âquen cõmati, içiuhca motlaloa, oc ceppa tepantli quêcaujtiqujça, qujmatocatiqujça, vncan oqujz in tlatolli ic neâio in iquac acame omoqualanjque, aço ic momjctiznequj, qujmolhuja: nocne ompa on tlalli ic njmjtzujtequjz, tlalli tiqujtototztiuetziz, timocuetzpaltempictiuetziz.

Likewise very solid[2] was his body — firm, hard, stout, robust, they said; lithe, mature, hardy, vigorous; and he was a good worker and diligent. He cared for and dedicated himself to not only one thing; indeed everywhere was returned that which made him rich.[3] He dealt in many things. Whatsoever it was, it resulted well. It was not apparent nor known how that which he required appeared.

No ioan vellachictic in jnacaio, pipinquj, tepitztic, chicaoac, chicactic, qujlhuja tlâtlalhoa tlâpaliuj, tlâpaltic, pupuxtli, ioan vel motlaiecoltia, iêel, açan centetl in qujmocujtlauja, in jpan mjxpoa, vel noviiampa mocuecuepa in tlein ic motlacamatia, mjiec in qujmonanauhtia, in catleoatl vel onmochioaz, ânezrica, âmachiztli injc neci itech monequj.

And Two Serpent, and Three Death — thus they proceeded, in order — Four Deer, Five Rabbit, Six Water, Seven Dog, Eight Monkey, Nine Grass, Ten Reed, Eleven Ocelot, Twelve Eagle, Thirteen Vulture: all these thus bring to a conclusion the two, three, [etc.]. Only one is the account of the various day signs here which go well and badly. When the family of day signs ended —[4]

Auh in vme coatl, ioan ei mjqujztli, inic tecpantiuh, navi maçatl, macujlli tochtli, chiquacen atl, chicume itzcujntli, chicuei oçomatli, chicunavi malinalli, matlactli acatl, matlactloce ocelutl, matlactli vmome quauhtli, matlactlomei cozcaquauhtli: in jxqujch in, injc ontlatlantiuh vme ey, çan centetl in jtoloca, in vncan izqujtetl qualtitiuh, ioan âqualtitiuh tonalli, in oqujz in cencalli tonalli.

1. *Tiqujtototztiuetziz: tiquipototztivetziz* in the *Real Palacio MS.*
2. *Vellachictic: vellalichtic* in *ibid.*
3. *Motlacatia* in *ibid.*
4. Here and in a number of later chapters, the concluding sentence is completed by the opening phrase of the next chapter.

Twenty-fourth Chapter, which telleth of the thirteen sign, named One Motion. And it was said [of] those then born that, if they performed penances and if they were well reared—it was said—good would befall them. But if they performed no penances, it was said that suffering would befall them.

—then set in One Motion. Of this they said that it was only half good. He who was then born, man or woman, who did penance well, who took good heed, who was well reared, succeeded and found his deserts and gifts.

But if he did not take good heed, and were not well reared, the opposite resulted. He met misery; it was visited upon him in good measure. He was a worthless person, who nowhere made an impression. He was a vagabond, wandering from place to place. Even as the night,[1] so nowhere did he show brilliance, etc.

And Two Flint Knife, and Three Rain, Four Flower, Five Crocodile, Six Wind, Seven House, Eight Lizard, Nine Serpent, Ten Death, Eleven Deer, Twelve Rabbit; and thus it came to an end with Thirteen Water. Later, then, they made them all favorable. So they regarded as good the conclusion of a series of day signs, as hath been told in many places. When this group of day signs ended—

Injc cempoalli onnavi capitulo: itechpa tlatoa, injc matlactetl omey machiotl: in jtoca ce olin, auh qujlmach in aqujque vncan tlacatia: intla tlamaceoaia, ioan intla uel izcaltiloia: qujl qualli ipan muchioaia: auh in amo tlamaceoaia, qujl netolinjliztli inpan muchioaia.

Niman oalmoquetza in ce olin: injn qujtoaia, çan chico qualli in aqujn vncan tlacati, in oqujchtli, in çioatl in vellamaceoa, in vel monotza, in uel mooapaoa, iehoatl qujçaia, qujttaia in jmaceoal, in jnemac:

auh intlacamo vel monotza, intlacamo uel mozcalti: çan icuepca in qujmonamictiaia icnoiotl, itech eoatinemj, çan nentlacatl, acan petzitl, çan quauhtlamelaoa, âanemj, çan iuh onioa, acan ixtona. Et[a].

Auh in vme tecpatl, ioan ie qujaujtl, navi suchitl, macujlli cipactli, chiquacen hecatl, chicome calli, chicuei cuetzpali, chiconauj coatl, matlactli mjqujztli, matlactloce maçatl, matlactlomome tochtli: ioan injc tlãtica matlactlomej atl, qujn cen vnpa qualtiaia, ic quiqualittaia in tonaltzontli, in iuh mjieccan omjto: yn ontlan jn cencalpan tonalli.

1. *Onioa*: *oyoua* in the *Real Palacio MS.*

Twenty-fifth Chapter, which telleth of the fourteenth sign, called One Dog. This, it was said, was a good day sign; and it was claimed that it was the day of Xiuhtecutli, whom they called Tlalxictentica.[1] They observed a very great feast day for him. And at this time the rulers were elected.[2]

Injc cempoalli on macujlli capitulo: itechpa tlatoa, injc matlactetl onnavi machiotl, in jtoca ce itzcujntli: inin qujlmach qualli tonalli, ioan qujl itonal catca, in xiuhtecutli: in qujtoaia Tlalxictentica, cenca vei ilhujtl qujchioaia: ioan ypan motlatocaaltiaia in tlatoque.

— then set in the one named One Dog. This, they said, was a good day sign. At this time, they dedicated the day to [the god of] fire, called Xiuhtecutli. They formed his image there in his temple. There they made offerings to it; before it they decapitated quail and spread incense. They adorned and bedight it in all manner of paper array. The fabrication [of the paper articles] was in charge of those called paper-cutters and designers. They provided it with feathers; they scattered feathers over it; provided it with various kinds of costly feathers and dispersed a variety of them over it. And they provided [the paper array] with green stones. They called the [ceremony] *nextlaualli.* All the food [and array of] Tlalxictentica[3] they burned before him.

Niman oalmoquetza in jtoca, ce itzcujntli: injn qujtoaia qualli tonalli, vncan qujtonaltiaia in tletl, in jtoca Xiuhtecutli: qujtlaliaia yxiptla in vmpa iteupan: vncan qujtlamanjliaia, ixpan tlacotona, copaltema, qujchichioa, qujccccncaoa, in jxqujch amatlatqujtl, inmac iecauja in moteneoaia amatecque, amatlamatque, qujviiotiaia, qujvitzetzeloa, qujnepapaniviiotia, tlaçoiujtica qujnepapanivitzetzeloa: ioan qujchachalchiuhiotia, quitocaiotia nextlaoalli, itlaqual in tlalxictentica, much ixpan qujtlatiaia:

And everywhere, in each family which was rich and had become wealthy, those of Pochtlan and Amantlan,[4] they made [the god] very important. Thus they did him honor: food and drink were provided. There was rejoicing. There were banquets. Very early in the morning, when it was still very early dawn, they burned the paper array. As was said, thus they fed the fire. Incense went with and accompanied [the offerings]. One basket at a time, or two baskets at a time, they cast into the fire clean, white incense. And they decapitated quail. It seemed that before the hearth, they kept fluttering and beating their wings. Their blood was scattered by their fluttering, so that the earth before the hearth was struck in various places. They spattered and poured forth their blood. Likewise they first made a libation of wine before the hearth, and later at each of the four corners of the hearth they made libations.

auh in noviian cecencalpan, in netlacamachoia, in necujltonoloia, in puchtlan, in amantlan: cenca qujveichioaia injc qujmaviztiliaia, tlatlaqualoia, aatlioaia, netlacamacho, necoanotzalo, oc ueca ioac, cenca oc tlaujzcalpan in qujtlatiaia amatl, in mjtoa ic qujtlamaca tletl, qujvicatiuh, qujtocatiuh in copalli, cecenpetlacalli, ovnpetlacalli in contepeoa tleco, chipaoac, iztac copalli: ioan qujncotona çoçoltin, iuhqujn tlecujlixquac tlâpatlaca, tlapapatlaca, ieço nemamacaooa, tlalli ic neujujteco tlecujlixquac qujtzitzicujtza, qujnonoquja in jmezço: ioan no achto tlecujlixquac qujtotoiaoa in vctli: auh çatepan tlecujlnacazco nauhcampaixti qujtotoiaoa:

1. Corresponding Spanish text: *"Este dezian: ser el signo del dios del fuego, llamado Xiuhtecutli, o tlalxictentica."*
2. *Ibid.*: *"los señores, y principales, que eran elegidos, para regir la republica: hazian la fiesta de su eleccion."*
3. *Ibid.*: *"cerca de la mañana, quemavan las ofrendas de papel, y copal, dezian: que con estas cosas, davã de comer al fuego."*
4. Monzón, *op. cit.*, pp. 50, 64, 68: *calpulli* of merchants, feather workers, etc.

And the commoners, the poor, only threw coarse incense into the fire. And finally the extremely poor, the poverty-stricken, the needy, the discontented, who came last, only cast aromatic herbs in the fire, thus making the offering in their own fires.[5]

auh in çan maceoaltzintli, in motolinja, çan copalxalli in tleco qujtema: auh in ça iequene qujtzacuja, in molhujicnotlacatl, tequjicnotlacatl, in âavia, in auellamati: çan ie in jauhtli tleco qujtepeoa, ic qujtlamaca in jxcoian itleuh:

And it is said that the lords and rulers were installed then, on the day One Dog; and there was a celebration, the royal ceremony, the rites of election,[6] on Four Reed. At that time the lords over the cities came from everywhere. There was feasting, by which it was made known that the new ruler had been installed. Many came in this manner: as their salutations, their gifts of greeting, they bore and carried wrist bands, capes, flowers, tobacco. For whatsoever their cities were famous and renowned, from wherever and howsoever far they traveled, they offered gifts and paid tribute to the ruler, and greeted him and paid him great respect. Their elders, the lords, the orators, the able speakers, who were seated, returned like for like and answered them for him.

ioan mjtoa in tlatoque vncan motecutlaliaia motlatocatlaliaia, in jpan in ce itzcujntli: auh ipan motequaltiaia, motecpacaia, motlatocapacaia, in nauhacatl, iquac noviian oalhuja, in altepetl ipan tlatoque, coanotzalo, ic machitilo in iancujcan tlatoanj omotlali, mjiec injc oalhuj, in jntetlapaloaia, in jntetlapalol qujoalcuj, qujoalitquj in macuextli, in tilmatli, in suchitl, in jetl, in çaço tlein imamaujzço, yximachoca imaltepeuh, in campa, in quexqujchca oaleoa, qujtlamamaca, qujtlatequjlia in tlatoanj, ioan qujtlapaloa, qujtlatlauhtia, oalmotlalia in jntechiuhcaoan, in tecutlatoque, in vellatoa, in tlatolmati, qujtlacuepilia, qujntlananqujlilia:

And in the same manner was it done and responded. Thus was returned their gratitude, in order to reciprocate, to acknowledge, to welcome, and to provide a repast. Flowers, tobacco, drink, food, and confections were presented. But the capes came in bundles. They were only in bales. Only by the bundle were they given and presented. Each brought out first the precious capes, appropriate to them, the ones to which they were entitled, made and completed in [the ruler's] house. Thereupon they gave them their choice and pleased them. What each thought best, or sought out, or what was fitting for him, or suited his liking, or his rank, they gave the lords over the cities; [the ruler's] servants thus honored and gave preference to each [of the lords] individually.

auh çan no iuj in chioalo, in namjco, çan ic mocuepa in jnnetlaçotlaliz, injc motlaneuj, injc mjximati, injc momalcochoa, injc mocoachioa, qujmomamaca in xuchitl, in jetl, in atl, in tlaqualli, in tlaqualtectli: auh in tilmatli çan qujqujmjliuhtiuh, çan qujqujmjlietiuh, çan qujmjltica in qujmomaca, in, in qujmotlauhtia, qujiaiacana in tlaçotilmatli, in tetechtilmatli, in vel intonal ĩcalitic ochioaloc, otlatlan, iquac impan qujnpepena, inpan qujnuelitta, qujntlatlattilia, qujmjipantia, qujnpapantia, qujnpapanjtia, in quenamj qujnmacazque altepetl ipan tlatoque: injc nononqua qujnmaujztilia, qujnvecapano, intetlaujcalhoan.

The gifts hurried, rushed, hastened, and sped borne on their backs, carried and transported by the tump lines. And the leavings, worth nothing, of no value,

tlaliuj, tlâtlaliuj, tlâtlalhujtiuj, tlâtlaliooa, in tlamamalo, in tlâtlatqujoa, quaquailpitiuh in netlauhtilli: auh in netlacaujlli, âtle tlaçotli, âtlatlaçotli, tla-

5. Corresponding Spanish text: *"Los pobres ofrecian un encienso, que llaman copalxalli, en su mjsmo hogar: y los muy pobres, ofrecian una yerva molida, que se llama yauhtli en sus mjsmos hogares."* — In Sahagún (Garibay ed.), Vol. IV, p. 371, it is *Tagetes lucida;* see also J. E. S. Thompson: *Mexico Before Cortez* (New York: Charles Scribner's Sons, 1944), p. 185.

Emmart, *op. cit.*, pp. 239-240, notes that Louis Raffour, in *La médecine chez les mexicains précolombiens* (Paris: Jouve and Boyer, 1900), p. 95, identifies *yauhtli* as a species of absinthe; A. Gerste, in *Notes sur la médecine et la botanique des anciens mexicains* (Rome: Imprimerie Polyglotte Vaticane, 1909), p. 54, says it is definitely narcotic. Jacinto de la Serna's "Manual de ministros para conocer y extirpar las idolatrias de los indios," in Jacinto de la Serna, Pedro Ponce, and Fr. Pedro de Feria: *Tratado de las idolatrías, supersticiones, dioses, ritos, hechicerías y otras costumbres gentílicas de las razas aborígenes de México* (México: Ediciones Fuente de Cultura, n.d.), p. 249, identifies *yauhtli* as *yerbanís,* which, according to Santamaría, *op. cit.*, Vol. III, p. 298, is *"Nombre vulgar que en el norte del país, en Méjico, se da a una planta parecida al cempasúchil* (Tagetes anisata), *cuyas hojas huelen a anís."*

6. Cf. Anderson and Dibble, *op. cit.*, Book VIII, "Kings and Lords," p. 64. Sahagún (Garibay ed.), VIII, 18, 14: *"la fiesta de su elección, que llaman* motlatoapaca."

went loaded upon their shoulders tied in bundles. Their cold things the lords caused to be carried away to where they came to be kept; and some of it was only entrusted to others.[7]

cujtlaputzmamalo, cujcujtlalpitiuh in jntlaçeujl, qujmjtqujlia tlatoque, in omopieco, ioan in cequjn çan otenepieltico.

7. Corresponding Spanish text: "*y quando hazia la fiesta este señor electo: dava muchas mantas, y maxtles ricos a los mesmos señores: que avjan venjdo: de manera que mas cargados yvan, de lo que recibian del: que no avjan venjdo, de lo que le avjan traydo. Las mantas que dava el señor: eran todas preciosas, hechas en su casa: y texidas, o labradas de diversas maneras: conforme a las personas, a quien se avjan de dar: tambien les dava mucha abundancia de comjdas, y yvan cargados de las sobras: para sus casas.*"

Twenty-sixth Chapter, in which it is told how these rulers (upon the day sign mentioned) proclaimed war. And at that time were sentenced those who were to die.[1]

When already the election ceremony had taken place, with festivity,[2] [the newly-elected rulers] disposed themselves for war to be declared. Also in this way it was said that for a second time, in war, the rulers would hold the election ceremony. Then to a considerable degree did the chieftains, the strong, cast their lot with him. They were urged and thrust upon him that they might show him their skill and aid him; so that they might take captives for him. This was because in this way they sought, dedicated themselves to, and gained their drink and food, and their capes, through the help of which they would live and have raiment; and he would honor them, etc. They would become his standard-bearing warriors, who, it was said, courted danger, hurled themselves against the foe, and joined in the fray.

And it was also said that on this [day sign] One Dog a court of justice was held. Then was sentence pronounced upon those who were to die. And at this time were released and freed those who had done nothing serious. And they absolved of their crimes those who had suffered injustice for no apparent crime or discernible fault, and had served and paid a penalty for it: those who had only wrongly been imprisoned for some invented wrong, who only paid and atoned another's fault or crime, or perhaps served in another's place. Perhaps they imprisoned one for another's fault. So they had been forced into bondage and had become slaves. At once they bathed there at Chapultepec to lay aside their crimes.[3]

Injc cempoalli on chiquacen capitulo: vncan moteneoa, in quenjn iehoantin tlatoque (in jpan in tonalli omoteneuh) iaotlatoaia, ioan vncan tlatzontequjliloia in mjqujztli ipan catca.

In jquac ie omotecpac tecoanotzaliztica: njman ie no cuele oalmotlalia injc iaotlatolo, no ic mjtoa ic oppa iaoc motecpacaz in tlatoanj, iquac cenca ipan mopepena in tiacaoan, in chicaoaque, ipan netotocholo, nemamalioa, injc qujtlamatilizque, qujpalevizque, injc iehoan uel qujtlamaltizque, ipampa ca qujxtoca, ipan mjxpoa, qujmototoqujlia in jauh, in jtlaqual, in jtilma, injc ipal nemjzque, ipallaquemjzque, qujnmaujzçotiz, Et[a]. itlaujcecaoan mochioazque in mjtoa: injc aqujtlaçotla in jntzontecon, in jmelchiqujuh, teca momotla, teujc mopetlatiuj:

ioan mjtoa no ipan tecutlatoloia injn ce itzcujntli, vncan tlatzontequjliloia in jmpan ca mjqujztli: auh iquac qujxtiloia, caoaloia, in amo cenca ovi ic cate, ioan qujntlatlacollaçaia, in tlatlacoti, in amo cenca melaoac, in amo uel ixnezquj, in amo cenca uel neztica ic tlacoti, ic tlanamjquj in aço çan tlapictli qujtzaqua, çan tlapiqujloque, çan ixpopoiotlanamjctiloque, ixpopoiotlanamjcque, aço çan tepan in tlaiecoa, aço çan tecujtl in qujtzaqua, injc cujtiloque in victli, mecapalli, injc victique, mecapaltique, iquac njman vmpa onmaaltia, in chapultepec, injc qujncaoa, intlatlacul:

---

1. Corresponding Spanish text: *"en el mjsmo sentenciavan a muerte, a los que por algũ gran crimen, estavan presos."*

2. *Ibid.*: *"En acabando de hazer la fiesta de la dedicacion de su señorio. . . . auja de mostrar la grandeza de su señorio."* Cf. also Anderson and Dibble, *loc. cit.*

3. Cf. *Florentine Codex,* Book VI, Chapter xli: *Ma chapultepec njnaalti.* In the Garibay ed., VI, 41, 67, the corresponding Spanish text reads: "Deseo irme a bañar a Chapultepec, o querría poder irme a bañar a Chapultepec. — *Este refrán dice el que ha tenido alguna gran enfermedad o algún cargo pesado, con deseo de verse libre de aquel cargo o enfermedad; dice*: Ma chapultepec ninalti, *que quiere decir, bañarme he ya en agua rosada cuando este cargo o enfermedad se me quitase.* Chapultepec *es una fuente que está cerca de México, muy buena; los que se bañan en ella piensan que les hace dios gran merced. Así, este adagio es de los mexicanos.*"

And one then born they hence regarded as fortunate and said that he would be rich. Our lord would reward him; through his grace he would buy slaves and ceremonially bathe them for sacrifice. Or many times he would have others sing and dance. And[4] when they gave him a name, they arranged it for Four Reed. Then they gave food to the young boys and had them perform the naming ceremony.[5] This was because that time was the time of the election rites, of the election of the rulers of the cities.

auh in aqujn ipan tlacatia, injc qujtonalittaia, qujtoaia: mocujltonoz, ipal iez, qujtlamaujçalhujz in totecujo: aço tecoaz, tealtiz, aço quezqujpa cujcujcaz teitotiz: uh inic qujtocamacaia, qujn no ipan qujmattiuja in naoacatl, iquac qujtlatlaqualiaia, qujxicvenquaqualiaia in pipiltotonti: ipampa in vncan motlatocapaca, in netlatocapacaian tlatoque, altepeme.

And also it was said that on One Dog the owners and breeders of dogs rubbed ochre on all the dogs' heads.[6]

No ioan mjtoa: in jpan in ce itzcujntli, in jxqujchtin chichime, qujnquatlaviaia in itzcujneque, in jtzcujnnemjtique.

And [the day signs] which followed it were Two Monkey, and Three Grass, Four Reed, Five Ocelot, Six Eagle, Seven Vulture, Eight Motion, Nine Flint Knife,[7] Ten Rain, Eleven Flower, Twelve Crocodile, Thirteen Wind. These were all the group of day signs.

Auh in qujtoqujlia vme oçomatli, ioan ey malinalli, navi acatl, macujlli oçelotl, chiquacen quauhtli, chicome cozcaquauhtli, chicuei olin, chicunauj tecpac, matlactli qujaujtl, matlactloce suchitl, matlactlomome cipactli, matlactli vmei hecatl, in jzqujtetl in cencalpã tonalli,

All were as in their account, as mentioned. Each day went related as to the manner of gifts of those then born. This is already explained; in many places hath it been made quite apparent. And when [these had] ended, thereupon set in —

ça ie much iuhquj in jtoloca omoteneuh, injc cecemjlhujpã tlapoaltitiuh, in quenamj innenemac ipan tlacati, ie omomelauh mjieccan vel omonenexti: auh in jquac onqujz in njman ic oalmoquetza.

4. *Uh*: *auh* is intended.

5. See Chapter 9, n. 1.

6. Corresponding Spanish text: "*Tambien tenjan una cerimonja: que en este signo, los que criavan los perrillos, que bivjan desto: los almagravan las cabeças.*"

7. *Tecpac*: *tecpatl* is meant.

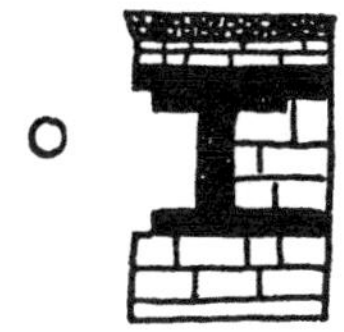

Twenty-seventh Chapter, in which is mentioned the fifteenth sign, named One House. And it was said to be evil. It was said that the men then born were thieves, patrons of vice and sin. All which befell them was bad. And it was said that the women [then born] were very lazy and much given to sleep, and did nothing useful.

Injc cempoalli on chicome capitulo: vncan moteneoa, injc caxtoltetl machiotl, in jtoca ce calli: ioan qujl amo qualli, qujl in vncan tlacatia toqujchti, ichtecque catca, teuhtli tlaçolli qujmocujtlaviaia: mochi amo qualli in jnpan mochioaia: auh qujl in çioa cenca tlatziujnj, cenca cochinj, njman atle qualli qujchioa.

— One House. This One House, they said, was a totally evil day sign, the breeding-place of vice and sin. And also, at that time, descended the so-called Goddesses; and what then came to pass hath already been told in many places. The midwives especially paid them honor; each one individually made offerings to them in her own home.

In ce calli: jnjn ce calli, qujtoaia, njman amo qualli tonalli, tlaçolli, teuhtli iiolian, ioan no ipan temoia in omoteneuhque cioateteo, auh in tlein vncan mochioaia, ie mjieccan omjto: in iehoan titici, oc cenca iehoan qujnmaujztiliaia, ceceniaca qujntlamanjliaia in jnchachan,

He who was then born, they fully expected, would thus come to a bad end: perhaps he would die in battle, or be taken captive; or perish at the crossing of the waters; or he would enter [among the foe] and be carried off. Perhaps he would be offered as a striped one in gladiatorial sacrifice, or be shot full of arrows; or his head would be burst in the fire, or he would be cast into the flames. Perhaps they would twist him in a net, or smash him, or tear out his entrails — violently tear out his entrails; or just destroy him like a water rat, pushing him under the water, spearing and stabbing him; or they would just cook him [in the steam bath].

in aqujn ipan tlacatia, cenca qujtlatenmachiliaia, injc ohujcan qujçaz, aço iaomjqujz, axioaz, iapaniocan popoliujz, anoço calaqujz, vicoz, aço oaoanaloz, oaoanoz, aco câcalioaz, aço quatlecueponjloz, aço tlepan tlaxoz, anoço qujmatlapatzcazque, quevitequjzque, anoço qujxicanazque, qujxicteteoanazque, anoço çan catoçanpolozque, catlanpapachozque, vncan qujxixilizque, tlatzotzopotztinemj, anoço çan qujtemazque,

And in this way he would come to a bad end. Perchance he would commit adultery. Perhaps he would covet a woman. Perhaps he would covet another's woman. Perhaps he would eat another's food, lift his head from another's [bed]. And the woman would be his companion in death; they would break and smash both their heads. Hence were adulterers called "broken heads" or "smashed heads."

ioan injc ovican qujçaz, aço tetlanximaz, aço tetlan aqujz, aço cueitl, vipilli tepan canaz, aço tetlaqualiz, tetlan quateujz: auh in cioatl imjqujztevical iez, vmextin qujnquatepipitzinjzque, qujnquatexaxamanjzque, ic tocaiotilo in tetlanxinquj, quatepitzic, quatexamac:

And so in this way he came to a bad end. Perchance he would sell himself, would eat and drink his substance, would swallow himself, would put an end to himself.[1] Discontented, nowhere did he feel tranquil. Thus he lived a thief. He robbed, he

ioan injc ovican qujçaz, aço monamacaz, moquaz, mjz motoloz, motlamjz, âcan avia, acan tlacaco tlamati, injc nemj, iichtequj, motlâtlacuja, tetlâtlatlalochtia, tetlacujcujlia, tetlatlaçaltia, tecacalxaputla, tequjqujmjliquanja,

1. Corresponding Spanish text: *"dezian: que seria esclavo, que el mesmo se venderia, y comeria, y beveria su precio."*

plundered and fled, he pilfered, he stole from people in the streets; he broke into people's houses; he deprived them of their raiment.

Living only in dangerous luxury, he was completely given to the rubber ball game, and to *patolli.* He continually played *patolli,* or the *tlachtli* game.[2] He lost; he lost the possessions of others. He was deceived. He deceived others or tried to deceive them. He detained others. He wagered everything which was in his home. He used up everything in *patolli* and *tlachtli.* All the treasures and support of his beloved mother and father he spirited away, even if some little thing had been hidden. In vain he practised deceit; to no purpose he wagered. There was no more that he could lay down as stakes, nothing more for him to wager, to match, to embarrass [rivals]. He no longer overcame others in *patolli* or *tlachtli,* or embarrassed, despoiled, or took all the wagers, even though he understood the language, the rules, of *tlachtli* and *patolli.*

çan iuh aviloujti, much qujmotequjtia in olli, in patolli, pâpatoa, ôollama, motlatlanjtoa, tetlatlanjtoa, moxixicoa, texixicoa, texixictlanj, ontetlatlalia, muchi qujtlanjtoa in jchan onoc, muchi patolco, tlachco, qujtlamja, in jntetzon, in jnnepachol itatzin, inantzin, muchi qujchteccaqujxtia, in açoc cana itlatzin tlatilo, çan nen qujpiquj, çan nempanca in motlanjtoa, aoc tle in qujxquetza, aoc tle in jtlatlanjtol, injc tlanamjctiz, injc vel oviti, aoc tepapatla, patolco, tlachco, oviti, chiquati, qujchiquatilia, anoçe qujmomachtia in ollatolli, patollatolli, ollatole, patollatole:

And he was not of good condition; he in no way excelled others. He was completely clothed in rags and tatters. He had no bowl nor jar. And he visited and inflicted pain, misery, and suffering on one.

auh amo ivian iectli, amo ivian tecauh, motqujtica tzotzomatli, tatapatli, âcaxe, âcome: ioan tecoco, tetolinj, cocoliztli qujteittitia, ic temotla:

And although he might take captives in war, it was said that he achieved only misery. Though he might become a seasoned warrior, he lived only in complete misery, torment, poverty, and need. He went about with his rags and tatters in pieces about his neck. His old maguey fiber cape hung from him in shreds. Indeed, he went about on earth very destitute.[3] Or else somewhere he would die a victim; he would die as a ceremonially bathed victim; he would be ritually bathed as a sacrificial victim.

auh in manellamaz iaoc, mjtoa çan icnoiotl in caci, in manel tequjoacati, çan icnoiotl ic mâpãtinemj, totoneoatinemj, in jiollo, aoneoatinemj, aonmonamjquj, in jtzotzoma, in jtatapa, iquechtlan cotontinemj, in jaiaçol qujchichiquailpia, uel ompa onqujztinemj in tlalticpac, anoço cana teumjquiz, tlaaltilmjqujz altiloz:

But if perchance something should be his deserts, it would not endure. He might become very deserving in his youth; at once, in his youth, the good counsel and teaching began. On emerging mature, not genuine on earth was the little which he might attain.[4]

auh intla ça noço itla imâceoaltiz, amo caxcanviz, vellamaceoaz, in jpiltian, çan njman ipan pilpeoaz in vel monotzaz, vel mozcaliz, çan vei qujçaz, amo iviian, tetitlan, quauhtitlan, in jtla qujcnopilhujz.

---

2. Cf. Anderson and Dibble, *op. cit.,* Book VIII, "Kings and Lords," Chapter 10.

3. Cf. *Florentine Codex,* Book VI, cap. xli: *vmpa onquiça tlalticpac*: *"He venido a extremada pobreza, o estoy en extremada probreza"* (Garibay ed., VI, 41, 36).

4. Corresponding Spanish text: *"por mucho que haga penjtencia, desde pequeño: no se podra escapar de mala ventura."*

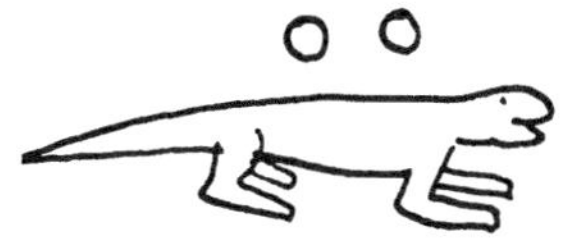

Twenty-eighth Chapter, which telleth still more of the nature and condition of women born on this sign.

And if it were a woman, similar were the deserts which visited her, and which were inflicted and laden upon her. She could do nothing. She could not twirl the spindle; she could not move nor raise the batten. She was incapable, witless, negligent, stupid, jeering, and impudent. She did nothing but talk in a loud voice; she went about snapping her chewing gum. She was of evil, inhuman tongue. Without effort, evil came from her lips.[1] Like flowing water she talked; her vile words swirled up like foam. Indeed, she was given to defaming people.

And she devoted herself only to sloth, negligence, and shiftlessness. She was a harlot, too lazy to do anything, careless, indolent, and a constant sleeper. And from what she did, they at once knew, and it was at once known, that her rearing was endangered and brought to shame, and that she delivered herself to servitude.

And in just the same way she achieved nothing and was not diligent at the place of her owner, where the slave-owner was. She could not prepare drink nor use the grinding stone for others. She was just uselessly attractive[2] and vain.[3] Furthermore, she was a great lump of flesh with eyes,[4] of no value and unteachable.

Wherefore they left her in the hands of the slave-dealers there at Azcapotzalco; she became a slave to be sold. And later she died, ceremonially bathed and sacrificed. This became her condemnation, her eternal fate.[5] She entered the place of the sacrificial stone.[6] For in truth her incorrigibility had been left to and had descended upon her. To no avail had

Injc cempoalli on chicuey capitulo: itechpa tlatoa, in oc cequj inieliz, in jmjuhcatiliz cioa in jpan tlacatia in machiotl.

Auh intla cioatl, çan ie no iuhquj in jmaceoalti, in jtech eva, injc movitequj, in jtech motzotzona, atle vel ai, avel qujtotia in malacatl, avel colinja, auel cacocuj in tzotzopaztli, maoolol, matetepo, ixqujqujmjl, ixtepetla, vetzqujztomac, âquetztzana, çan ic nemjntlapitzaoa, itzic qujtlatlatztzatinemj, tentlaueliloc, âtentlacatl, atle ovi in qujcacamacaoa: iuhqujn acontetemoa qujtoa, iuhqujn qujmonolotza itlaellatol, vel tepapacanj:

auh çan qujxcauja in cujtlaçotlaoatinemj, tlatenmattinemj, moquêquêquetza, maaviltia, aiel itla aiz, cujtlatzcopic, cujtlaçotlac, cochmjmjl auh in ie oqujchiuh, çan jc qujmati, çan ic imachitilo, in movicanaquja, in movitilia, in oalmozcalia, ic tevic, ic temecapal muchiuhtinemj:

auh çan no iui aontlaiecoa, aontlaeltia, in jtecuacan in vmpa tetlacauh, âvel atl, âvel metlatl contechiujlia, çan neian qualpul, qualtepul, ixtimalpul, iece çan molhuj tlacamjmjlli, atle inecoca, atle ic temachilo:

ic njman inmac concaoa in tlacanecujloque in vmpa azcaputzalco, tlacanecujlolli muchioa, auh çatepan tlaaltilmjquj, icoatl ipopoliuhca, yceniaca muchioa, vncan tzomoccalaquj, ca nel iauelnenotzaliz in oconcaujli, in ocontemovi, aocmo tlatollin tlatolli, avmpa oqujttac in jzcaliloca, çan jpan otlamelauh in iuhquj itonal, in jpan tlacat:

1. Corresponding Spanish text: *"salen de la boca, las malas palabras."*

2. *Neian*: *nenyan.*

3. *Ixtimalpul*: cf. *Florentine Codex,* Book VI, cap. xli, fol. 192 (*ixtimal*), and Sahagún (Garibay ed.), VI, 41, 58: Tiene buena cara: tiene buena apariencia. — *Este refrán se dice de las personas que en su gesto y disposición parece que son para mucho, y no son para nada en la verdad, o son para poco; de éstas se dice por vía de mofa* ixtimal, *cara gloriosa."*

4. Sahagún, "Memoriales con escolios," p. 215, gloss No. 12 (*tlacamimilli*): *"lo que dezimos pedaço de carne con dos ojos."*

5. *Ycenyāca* in the *Real Palacio MS.*

6. *Tzomoccalaqui*: we have interpreted *tzomoc* as *tzonmolco;* cf. corresponding Spanish text: *"āsi venja a murir en el tajon, de los ydolos."*

been repeated counsel. She had ignored her rearing. Just so was it substantiated upon her as was the day sign on which she was born.

But in order to improve one's day sign somewhat, they bathed one on Three Serpent, for the reason that was told of all the third day signs. If they waited a day, they made it good. And if still they should wish it, perhaps they bathed him later, on Seven Water, likewise because of the goodness of each individual day sign with the number seven, as [is said] above.

And so we shall not repeat uselessly[7] nor reopen the discussion. Not just mixed, twisted, disordered, unconsidered, and profitless discussion shall we make use of or continue to work over.[8] And in order not to do this, we shall continue to mention, return, and go back to all that was said and stated. Here only one part is mentioned.[9] A word is said of the account. For all are just as in the separate accounts. All hath been mentioned — how one by one they proceeded in order: the day sign which came as good, or as somewhat good, or as in no way good. All thirteen thus go to their conclusion; because of this, all of the day signs are brought together in one group, beginning with One House, and [then] Two Lizard, Three Serpent, Four Death, Five Deer, Six Rabbit, Seven Water, Eight Dog, Nine Monkey, Ten Grass, Eleven Reed, Twelve Ocelot, Thirteen Eagle. And when all these days had ended, then set in —

auh inic achi qujqualtilizque itonal, ipan caltiaia in Ei coatl: ipampa omjto, in jxqujch eei tonalli, intla cemjlhujtiltia qujqualittaia: auh intla noço qujnequjzque, aço qujn jpan caltizque, in chicome atl: no ipampa in jqualtica in jxqujch chichicovme tonalli, vt supra.

Auh injc amo ça nen totlatlatozque: titlatolçacamuzque, in amo çan tlatolxaqualli, tlatolnechicolli, tlatolnenel, iliviztlatolli, çan nen tlatolli toconnemjtizque, ticcueptinemjzque ioan injc amo çan ieehoatl, tiqujtotinemjzque, ticcueptinemjzque, ticcujtlacueptinemjzque in jxqujch omjto, omoteneuh, ça njcan onmocenteneoa, onmocencamaitoa, in tlatolli, ca çan ie much iuhquj in jtlatlatollo ixqujch omoteneuh, in iuh tetecpantivi, in vncan qualtitiuh tonalli, ioan in achi qualtitiuh: ioan in njman amo qualtitiuh, in jxqujch ic ontlatlantiuh, matlatlactlomeei: ipampa in ça njcan onmocentlalia, izqujteme cencalpã tonaltin, in qujnpeoaltitica ce calli, ioan vme cuetzpalin, ei coatl, nauj mjqujztli, macujlli maçatl, chiquacẽ tochtli, chicome atl, chicuei itzcujntli, chicunauj oçomatli, matlactli malinalli, matlactloce acatl, matlactlomome ocelutl, matlactlomej quauhtli, auh in jquac ontlan izqujlhujtl in, njman oalmoquetza.

7. After *injc,* the *Real Palacio MS* has *amo ça yliviz.*

8. *Ticcuentinemizque* in *ibid.*

9. *õmocenteneva* in *ibid.*

Twenty-ninth Chapter, which telleth of the sixteenth sign. It was said to be a good day sign; and it was said that those then born became aged. Nevertheless, it was not certain that this would so come to pass, because many then born soon died.

— One Vulture. This Vulture was said to be the day sign of the aged, as hath been told in its account in various places. Whoever was then born they regarded favorably; they said he would become an old man or an old woman. He would partake; he would go partaking of happiness. And he would be wealthy and admired on earth.

But even though one who attained this (day sign) might so realize, nevertheless, many people born at this time died.

And if there were at hand perishable and expendable things, good food, wherewith to gather, assemble, arrange, acknowledge, render homage to, and banquet others, then at once they bathed [the child] on this day sign and therefore called him Cozcaquauh. But if there were nothing to expend, the parents still deferred while they acquired wealth and provided all the different things to be required. They bathed [the child] later, on Seven Wind.

And Two House[1] followed [One Vulture], and Three Flint Knife, Four Rain, Five Flower, Six Crocodile, Seven Wind, Eight House, Nine Lizard, Ten Serpent, Eleven Death, Twelve Deer, Thirteen Rabbit.

Of all of these, their designations were the same, as they proceeded in proper order. No longer is it necessary for us to continue repeating only worn-out, useless discussion, so much unfit talk, so many lazy words. Hence a few short words concerning only the beginning day sign, whereby we make manifest how it was to be considered all the twenty times it fell, as each group marched along its course and went following in order. When the group of day signs ended, which became as one week, considered as a Sunday, then One Water set in and took up its task and labors.

Injc cempoalli on chicunavi capitulo: itechpa tlatoa, injc caxtoltetl oce machiotl: qujlmach qualli tonalli: auh qujlmach in aqujque vncan tlacatia, vecaoaia, iece amo nelli iuh muchioaia, iehica ca mjequjntin iciuhca mjquja, in vncan tlacatia.

In ce cozcaquauhtli: injn cozcaquauhtli, mjtoa veue tonalli, ca quezqujcan omjto, in iuhquj itlatlatollo: in aqujn vncan tlacatia, qujquallittaia, qujtoa veuetiz, ilamatiz, qujtlamjz, qujtlamjteoaz in paqujliztli, ioan mocujltonoz, tlamaujçoz in tlalticpac:

auh tel çan no ipantia, in aqujn iuhquj ipan mochioaia, iehica ca mjec tlacatl mjquja, in jpan tlacatia:

auh intla onca poliujnj, popoliujnj, in qualonj, tenechicolonj, tecentlalilonj, tetemolonj, teiximachonj, tetlacamachonj, tecoanotzalonj, njman iquac caltia in jpan itonal ic qujnotza Cozcaquauh: auh intlaca ie tle popoliujz, oc conchololtia in pilhoaque, oqujc onmotlamachia, oqujc conjhimati, in jxqujch monênênequjz, qujn jpan caltia in chicome hecatl.

Auh in contoqujlia vme calli, ioan ei tecpatl, nauj qujavitl, macujlli suchitl, chiquacen cipactli, chicome hecatl, chicuei calli, chicunauj cuetzpalin, matlactli coatl, matlactloce mjqujztli, matlactlomome maçatl, matlactli vmei tochtli.

In jxqujch in,çan ie centetl in jnteneoaloca, in iuh tecpantiuj, aocmo monequj in ça tlatolçolli, ça nentlatlatolli, in omachcamatzopetziuh, omachtlatziuh tlatolli tiqujtotinemjzque: ipampa in çaiio tonalpeoallotl, achitzitzin tlatolli ic toconnextia, injc mottaz, in jzqujpa vetzi cempoalpa, injc cecencalpan otlatocatiuj: ioan oalmotoqujlitiuj: in jquac ontlan in cencalpan tonalli, in iuhquj ce Semana muchioa, in jpan machoia ce Domingo: njman ic oalmoquetza, vmpeoa, ontequjana, ontequjcuj in ce atl.

1. Two Motion should follow One Vulture. In Chapter 32, Two House is in correct sequence.

Thirtieth Chapter, which telleth of the seventeenth sign, called One Water. It was said to be an evil day sign. And it was said of those then born that they rejoiced a little only at the beginning of their lives, and that they ended in evil. And it was said always to be evil when they died. And it was said to be the day sign of Chalchiuitl icue, whose feast day the water folk observed.

One Water. This One Water, they said, was also evil. And they said it was quite varied, of different qualities, all good or all bad.

At this time they made offerings to the one named Chalchiuhtli icue, who represented the water. Especially did the sellers of water, the owners of boats — those who transported water with boats — and those who launched boats, made offerings to her. These formed her image; they set in place the framework [for her image] at her temple, in her *calpulco.*

And thus was it said to be diverse [in fortune], one which could not attain and carry with it very much good. That is to say, of the one then born, very few resulted great and fortunate at this time. For according to his deserts, his day sign, he was only all evil, completely surrounded by vice. And in evil he would go; in it he would die. Perchance somewhere he would be stoned — he would be felled by a stone; or else he would be drowned — he would perish in the water.

But even if, on the other hand,[1] he merited some reward, only for a miserable moment, only for a short time, a very short time, and frequently for a brief space, a moment, for a time only, would he partake of his riches.[2] So of him were said the words of the talkative inhabitants, that in the world there are bad days. Sometimes one succeeded; sometimes one failed; if, in his childhood, he should suffer

Injc cempoalli on matlactli capitulo: itechpa tlatoa, inic caxtolli omome machiotl, in jtoca ce atl: qujlmach amo qualli tonalli: auh qujl in aqujque vncan tlacatia, çan ipeuhian in jnnemjliz achi paquja: auh injc tzonqujçaia amo qualli, auh qujlmach mochipa, amo qualli, injc mjquja: auh qujl itonal catca in chalchiujtl icue, qujlhujqujxtiliaia in atlaca.

Ce atl: injn ce atl: qujtoa, amono qualli: yoan qujtoa, çan chictlapantli, chictlapantica: ixqujch qualli, ixqujch amo qualli:

vncan qujtonaltiaia: in jtoca chalchiuhtli ycue, in jpan mjxeoaia atl: oc cenca iehoan qujtlamanjliaia, yn anamacaque, in acaleque, acaltica atlacuj, yoan acalquetzque: iehoan qujxiptlatiaia qujtlaliaia ycoloio in jteupan, in jcalpulco.

Auh injc mjtoa çan chictlapanquj yn amo vel macitica motquitica ic qualli, quitoznequi in aqujn ipan tlacatia, çan vej quiçaia cenca çan aca in vncan qujçaia tlacnopilhujani, ca in juh ca vel inmaceoal, itonal çan muchi âqualli in cololotica motquitica teuhtli, tlaçolli, auh amo qualli ynjc iaz, inic miquiz, aço çan cana tetepacholoz, tetica uetziz, anoço, atocoz, atlan mjqujz,

auh intla ça noço itla imaceoaltiz, çã cotocpol, çan cuel achic, can cuecuel achic, çan achica, çan achitonca, çã achitzinca, çan ixqujch caujtl in, in jxpan onqujçaz in jnecujltonol, ic ipã mjtoa, in jntlatol tlalticpac tlatlatoanj, çan tatacapitz uel in tlalticpac, quẽman veli, quenman aveli, intla ipiltian motoliniz, qujn itzonco in achi moiollaliz:

1. *Intla ça noço*: Biondelli, *op. cit.*, has *etsi* (although, yet) or *quamvis* (as you will) for *intlaça,* and *neque* (and not) for *noço.*

2. Corresponding Spanish text: *"y si algunos bienes deste mundo: tenjan poco tiempo, los gozauan el mejor tiempo, se les acabaua la vẽtura."*

misery, later, in the end, he would be somewhat content.[3]

But if by chance his wealth began in his childhood, his youthful years, he received, in exchange, destruction, a miserable portion, and ended and finished with misery. And if it were a merchant, it was said, perhaps his goods would be swept away by a river and lost. And if one then, at this time, lacked zeal, it was as if his life were swept away and immersed in evil. For just of that nature was his day sign, One Water.

But we shall speak in a few places and take the matter up. We shall go returning to,[4] explaining considerably, and explaining much, the expressions which are different. We shall hang on to it. We shall reflect much; we shall repeat, like one not tired of talking or of lazy tongue. We only merely quickly develop and superficially dispense with, hastily and superficially dispense with the above words which are quite apparent and manifest, *ut supra.*

He who was then born was, like the day sign, evil. They later sought out and importuned a time of good. Then they bathed him. It was said that thus in part they reversed and made good his birth. No one knew nor understood whether perhaps something would be his reward, if he would perform his penances well, etc.

For so are evident the many places, if there have been as many times, where each of the day signs known as good, go. Because here are assembled and mentioned together the different ones which were made to proceed and go along in each series, each group.[5] For Two Dog taketh second place and followeth. Then come in order, following along, Three Monkey, Four Grass, Five Reed, Six Ocelot, Seven Eagle, Eight Vulture, Nine Motion, Ten Flint Knife, Eleven Rain, Twelve Flower, Thirteen Crocodile.

When the different days which followed along at this time had laid down their burdens, ceased their labors, ended their functions, and run their course, then set in and took up the burden —

auh intla noce njman ipã pilpeoa, qujpilpilpeoalti inetlamachtil, çan tlantica, çan cotocpol, injc conmotlanevia: auh ça icnoiotl: injc ontlatzonqujxtia, ontlatzontia: auh intla puchtecatl, mjtoa, aço cana tlaatoctiz, tlapoloz: auh in aca çan njman ie atle onqujça, çan iuh amoiaoa, aujlqujça in jnemjliz: ipampa ca njman iuhqujn itonal ce atl:

auh injc amo cenca oc noujian tontlatozque, tontlaanazque in amo çan iee tlatolli ticcueptinemjzque, tictequjmattinemjzque, tictequjmatizque, ipan tompipilcatozque, titotequjmatizque, titlatlatozque, in iuhquj atotenquauhtinj, atitentlatziujnj, ça ixqujch ic onmaantiqujça toconpapanqua, toconpapanquatiqujça, in çan uel neneztica, ixneztica, panj caca tlatolli vt supra.

In aqujn ipã tlacatia, in iuhquj in tonalli, in amo qualli, qujn jpan contlatotoqujliaia, vmpa qujn contlatequjviaia, in qualcan, iquac caltiaia, mjtoa ic qujchicoqujxtia, qujqualtilia, in jtlacatiliz, aiac qujmati, aiac ontlamati, in aço ça itla imaceoaltiz, intla uellamaçeoaz. Et[a].

Ca ic neztica in quecizqujcan intla quecizqujcaiopan ieietiuh in moteneoa qualli tonalli: ipampa in ça njcan onmocecentlalia, onmocenteneoa in izqujteme in tlaotlatoctia, tlanenemjtia cencalpan, cencallopan: ca iehoatl ontlaoncaiotia, ontlatoqujlia, in vme itzcujntli, ic tecpantiuj, mototoquilitiuh in ey oçomatli, nauj malinalli, macujlli acatl, chiquacen oçelotl, chicome quauhtli, chicuey cozcaquauhtli, chicunauj olin, matlactli tecpatl, matlactloce qujavitl, matlactlomome suchitl, matlactlomei cipactli:

in jquac onuetz intequjuh in in ontequjcauhque in oconmotlaxilique in tlanenemjtiaia in jzqujlhujtl vncan tlaotlatoctia njmã oalmoquetza, ontequjana.

3. *Ibid.*: *"y por esta causa se levãto el refran, que dizen: que en el mundo un dia bueno, y otro malo."*

4. *Ticcuentinemizque* in the *Real Palacio MS.*

5. Corresponding Spanish text: *"a los que nacian en este signo: no los baptizauan, luego, difirianlos: para el tercero dia, o para el seteno, o para el deceno, o para alguno, de los que siguen. Porque dezian: que todos estos, hasta el trezeno, tenjan algunn bõdad."*

Thirty-first Chapter, which telleth of the eighteenth sign, named One Wind, and the evil, the bad, which was with it. It was said that those then born gained as reward an evil day sign.

— One Wind. This One Wind, they said, was evil. At this time they made offerings to the one called Quetzalcoatl, who was the representative of the wind, the whirlwind.

And of him who was then born, they said that, if he were a nobleman, he would be a wizard,[1] inhuman; an astrologer,[2] one who had spells to cast.[3] It was evident to them that he was a man; nevertheless he was evil, corrupt, one who deluded, laid enchantments — the devil's works. He breathed [evil] on people, or cast the evil eye at them, or said spells over them, brought harm on them, or invoked the god [to do evil] to one. All his doings he mastered — all. Perhaps his was the disguise of a fierce beast, or a coyote, etc.

And if it were a commoner, in just the same way it was said of him that he was a demon; he caused one to be possessed, or to become demented; he danced with the arm taken from a woman dead in first childbed; he was a destroyer of men; he burned images for one.[4] Likewise, if it were a woman, she could enchant by taking apart or disarticulating the bones of the foot,[5] etc.

Injc cempoalli on matlactli oce capitulo: itechpa tlatoa injc caxtolli vmei machiotl, in jtoca ce hecatl: ioan in amo qualli, in amo iectli in jtech ca: qujl amo qualli tonalli qujmâceoaia, in vncan tlacatia.

In ce hecatl: inin ce hecatl, qujtoa amo qualli, vncan qujtonaltiaia, in moteneoa quetzalcoatl, in jxiptla catca hecatl, hecamalacotl:

auh in aqujn vncan tlacatia, qujtoa intla pilli, naoalli iez, amo tlacatl, tlaciuhquj, nenonotzale, impanj neçi ca tlacatl, iecê amo qualli, itlacauhquj, itla qujmati, tlacatecolotlatolli, tlacatecoloiotl, teipitzanj, texoxanj, tetlachiujanj, tetlanonochili, tetlateononochili, much ichiujl much qujmati, aço tequannaoale, coionaoale. Et[a].

auh intla maceoalli çan ie no iuhquj iehoatl in mjtoa: tlacatecolotl, tetlatlacatecolouja, tepupuxaquavia, temamacpalitotia, tepoloanj, teeujllotlatia: no iuhquj intla cioatl mometzcopinquj, mometzcopinanj. Et[a].

---

1. Corresponding Spanish text: *"seria enbaydor . . . se transfiguria en muchas formas . . . seria nigromantico, y hechizero, y malefico."* Seler (*Collected Works*, Vol. II, Pt. 1-2, p. 55) classifies the *naualli* as a magician and soothsayer of high class. His attributes marked him since his youth; he knew the hidden things of heaven and hell; he had supernatural powers, such as of forecasting rain, dispersing hail and pestilence, and protecting against wicked magicians; he lived unmarried, as a priest, in a temple, and advised the king and the people; he fasted, and for his arts used tobacco and such narcotics as *ololiuhqui* and peyote.

See also Chapter 11, n. 4, *supra.*

2. *"Nombre más o menos relacionado con* [*teciuhtlazqui, tecihuero, granizero,* hail-thrower]. *La raíz* ciuh, *parece denotar fenómenos meteorológicos"* (Garibay, "Paralipómenos de Sahagún," *Tlalocan,* II, 2 [1946], p. 171). Siméon, *op. cit.,* defines *tlaciuhque* as *"familiers ou pareils des dieux, qui étaient très-puissants chez les Otomis et que l'on venait consulter de fort loin* (Sah.)."

3. Cf. Molina, *op. cit., tlanonochilia. Nenonotza,* however, could imply a pact or an understanding with the *demonio* as in Chapter 11, n. 4.

4. Cf. *supra,* Chapter 19.

5. *Metzcopina,* in Harold Key and Mary Ritchie: *Vocabulario mejicano de la Sierra de Zacapoaxtla, Puebla* (México: Instituto Lingüístico de Verano and Dirección General de Asuntos Indígenas, 1953), is defined as *se zafa* (*el pie*); *zafarse,* in Santamaría, *op. cit.,* Vol. III, p. 308, is *"Descoyuntarse, desarticularse los huesos."*

Seler, *op. cit.,* p. 56, describes one who "cuts himself up. He lays his hands and feet in separate places. He dislocates all the joints. Then he covers the mangled members with a light cloth, and then they begin to sprout and to grow again, so that it seems as if he had not been cut up, and thus he proves that this too is a juggler's trick."

See also *Mometzpinque* in Sahagún (Garibay ed.), Vol. IV, p. 344.

And when he brought destruction on one, then he chose an evil day sign; he sought and searched it out. They said that he did great evil to one on Nine Dog, or Nine Death, or Nine Grass, and indeed on all the ninth positions, and the other bad day signs mentioned — each of the different positions named.[6]

auh in jpan tepoloaia, vncan qujmattiuja in aqualli tonalli, iehoatl contotocaia, contlatotoqujliaia, qujtoa cenca ipan tepoloaia in chicunauj itzcujntli, anoço chicunauj mjqujztli, chicunauj malinalli: ioan in ie muchi chichicunanauj, ioan in oc cequj moteneoa aqualli tonalli, in jzqujcan omoteneuh,

And of such different positions, it is told that he who had work of this sort, whose labors became these separate tasks, who undertook these various burdens, was never content. He had no food. He lived only in poverty, destitute, without a house or home; nowhere was he a householder; nowhere was he of a happy home, a householder of tranquility. He went looking forward only to misery. He went eating and consuming food for himself only if somewhere something were given him, if he were offered something in order to destroy people as a reward for doing evil to them. Perhaps somewhere he was seized when already he became negligent, slothful, or developed an aversion [to evil]. Then he was seized, and they cut hair from the crown of his head; they took his renown from him and damaged his day sign for him. Thus he was abandoned to his death by the hands of others.

auh in iuh quezquican omjto, in aqujn iuhquj in itequjuh, itetequjuh muchioa, qujmotetequjlia, aic auja, atle qujquanj, çan motolinjtinemj, aoneoatinemj, âcan ichã, âcan chanca. amo chane caca, acan chantlamattica: acan chane ca tlamattica, çan icnoiotl qujtztinemj, çan ic conquatiuh, çan ic onmotlamjtiuh, intla cana itla maco, nemaqujlilo injc tepoloa, injc netlaquevilo: ânoce cana axioa in jquac ie otlatlatziujti, ie ontlaxujti, ie otlatlatzilhuj, vncan ano, qujtzoncuj, qujtleiocujlia, qujtonalitlacoa: ic ça temac onmomjqujzcacaoa:

And the ones known as men who danced with a dead woman's forearm, who crazed people,[7] when perhaps they would commit a robbery somewhere and spirit something from someone's home, would adorn the image of One Wind [Quetzalcoatl]. It went as their guide, at their head, guiding, marching in front. And they went bearing with them the forearm[8] of a woman who had died in childbed, and could not give birth to what was in her womb. When they took it from the one who had died, they only stole it during the night; they cut it off at midnight.

auh in iehoantin moteneoa, temamacpalitotique, tepupuxaquaujque, in jquac tla cana ichtequjzque, techan tlaqujxtizque, qujchichioaia in jxiptla ce hecatl: qujniacantiuja iniacac, imjxpan icatiuja, ioan qujtqujtiuj in jmacpal moçioaquetzquj, in iti ic iauh in auel mjxiuj iquac qujcujliaia in qujn onmjquj, çan oqujchteccacuja, ioaltica in qujtequjliaia, iooalli itic,

And so did they bury her, not at her home, but only leaving her there in the road; there at the very crossroads they buried her. They went skirmishing, fighting over her, and howling as they carried her. And as they brought her out of her house, it was not from the front; only at the back of the house,

auh injc qujtocaia amo ichan, çan vmpa concaoaia in vtlica, vncan in uel omaxac contoca, qujnêcaliltitiuj, ipan necalioatiuh, coiovitiuj injc qujujca: auh injc qujoalqujxtia ichan, amo ixcopa in jcal, çan qujcujtlacoionja in calli, vmpa qujqujxtia injc concaoa vmaxac:

6. *Omoteteneuh* in the *Real Palacio MS.*

7. Corresponding Spanish text: *"temacpalitotique, o por otro nombre tepupuxaquaujque."*

8. *Ibid.*: *"Un braço desde el codo, hasta la mano, de alguna mujer: que oujesse muerto, del primer parto: las cortauan, a hurto, el braço yzquierdo."* Seler, *loc. cit.*, describes hypnotists "who knocking on the threshold of a house with the hand of a woman who died in childbed, send the entire household into a paralysed and immovable state, and then plunder with impunity the whole house and commit every possible infamy upon its inmates."

they broke a hole, through which they removed her so that they could leave her at the crossroads.[9]

And when those who danced with the forearm would somewhere destroy or rob people, one person carried and bore the forearm of the woman who had died in childbirth, on his shoulder. It was the one on her left, her left forearm. When he came to reach one's home, but had not yet entered the house, first of all he struck the mid-point of the courtyard with the forearm. Twice he struck. On reaching the entrance of the house, he struck the portal, the lintel, and then he passed by the square, wooden pillar. Then he once again struck there before the hearth.

When such came to pass, it was said, no more did one speak out. No one could be aroused. Verily, the householders had swooned with fear. And some of them were in a deep sleep, snoring and rumbling; there was sleeping as if one's nose were broken. And if now some only in vain sat looking, they could not move, nor stir, nor resist. They were stunned; their arms and legs were deadened. For verily they were spread out gazing upward with unseeing, glassy, and staring eyes.

And these great, evil thieves thereupon lit up the torches and sought out the food. First of all they ate; they took it for themselves. None could restrain them. For in truth they had overcome and bewitched the people. When they had satisfied themselves, then they entered the storerooms, the storage chambers, and bundled up and removed all the capes; the large, cotton blankets; the green stone; the gold. Indeed, everything that had been hidden away — the treasures, the guarded things, — all was laden on their backs; all was appropriated and sorted out. Whatsoever it was, they placed as much on their backs, and with it arrayed themselves.

And in very truth, so it is said and so it is known, they did not leave them having done nothing; nor, with no result, did they take their pleasure with them taking advantage of their sleep, of the sleep into which the common folk had been thrown, to hang on to [the women], line them up, rolling them aside and enjoying another's place. There where each one lay apart, where she was stretched out, they simply rolled her over to another place. How much the wicked ones made sport of them cannot be said.[10]

auh in ieoantin in temamacpalitotique, in jquac cana tepolozque, ichtequjzque, ce tlacatl conquechpanoa conmoquechpanoltia in jmacpal, mocioaquetzquj, iehoatl in in jopuch, iopuchma, in jquac oacito techan, in aiamo calaquj calitic: oc ie achto itoalnepantla ic tlaujtequj in macpalli, ic oppa tlaujtequj, in oacique, caltempan, qujujtequj in calixquatl, in tlaixquatl: njman iee in tlaquetzalli, ic conmocaoa in tlecujlixquac, oc ceppa oncan tlaujtequj,

in jquac in iuh mjtoa njman aocac naoati, aocac uel mopoçaoa, vel ioiolmjquj in chaneque, auh in cequjn çan vel cocochmjquj, tlacotaliuj, tlaquaqualaca, iuhqujn neacatzaianalocochioa, auh intla ça oc aca nenitztoc, aoc vel molinja, aoc uel mocuechinja, aoc vel momapatla, vel çoçotlaoa, çoçotlacmjquj yn jnma, in jmjcxi, ca nelli mach in acopa teiitztoque, ixtepepetzme, ixpepetzteme onoque, ixpepetzintoque:

auh in iehoantin ichtecpatlachpopul, njman ie ic tlepitza, qujtemoa in tlaqualli, achtopa tlaqua, vel motlacauja aiac qujmelleltia, ca nel oontepoloque, ontepuxaquaujque in jquac onmoiollalique njman ic calaquj in tlecopa, in tlatlatilcali, tlamaololoa, tlaqujxtia in jxqujch tilmatli, in quachtli, in chalchiujtl, in teocujtlatl, in ie ixqujch tlatilonj, in tetzontli, in pielli, netlacujtlaputzmamaltilo, netlanênectilo, netlatlattililo, in çaço ac quexqujch ic conmotlamamaltia, ic onmuchichioa:

auh in nel cenca iuh onmjtoa, in iuh onmachizti, amo nentecaoa, amo nenqujça, teca maujltiteoa in iuh cochioa, necochitilo maceoalpan pilcoatoc, vipantoatoc, teiiquanja, tepapatla, in vncan ceceiaca ionoia, inetecaia, oc ie cecni conteca, amo vel mjtoz, in quexqujch ic teca maujltia tlaueliloque:

9. Cf. account of the *mociuaquetzque* in Seler, *Einige Kapitel,* pp. 306 ff.

10. Corresponding Spanish text: *"hazian muchas suziedades, y desonestidades en las mugeres, de aquella casa."*

And as they went along the road, nowhere did they rest or refresh themselves. They immediately sought out their homes. It was so said and affirmed that if any of them rested by the road, he could no longer go, rise up, nor travel. There the dawn would overtake him. He would betray his fellow thieves. They would be seized; each one seized and imprisoned, despoiled, and firmly bound.[11]

auh injc vi otlica acan moceuja, âcan mjxquacevia, ça qujn cẽ vmpa qujmattiuj in jnchan: iuh mjtoa, qujlmach intla aca moceviz vtlica: aioc vel yaz, aio uel meoaz, aioc vel otlatocaz: vncan ipan tlathujz, qujnnexotlaz injchteccaicnjoan, anozque, çaçacozque, namoialozque, tecâcatzilpiloz.

11. The reader may prefer to use the translation of *temacpalitotia* and derivations used by Alfredo López Austin in "Los tempacpalitotique," *Estudios de cultura náhuatl,* IV (Mexico: Instituto de Investigaciones Históricas, Universidad Nacional Autónoma de México, 1966), pp. 97-117, and others (*"Hace bailar a la gente en la palma de la mano"*). In view, however, of illustration No. 67 in Book X of the *Florentine Codex,* showing the carrying of an arm, and of the context of the corresponding Spanish text emphasizing the thieves' dancing, we leave our original translation unchanged, even though the etymology of the term would justify doing so. *Translators' note to the 1979 reprinting.*

Thirty-second Chapter, which telleth of the tears, the lamentations, and the misery of those who had been robbed, whom those who had danced with the dead forearm had plundered; and of the rest of the houses belonging to [One Wind].

Inj cempoalli ommatlactli omome capitulo: ytechpa tlatoa in jnchoqujz, in jntlaocul, yoan in jnnetolinjliz in jchtequjliloia: in qujmjchtequjliaia in temamacpalitotique: yoan in oc cequj calli, in jtech pouhquj yn.

And those who had been despoiled later then revived, moved, continued to stir, and rose up; they arose one by one. They to whose home the thieves had come stood up. They looked into the hearth, and into their coffers, woven reed containers, and palm leaf baskets. The bracelets, the green stone, and the quetzal feather mats, the mats of quetzal feathers, no more lay about. All was bare and laid waste.

Auh in iehoantin otlaqujxtililoque: qujnjquac muzcalia, moôlinja, mocuecuechinja, meoa, meeoa, meoatiquetza, in oacique inchan ychtecque: yn ontlachia in tlecopa, yoan yn jntopco, in jnpetlacalco: in jtanaioc in maqujztli in chalchivitl: auh in quetzalpetlatl, yn jpetlaioc in quetzalli, aioc tle onvetztoc, ça câcactoc, ça nemjuhian:

They had carried away all the goods with them. All was gone. They had borne all away from them. They had heaped and massed the goods together, had robbed and looted them; they had stripped all of value. They had caused ruin and left them bare. They had worked thoroughly and wrought misery for them. They had plunged them into misery, destroyed them, and brought them to disaster.

otlacemjtqujque, otlaceia, oqujmontlacemjtqujlique, ontlamaololoque, oqujmontlamaololhujque, ontlanamuxque, oqujmontlannamojelique, otlanavac ontlavicaque, ontlanemjuhcantilique, oqujmonpetztoccauhque, ovelqujmonchiuhque, oqujmonjcnochiuhque, icnoiotl oqujmontlaxilitiaque, oqujmontlaixpulvique, oqujmontlacecemmanjlique:

In vain there was desperate searching. The women raised wails and howls, continuous howls; they raised a cry, beat their hands, pounded with their fists, and wept tears. Verily, how could it be? What could they do? Truly, of what profit was it? Of what profit was their work? What was left? What still could they say? Nothing more could be said. Where in truth could it be told? Each one even threw herself to the ground, cast herself on her face, beat her face, and wept, for it was carried away, scraped all together,—scraped clean—swept bare. They had stripped the necessities of life [procured] by drudgery; the things arduously established and founded; the solace of [the labor of] the elbow and the knee; that which had appeared and accumulated with effort, to increase and augment the property and possessions of our lord, etc.

çan êia, ça nelli mach in mootta, tlachoqujztleoa, tlatecoiooa, tlatetecoiooa, tlatzatziztleoa, momamatlatzinja, momamapuztequj, mjxaiopatzca in cioa: que çan nel oc nen, quen oc, tle ça nel nen, tle ça nen, tle oc nen, tle oc ytlatollo: ac onnelhujloz, campa nel onmjtoz, in manel momamaiavi, motetentimaiavi, mjxtetzotzona choca, ca onitqujoac, ontlacemjchictia, oncemjchictia, ontlachichictiaque, oconcemjchictiaque, yn atlaaxcavilli, in aiaxcaio, in aiaxcan otzintic, oneloaiooac, in jpatiuh in molicpitl, in tetepuntli, in aiaxcan onez, oçaçaliuh: injc omacoquetz, omotlapivi in jcococauh in totecujo in tlatqujtl et[a].

In this manner they said that those who danced with a dead woman's forearm destroyed people, those known verily as genuine thieves, struck-by-

Iujn in qujtoa tepoloaia: in moteneoaia vel teuichtecque, tetzôtzonme, tepatlachti: in iehoantin temamacpalitotique. Auh injc tocaiotilo tetzotzonme:

stones, crushed-by-stones. And hence were they named "struck-by-stones"; if somewhere they could be taken, they just stoned them. They set upon them with stones; they were felled by stones; they beat and mangled them with stones; they crushed their heads with stones. Then and there were taken and plundered practically all their stolen goods and loot, etc.

intla cana ovel anoque, çan qujntetepachoa, qujntecicali, tetica vetzi, qujntetzotzona, qujntepatzca, qujnquatepipitzinja: yquac vncan cujtilo, namoialilo in amo çan quexqujch imjchtech, intlaqujxtil. et[a].

And as was said above, so that it be not mere idle words, we shall consider it, and it will be discussed and explained in detail; we shall elucidate and explain at great length, expound it, develop it, and enlarge upon it. That which is different we shall go on explaining in detail; we shall do it twice, thrice, or four times. But to make it clear, we reflect upon, try to realize and give form to that not yet apparent, and not determined above; that which is still being established, considered, denied;[1] that which is not yet in one's heart, not yet understood or comprehended — not yet taken to heart, the discussion not yet clear. For many times we have gone hurrying back to all which hath been told. For that reason, that which is here present we pass over, we quickly skip over, we hurriedly leap over the fragment. No more do we correct or deal with what hath been mentioned: the different accounts of the day signs each in its proper place. So only here they are gathered, assembled, brought together, amassed, and arranged in succession. We place them in clusters and join and put them together. So only these are being clustered, brought together, joined together, set separately, arranged in procession and in succession, the different numbers of the series, with their assigned tasks: Two House, Three Lizard, Four Serpent, Five Death, Six Deer, Seven Rabbit, Eight Water, Nine Dog, Ten Monkey, Eleven Grass, Twelve Reed, Thirteen Ocelot.

Auh in juh omjto tlacpac: injc amo çan iliujztlatlatolli toconnemjtizque, onmijtoz, onmotetequjmatiz, ipan tontlatepeoazque, tontlatequjtepeoazque, tocontlatepeoaltizque, tocontlaaaqujlizque, tocontlatlatlalilizque: in amo çan ieehoatl tictoqujmattinemjzque, ticovppavizque, tiqueexpavizque, ticnanappavizque: çan iehoatl ipan tontixpoa, tontoiolpoa, toconjxtoca, ipan tontlaneiocolia, in aiamo neci, in aiamo panj oalmotlalia: in oc tlapachiuhtica, mocujlitica, mocujcujlitica, in aiamo teyollipan, in aiamo teiollo qujnamjquj, in aiamo teiollo contoca, in aiamo teiollo contoca, yn aiamo teiollo itlan qujça, teiollo ipan iauh tlatolli: ca mjiecpa omocujcujtlacueptinen, in jxqujch omjto: ipampa in ça njcan ixco tonqujça, toconchôcholhujtiqujça, toconcuechcholhujtiqujça. Aiocmo vmpa tontlavica: aiocmo toconiehoailhuja yn omoteneuh, injc nononqua tlatollotoque izqujteme tonalti: yn çan njcan ommocentlalia, ommotecpichoa, onmonechicoa, onmocenqujxtia, onmototoqujlia, tiqujmonnenetzollalia, tiqujmonnenetechçaloa, tiqujmonnenetechtlalia: ic çan onnenetzolcate, nenetechcate, nenetech çaliuhticate, moquequetzticate, mototocaticate, mototoqujliticate, yn jzqujteme njcan cencalpan tequjppaneque: in iehoatl vme calli: ey cuetzpalin, navi coatl, macujlli mjqujztli, chiquacen maçatl, chicome tochtli, chicuei atl, chicunavi ytzcujntli, matlactli oçomatli, matlactli oçe malinalli, matlactli omome acatl, matlactli omey ocelutl.

When the count of these different days, the time of each one of the days, had ended, then set in —

Yn jquac oontlan izqujlhujtl, yn, intlapoalpan: yn jntlacecemjlhujtiltiaian: njman oalmoquetza.

1. Repetition of *in aiamo teiollo contoca* is lightly crossed out in the Nahuatl text.

Thirty-third Chapter, in which is mentioned the nineteenth sign, named One Eagle. It was said to be an evil day sign, and he who was then born was boastful, and brave, daring, fearing nothing and no one. And it was said that the women also were daring, of ill fame, of evil tongue, shameless, and immodest. And it was said that at this time descended the lesser Goddesses; and they did evil to the small children. Hence they did not let them go out of doors, nor did they bathe them at that time.[1]

— One Eagle. This One Eagle, it was said, was an evil day sign. Also at that time descended those named the "Goddesses." It was said, and it was so stated, that they were only the youngest ones, only the sisters,[2] who then came down. Nevertheless, [the people] took great fright, because it was said that they were very harmful, furious, hateful, hostile, and merciless. As they could not be resisted, so they made sport of people, as is told in various places and mentioned here and now. None of the small children might go naked. They were carefully watched, because at this time they might be violently possessed, their lips twisted and withered, their eyes crossed and cloudy, their noses crooked, etc.

And therefore they paid them great honor there in the places where they were awaited, there in the different Goddesses' temples. In each neighborhood, in the house clusters and their vicinities, reeds were strewn and scattered; sand was sprinkled on the roads and at street crossings and crossroads — places where roads came together.

One who made a vow to them that he would cover and wrap them, adorned their offerings, the paper banners of the Goddesses painted and spattered with liquid rubber. There he covered the different images of the Goddesses, as they were arranged in order. It was at midnight, just at the dividing of the night, that the making of offerings

Injc cẽpoalli õmatlactli vmey capitulo: vncan moteneoa ynjc caxtolli vnnavi machiotl, yn itoca ce quauhtli: quil amo qualli in tonalli, auh in ipan tlacatia, mochachamaoanj, yoã chicaoque, aiac ixco tlachia, atle ypan tlatta, atle ypã teitta: yoan quil in cihoa, ano tle ypã tlachia, yoan cenca tlavilqujxtianj, tentlaveliloque, ixquauhti, amo pinaoanj: auh quil yn iquac, oaltemoia yn aquique tepitoton cihoateteu: auh quintlaueliaia in conetotonti, yc amo quinoalquixtiaia in qujiaoac, amono quimaltiaia yn iquac.

In ce quauhtli: ynjn ce quauhtli, mjtoa amo qualli tonalli, no vncan temoia, in qujntocaiotia cihoateteu, quilmach yn juh onmjtoa ça xoxocoio, ça teiccaoan yn vncan temoia, iece cenca vellamauhtiaia, ypampa quil cenca ihjioque, tlaveleque, tetlavelique, amo ellelceuhque, amo icnooaque, njman aixnamjquizti, ynjc teca maviltianj, yn juh omjto quezquican: yn juh conitoa in iquac hin, njmã aiac vel petlauhtinenca in pipiltotõti, cenca malhujloia, ypampa cenca tlaquauh vncan tetech quineoaia, tennecujlooaia, tempatziooaia, ixnecujliooaia, ixcatziooaia, iacanecuiloaia. et[a].

auh injc cenca qujnmaviztiliaia in vncan inchielpã yn izquicã cicihoateucalco, in tlatlaxilacalpã, tetlatlaxilacalloc, tetlatlaxilacaltian, tôtoltzetzelolo, tlatoltzetzelolo, tlaixalhujlo yn vtlica, yn vmaxac, yn inepanivjian vtli.

Jn aqujn invicpa monetoltia: in qujnquentiz qujntlaquentiz, qujnchichivilia yn jnnextlaoal, in cihoateuitl amatl, tlaoolxaoalli, oolpeiaoac, vmpa qujmoquequentia yn izqujteme, tecpantoque, yn inixiptlaoan iooalnepantla, çan jc onxellivi, iooalli im peoa tlamanililo, auh iquac mocaoa yie nepantla tonatiuh, yie tlaqualizpã auh in aqujn amo qujntlaquentia, çan

1. Corresponding Spanish text: *"no los dexavan salir de casa, nj bañarse, el tiempo que este signo reynava."*

2. *Teiccavan*: see "Memoriales en 3 columnas," p. 212.

began. And when it ceased, it was midday, when it was already time to eat. And he who did not cover them only offered and arranged a little drink and food, or white incense, or coarse incense. The youths, the young seasoned warriors, the masters of the youths,[3] the guardians there at the Goddesses' temple, who watched and kept vigil for one night, kept the food as a gift, took and appropriated it to themselves.

atzintli, tlaqualtzintli in cõmanaia, in contecpanaia, anoço iztac copalli, copalxalli, in tlaqualli iehoã qujmovevenja qujmocuilia, quimotechtia in telpupuchti, telpuchtequjoaque, yoan titiachcaoã, in vmpa tlapixtoque cihoateucalco, in vmpa ceiooal oyxtoçoque, otoçoque,

And when silence fell, when at each place there was a cessation of offerings, then forthwith began the libations. Only in each person's home, each person's house, was it done. No more did one practise restraint: no more were there inhibitions. They made the old men and the old women drink and poured out the wine for them. So there were tearful greetings of one another and animation of one another, etc.

auh yn ocactivetz, yn onecacaoaloc tlamanalo, njman ic peoa ĩ tlatlatoiavililo, ça techachan, ça tecacaltic yn muchioa, aocac õtemamati, aocmo onnemamacho, iehoãti qujntlaoanilia, qujntlatoiavilia yn vevetque, yn ilamatque, ic mochochoquiztlapaloa, meellaquaoa et[a].

And it was said that he who was then born, was perverted. If a man, he became a chieftain, a man-at-arms, debauched, evil, and daring. Only his exploits, his chieftainship, did he relate and make public. He considered that no one rejected him. He pretended to excel others. He respected no one. He wished others destroyed. He despised others. He became presumptuous. And then, being of ungovernable tongue, he interrupted people and belittled the word of others, and scoffed and grumbled at them. He rose up in rage; he constantly shook his head; he interfered in others' affairs; he pretended to know all; he praised himself. He pretended that he spoke well and truthfully. He would not be outdone in talk. He was vainglorious; he was a flatterer. He pretended to be virtuous, but to see no virtue in others. He belittled others' words. He contradicted, denied, and twisted his own words. All his works, all corresponded to him; he merited all; all indeed became him: vices, drunkenness,[4] and corruption. And sometimes, if he became neglectful, he was captured and imprisoned, or died in battle, etc.

Auh mjtoa yn aquin vncan tlacati, atlacacemelle, intla oqujchtli, tiacauhti, oqujchti, âquen tlatta, âquen tlatlatta, aiac ixco tlachia, çan jioqujchio, ytiacauhio in conpopoa, yn jxco quimana, njman aiac qujmotlaçaltoca, motepanaviltoca, aiac tle compoa, motepololtoca, atle ontepoa, cenca iz moquixtia, yoã njmã âtentlacatl, vel tepâpatzoa, tepâpatzaoa, tetlitlivia, tequiquinatza, mîitleoa, moquaquacuecuechoa, motlâtlamachiztia, motlatlamachitoca, motlatlanitztia, movevellatoltoca, moieiectlatoltoca, âmotẽpanavillanj, momamachotla, temâmachotla, moiêiectoca, âteiectoca, tetẽpatztlatoa, motêtencuepa, tlatlatolcuepa, tlatlatolmalacachoa, much ychivil, much qujmopanjtia, much quimolhujltia, much vel itech muchioa in tlatlauelilocaiotl, yn ehi iujntiliztli, yn avilquizcaiotl, auh in quẽman intla otlatlatziviti vico, calaqujlo, iaomjquj et[c].

It was just the same if it were a woman. She was truly of evil tongue, vile-mouthed, inhuman in speech — big-mouthed, of biting words. Her great joy, her great pleasure, was evil speaking. She was one who vituperated others, who insulted and affronted them. Like a dog, [she let] no one head her

Çan ie no iuhquj intla cihoatl, vel tentlaveliloc, camatlaveliloc, ahtentlacatl, tenxaxacal, camatlatecoa, cenca ipac, cenca ivelmach yn tentlauelilocaiotl, vel tepapacanj, tenovjiantocanj, tepacçotlaoanj, iuhqujnma chichi aiac vel qujiacaolinia, qujiacapeionja, yntlaca itech onaci, njmã quitlecavitiquiça, ytech mo-

3. Corresponding Spanish text: *"los mjnjstros, de aquellos oratorios."* — Cf. Anderson and Dibble, *op. cit.*, Book II, "The Ceremonies," p. 102.

4. *Eihiuitiliztli* in the *Real·Palacio MS.*

off or trap her. If someone approached her, at once she quickly sprang on and clung to her. She gripped her, and scratched, clawed, tore, and hacked her face; she divested and stripped her face; she pricked, beat, smashed, and struck it. She smashed and banged her head. It was as if she shattered the grey-haired head. She tore out, plucked, pulled, and jerked out her hair. She struck her nose; she bloodied her nose. She struck and broke her teeth. She broke her jaw. She struck her in the face. She tore up her clothes; she rent her clothes into pieces; she ripped them into fragments and made bits of them. Each rag she destroyed. She tore her cape and shift into tatters and disrobed her.

piloa, quiteteuhtzitzquja, quixtataca, qujxmomotzoa, qujxcocotona, qujxcocototza, qujxcujcui, quixnamoia, quitztzeltilia, quitzotzona, quixtitipitza, quitzitzilitza, quiquatitipitza, quiquatzitzilitza, iuhqujn tequaiztatlapana, tequamomotzoa, tequaçacamoa, tequaçacapi, tequavivilana, tequavivitla, teiacatzotzona, teiacachachaquanja, tetlantzotzona, tetlanpepetla, tetenaana, teitztzotzona, tetlatzatzaianilia, tetlatetetzomuchilia, qujtetetzomotza, achchiqujtlalia, cēcēçotl qujvica, qujtzeltilia yntetilma, inteujpil, teixnamoia

Thirty-fourth Chapter, in which are told and mentioned what they did when they visited women recently delivered, and other things which were done where a woman recently delivered dwelt.

And here it is told that when a child was born, and when [the mother's] relatives knew of it, and it was known and the news spread and was noised abroad, her family and blood relations were assembled and brought together. They set forth, and came and proceeded to visit the much revered child.

When they entered, at the very first, they took ashes; they anointed their knees with ashes; they rubbed themselves. And also they put ashes on the knees of their children yet in the cradles; or those still crawling, going on all fours; those who stood, who already took to their feet; the boys, girls, youths, young men, unmarried girls, and young women. Everywhere, on all parts of the body they placed ashes; on every joint and articulation: their ankles, their elbows, their buttocks, over the kidneys, the napes of their necks, their shoulders, but especially their knees.

And it was so said and averred that thereby they would not become lame. But if this were not so done, they would become lame, and all the joints, in every place, would creak.

And also for four days they carefully watched the fire. It never went out. It continued to flare up, to grow and increase, to flare red. They thus carefully started it; it was well set. And no one might take the fire. And if anyone wished to take the fire, or a light, they would not give it to him, lest he take renown from the child who had been born, until the four days had ended, or for still a few days, when they bathed him.

Injc cempoalli ommatlactli onnavi capitulo, vncan mjtoa, moteneoa: in tlein qujchioaia in qujmontlapaloaia in mjxiuhque: yoan in oc cequj in muchioaia, in vncan onoca mjxiuhquj.

Auh njcan mjtoa: in jquac aqujn tla otlacat piltontli: in oconmatque yoaiolque, in onmachoc, in otepan ocenman, in otepan onmotecac. Niman ic nenechicolo, necenqujxtilo, in jtlacaiooan, in jcujtlaxcolloc eoa, viloa, pipiliooa in qujtlapalozque, in jxco, ijcpac, tlachiazque piltontli.

In iquac oncalacque, oc ie achto concuj in nextli: ic onmotlanquanexvia, onmomamatiloa: yoan no qujmontlanquanexuja in inpilhoan, in oc coçulti, anoço in ie movilana, coionenemj, in ie moquequetza, in ie imjcxi caana in oqujchpipiltotonti, in cioapipiltotonti, in telpupuchpipil, telpucatoton, ichpupuchpipil, ichpucatoton: novian qujntlatlalilia in nextli, in jzqujcan inçaçaliuhian, in jmjhilpicaiocan, in jnquequeiultitech, in jnmolicpi ytech, yn jntzintenpan, in incujtlacaxiuhian, in jnquechtepultitech, in jmacolpan: oc cenca iehoatl in jntlanquac.

Iuh mjtoa, qujlmach ic amo tlanquananatzinjzque: auh intlacamo yuh muchioa, tlanquananatzinjzque: yoan nanatzinjz, in jzqujcan in çaçaliuhian.

Auh yoan navilhujtl in vel qujpia tletl aquēman cevi, xotlatica, oalantica, oaoalantica, mopipitztica, vel qujcpeoa, vel ic peuhtica: yoan aiac vel ontlecuj. Auh intla aca ontlecujznequj tletlecujc: amo qujmaca, injc amo qujtleiocujlizque piltontli, in otlacat: ixqujchica in ontlamj navilhujtl: anoço in oc izqujlhujtl caltizque.

Thirty-fifth Chapter. Here is told what was done when they bathed their children, and how food was eaten when they gave them their names; and the discourse which the old people gave when they addressed the child and the mother.

And when he was bathed, quite early in the morning, in the morning light, when the sun appeared, they had the small children perform the naming ceremony. They went out shouting and panting on the roads; to the entrances they ran. Thus they went calling out what he had been given as a name, as hath already been mentioned, in a certain place. They took the naming ceremony gift, parched maize toasted with beans. They provided it with beans, many beans, offered in a vessel.

And it is said that so was the custom if someone were born on a day sign beginning in the first position (as hath been said in many places). If it were a good time, then at once they quickly bathed him. Or later, they set it aside and skipped a day, so that they could make good the feasting and drinking for the child.[1]

But if they could not do so then, they bathed him later, on the third day sign. As here it appeareth in [the series of] One Eagle, the one perhaps then born they would bathe later, on Three Motion.

Those whose fathers and mothers were poor, the indigent, who were in misery, and had nothing to use, with which to gather together and assemble people, only with affliction, sickness, and misery bathed their child. For they only aggravated and worsened it when they did not delay, defer, retard, procrastinate, or postpone [the day of bathing].

But if the fathers were rich and prosperous, if there was wherewith to eat, they selected for one a later date, on the seventh day sign; at that time they bathed the child and placed him in the cradle. This was because, as hath been said, they always considered the seventh day sign good. At that time they held an important banquet. There was drink and

Injc cempoalli on caxtolli capitulo: vncan mjtoa yn tlein muchioaia, yn iquac quimaltiaia impilhoan, yoan injc tlaqualoia yn iquac qujntocamacaia: yoan in tlatolli in qujtoaia vevetque, in quilhuiaia, piltontli: yoan in tenã.

Auh in iquac maltia, çan iooatzinco, tlavizcalpã, iquac yn oalmomã tonatiuh, quixicvenquaqualia im pipiltotonti tzatzatzitiui, yhicaoaca, yn vtlicapa, quiaoacpa, motlatlaloa, ic quinotztiui, in tlein õtocaiotiloc piltontli, in juh ie omoteneuh, ceccã qujnanamoia, in xicventli, izquitl in quicequi, heeio, quêeiotia, moca ietl, xicaltica quimana.

Yoã mjtoa iuh tlamanca intla aca ipã otlacat ynjc cemilhuitl vmpeoa tonalli (ca mjeccã omito). yntla qualcan njmã iciuhca conaltitivetzi, auh qujn nonqua, contlalilia oc concholoYtia, ynjc quitlatlaqualia, pillaqualo, pillaoano:

auh intlaca ie moveliti, quin ipã caltia yn Ey tonalli, yn juh nican neci ipã ce quauhtli, yn aqujn tla ipã otlacat, quin ipã caltizque in Ey olin,

iehoã in çã tlacococavia ytahoan ynãoã in çan icnotlaca, in ça quitzacuia icnoiotl, atletzin in polivini, in tecentlaliloni, in tenechicolonj, ic çan cococatzin, cocaiotica, icnotlacaiotica conaltia yn jnconeuh, ipãpa in çan quitototztivetzi, quitototztiquiça, in aocmo cõvecatlaça, cõuecatilia, cõnechcatilia, cõnechcatlaça, cõchololtia,

auh intla motlacamati, mocuiltonoa tetahoã, in vncã quiquanj, qujn ce vmpa quimattivi yn ipã chicome tonalli, yquac caltia, yoan quicoçolaquja im piltontli, ypampa yn juh omjto muchipa quiqualittaia yn 7. tonalli, yquac quivejchioa in tecoanotzaliztli, atlioa, tlaqualo, novjiampa, xoxochitlano, oalhuj in xochicauhque, nequequeçalo, nepopotzolo, auh in

1. Cf. Sahagún (Garibay ed.), I, 13, 11, and II, 38, 7-8; also Anderson and Dibble, *op. cit.* Book II, "The Ceremonies," pp. 152-153.

food. From all parts flowers were taken; all the flower bearers came. There was jostling and crowding. And the old men and old women greeted the small boy and his newly delivered mother. They said:

"O my beloved grandson, thou hast endured suffering and fatigue. For thou hast come here to earth; thou hast appeared on earth. Thou shalt behold, come to know, and feel pain, affliction, and suffering. It is a place of torment and affliction; of constant torment and affliction; a time of torment and a time of affliction to which thou hast come; a place of bitterness, a place of much work and affliction. Perhaps we shall receive as merits and as good deserts that for a short time thou shalt be lent to us. For thou art the living image, the likeness, the noble child, and the offspring[2] of thy ancestors, thy beloved grandsires, thy great-grandsires, thy great-grandmothers, the grandfathers of thy nephews, who already have gone beyond, who a short time ago came to stand guard for a little while, here where thou liest and hast endured suffering and fatigue, O my beloved grandson. For our lord hath sent thee."

Forthwith they petted him and stroked him with their hands, to show that they loved the child. Also at once they addressed and greeted his newly delivered mother. They said:

"O my daughter, O my beloved daughter, my lady, my beloved lady, thou hast endured suffering and fatigue. For in some way thou hast separated thyself from and left the jeweled necklace, the precious feather which was within thee. Now that he is come forth on earth, you are not indivisible; you will not be joined together, for you are separated. What will our lord require? Perhaps for a little day we shall take him as lent to us. We shall love him like a precious necklace or a precious stone bracelet. Be calm and modest; take care. Do not relapse into sickness nor let accident befall thee. Do not try to be up and about. Be careful, in convalescing, when they place thee in the sweatbath. And do not neglect the child. Take care of him. Even in thy sleep, be fearful for him. Do not pierce his palate, [in nursing him]; do not crush him in thy sleep; do not let him sleep unwatched, so that thou nowhere

piltontli quitlapaloa in vevetq̃, yn ilamatque, yoã in inãtzin mixiuhquj, Quilhuja.

Noxhujuhtze, otiquihjiovi, oticçiauh, ca otioalmovicac in tlalticpac, otimotlalticpacquixti, tiquittaz, ticmatiz, ticiehecoz, in tecoco, in tetolinj, in tlaihjoviliztli, ca tetoneuhcã, techichinatzcan, tetotoneuhcan, techichichinatzcã, tetoneuhian, techichinatzian, yn otioalla, cococ yieoaiã, teicnotlamachtican, aço titolhujltiz, titomâceoaltiz, aço achitzinca timitztotlanevizque: ca timixjptla, timpatillo, timezço, tintlapallo, tintzicuevilo in motechiuhcaoã, in mocoltzitzinoa, ỹ machtooã, yn mopiptooa, in machcocolhoã, yn ie nechca mantivi, yno cuel achic, yno cemilhujtl, ontlapieco, yn vncã timonoltitoc, otiquihjiovi, oticiauh noxhujuhtzine, ca omitzoalmioali in totecujo,

njmã ic compêpetla, cõmapêpetla, ic quinextia, ynjc cõtlaçotla piltontli. Nimã no ic cõnotza contlapaloa yn inãtzin mixiuhquj, Quilhuja.

Nochputze, nochputzine, ciuapille, cioapiltzintle, otiquihjiovi, oticiauh, ca oquẽteltzin mitztlalloti, mitztlalcavi in cozcatl, in quetzalli, ynjc otimapãticatca, ca otlalticpacquiz, acenononqua yn amonmotlanamjctizque, ca oanmotlallotique, quẽ qujmonequiltia in totecujo, aço cemilhujtzintli, tictotlanevizque, ticozcateuhtlamatizque, timacuexteuhtlamatizque, ma oc yvjiã, ma oc iocuxca, ma oc xõmomalhuj, ma tõmocaxanj, ma tõmonevjiavi, macamo xõmopûpuxcanequj, ma yvjian in tioalmimatiz, in temazcaltzinco mitzoncalaquizque, auh ma tocõmoxiccavili in piltzintli, ma xocõmocuitlavi, ma oc mocuchpan xocõmamatto, ma tocõtẽtzoponj, ma tocõcochpacho, ma toconcochcauh, ma çã tehoatl tocõneviãvi, ma çã ic tocõquelo, ca oqujmomacavili in totec.°

2. Cf. Sahagún, "Memoriales con escolios," p. 208: *"quebradura de la piedra que se labra o nieto o hijo."*

mayest bring mishap to him. Do not do so intentionally; for our lord hath given him."

Thus only briefly they greeted her, lest they tire her by useless talk.[3]

Yc çan achitzin ic contlapaloa, injc amo quitzonteconeoazque.

3. Corresponding Spanish text: "*esforçados hija, y tened cuydado de vuestra salud: mjrad no cayais en enfermedad por vuestra culpa: y tened cuydado de vr̃o hijto* [*sic*]. *Mirad que las madres, mal aujsadas: matan a sus hijos dormjendo, o quando maman: si no les qujtan la teta, con tiento: suelense agujerar el paladar, y mueren. Mirad que pues: que nos le a dado nuestro señor: no le perdamos, por vuestra culpa: y no es menester fatigaros, con mas palabras.*"

Thirty-sixth Chapter, which telleth how a feast was held, and what the order of service was, and how there was drinking of wine.

And as to the invited guests: already there was jostling among the guests. All took their respective places; the houses were entered. There was disorder and scattering about; there was wandering and there were disputes, rushing about like fools, hurrying, hastening, and unrest.

For everything, assignments were made and work distributed. First came the tobacco servers. Tobacco was served; one was provided with tobacco; tobacco was smoked. Then the flower servers followed them. They provided and gave them flowers; they favored them with crowns and garlands of flowers; they provided them with flower crowns and garlands. They arranged before them bowls with tobacco tubes. They sat smoking, inhaling the fragrance. All smelled it. There was a pleasant and fragrant odor.

And thereupon went the server, and following him those who changed the courses and carried [the food] in their arms. They served the people, placed them in order, went placing the people in line, putting them all in line. Thereupon all ate. [But] first they cast on the ground [a mouthful of food].[1] Later something was reserved, put aside for their servants.[2]

And thereupon also went the chocolate[3] server. In just the same way he went arranging the people in order, placing them in line. He neglected no one; he was very careful with each one. He went placing for each one the stirring sticks with which the chocolate was beaten, whereby the chocolate was consumed. Chocolate was put aside for each of them — they put aside chocolate for their servants, [as well

Injc cempoalli on caxtolli oce capitulo: ytechpa tlatoa yn juh mocoanotzaia, yoan in juh catca tlatecpãtli, yoan in juh tlaoanaia.

Auh in tlacoanotzalti, ie cuel iê, nequequeçalo in coame, netêteco, calacoa, tlaixnelivi, tlaixmoiaoa, neixpololo, neixnanamico, tlaixtomaoa, tlâtlacivi, ycioa, netetequipacholo,

cecentlamãtli ipã neyhixquetzalo, netetequjmaco, iacattiuh, in teyiemacac, teyiemaco, teyietilo, yietlatilo, njmã contoquilia yn texochimacac, texochitia, texochimaca, conteaquia in icpacxochitl in xochicozcatl, teicpacxochitia, texochicozcatia, teixpãmomâmana yn jiecaxitl, tlachichinalotoc, tlanecutoc, tlaneco, tlaaviaxtoc, tlavevelixtoc:

auh njmã ie ic iauh in tetlamacac, qujtocativi, in tetlanamjctilique, in tlanapaloque, tetlamaca, tevipana, tepilotiuh, tecempilotiuh, njmã ie ic tlaqualo, achtopa, ontlatlatlaça, çatepã netlacavilo, ic tlaquanja yntetlavicalhoã:

auh njmã ie no ic iauh in teamacac, çan ie no ivi tevipantiuh, tecempilotiuh, aiac quixcaoa, vel mixpepetztza, contetequilitiuh in aquavitl, ynjc moneloa cacaoatl, ic ahatlioa, teaatlacavilo, qujmatlacavjia, intetlavicalhoã, in viconj, in tlacaoanj, in quitquinj netlacavilli,

1. Corresponding Spanish text: *"antes que començassen a comer: los combidados, la comjda que les aujan puesto: tomauan un bocado de la comjda, y arroiauanle al suelo: a honrra del dios Tlaltecutli."*

2. *Ibid.*: *"los servjdores de la comjda . . . trayan comjda a cada uno, segun su comjda* [*sic*]: *y la ponjan delante, del que estaua asentado: una orden de chiqujvites, con diversas maneras de pan: y pareados en los chiqujvites: otros tantos caxetes, con diversas maneras de cazuela, con carne, o pescado. . . . Aujendo comjdo, dauan las sobras a sus criados, y tambien los caxetes, y chiqujvites."*

3. *Atl* is sometimes used to mean chocolate. Cf. Molina, *op. cit.* (Spanish-Nahuatl section), *"Bever agua, vino o cacao. n, atli."*

as] the vessels to carry, keep, and transport the leavings.[4]

Then, for a short time, all sat relaxed, watching; all sat content in the place of lingering, in the banqueting place. But if some were not well satisfied, nor happy, nor content, with the chocolate, the food, the flowers, and the tobacco, etc., they only ran away angry. They quickly arose and sprang to their feet, leaped up, glared in rage at the drink and food, and went about chattering, babbling, jabbering, multiplying it and shouting, doing it in crescendo.[5] Thus oppressed and troubled, they went to seat themselves at their homes and in their houses. And those who had left in such a manner, those who had only become enraged, if they were noted, later, next day, once more they received them[6] and brought them in, consoled them, when it was the time of finishing the food.[7] In their behalf it was celebrated; they were consoled and made joyous.

vncã achitzinca ompacoatoc, nepielotoc, vellamachotoc in nepieloian, in tecoanotzaloian: auh in cequjn in amo cenca tlavelmati, vellamati, movelmati, yn atica, tlaqualtica, xochitica, yietica et.[a] çan motlavellaloa, moquetzteoa, moquetztiquiça, choloteoa, maçoma, motlaqualçoma, tlâtlatotivi, popolocativj, tlatetotiuj, tlâtlanauhtiuj, tlanauhtiuj, tlanauhpactiuj, ic oallatepachoticate, moxixicoticate, yn omotlalito inchã, yn jncalitic: auh intla oittoque in iuh oquizque, in çan oqualantiaque, quin imuztlaioc oc ceppa qujnana, qujmonjcxiana, qujniolceuja, in iquac ie apeoalco, inca nechioalo, iollalilo, papaquiltilo,

And the women only drank a gruel, perhaps a gruel of wrinkled *chía* cooked with maize, or a drink of pinole mixed with *chía*,[8] which they drank. They gave them [gruel] topped with honey, or with chilis, yellow chilis, small hot ones, or hot green ones, or with squash seeds on it.

auh in cihoa çan tlayia, aço chiantzotzolatolli, anoço chianpinolli in quia, in qujnmaca, necpanj, anoço chilpanj, chilcozpanj, chiltecpimpanj, chilchopanj, aiooachpanj,

And when it grew dark, the old men and women drank wine. They gathered around and congregated. They set up before them that from which they drank, called the flower vessel, and their drinking bowls and wine cups, the serving vessels.[9]

auh yn oioac in vevetque, yn ilamatque, tlatlaoana, mohololoa, mocecentlalia, ymjxpan quioalquetza yn intlaoanaia, yn jtoca xochcomitl, yoã yn intlaoancax, in jntetlaoã, in tetlamamaconj,

The wine server, the server, first began; so he went to the one of highest rank, the first in rank, the one in first place. So he went in order, going in line, and so were left those of lesser rank, of inferior station, in last place. He continued serving the wine, perhaps white, or watered, or honeyed;[10] those which were stored and prepared for the drinking ceremony. It was carried there in jars for dregs, in wine jars and dipping vessels.

achto iê vmpeoa in tetlaoanti, in tetlamamacac, njmã ie ic iauh yn jiacac, in tlaiacac, yn jiacaiocã, ic tevipãtiuh, tecempilotiuh, ic ommocaoa in icuitlapilco, in tlacuitlapilco, in tlatzaccan, quioaltecatimanj in vctli, aço iztavctli, anoço aivctli, tlachioalvctli, yn otlaliloc ochichioaloc ic pillaoanoz, ontlaçaçaco inxaiocomjc, inoccomjc, intlatemovilcomjc,

4. Interpretation is provisional. For this, Sahagún, in the corresponding text, writes: *"y las sobras del cacao, dauan a sus criados."* See n. 2.

5. The term is apparently incompletely corrected to read *tlanappactiuj*; cf. *Real Palacio MS.*

6. *Oc ceppa quimonana* in *ibid.*

7. Corresponding Spanish text: *"a este dia llamauan, Apeoalco: porque en el, se acabaua todo el combite."* Cf. also Anderson and Dibble, *op. cit.*, Book I, "The Gods," p. 23, and Sahagún (Garibay ed.), Vol. IV, p. 321. In *ibid.*, I, 21, 24, it is referred to as *"añadidura a lo que estaba comido y bebido."*

8. Cf. Anderson and Dibble, *op. cit.*, Book VIII, "Kings and Lords," p. 39; Book II, "The Ceremonies," p. 91 (*chianpinolli*).

9. In the *Real Palacio MS, yn tlavanoni, ỹ netlamamaconi* follows *tetlamamaconj.*

10. Corresponding Spanish text: *"hechizo de agua, y miel cozido, con la rayz: al qual llaman ayuctli, que qujere dezir, pulcre de agua: lo qual tenja aparejado, y guardado el señor del combite: de algunos dias antes."* See also Oswaldo Gonçalves de Lima: *El maguey y el pulque en los códices mexicanos* (México: Fondo de Cultura Económica, 1955), *passim,* and esp. pp. 107 ff.

And the wine server, if he saw that those whom he gave wine did not become intoxicated and in a stupor, but only sat staring and grimacing, once again turned to the left, made a beginning from the left — that is, beginning where he had left off, with those of last place, the lesser in rank. So at that place he made a beginning in order to make them drunk. Thus he went reversing and rearranging the process of making them drunk.

auh in tetlaoanti intla quimjtta quintlaoantia, yn amo ivinti, in amo iamanja, in çan itztoque, ixpepeiontoque, ie no cuel iê copuchilochtia, tlaopuchcopa quipeoaltia. q. n. in vncã oquicauh, in tlatzaccan, in tlacuitlapilco, ic nê vncan quipeoaltia, ynjc tetlamamaca, ynjc tetlaoantia, ic quicueptiuh, quipapatlatiuh in itetlaoãtiliz:

So there was singing: there were songs of sadness and tears; or only broken singing, each one as he liked, each outdoing the others. There was the giving of pleasure, of much contentment. There was the encouragement of one another, and tearful greetings. And some only hummed, singing secretly, or did nothing. And some did nothing else but sit content and rejoicing, laughing and making witty remarks, making others burst into laughter as if their sides were sore. They sat exhausted with mirth[11] if they heard something which moved them to or diverted them with laughter. It was as if dogs were barking.[12]

ic necuicatilo, netlaoculcujcatilo, nechoquizcuicatilo, anoço çan cuicaçacamolo, no çac tle queoa, necujcapanauilo, necemeltilo, nececemeltilo, neellaquaoalo, nechoquiztlapalolo, auh in aca çan têtencuicatica, yhichtacacujcatica, aiac ica quichiuhtica: auh cequjn çan qujxcavia in pactoque, im papactoque, vevetzcatoque, camanalotoque, vetzquiztequittoque, iuhqujn inxillã quaquauhti, ommimjctoque in veutzca, yn onoitla quicacque, in tevetzquiti, tevetzquiceuh, iuhqujn tlananalco.

Just so was it done at banquets and feasting, and assemblages and gatherings of people, and their recreation and the giving of dances, etc., when someone had a feast for the child to place it in the cradle, and the place where he was put in the cradle was watched.

Oyvin in muchioaia coaiotl in tecoanotzaliztli, in tecẽtlaliliztli, tenechicoliztli, teceviliztli, teittotiliztli. et.[a] Yn iquac aca quitlaqualiaia in piltzintli, ynjc tlacoçolaquja, tlacoçolaquiloian nepielo.

11. *Veuetzca* in the *Real Palacio MS.*

12. *Tlananal vetzco* in *ibid.*

Thirty-seventh Chapter, in which is mentioned how the festivity was performed; and how the rulers and merchants of old provided banquets, even as to this day they have been doing.

And the manner of doing nowadays: when one holdeth a banquet for the sake of his child, so it is said, they baptize; the head is washed; food is given. So was it done; just so were guests procured and invited; [as] in other banquets were the distribution and the seating according to rank.

So here a little is divulged of the invitation to banquet. But among the rulers, the princes and noblemen, those of illustrious lineage, or when somewhere riches and wealth had been procured, then there was avarice, among the merchants of Pochtlan, [or among the artisans, the craftsmen,][1] the skilled workers, by each group separately there was bringing of goods according to custom; guests were procured, wealth was procured, and there were invitations.

When somewhere there was great congregating, there was indeed trampling, shoving, and crowding. Entry was impossible. There was no recognition of the invited guests. Indeed, there was trampling, crowding, jostling, and shoving to one side. Nowhere were available seating places, spaces to occupy, or seats to use.[2]

However, it was the task, concern, and charge especially of the attendants, those who greeted [the guests] — their great concern — to search and watch well. [The host] commissioned them each as servants, officials, and servitors, so that they could look with care to recognize one, no matter from where the banquet guests, those bidden to the feast, the invited ones, had come.

These ascertained well what could be done for them, so that they might be well received, and that, in the distribution of goods, none might be forgotten. All which they came by and received as gifts,

Injc cempoalli on caxtolli omvme capitulo: vncan moteneoa in cujcujcaliztli catca in quenjn muchioaia, yoã in juh tecoanotzaia in veveintin tlatoque, yoan in pochteca, yn juh noma axcan quichioaia.

Auh in axcã ie ic tlamanj yn iquac aca ypampa tecoanotza ypiltzin, ie mitoa tlaquaatequia, tlaquatequiloia tetlatlaqualtilo, çan ie muchioaia, çan ie iuh coatioaia, çan ie iuh tecoanotzaloia yn oc cequj ypan cooaiotl, tetlacamachiliztli, tetemoliztli.

Jc çan njcan tepiton onmonextia in tecoanotzaliztlatolli, tel in tlatoca, im pilpã, im pillovã, tecpilpan, yn anoço cana netlacamachoian, necuiltonoloia, tlatlamepã, im puchtla, in puchtecapã, toltecaiopan, cecentetl injc netquioaia, ynjc tlamanja, ynjc tlamanca, ynjc cooatioaia, netlacamachoia, necoachioaloia,

in cana vel moveychioa, vel môocça, tzîtzica, câcatzca, aonneaquilo, ahmiximati, yn tlacoanotzali, vel nequequeçalo, nepopotzolo, nexoxocolo, ahujc xoquiooa, âcan veli, in netlaliloia, in ieloaia, in tetlaliloia,

oc cenca iehoan intequjuh, innecuitlavil, ymix intequjuh, vel innecuitlavil, vel mixpetztza, mixpetzoa, quimiîcaniantia, quintetequippantia, quincôcocoltia in techixque, in tetlalique, ynjc iehoan vellachia, teiximati, in cãpa iê ooallaque coame, tlacoanotzalti, tecooaoa,

iehoan vel quiteilhuja, ynic inca nechioaloz, ynjc vel namicozque, aiac ilcaoaloz, ypan tlacotoniz, much intech aciz, yn nemactiz, yn jxquich ic otlatequililoque, in chieltilo, ynjn ca oytoloc, yiemacoz-

1. In the *Real Palacio MS*, the words *anoço tlachichiuhcapan, toltecapan,* follow *puchtecapã.*

2. In *ibid., tel* follows *tetlaliloia.*

all the things which had been set aside and placed apart [by the host] — this hath been told. They would be given tobacco; they would be plied with and provided tobacco; they would be plied with and given flowers. They would be feasted; they would be given to drink. They would be plied with gifts — capes, clothing, vestments, mantles, and breech clouts. And after they had rejoiced for a little while, they would be provided with dancing, and they would set out in the sun for them the flowers, the tobacco, the capes, and the breech clouts, in order to meet the obligations of banqueting, lest it be said [of the host] that the guests were slighted and found discontent there.

que, miietizque, yietilozque, moxochimacazque, moxochitizque, xochimacozque, tlaquazque, atlizque, motlauhtizque, motilmatizque, moquentizq̃, motlaquentizque, motlalpilizq̃, momaxtlatizque: auh çatepã ymellel onquiçaz achitzinca, õmitotizque, ontlatotonizque, yn xochitl, yn jietl, in tilmatli, in maxtlatl, injc conjxtlaoa, cooaiotl, ontlaiolpachivitia, injc amo itolozque, ca çã moiolitlacoa, ahtlavelmati.

And where, in this manner, there was considerable congregating, one augmented, increased, and multiplied the flowers and edible things. It was as if his nourishing goods rested everywhere, covered and spread over the ground, spread all about; as if the food brought there spread souring; all the tamales became mouldy. Musty were the tamales which had been set out.

Auh in cana tel çan ie no yui, vel moveichioa, tonacatica miequia, tlapiviia, ĩ suchitl, in qualonj, iuhqujn papachivi, tlalpan aci, tlalpan actimoteca, tlalpan acitimoteca, yn jcococauh ipalnemoanj, iuhqujn tlaxoxocoiaxtoc, yn vmpa oalquiça tlaqualli, ixqujch pupuxcavi in tamalli, tamalpupuxcauhqui, yn temaco,

But there at the flower places, where the flowers were placed and arranged, the pleasing odor and fragrance spread to all parts. No one wished to be deflated or to lose stature. All persons wished[3] that they be given recognition, fame, and distinction; that they might not, on the contrary, be shamed, receive blame, be embarrassed, confused, belittled, confounded, or excluded from others. Each and everyone paid attention to, took great care with, [and] gloried in his invitations to others. Each and everyone therefore made him resplendent and admirable, each one separately proceeding with exclusive and undivided attention to feasting. They exalted and raised themselves; they surpassed and much exceeded themselves. There was vying and competition.

auh in vmpa yonoia, itecôia, ivipanaloian suchitl, iuhqujn tlavevelixtimanj, tlaavjiaxtimanj, aiac mopatzaoallanj, aiac patzactzintli ieznequi, muchi tlacatl iuh connequi, in ma ça vel onixpatlaoa, onteiooa, onitauhcaiooa, in maca tle ic õmopinauhti, ompinavizcui, ompinaviztlamati, ommomamati, ontzinquiça, ommixtilquetza, ic tevicpa ontzicolo, muchi tlacatl cecentetl ic qujmati, quitlamachia, quiveilia, yn itecoanotzaliz, muchi tlacatl cecẽtetl ic quicueponia, ic tetlamaviçoltia, nonõqua mîcauhtiuh, mîcauhcaiauh in coaiotl, macoctiuh, macoquetztiuh, mopanavitiuh, mopapanavitiuh, nepanaviltoco, nepapanavilo,

On the other hand, one might not wish to do it, preferring not to enter into it, and not desiring it, lest his favors should fall away or fail. And if it was not brought about, everyone wondered, was chagrined, and made much of it. This same one, when he learned of it, became troubled and continued in fear[4] that possibly his efforts would fail, pass away, or miscarry. O that none might ever speak to him of

noçac yn âconnequj, acõâquinequi, aqujn maca quinequi, yn ma vel onvetzi, onquiça itlaocul, auh yn aiamo muchioa muchi tlacatl, motẽmati, tlatẽmati, tlaveymati, çan iê in qujmati, ic motequjpachoa, q'nmattinemi, in quẽmach nenti onquiçaz, contlalcaviz ynetequipachol, macaiac tle ic conitotiaz, conixaoatiaz, conjxmotlatiaz, onahioz, onteputzcomoniloz.

3. In *ibid.*, *ỹ ma ça vel onneci ycoayo* follows *iuh connequi.*

4. *Quimamattinemi* in *ibid.*

it, or reproach or revile him; [that he not be] cried out at, or in bad grace.

And when already it had dawned, guests would be procured; there would be receptions, and there would be invitations to dine. There was much preoccupation and bustling. All was put thoroughly in order. Paths were adorned; the courtyard was prepared; the ground was leveled and smoothed; earth was scattered on it; it was wet and sprinkled; sand was strewn on the surface; reed tips were arranged, suspended, laid out, and draped. There where there was to be dancing they were scattered.[5] This was the task and obligation of the musicians, who were in charge.

auh in ie oallathui coatioaz, nepieloz tecoanotzaloz, cēca neahamanalo, netetequipacholo, tlatlacencaoalo, vchichioalo, ithoalchichioalo, tlatlaixmanalo, tlatlaltemalo, tlatlacujcujoa, tlaatemalo, tlaavililo, tlaatzelhujlo, tlaixxalhujlo, tolquatecteco, tlapipilolo, tolquatectli moteca, mopipiloa, ī vncā netotiloz, tlatzetzelolo, ỹin iehoā intequjuh incocol, cocoltilo, in cujcanjme.

And some plucked and removed the feathers from birds, and dressed them; or slew, singed, and dressed dogs; or prepared and cooked meat, and braised it in pots. Some ground and powdered tobacco and with a heavy straw filled tubes with it. And among the ashes was the labor of the old women. They made tamales and wrapped them in husks. They made tamales using dried grains of maize; they made white ones with beans forming a seashell on top, and meat cooked with maize. They made tamales of meat. Some cooked the tamales in an olla. Some washed the maize grains which had been cooked in lime. Some carried and drew water, or poured it. Some broke up, ground, and pulverized cacao beans. Some mixed cooked maize with chocolate. Some cooked stews, or roasted chilis — different kinds of chilis. All night they remained there. Vigil was kept. They kept watch. There was constant awaiting of the light. They sat holding vigil and chattering.

auh in cequjn tlavivitla, totolhuivitla, totolchichioa, itzcujnmjctia, itzcujnchichinoa, itzcujnchichioa, nacachichioa, nacapaoaci, côcontlatia, in cequjn yietlalchioa, yietlalxaqualooa, yietema teçacatica, auh in nextitlan, iehoan intequjuh yn ilamatque quichioa tamalli, piqui, tamaloa, tlatlaoiotia, quatecuicuilli quichioa, nacatlaoio, nacatamalli quichioa, cequjn tamalpaoaci, cequjn nextamalpaca cequjn açaçaca, atlatlacuj, ateteca, cequjn cacaoatl quixamanja, cacaoateci, tlacuechoa, cequjn tlanextlamalneloa, cequjn molchichioa, chilixca, chichilixca, çan iuh ceiooal in nemoa tozçolo, tozçoa totozçolo tlavilli quiztoc, chachalacoatoc,

And when it had dawned, thereupon there was sweeping in all parts, the laying out of straw mats in all places, and the setting out of seats. Straw beds were spread out, frayed and interwoven at the edges. Already was prepared and lined up all which might be required.

auh yn otlavizcalleoac, njman ie ic tlatlachpano, petlateteco, icpalteteco, çacapechtli moteteca, motevimoloa, tlatenvimollolli, ie ic tlaonoc, ie omocuecuentilli, in ixqujch monenequiz,

Already arranged in order, in their respective places, and assigned to their proper tasks, were those who were to be waiters, who were to serve. No longer was the host, he who had invited the guests, concerned; the care, all provision of comfort to others, had been assumed and taken over for him, so that there would be no neglect or carelessness.

ie omotetecpanque, ie in mâmania, omotêtequippantique, in tlatequipanozque, in tenamiquizque, aocmo quen ipā in tecoanotzqui, in tecoanotzanj, ça ixqujch ynecuitlavil in teca muchioa, ī tepantlatoa, in maca onxiccaoalo, onjxcaoalo,

5. In *ibid.*, *toltzetzelolo* follows *tlatzetzelolo.*

Poised and prepared were the tobacco servers, who provided tobacco; the flower servers, who provided flowers; the servers, those who changed the servings; the bearers. Then there was the chocolate drink maker, who prepared chocolate; who made it foam and froth; and the server of chocolate. Then there were the attendants, those who greeted the guests.

ie vncan ie ic hicac yn teyiemacac in teyieti, in texuchimacac, in texuchiti, tetlamacac, tetlanamjctili, tlanapaloque, njmã ie iehoatl yn achiuhqui, aquetzque, tlaamjnquj, tlaaminanj, yoan in teamacac, njmã ieeoan in techixque, in tetlalique.

But among those who were only commoners, among the poor folk, among the workers of the fields and the water folk, it is already told, only miserably, in poverty and want, were receptions and invitations made. Not as much was offered one as was required and customary; as was possible or of one's capability. Many things were omitted or spoiled. Thus [the feast] was a failure and fruitless when someone received or realized nothing more. Perhaps only old, withered flowers could he find or come by; perhaps only leftover, bitter sauces, and stale tamales and tortillas were offered them.

auh in çan maceoalpã, in çan jcnotlacapã, millacapã, atlacapan, ie omjto çan cococatzĩ, icnoiotica, icnotlacaiotica, in tetlacamacho, in tecoanotzalo, amo cenca onteaxioa yn juh monequj, in ie ivi, in ie vel ivi, in ie teveli, mjiec tlamantli mjxcaoa, ytlacavi, ic tlatlacavi, tlâtlatlacavi, yn aca aoc tle ipan aci, aoc tle ipan mopooa, aço ça xuchiçolli, tlacevilli yn ipanti, in quipantilia, yn ipã mopoa, yoan aço ça mollacaoalli, molchichictli, tamalçolli, tlaxcalçolli, yn nemaquililo,

And if one had been sitting to no purpose and in vain, [he was] only forgotten there for a long time, for a considerable time. And when he grew tired of waiting, he only continued vexing himself, anxious to go, no longer able to endure it, continuing to stir, unable to sit anywhere. His seat was benumbed, stiffened, tired of sitting. So he leaped up, sprang to his feet, and ran off discontented; because perhaps whatever was served had come to an end; the banqueting had increased and grown in numbers, and become crowded. And he simply entered various houses and visited different places, begging and asking alms at each one, etc.

auh intla ça oc nẽ tlalilo, nempancatlalilo, vecauhtica, ieoatica, çan vncã ylcaoalo: auh yn õmopatlac, ça motetectica, yiollo cholotica, injc iaz, aocmo ontlaiecoa mocueptinemj, achcan vel motlalia, itzintepitzquâquauhti, quâquauhtitica, tzintepitzquâquauhtitica, ic choloteoa, moquetzteoa, motlauellaloa, ypampa aço otlatlatlan, acaçoc tlẽ temaconj, omiequix, otonacat, omoquequez in tlacoanotzalli, yoan in çan cacalacquj, tetlatlapalo, motlatlaievi, motlatlaitlanj. et.ª

In this place is only mentioned Two Vulture, which followed and came in second place after One Eagle. All these, the companion day signs in the series, have been chronicled and mentioned here. Of this, Two Vulture, there is no more need to relate anything, just to please; to invent, arrange, and contemplate some brief words. For already hath been mentioned the manner of the separate accounts of all day signs in the second [position]. For indeed all are similar as they proceed and go together there. Similar are their accounts as they advance in order, as all the days accompany one another.

Nican ça onmoteneoa in vme cozcaquauhtli, in contoquilia, in cononcaiotia ce quauhtli, yn jxqujch in, ic omotlatlatolloti nican omoteneuh, ynjc cencalpan tlavica tonalli, yn iehoatl y, 2. cozcaquauhtli, aocmo monequj yn itla ic motlatollotiz, in ça onmoqualittaz, onmovelittaz, ommopipiquiz, ommovevellaliz, itlatlatoltotonti, ca ie omoteneuh in quenamj intlâtlatollo ixqujch ôvme tonalli, ca çan ie much iuhquj, çan much vmpa itztivi, çan much vmpa tlavica, çan ie cẽtetl yn imitoloca, yn juh tetecpantivi, ynjc tlavica cecemilhujtl,

So here we have only added and mentioned as a group the different day signs, which went in their courses as a series, as each day went traveling, following along, and changing: Three Motion, Four Flint

ypampa in çã njcã, tiqujmontecpichoa, tiqujmõcenteneoa yn izquiteme in tonalti, in njcã cencalpan tlaotlatoctia, ynic cecemilhujtl motztiui, motoquilitivi, mopatlativi, in iehoatl Ey olin, 4. tecpatl, 5. quj-

Knife, Five Rain, Six Flower, Seven Crocodile, Eight Wind, Nine House, Ten Lizard, Eleven Serpent, Twelve Death, and Thirteen Deer.[6] When the day sign ended, then —

iavitl, 6. suchitl, 7. cipactli, 8. hecatl, 9. calli, 10. cuetzpalli, 11. coatl, 12. miquiztli, 13. maçatl. 11. 12. 13. yn õtlan jn tonalli, njma.

6. The figures "11. 12. 13." are part of an extraneous 3-13 series in *ibid.*

ILLUSTRATIONS

BOOK IV

Libro. 4°.

Y esta astrologia, o nigromancia fue tomada, y ouo origen de vna muger: que sellama Oxomoco, y de vn hombre que sellama cipactonal. Y los maestros, desta astrologia, o nigromancia: que contauan estos signos, que sellamauan tonalpouhque: pintauan a esta muger oxomoco, y a este hōbre cipactonal: y los ponjā en medio de los libros: donde estauan escritos, todos los caracteres de cada dia; porque dezian: que eran señores desta astrologia, o nigromancia, como principales astrologos: porque la inuentaron, y hizieron esta cuenta, de todos los caracteres.

¶ Capitulo segundo, del segundo signo: llamado ce

oan, iaopan concaoaia: vel oncan mncecahoa, intlatecolo, yniapan locan contocaia. Auh in tlacioatl otlacat: ynjc caltiaia imalac, ichcauh, itzaoalcax, ioan ipopouh, icchpanoaz ipan contemaia ynjnealtilcax, ynj nealtilapaz: yc quinextiaia, in icampa iarj cioatzinth, cancalli ichan: ic canmetlatitlan. Hecuyl nacasco contocaia ynjxic. Auh inin tonalpoalli, iuh mjtoaia: tehoan intlanexhil, ichoan quijtemacaque, in vmentin tencoalo, intoca Oxomoco, ioan cipactonal: in Oxomoco cioatl micquijcujlo aia: auh in Cipactonal oquijchi: in tonalpouhque catca, ynjn tonalamauh quijiollotiaia; ynj mjxiptla, ynepantla quintlaliaia, ynjc quijnjcujlaiaia: ca iuh mjtoaia; vncan tlatoque muchi oa ynjpan ixquijch tonalpoalli.

Injc vme capitulo: itech pa tlatoa, injc vntetl mo:

Page from *Florentine Codex,* Book IV.

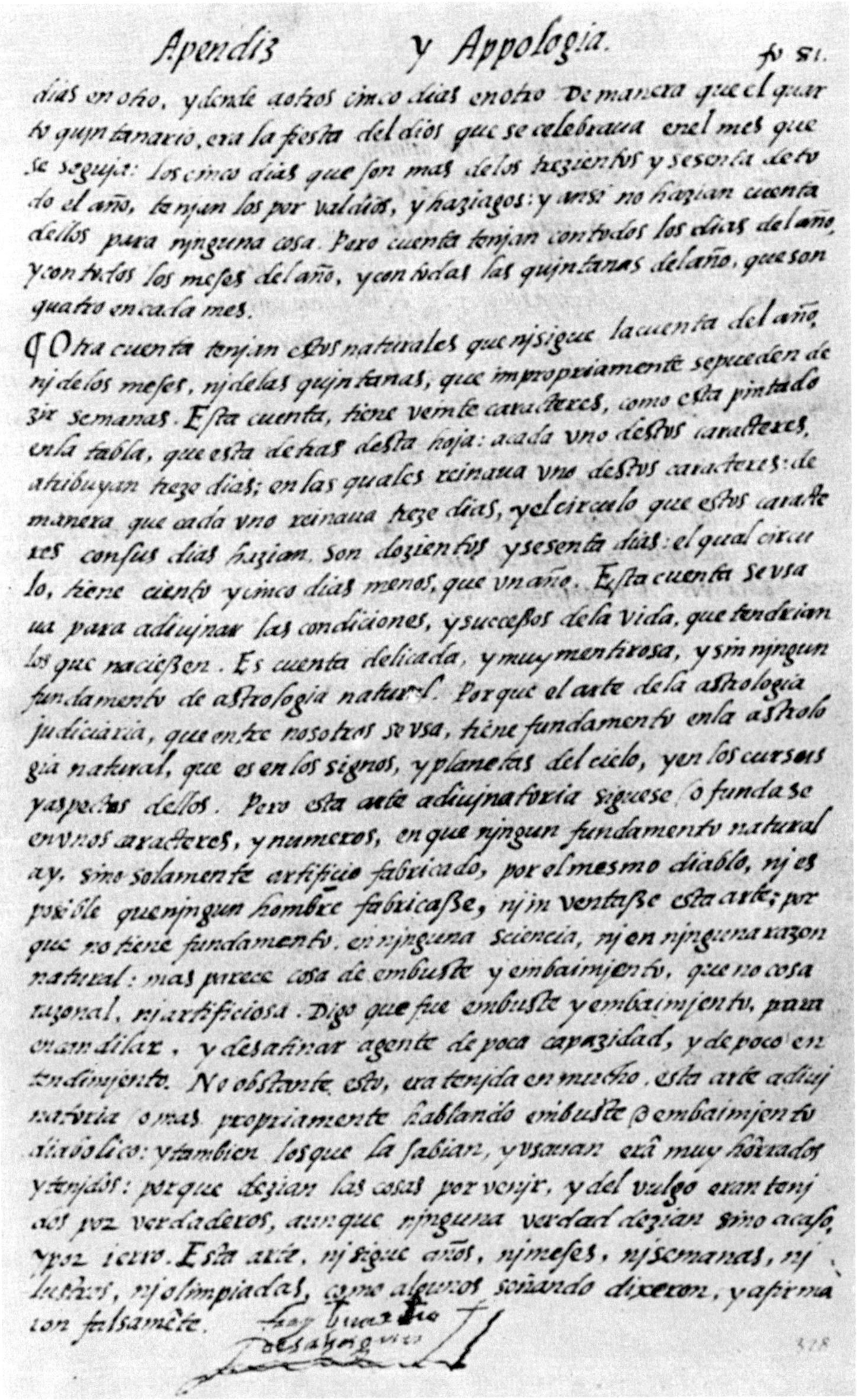

Apendiz y Appologia. fo 51.

dias en otro, y dende a otros cinco dias en otro. De manera que el quar
to quintanario, era la fiesta del dios que se celebraua en el mes que
se seguja: los cinco dias que son mas delos trezientos y sesenta de to
do el año, tenjan los por baldios, y haziagos: y ansi no hazian cuenta
dellos para njnguna cosa. Pero cuenta tenjan con todos los dias del año,
y con todos los meses del año, y con todas las quintanas del año, que son
quatro en cada mes.

¶ Otra cuenta tenjan estos naturales que nj sigue la cuenta del año,
nj delos meses, nj delas quintanas, que impropriamente se pueden de
zir semanas. Esta cuenta, tiene veinte caracteres, como esta pintado
en la tabla, que esta detras desta hoja: a cada vno destos caracteres,
atribuyan treze dias; en las quales reinaua vno destos caracteres: de
manera que cada vno reinaua treze dias, y el circulo que estos caracte
res con sus dias hazian, son dozientos y sesenta dias: el qual circu
lo, tiene ciento y cinco dias menos, que vn año. Esta cuenta se vsa
ua para adiujnar las condiciones, y sucessos dela vida, que tendrian
los que naciessen. Es cuenta delicada, y muy mentirosa, y sin njngun
fundamento de astrologia natural. Porque el arte dela astrologia
judiciaria, que entre nosotros se vsa, tiene fundamento en la astrolo
gia natural, que es en los signos, y planetas del cielo, y en los cursos
y aspectos dellos. Pero esta arte adiujnatoria siguese o funda se
en vnos caracteres, y numeros, en que njngun fundamento natural
ay, sino solamente artificio fabricado, por el mesmo diablo, nj es
posible que njngun hombre fabricasse, nj inuentasse esta arte; por
que no tiene fundamento, en njnguna sciencia, nj en njnguna razon
natural: mas parece cosa de embuste y embaimjento, que no cosa
razonal, nj artificiosa. Digo que fue embuste y embaimjento, para
encandilar, y desatinar a gente de poca capazidad, y de poco en
tendimjento. No obstante esto, era tenjda en mucho. esta arte adiuj
natoria o mas propriamente hablando embuste o embaimjento
diabolico: y tambien los que la sabian, y vsauan eran muy honrados
y tenjdos: porque dezian las cosas por venjr, y del vulgo eran tenj
dos por verdaderos, aunque njnguna verdad dezian sino acaso,
y por ierro. Esta arte, nj sigue años, nj meses, nj semanas, nj
lustros, nj olimpiadas, como algunos soñando dixeron, y afirma
ron falsamente. fray bernardino de sahagun

328

Page from the Appendix of Book IV, with Sahagún's signature.

— After Paso y Troncoso

1. Oxomoco and Cipactonal (Chapter 1). 2-5. One Ocelot and following signs (Chapter 2). 6. One Deer (Chapter 3). 7. Mother with child (Chapter 3). 8, 9. Two Rabbit: drunkenness and drunkards (Chapters 4, 5).

— *After Paso y Troncoso*

10-13. Two Rabbit: drunkenness and drunkards (Chapters 4, 5). 14, 15. One Flower: musicians, entertainers, embroiderers (Chapter 7).

— After Paso y Troncoso

16-20. One Flower: musicians, entertainers, embroiderers (Chapter 7). 21. Seven Rain (Chapter 8). 22, 23. Eight Flower and bathing of child (Chapter 8).

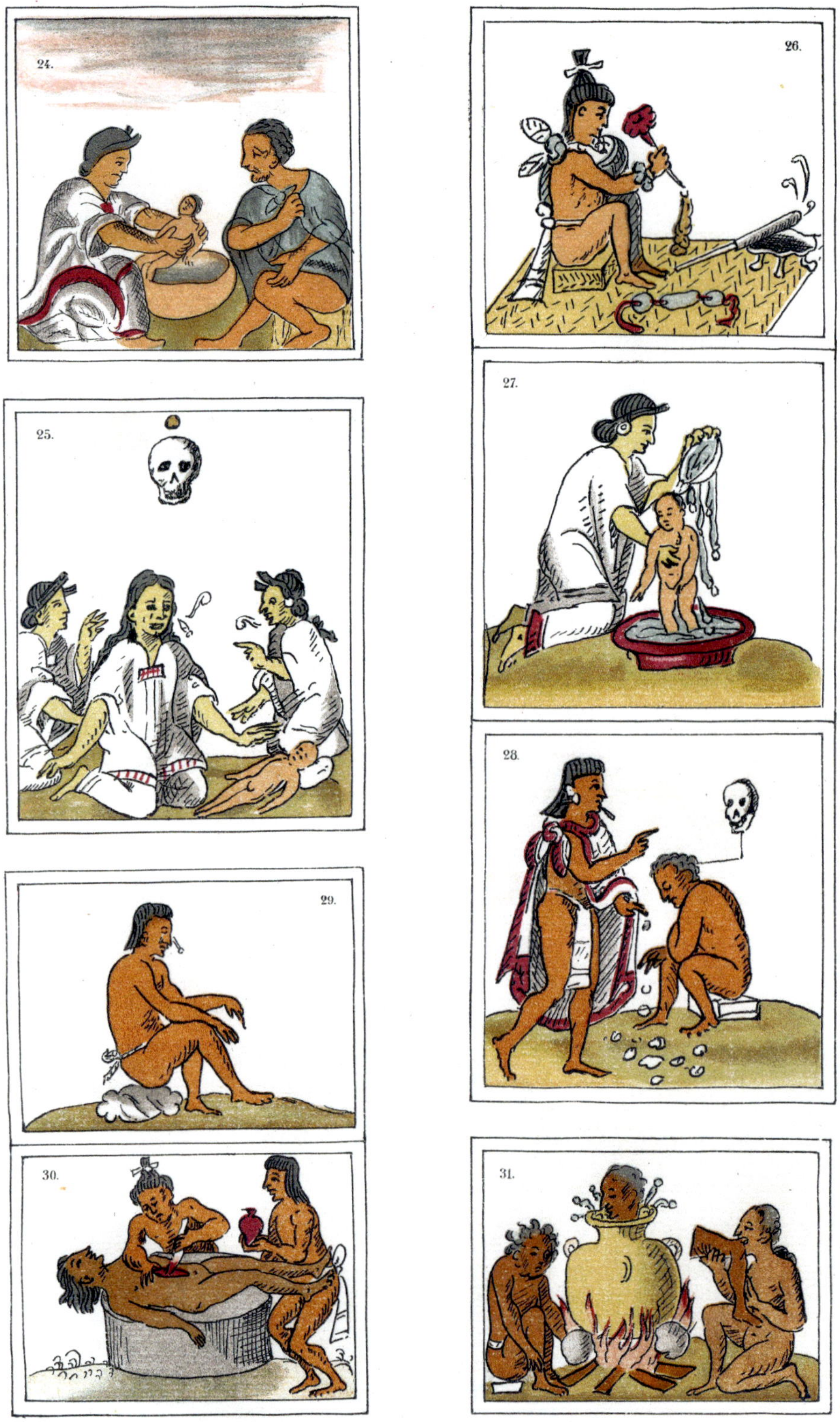

— *After Paso y Troncoso*

24. Eight Flower: bathing of child (Chapter 8). 25-31. One Death and associated good and ill fortune (Chapter 9).

— *After Paso y Troncoso*

32. Eight Water (Chapter 10; the text correctly refers to Eight Reed). 33, 34. Nine Ocelot and bathing of child (Chapter 10). 35, 36. Ten Eagle and bathing of child (Chapter 10). 37. One Rain (Chapter 11). 38. Descent of the "Goddesses" (Chapter 11). 39. Imprisoned evildoers (Chapter 11). 40. Bathing of child (Three Crocodile; Chapter 11).

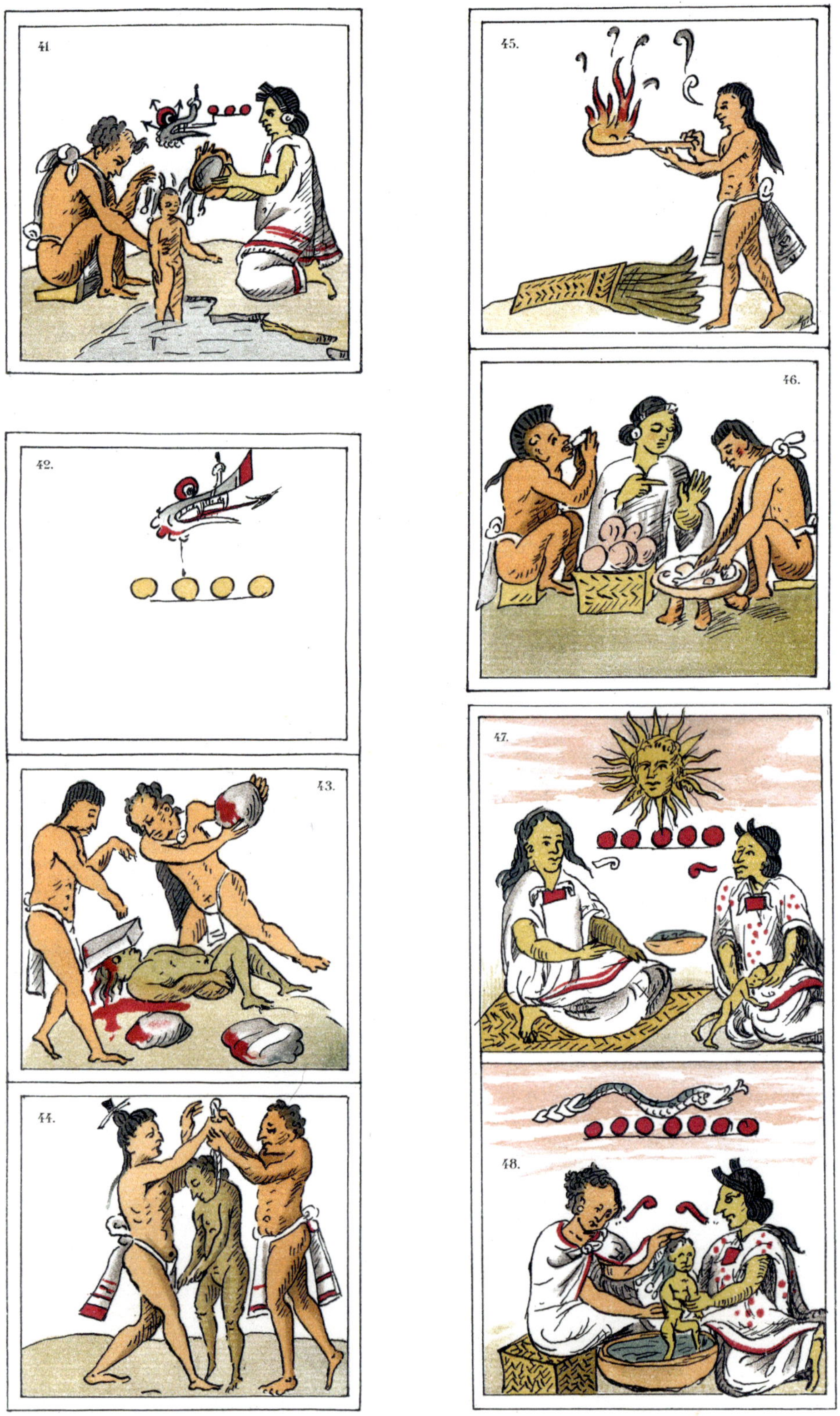

— *After Paso y Troncoso*

41. Bathing of child (Three Crocodile; Chapter 11). 42-46. Four Wind and associated scenes (Chapter 12). 47. Macuilxochitl (Chapter 13). 48. Seven Serpent (Chapter 13).

— After Paso y Troncoso

49-51. Eight Death and Nine Deer, and bathing of child (Chapter 13). 52. Ten Rabbit (Chapter 14). 53-55. One Grass and its miseries (Chapter 15).

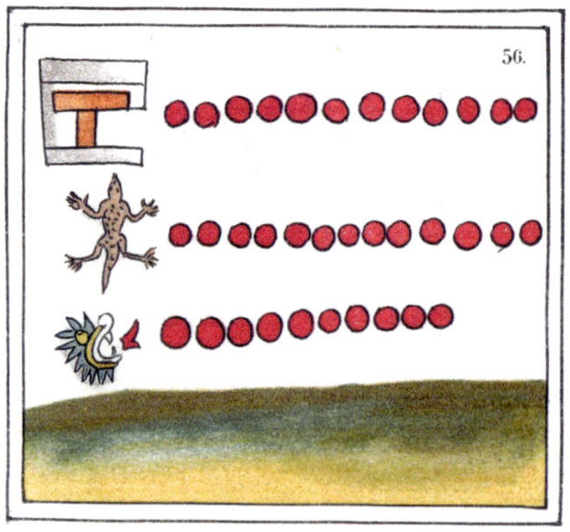

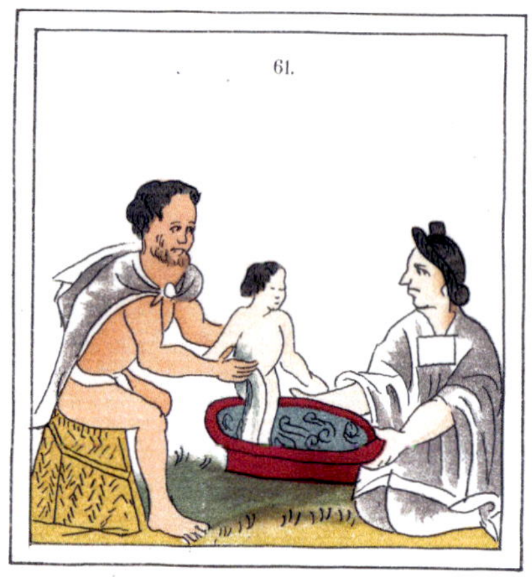

— *After Paso y Troncoso*

56. Twelve House, Thirteen Lizard, and Ten Crocodile (Chapter 15). 57. Uitzilopochtli (Chapter 17). 58, 59. Merchants (Chapter 18). 60, 61. Three Deer and bathing of child (Chapter 19). 62. Uitzilopochtli (Chapter 20).

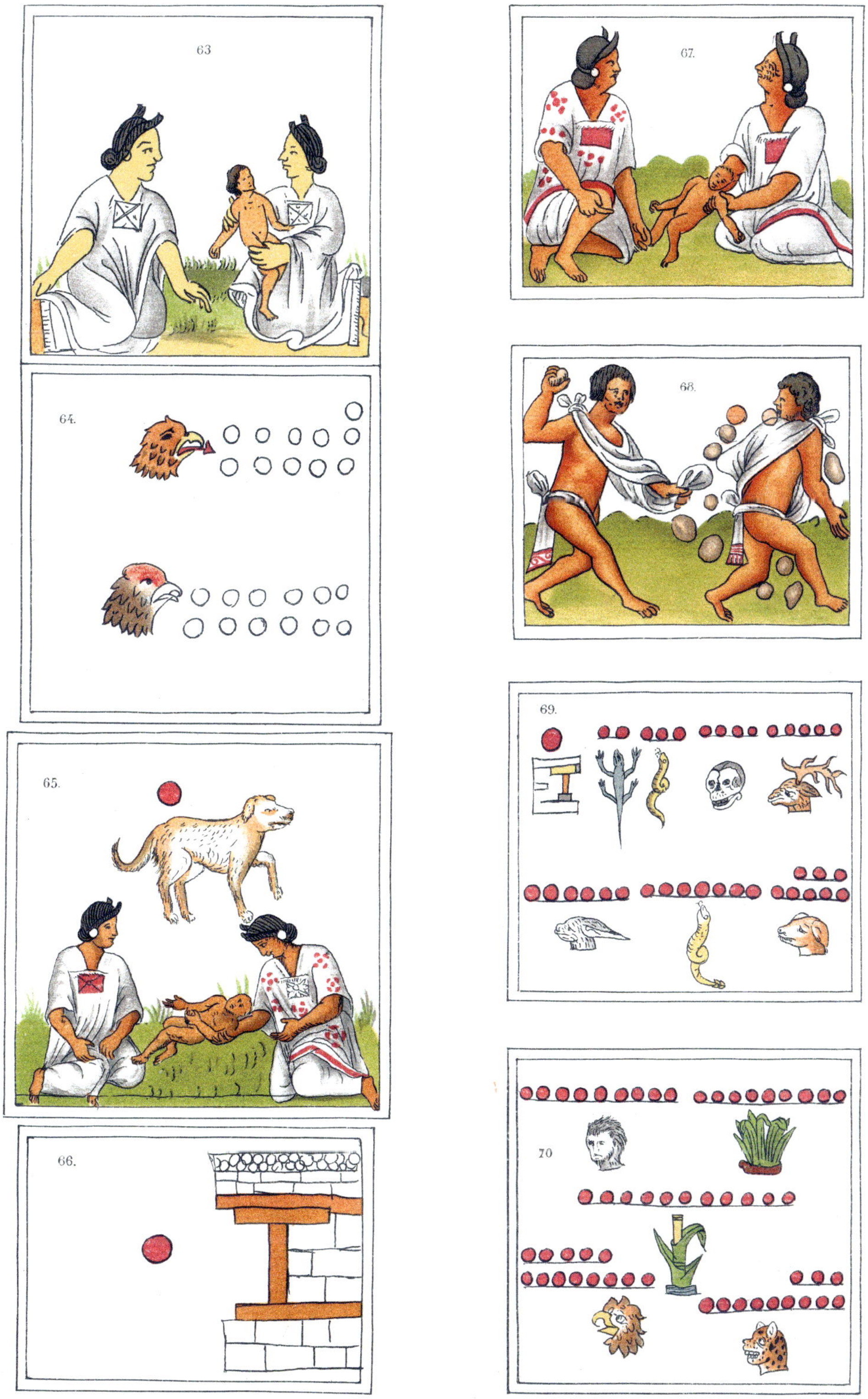

— *After Paso y Troncoso*

63. Women and child (Chapter 20). 64. Eleven Eagle and Twelve Vulture (Chapter 20). 65. One Dog (Chapter 25). 66. One House (Chapter 27). 67, 68. Women and child; men brawling (Chapter 28). 69, 70. One House and following day signs (Chapter 28).

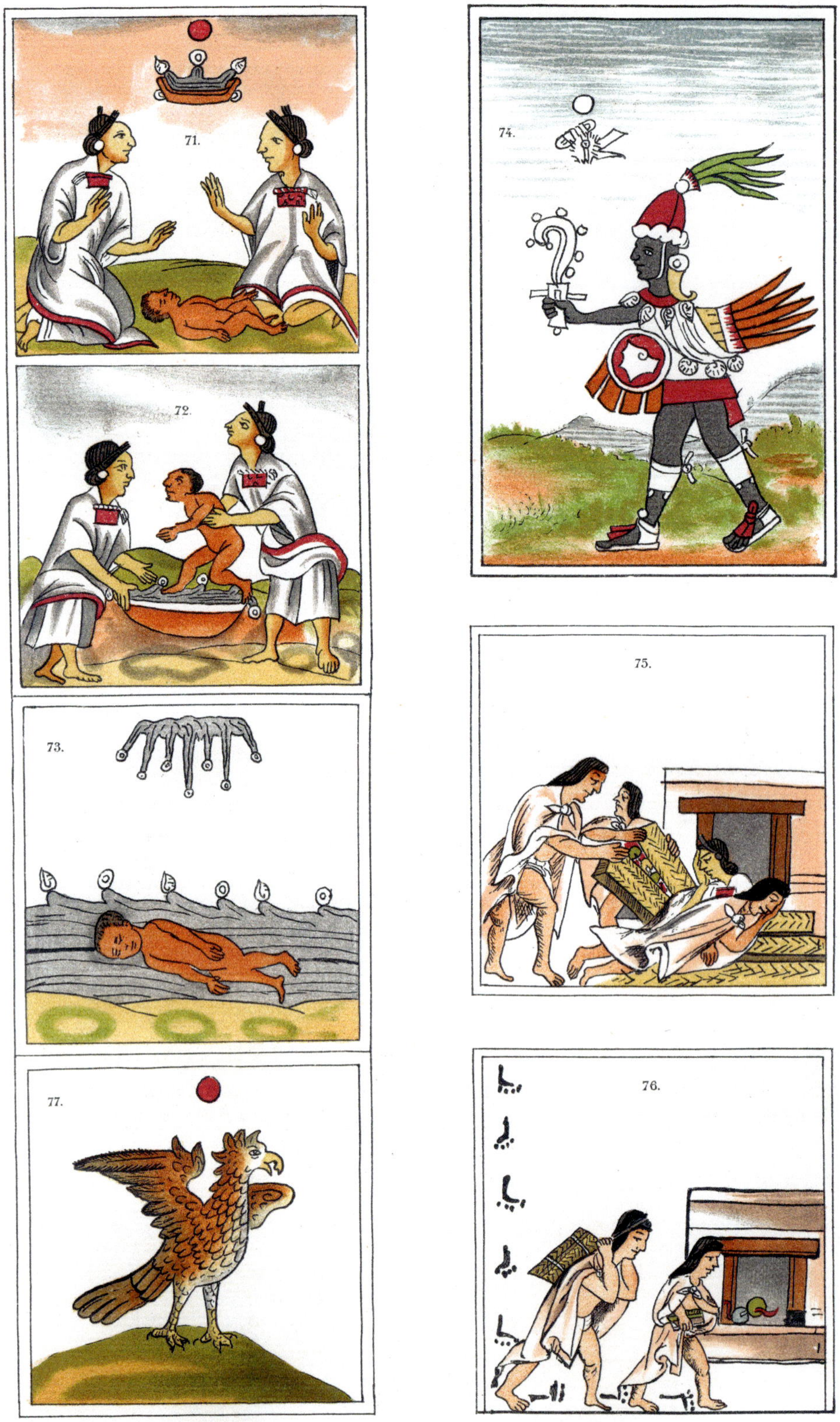

— After Paso y Troncoso

71, 72. One water and bathing of child (Chapter 30). 73. [Eleven] Rain (Chapter 30). 74. One Wind and Quetzalcoatl (Chapter 31). 75, 76. Thieves (Chapter 32). 77. One Eagle (Chapter 33).

— *After Paso y Troncoso*

78-82. Descent of the "Goddesses" and attendant ceremonies (Chapter 33). 83-85. Visit to the recently delivered mother (Chapter 35).

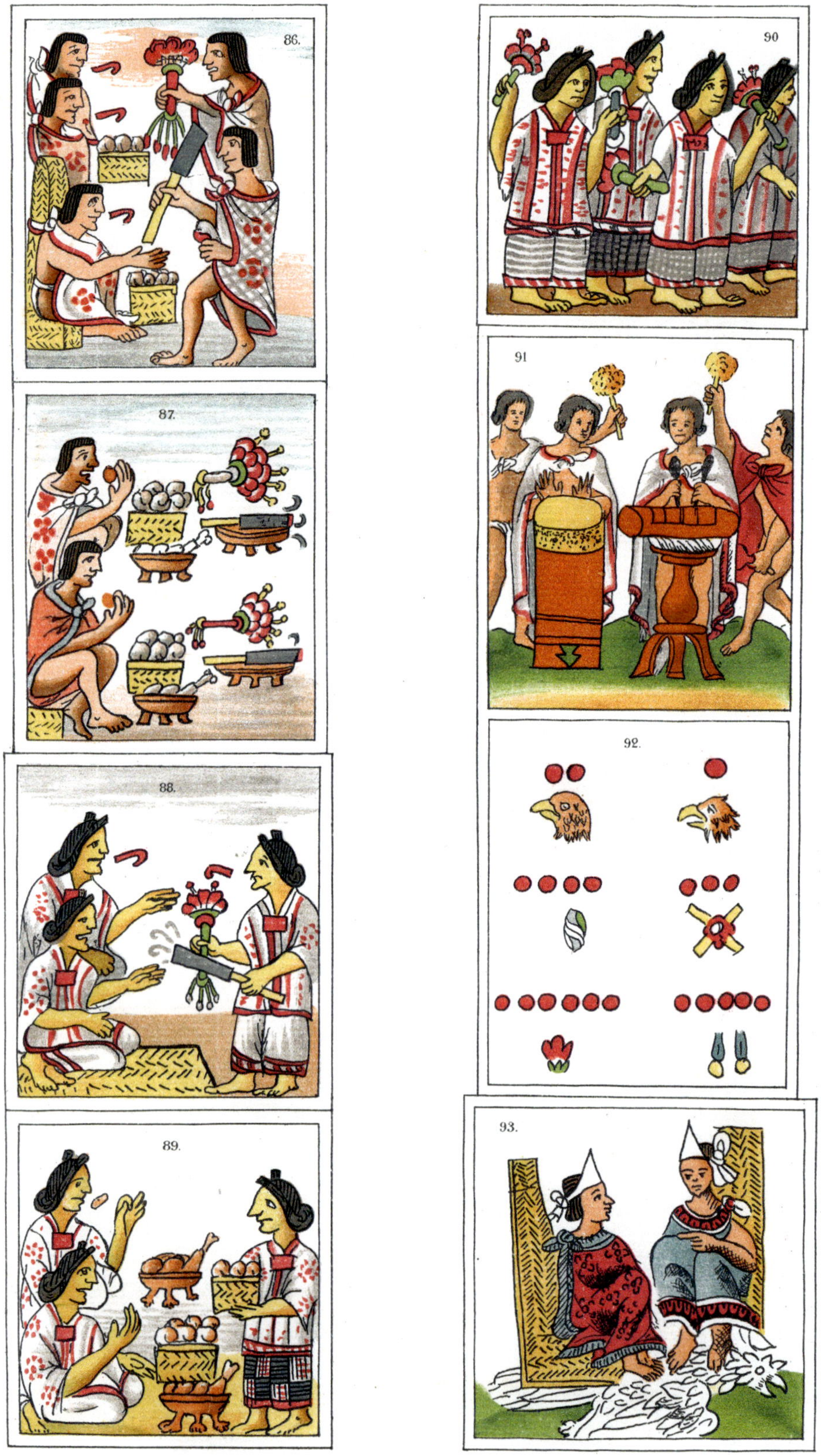

— *After Paso y Troncoso*

86-91. Feast in honor of a new-born child (Chapter 37). 92. Two Eagle and following day signs (Chapter 37). 93. One Rabbit's good fortunes (Chapter 38).

— After Paso y Troncoso

94-101. One Rabbit's good fortunes (Chapter 38).

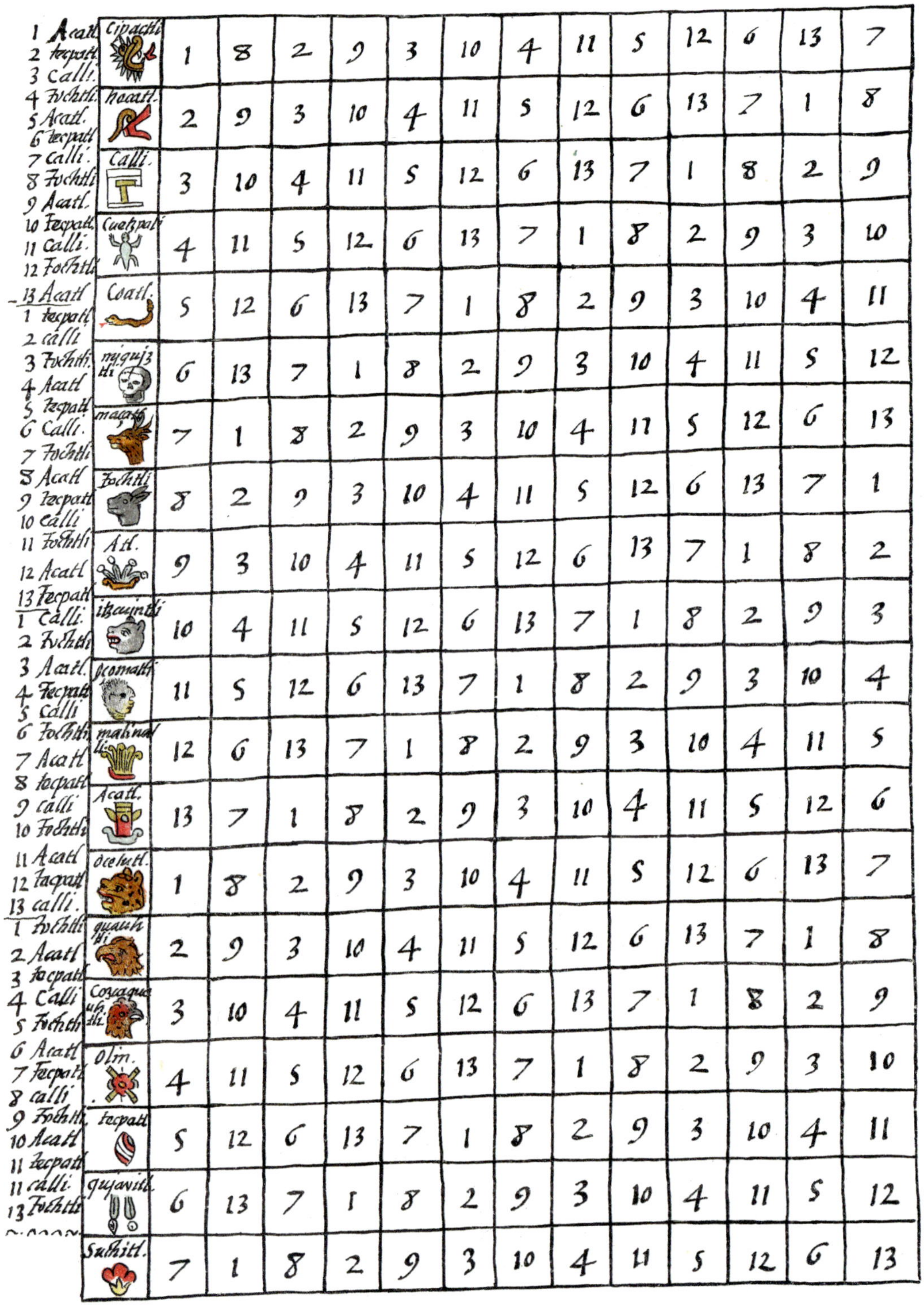

— *After Paso y Troncoso*

102. First chart for reckoning the day sign count (Appendix).

— *After Paso y Troncoso*

103. First half of second chart for reckoning the day sign count (Appendix).

— *After Paso y Troncoso*

104. Second half of second chart for reckoning the day sign count (Appendix).

ILLUSTRATIONS

BOOK V

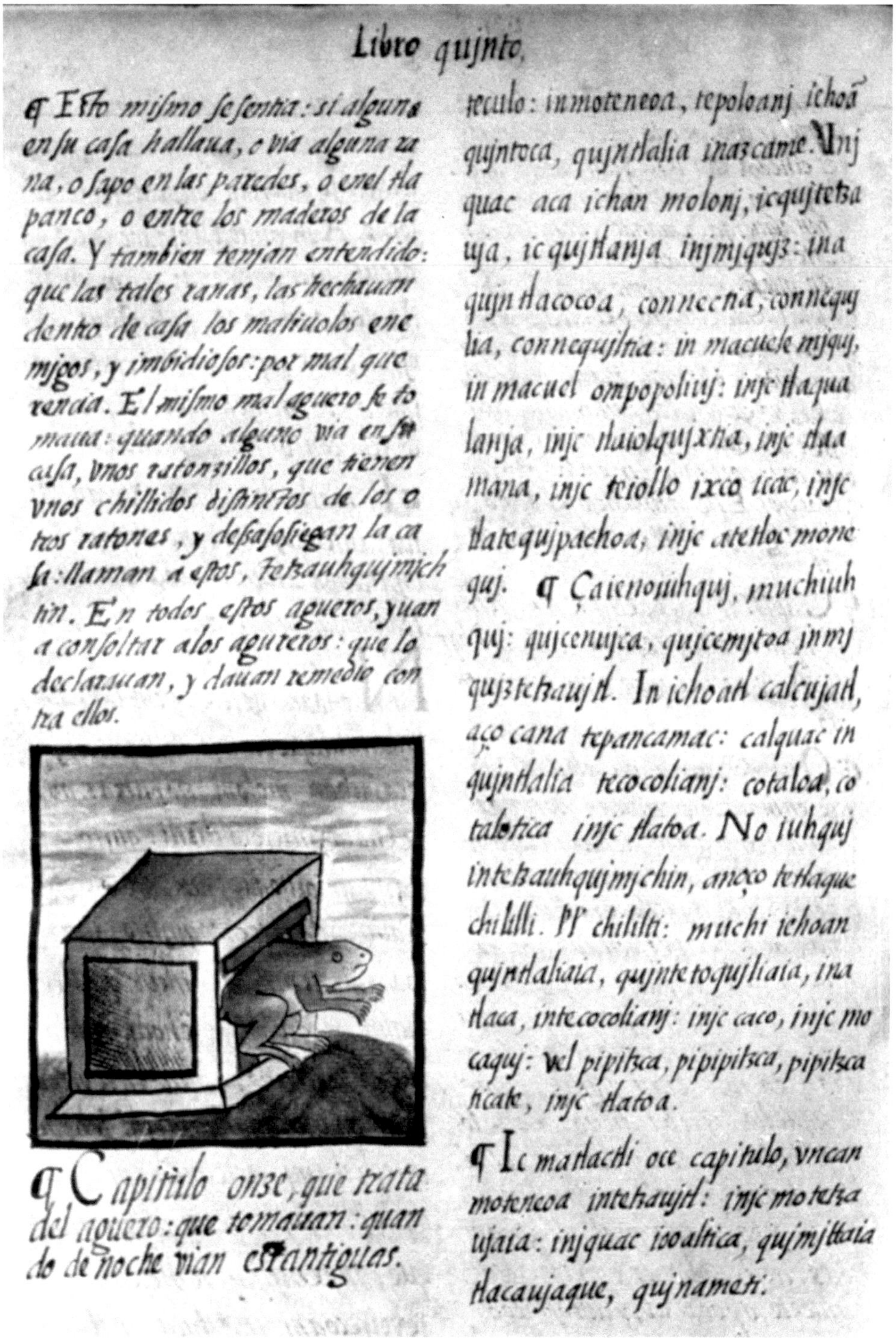

Libro quinto.

¶ Esto mismo se sentia: si alguno en su casa hallaua, o via alguna rana, o sapo en las paredes, o en el tlapanco, o entre los maderos de la casa. Y tambien tenjan entendido: que las tales ranas, las hechauan dentro de casa los malüolos enemigos, y imbidiosos: por mal que rencia. El mismo mal aguero se tomaua: quando alguno via en su casa, vnos ratonzillos, que tienen vnos chillidos distinctos de los otros ratones, y dessasossiegan la casa: llaman a estos, tetzauhquimichtin. En todos estos agueros, yuan a consoltar alos agueros: que lo declarauan, y dauan remedio contra ellos.

¶ Capitulo onze, que trata del aguero: que tomauan: quando de noche vian estantiguas.

teculo: in motenehoa, tepoloanj ichoa quintoca, quintlalia inazcame. Vnjquac aca ichan molonj, icquitetzauja, ic quitlanja injmjquiz: inaquin tlacocoa, connectia, connequjlia, connequjltia: in macuele mjquj, in macuel ompopolivj: injc tlaqualanja, injc tlaiolqujxtia, injc tlaamana, injc teiollo ixco icac, injc tlatequjpachoa, injc atetloc monequj. ¶ Çaienouhquj, muchiuhquj: qujcenujca, qujcemjtoa jnmjqujztetzaujtl. In ichoatl calcujatl, aço cana tepancamac: calquac in quintlalia tecocolianj: cotaloa, cotalotica injc tlatoa. No iuhquj intetzauhqujmjchin, anoço tetlaquechilitli. pc chilitli: muchi ichoan quintlaliaia, qujntetoqujliaia, inatlaca, intecocolianj: injc caco, injc mocaquj: vel pipitzca, pipipitzca, pipitzcaticate, injc tlatoa.

¶ Ic matlactli oce capitulo, vncan motenehoa intetzaujtl: injc motetzaujaia: injquac ioaltica, qujmjttaia tlacaujaque, qujnametl.

Page from *Florentine Codex,* Book V.

— After Paso y Troncoso

1. The howling beast (Chapter 1). 2. The night axe (Chapter 3). 3. The owl (Chapter 4). 4. The frog (Chapter 10). 5. The towering man (Chapter 11). 6. Cuitlapanton (Chapter 13). 7. The corpse in wrappings for the dead (Chapter 13). 8. Placing maize in the cooking pot (Appendix, Chapter 4). 9. The elder brother drinks before the younger (Appendix, Chapter 6).

Thirty-eighth Chapter, which telleth of the twentieth and closing sign, called One Rabbit. It is said that those then born were ample providers, good workers, and rich.

— One Rabbit set in, with which ended all the twenty houses of day signs carried together in groups of thirteen.

It was said that this One Rabbit was a good day sign. He who was then born would be rich. There was what he might eat. But his wealth he did not just appropriate without purpose, nor fail to take; neither did it just fall to him. He took to everything and exerted his utmost efforts, such as not lying down, hurrying, and hastening.

Never suffering from being defrauded, not losing anything through mismanagement, he sought diligently in all parts for advantageous dealings, and continued to seek them out. He bought all things in all places, all things for gaining a livelihood. He was very diligent, careful, and vigilant. He sought and dedicated himself not to only one thing. He never tired; he was not lazy nor listless. Indeed, he attended to his affairs day and night. Not vain nor futile was his work. He labored industriously to gain sustenance, his daily bread, his trail rations, his livelihood, his maintenance, the source of life, the means of living, and provisions for traveling. He looked to the future and saw before him that sometimes poverty and misery would develop for and strike him. He would meet it.

He saved up wealth to protect and divide justly among his children.

Everything frightened him, lest sometime something be brought upon him: gossip, calumny, slander, perjury, covetous deeds, greedy dealings. Perhaps they might thus snare or snatch something of his goods and property. They might covet or seek after it. Or in something justice might be demanded; there would be accusations, and it would be made public. Then he might have to pay; he would lose

Injc cempoalli on caxtolli vmey capitulo: ytechpa tlatoa, ynic cempoaltetl: yoan in ça ontlatzacuja machiotl yn itoca ce tochtli: quilmach yn aquique vncan tlacatia cenca motlaecoltianj, tlatequipanoanj mocuiltonoanj.

Ic oalmoquetza yn ce tochtli yc ontlamj in izquitetl cempoalcalli tonalli, yn matlatlaquilhujtl vmeEy tlauica,

mjtoa injn ce tochtli qualli tonalli, yn aqujn vncã tlacatia mocuiltonoanj, õca quiquanj, auh amo çan quinencuj, câcuj, amo çã ixpanvetzi yn inecujltonol, vel ixqujch caana, ixquich itlapal quichioa, iuhqujn âmo teteca, vel õpilcatoc, õtlalhujtoc,

njmã âmonenencaoa, âmoxixiccaoa, vel noviiampa mixpetzoa, mixpepetztza, tlacentoca, tlacencoltoca yn jxqujch netlaiecoltiloni, cenca yiehel, motlacujtlavianj, cochiçanj, tlâcelianj, âçan centlamãtli in qujxtoca, yn ipan mixpooa, njmã âmo ciiauhcanequinj, âmo tlatziuhcanequini, amo tlaquelchioanj, vel quitemachia in cemilhujtl, in ceiooal, amo nẽvetzi, amo avetzi, in itlapaliuiz, vellaixnextia, injc qujtemoa, ycochca, yneuhca, yn icemilhujtiaia, yn iotlatocaia, yn inẽca, yn nẽcaiotl, in nemoanj, in nemoalonj, yn otlatoconj, vehca õmotlachielia, ixpan õtlachie, yn ma quenmanjã ytech eoa, itech motzotzo, qujmonamjcti netoliniliztli, icnoiotl,

qujtetzontia, qujntlapachilhuja, qujntlatlamachia ympilhoã

much iê in qujmauhtia in ma quẽmanjan itla ipan oalla tlacatlatolli, tetlatoleviliztli, tetlatolchichivililiztli, tetlatoltequililiztli, netlaixtoquililiztli, tetlaixtoquililiztli, yn aço itla ic quitzouizque, quitzouilizque yaxca, ytlatquj, quixtocazque, qujxtoquilizque, anoce itla ic teilhujloz, tlatoleviloz, teixpannemitiloz, vncan tlacalaquiz, tlapopoliviz, tlaixpoliviz, tlaamoiaoaz, can nen onmanaz, can onmaiaviz, can onmaçooaz,

all, lose his property, scatter it. Where could he save himself, find repose, or extend his arm? What could he quickly take? Well did he save, hide, and store his sustenance for himself.

tlê concuitivetziz, vel motêtetzõtia, monepacholtia, quitetzontlalia, yn inenca,

Everything frightened him lest pestilence sometime come upon him: fearful sickness, the gout, lameness, cramps, paralysis; sickness of the eyes — ophthalmia, or crossed eyes, or watering, withered, or shattered eyes, and blindness; or cancer,[1] piles, some major corruption; or the king's evil; or inflammation of glands might settle in and affect his throat, scarring and marking it;[2] or a bloody flux and loss of blood;[3] or a sore throat, and hoarseness; or pustules, etc.; or possession by a demon and insanity.

muchi iê ynjc motlamauhcaittilia in ma quẽmã ipan oalla in temuxtli, hecatl, in temamauhti cocoliztli, in coaciviztli, in cocototzaviliztli, in oapaoaliztli, quâquauhtiliztli, yn anoço ixcocoliztli, ijchichitinaliztli, in teixcuecueponi, in teixcatatili, teixpatzauh, teixcacaxo, tlaiooaiantetlali, anoço qualocatl, xochiciviztli, itla veypalanaliztli, anoço toçanpotzalli, coatetl in tequechtlanmotlalia motlattilia, tequechtitilo tequechtitiqujlo, tequechmomotzolo, anoço tlaelli, ezcuicuiltic, anoço tozcamiiaoaciviliztli, yçaoaquiliztli, nanaoatl. et.[a] anoço tetechquineoaliztli, iollotlavelilocatiliztli.

This man was the one on whom these ailments did not settle; who benefited and provided for himself, and provided for and benefited his children and grandchildren; who lived in wealth.

Jehoatl in ynic âmotlatlalia, ynic mocnelia, ynjc monavilia, yoan qujnnavilia, quĩmjcnelia yn ipilhoã, yn jxvioan, ynjc motlâtlamachitinemj,

And if he were a gardener, a worker of the soil, a laborer, one who tilled the land, one who broke and reworked the fields, he planted and sowed all things on his land, in his garden, in his worked fields. And when [the seed] had sprouted, and formed shoots, he hoed the ground; he built up mounds; he broke the clods of earth, and went stirring up the dust.

auh intla millacatl, tlalchiuhquj, elimjcqui, elimiquinj, çacamo, çacamoanj, ixquich qujtoca, ontlatepeoa, yn imilpan, yn imilco yn icuentla, auh yn oixhoac, in ie papatlacatoc, ytoc, tlapupuxoa, tlatlalhuja, tlacuentlapana, ixtlalilhujuhtinemj;

And if it were irrigated land, he opened his plot for irrigating. And if he had swamp land, and were a dweller in swamp country, he cultivated and planted maize for tamales, transplanted and set out chilis, and fertilized the land.

auh intla amilli, câatlaxilia, auh intla chiname, chinãpanecatl, cintamaloa, cintamalaquja, chilteca, chilquetza, tlaçoquipachoa,

After this, he witnessed the successful results of his fatigue and pains. Thus he attained his wealth and his contentment. When he had realized and procured his products of the soil, he was content, rejoicing, and happy.

ie vncan jnin quitta, yn amo nenvetzi, yn iciaviz, yn inecôcol, ynjc qujtta ynecuiltonol, yneiollaliliz, yn otlamuchiuh yn oquittac itonacaiouh, moiollalia, paqui, vellamati,

He stored it; everything he stored up: his ears of maize, black, white, yellow, or red. And when he harvested and gathered it, he put aside, sorted out, and chose the large ears of maize. Some he formed into clusters, separate clusters; some he formed into caltrops. On the beams at the front of the house he hung the bunches and the caltrop-shaped bunches.

tlacalaquia, ixqujch quicalaquja yn icin in iauitl, yn iztac, in coztic, in xiuhtoctli, auh in iquac pixca, in tlacuicui nononqua quitema, quicẽquixtia, quipepena, in vevej cintli, cequi cochollalia, côocholalia, cequi colchicaloa, ycalixquac qujpipiloa yn iochol, yn iolchical, iuhqujn tlapipilcac ocholli, yn olchicalli, auh in molquitl nonqua quitema, yoan im popoiotl

1. *Cualocatli*, in Sahagún (Garibay ed.), Vol. IV, p. 331, is *"Niguas, parásitos que se introducen bajo la piel. Dermatophylus pulex penetrans L."*

2. *Motlattilia, tequechtitilo* does not appear in the corresponding *Real Palacio MS* text.

3. *Ezcuicuiltic* in *ibid.;* it is followed by *anoço amintli, neaminaliztli* (possibly meaning "or a bad taste in the mouth"; cf. *amina*).

It was as if the clusters and caltrop bunches hung suspended. And the undeveloped ears he laid apart, as well as the smutty ones. He kept all, he left nothing. He removed all the grains of maize, and the various things which were with the grains of maize.

And the harvesters, those who gathered the harvest, he provided with and gave bunches of ears of maize. He garlanded them with clusters of ears of maize. The harvesters, those who harvested for him, were provided and given clusters of ears of maize; they were garlanded with clusters of ears of maize, and with [single] ears.

And some walked about as gleaners. They gleaned, gathered, and searched for themselves the forgotten ears of maize, or the small, undeveloped ones, which the harvesters had not gathered. They hurried to all places[4] and went everywhere, feeling with their feet among the dry maize stalks, the leaves, and the husks, in order to place their gleanings in the fold of their capes.

And the owner of the garden then filled storage bins. He packed and filled his storage bins with his amaranth,[5] his *chía,* his beans. First he threshed, purified, sorted, and gathered them up, and winnowed and fanned out the chaff; he let the wind carry off and scatter the impurities. He threw away the dirt among the bean pods. Then he filled up each vessel. He filled the vessels with his food, sealed them up separately, etc.

atle quixcaoa, tlacētoca much cohoia, yn izquitetl ytech caca tlaolli,

auh in pixcaque in quipixquilia, quimochavia, quimocholtia, quimocholcozcatia, mochavia, mocholtia, mocholcozcatia, mocĩcozcatia, in pixcaque, in tepixquilique,

auh cequjn onnemj motitixique, qujmotitixia, qujmocuicuilia, qujmotetemolia in çan oilcaoaloc cintli, anoço molquitotonti, in amo quicuicuique pixcaque, tlacencoltoca, qujpanocvitivi, tlatlacxitemotivi in ooaquauhtitlan izoatitlan, totomochtitlan, ic moxixiquipilquentia yn jntitix,

auh in mile çatepan tlacuezcõtema, tlacuecuezcontema, tlacuezcomatema, yn iiaouh, yn ichie, ym ieuh achtopa quivitequi, quiiectia, quitlaiectilia, quitlacuicuilia, câcana, quehecaquetza, quêcatoctia, quitepeoa in polocatl, quitlaça yn exotlaçolli, çatepã tlacocõtema, qujcocõtema, quipepepechoa, in ie ixqujch itonacaiouh. et.[a].

4. After *qujpanocvitivi* the *Real Palacio MS* reads: *in milli noviyã tlaxexelotiui . . .* This would change it to read: *they hurried to all places and went from field to field. Everywhere they went stirring, feeling with their feet . . .*

5. *Ivauh* in *ibid.;* otherwise (*iiaouh*), his aromatic herbs.

Thirty-ninth Chapter, which speaketh of all the day signs (those which have been mentioned).

Here, in only a word, a statement, is made plain, as hath many times been told, the manner of its significance, its account, exposition, history, and discussion; and in what manner the sign of each day came to pass, how they proceeded in order, so following along; those which came good; and the evil, of unfavorable time. For not for the first time, nor the second; not for the four hundredth, nor the eight hundredth time, nor for countless times, but for very many times hath it been told of the various groups of day signs, the twenty which went beginning and becoming the starters. In many places they have been discussed. For all these same ones proceeded, changing places, changing one by one; substituting, substituting one by one.

The order, the designations, of the twenties, or scores, all remained the same. But each one fell once, each one took the lead once. Sometimes it became good; sometimes it was not harmful, not complete destruction. Sometimes it fell in two ways, they said: perhaps good, perhaps evil; if good, also perhaps evil, or only indifferent. And elsewhere are told the good aspects and characteristics of each of the day signs which accompanied it.

All that then happened hath been told. If it was a good time, they then bathed the one born at this time. But if not, they still sought one of the day signs on which he was to be bathed. So the old men sought to make it good — the little, shriveled, old men, wicked and vile, decrepit, stupid, and foolish, who came to live in obscurity and darkness,[1] in practising deceit, and losing their reason, living in error, crazed by omens.

Wherefore here we quickly come to agreement so that we shall not afflict one's ears without need, or trouble them with useless talk; nor be repulsive, opinionated, and headstrong. As food is considered a discourse, which, [if] all is repeated, [is like food which is] soft, warm, savory, pleasing to smell; and crude, hard, rough, coarse, cooled, chilled, cold, and

Injc cempoalli on caxtolli õnavi capitulo: yntechpa tlatoa yn ixquich yn machiotl (yn omoteneuhque).

Nican ça cencamatica, cententica onmonextia, in quenjn cenca ie mjiecpa omjto, yn juhquj inenezca, ytoloca, yteneoaloca, ytlatollo, ytlatlatollo: yn quenamj cecemjlhujtl tonalli ipan muchioa, in juh tecpantivi, yc otlatoca: yn vncan qualtitiuh, yoan yn amo qualli, in amo ieccan, ca amo qujn ceppa, amo qujn vppa, amo qujn centzompa amo qujn vntzompa, amo qujn tlapoalpa: ca cenca ic vel mjiecpa omjto, in jzqujcalpan izqujtctl tonalli cempooaltctl in tlapeoaltitiliuj, in tonalpeuhcaiome muchioa: ca mjieccan otlatlatolloaque, ca çan ie much iehoan, çan mopatlativi, mopapatlativi, mopatilitivi, mopapatilitivi, mopatilicavi

yn jzqujteme cempoaltetl, cempoalteme: in tlatecpantin, tlateneoaltin much iuhticate: ca muchtin ceceppa vetzi, ceceppa teiacana: in quenman qualtia, in quenmã amo itlacavi, cempopolivi, in quenman vme vitz quitoa, yn aço qualli âcanoçomo qualli, intla qualli, intlacanoçomo qualli, yn anocê çan iliviz, yoan in cequi omito, in vel nenezqui, yn juh ynneixcavil cecemilhuitl ic tlavica tonaltin,

ca omuch mjto in tlein vncan muchichioaia, intla qualcan, njman caltiaia yn ipã otlacat. auh intlacamo, oc quitemoaia in catlehoatl tonalli ipan maltiz yn iuhquj ic quiquallittaia vevetque, veventoton, vevenpipil, tlahelvevetq̃, avilvevetque, aoc quimati vevetque, nextecuilvevetque, totumputlavevetque: yn onemico mixtecomac, tlaiooa, ynjc omoztlacavitinenca, omotlapololtitiaque, omixcueptiaque, omixtetzappolotiaque.

Jpampa yn ça nica tocõcemitotiquiça, ynic amo ça nen tictequipachozque tetlacaquiliz, titenacaztititzazque, ça yliviz tlatoltica titetzontetilizque, titotzontetilizque, titzontetiezque, yn ma iuh tlaqualli momati tlatolli, ca omuch mito in iamanquj, in totonqui, in velic, in avjiac, auh in oapaoac, yn oapactic yn oquappitzauh, in quappitztic, yn oitztix, yn ocecex, in itz-

1. *Tlayovaya* in the *Real Palacio MS.*

frozen; or to be like bad tortillas, burning with lime, which scald the mouth, badly made, with coarse meal; or like tamales, hot, burning, scalding the roof of one's mouth, those with the steam still rising — the hot foods; or like stale tamales, cold, soggy, slimy and slippery, sticky, and stinking, [so] is all that hath been said.

Wherefore here we shall abbreviate and shorten the discourse, in order to bring it to a close, in order no longer again to repeat all the small statements which have been recalled, which are as prattling. Like a wall is the account constructed. Little, a little at a time, was it laid on and joined. In part it was well joined, constructed, and leveled off. When finished it was ordered, completed, and made good in all parts. It was given a core of rock, and filled with small stones; with small stones [set in] a core of rock, and chinked with clay. [So] with the separate words. But in part they were only broken, reduced to fragments, in pieces, dismembered, with holes; with unevennesses and breaks; not regarded as complete; with interruptions; bruised, altered, and changed. [So] each group proceeded on its way; all the day signs mentioned, of which there hath been discourse and discussion.

tic, in cecec, yn anoço pâpaian, in nexcococ, in cocopatic, yn âvmpa ieheoa, yn acuechtic, yoan in anoce iuhquj tamalli, in totonquj, ĩ totontlapetztic, in techichino, in tecopacchichino, yn oc ipotocquiztivitz, in totoncatlaqualli, yn ânoce, ça tamalçolli, tamalcecec, yn opuxcauh yn oalaoac, oalactix, yn oçaçalix, yn oiiax, ca omuch mjto.

Jehica yn ça njcan ontitiquiltzopi, tocontitiquiltzopa tlatolli, ynjc ontlatzonquiça, ynjc aocmo ceppa, ticceceppavizque, yn ixq'ch cecencamatotonti omolnamjc, in juhqui omoçaçanilo, in ma iuh tepantli ooalmochiuhtia tlatolli, achchi, achchitoton ooalmotlalitia, ooalmoçalotia, cequj vel omoçaçalo otzotzop, otzotzõma, yn itlamjã vel omotlamamacac, omotlaaquili, omotlatlaqualti, omoteiolloti, omotetzicueoalloti, tetzicueoaltica, teiollotica, ynjc vel ooalçoquicoallotia tlatlatoltica, auh cequj çan omococoton, omocecototz, côcotonqui, cocotontica, cocotocatica, cocoiontica xixipuchauhtica, xixipuchauhtoc, amo centlachixtoc, xixiquipiltic, xixiquipiliuhtoc, cocomotztic, cocomotzauhtoc, ynjc cecencalpan ooallotlatocac, in ie muchi tonalli omoteneuh, yn ipan otlatlatoloc, otlatlatolloac.

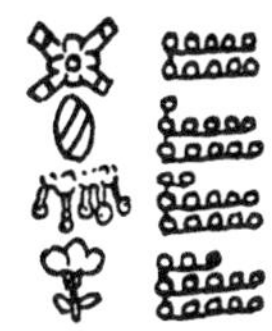

Fortieth Chapter, which telleth of the rest [of the day signs] which formed a part of the day count; those still remaining, belonging to the day sign [One Rabbit]. Also it telleth of the chart and the counters of the different day signs, and of the thirteen [numbers] which belonged to the day sign.

And now when already is ended and concluded just this one day sign starter, the one here named One Rabbit, and the different companions, which follow it, then nothing more appeareth of what is well concluded, well finished, and well terminated. Because of what hath been said, it is only abbreviated. Thus the other brief statements which are here, are pieced together. Moreover, there are still ideas yet to appear, which are still being guarded and hidden, yet to be unearthed, which have not been apparent; as may be said, like captives yet in bonds, who thus can be brought to an end and arranged.

Wherefore, for the moment, we have here only gathered, hastily brought together and assembled, [the day signs], as if they were a necklace, a bracelet. Here like a precious necklace or bracelet, with paintings, we have strung and threaded them together. We strung them into necklaces and placed them in sequence. Hence it is no longer very necessary that each separate day sign be dealt with and chronicled separately.

So here, quickly and without reflection, as if in a hurry, as if in our boredom and desperation, frenzy and despair, we have rapidly repeated these different [day signs]. Here they end and conclude; selected, brought to a head, and made known (for so the discussion is already arrived to the time of its maturity), are these named here: the second, taking second place, Two Water, and Three Dog, Four Monkey, Five Grass, Six Reed, Seven Ocelot, Eight Eagle, Nine Vulture, Ten Motion, Eleven Flint Knife, Twelve Rain, and Thirteen Flower.

Injc vmpoalli capitulo: ytechpa tlatoa yn oc cequi ic xexeliuhtoc tonalpoalli yn vc mocaoa yn itech povi in tonalli, no itechpa tlatoa yn itabla, yoan in ipoaloca in izquitetl tonalli, yoã in matlaquilhujtl vmey in itech povia in tonalli.

Auh in axcan in ie ic õtlami yn ie ic ontzonquiça in çayio tonalpeuhcaiotl nican omoteneuh y iehoatl ce tochtli, yoã in izquiteme ytlavilanoan, in quitoquilia, ca aoc tle neci in vel ic tzopiz, vel ic tlamiz, vel ic iecaviz, ypampa in mitoa ça ontitiquiltzopi, ic ommochîchichi yn oc quezqui camatotonti, nican omolnamjc, ca tel vncah in tetlalnamiquiliz, yn oc neciz, yn oc motlatitica, yn oc tlapachiuhtica, yn oc motatacaz, yn âneztica in mitoa iuhquj oc vixtoylpitica, in vel ic tzotzopiz, in vel ic mocencaoaz.

Jehica yn axcan ça nican tiqujmoncentlalia, tiqujmõcentlalitivetzi, tiquimoncentlalitiquiça, tiqujmontecpana, tiquimontecpantivetzi, timoquimontecpantiquiça in ma iuh cozcatl, macuextli, nican cozcateuh, macuexteuh, tliltica, tlapaltica, tlilantica, tiqujmonçoço, tiquimoncẽço, tiquincozcaço, tiqujmoncenvipana, ynjc aocmo cenca monequj nonõqua ontlatlatolloaz, õmotlatlatollotiz, yn cecentetl tonalli,

yc ça njcã yciuhca, ixtomaoaca, ça iuhqujn netlalolpã, yoan ça iuhquin tonepatlalco, tonexiuhtlatilco, tonexiuhtlatilcopa, tonexiuhtlaticopa, tiqujmocemitotivetzi yn izquiteme in njcan ontlatzonquixtia, ontlatzopa, ontlatzõmana, ontlatzonmjiaoaiotia, ontlapantlaça (ynjc ie ixiloiocan, yn imjiaoaiocan oacico tlatolli), yn iehoantin nican moteneoa, yn vncan in tlaoncaiotia 2. atl, yoã Ey itzcuintli, 4. oçomatli, 5. malinalli. 6. acatl. 7. ocelutl. 8. quauhtli. 9. cozcaquauhtli. 10. olin. 11. tecpatl. 12. quiavitl. 13. suchitl.

APPENDIX

Apendiz del quarto libro

APPENDIX OF THE FOURTH BOOK, IN THE SPANISH VERNACULAR, WHICH IS JUSTIFICATION IN DEFENSE OF THE TRUTH CONTAINED HEREIN.

APENDIZ DEL QUARTO LIBRO EN ROMÃCE Y ES VNA APPOLOGIA EN DEFENSION DA LA VERDAD QUE EN EL SE CONTIENE.

Because some have been deceived, and the delusion even today endureth, concerning certain [systems of] counting which these natives used in days of old, I consider it helpful to place here an explanation of three kinds of counting [systems] which they used and in some places still use.

Porque algunos se an engañado, y aun todavia dura el engaño, cerca de ciertas cuentas, que estos naturales vsauan antiguamente: tengo por cosa prouechosa poner aquj, la declaracion de tres maneras de cuentas, que vsauan, y avn en algunas partes las vsan.

The first count is the division of the year into its months. The fact is that they divided the year into eighteen parts, and to each part they gave twenty days. These may be called months. Thus their year had eighteen months, which comprised three hundred and sixty days. The five left over to make a full year are not counted: rather, they called them idle and unlucky days, because to no god were they dedicated. The purpose for which they established this division was that they dedicated each month or [period of] twenty days to a god, and during each they held celebrations and made sacrifices; except that in two of the months they celebrated the feasts of four gods, [in each] assigning ten days to one and another ten to the other. And so, although there were eighteen months, the feasts celebrated in them were twenty. This count is called a calendar in which all the days of the year are dedicated to the gods except the five which, as is told, they considered idle and of evil fortune. This count, which is the calendar these natives had had from time immemorial, has nothing to do with the other two counts which will now be described.

Es la primera cuenta, la division del año por sus meses. Es el caso que ellos repartian el año, en deziocho partes, y a cada parte, le dauan veinte dias; estos se poeden llamar meses: de manera, que su año tenja deziocho meses: los quales contienen trezientos y setenta [*sic*] dias, y los cinco que sobran, para ser año cumplido, no entran en cuenta, sino llamauanlos dias baldios, y aziagos, porque a njngun dios eran dedicados. El fin a que enderecauan [*sic*] esta diujsion es, que cada mes o cada veinte dias, los dedicauan a un dios, y en ellos le hazian fiestas, y sacrificios, exceto que en dos meses hazian fiesta a quatro dioses, dedicando diez dias a al vno, y otros diez al otro. Y ansi con ser los meses deziocho, las fiestas que celebrauan en ellos eran veinte. Esta cuenta, se llama calendario, donde todos los dias del año, se dedican a los dioses, excepto los cinco que como esta dicho los tenjan baldios y aziagos. Esta cuenta, que es el calendario que estos naturales tenjan de tiempo sin memoria, no tiene que hazer, con las otras dos cuentas, que luego se dirã.

The second count which these natives used is called the year-count, because [by it] they counted a certain number of years in the following way. They had four characters placed in four positions with respect to a circle. One of these characters they called Ce acatl, meaning One Reed. This character was represented as a green reed, and, with reference to the circle, was to the east. The second character they called Ce tecpatl, meaning One Flint Knife. [It was] made in the manner of a lance head, half of it blood-stained. This was placed to the north with

La segunda cuenta que estos naturales vsauan, se llama cuenta de los años, porque contauan cierto numero de años, por la forma que se sigue: tenjan quatro caracteres, puestos en quatro partes en respecto de vn circulo redondo. A al vno destos caracteres llamauã, Ce acatl, que quiere dezir, vna caña: este caracter, era como vna caña verde pintada, y en respecto del circulo, estaua hazia al oriente. Al segundo caracter, llamauan ce tecpatl, que qujere dezir vn pedernal: hecho a manera de hierro de lança tiñjdo la mjtad del con sangre: este estaua puesto

reference to the circle. The third character was the representation of a house, which they call Ce calli [One House]. It is placed to the west with reference to the circle. The fourth character is the likeness of a rabbit, which they call Ce tochtli [One Rabbit]; it is placed to the south with reference to the circle. By means of these characters they counted fifty-two years, assigning thirteen years to each character. And they counted in this manner, One Reed, Two Flint Knife, Three House, Four Rabbit, and so on, so describing circles by means of these characters, until each one attained thirteen years. These, altogether, make up four times thirteen and equal fifty-two years. The purpose or intention of this count is to renew, every fifty-two years, the covenant, contract, or vow, to serve the idols. Because at the end of the fifty-two-year [cycle] they observed a very solemn feast and made new fire, and extinguished all the old [fires]. And all the provinces of this New Spain took of this new fire. Then they renewed all the statues of the idols and all of their adornment, as well as the intention of serving them for the next fifty-two years. And also they had a prophecy or oracle of the devil that at [the end of] one of these periods the world would come to an end.

The third count which these natives used was the art of divination of the fortune or luck which those born would have, whether men or women. It was done in this way. They had twenty characters. The first they named Crocodile, the second Wind, the third House, the fourth Lizard, the fifth Serpent, etc., up to twenty, as is represented in the chart at the end of this Appendix.* They said that each of these characters reigned thirteen days, so that all together are two hundred and [sixty] days. Some say that these thirteen-day [periods] are weeks of the month, but this is not so. Rather they are the number of days in which the sign or character reigneth. The weeks of the month are of five days, and so there are, in each month, four weeks; and the *tianquiztli,* or markets, are fixed according to this number of days, or used to be so fixed. So that by periods of five days they established the markets or fairs. And so they had no weeks [of seven days], but rather periods of five days. And nowadays, in many places, they set the markets and fairs according to our seven-day weeks. In this illicit soothsaying

* See Plates 102-104.

hazia la parte del septendrion en respecto del circulo. El tercero caracter era vna pintada que ellos llaman ce calli, esta puesta hazia la parte del occidente, en respecto del circulo. El quarto caracter es la semejança de vn conejo que ellos llaman ce tochtli: esta puesto hazia la parte del medio dia, en respecto del circulo: contauan por estos caracteres cincuenta y dos años, dando a cada vno de los caracteres treze años, y contauan desta manera, ce acatl, vme tecpatl, ei calli, navi tochtli, y ansi dando bueltas, por estos caracteres, hasta que en cada vno se cumpliessen treze años, los quales todos juntos, son quatro vezes treze que hazen cincuenta y dos años: el fin o intencion desta cuenta es, renouar cada cincuenta y dos años, el pacto, o concierto, o juramento de servjr a los idolos. Porque en el fin de los cincuenta y dos años, hazian vna muy solemne fiesta, y sacauan fuego nueuo, y apagauan todo lo viejo y tomauan todas las proujncias desta nueua españa fuego nueuo; entonce renouauan todas las estatuas de los idolos y todas sus alhajas, y el proposito de serujrlos otros cincuenta i dos años. Y tambien tenjan profecia o oraculo del demonjo, que en vno destos periodos se auja de acabar el mundo.

La tercera cuenta que estos naturales vsauan, era el arte para adiujnar la fortuna o uentura, que tendrian los que nacian hombres y mugeres. Era desta manera que tenjan viente caracteres: al primero llamauan cipactli, el segundo hecatl, el tercero calli, el quarto cuetzpali, el qujnto coatl. &c. hasta viente como esta pintado en la figura, que esta al fin deste apẽdiz: dezian que cada vno destos caracteres, reinaua treze dias, que todos juntos son dozientos y setenta [*sic*] dias. Algunos dizen que estos treze dias son semanas del mes y no es ansi sino numero de dias en que reina el signo o caracter: las semanas de los meses son cinco dias y ansi ay en cada mes quatro semanas y los tianquez, o mercados por este numero de dias se señalla, [*sic*] o solian señallarse, que de cinco en cinco dias hechauã los mercados, o ferias, y ansi no tenjan semana, sino qujntana, y agora en muchas partes hechan los mercados y ferias por nuestra semana de siete en siete dias. En esta cuenta adiujnatoria i no licita entreponense los caracteres de la cuenta de los años; conviene a saber, aquellos quatro caracteres de que arriba se hizo mencion, que es caña,

count are interspersed the characters of the year-count; that is, those four characters mentioned above, which are Reed, Flint Knife, House, and Rabbit, by which they counted the hebdomad of their years, which is fifty-two.

pedernal, casa, conejo, por donde contauan la hebdomada de sus años, que son cincuenta y dos.

This very pernicious count, superstitious, and full of idolatry, as is to be seen in this Fourth Book, some praise highly, saying that it was very ingenious and contained no blemish. This they said because they did not understand for what purpose this count, which is very evil and idolatrous, was established. Little did they appreciate the multitude of superstitions, feasts, and idolatrous sacrifices involved in it. And they called this count the calendar of the Indians, not understanding that this count doth not extend through all of the year; because it hath only two hundred and sixty days in its round, and then cometh back to its beginning. And so it cannot be and never was a calendar; for the calendar, as hath been said, is represented in the opening of the Second Book, and containeth all the days of the year, and [all] the feasts of the year. And this they who say that this soothsaying art is a calendar, do not know. And surely it was great carelessness and culpable ignorance to praise by word of mouth and in writing something so evil and full of idolatry.

Esta cuenta muy perjudicial, y muy supersticiosa, y muy llena de idolatria, como parece en este libro quarto, algunos la alaban mucho: diziendo, que era muy ingenjosa y que njnguna macula tenja, esto dixerõ por no entender a que fin se endereza, esta cuenta el qual es muy malo ydolatrico de poco entendieron la muchedumbre de supersticiones y fiestas y sacrificios idolatricos, que en ella se contienen, y llamaron a esta cuenta, el calendario de los indios: no entendiendo que esta cuenta no alcança a todo el año, porque no tiene mas doscientos y sesenta dias de circulo, y luego torna a su principio, y ansi no poede ser calendario y nj nunca lo fue, porque el calendario, como esta dicho, y esta pintado, en el principio del segundo libro, contiene todos los dias del año, y las fiestas del año: y esto ignoraron los que dizen que esta arte adiujnatoria es calendario: y cierto fue grande inaduertencia, y culpable ignorancia loar por palabra, y por escrito vna cosa tan mala y tan llena de idolatria.

The zeal for truth and for the Catholic Faith compels me to place here the very words of a treatise which a member of one of the religious Orders wrote in praise of this art of soothsaying, declaring that it is a calendar; so that wherever one may see it, he may know that it is something very pernicious to our holy Catholic Faith; and it may be destroyed and burned.

El zelo de la verdad, y de la fe catholica, me compele a poner aquj, las mjsmas palabras de vn tratado, que vn religioso escriujo en loor desta arte adiujnatoria; diziendo que es calendario, para que dondequjera que alguno le viere, sepa que es cosa muy perjudicial, a nuestra sancta fe catholica, y sea destruydo, y quemado.

The following is the introduction of the aforementioned treatise.

Siguese la introducion del tractado sobredicho.

Introduction and explanation, newly made, of the calendar of the Indians of Anauac, that is, of New Spain.

By means of the wheels reproduced above, the Indians count their days, weeks, months, years, olympiads, five-year periods, indictions, and hebdomads, starting their year, like ours, with the beginning of January. In [their system] are found the means of reckoning time which all nations have had. And as is seen, the Indians who established and knew it well certainly showed themselves to be natural philosophers. They were at fault only as to the leap year.

Introducion, i declaracion nueuamente sacada, que es el calendario de los indios de Anaoac, esto es de la nueua españa.

Por las ruedas aquj antepoestas, cuentan los indios sus dias, semanas, meses, años, olimpiadas lustros indiciones, y hebdomadas: començando su año, con el nuestro desde el principio de henero: en la qual se hallan las maneras de contar los tiempos que tujeron todas las naciones, y segun parece los indios que la composieron, y sabian bien, ciertamente se mostraron philosophos naturales, solamente faltaron en el bixesto: pero tambien paso el gran philosopho

But this was the case also as to the great philosopher Aristotle and his teacher Plato, and many other wise men who did not attain [knowledge of] it. And it should be known that in this calendar there is nothing idolatrous; and this is praiseworthy for many reasons, but to mention one will be enough. And it is that in this land it was not very many years ago that idolatry began. And this calendar is exceedingly ancient, and if the names of the days, weeks, and years, and their representations, are of animals and beasts, and other creatures, it is nothing to wonder at; for if we look at ours, they also are of planets and of gods which the pagans had. Even if many rites, falsehoods, and ancient sacrifices are written of here [in connection with] a thing so good, of such excellence and truth as these natives possessed, there is no reason to condemn it. For we know that all good and truth, no matter who expresseth it, is of the Holy Ghost.

Aristotiles, y su maestro platon, y otros muchos sabios que no lo alcançaron. Y es de saber, que en este calendario, no ay cosa de idolatria: y esto se poede de alabar, por muchas razones, pero bastara dezir vna: y es que en esta tierra no ha muy muchos años, que començaron las idolatrias: y este calendario es antiquissimo y si los nombres de los dias, semanas, y años, y sus figuras, son de anjmales, y de bestias, y de otras criaturas; no se deuen maraujllar, pues si mjramos los nuestros: tambien son de planetas, y de dioses que los gentiles tuujeron: y pues que aquj se escriuen muchos ritos, ficciones, y antiguos sacrificios, vna cosa tan buena, y de tanto primor, y verdadera que estos naturales tuujeron: no es razon de reprobarla: pues sabemos que todo bien y verdad, qujenqujera que la diga, es del espiritu sancto.

Refutation of the above[1]

As to what he first saith, that by means of this count the Indians reckoned [their] weeks, months, and years: this is most false. For this count containeth only two hundred and sixty days, and lacketh one hundred and five days to be the count of an entire year. Neither did they reckon their months by this count, because their months are eighteen in a year, and each one hath twenty days, which maketh three hundred and sixty days. This count doth not reach that number. Neither do they reckon their weeks by this count; for what they say, that they had thirteen days in a week, is false, because thus there would be a week of thirteen days and another week [which] would go into the next month with three days,[2] and so no month would have two entire weeks. But more important, their weeks were of five days, which were better called five-day periods than weeks, and there are in each month four of these five-day periods.

What he saith of olympiads, five-year periods, indictions, and the like, is false and pure invention.

What he saith, that the year started in January, like ours, is most incorrect; for what they call a year by this count is of only two hundred and sixty days,

Confutacion de lo arriba dicho.

En lo primero que dize, que por esta cuenta: los indios contauan seis [*sic*] semanas, meses, y años, es falsissimo: porque esta cuenta no contiene mas doscientos y sesenta dias, y faltale ciento y cinco dias, para ser cuenta de vn año entero; nj tanpoco contauan sus meses por esta cuenta, porque sus meses son deziocho en vn año, y cada vno tiene viente dias que son trezientos y sesenta dias; al qual numero, no llega esta cuenta; nj tampoco cuentan, por esta cuenta sus semanas, porque aquello que dizen, que tenjan treze dias por semana es falso, porque desta manera seria vna semana de treze dias, y otra semana entredia con tres dias en el mes sigujente, y ansi cada mes no tendria dos semanas enteras: mayormente, que sus semanas eran de cinco dias las quales mejor se llamaran quintanas, que no semanas, y ay en cada mes quatro destas quintanas.

Lo que dize de Olimpiades, y lustros, y indiciones o la mesma razon es falso, y mera ficciõ.

Lo que dize, que el año, comencaua [*sic*] en Enero, como el nuestro, es falsissimo: porque lo que llaman vn año por esta cuenta no son mas doscientos y sesenta

1. On the controversy between Sahagún and Motolinía regarding the nature of the calendar, see L. Nicolau d'Olwer: *Fray Toribio de Benavente* (*Motolinía*): *Relaciones de la Nueva España* (México: Ediciones de la Universidad Nacional Autónoma, 1956), pp. LV-LVI.

2. Sahagún (Garibay ed.), IV, Ap. 6, has *entraría.* Santamaría, *op. cit.*, Vol. I, p. 612, defines *entredía,* as used in Cuba, by saying *"Dícese . . . de cualquier momento del día solar."*

and of necessity it would have to end one hundred and five days before our year. And so it could not start with our year, except with some, and very rarely.

As to what he saith, that the Indians [who] devised this count showed themselves to be natural philosophers: this is most false. For they do not carry out this count according to any natural order; for it was an invention of the devil and an art of soothsaying.

As to what he saith, that they lacked the leap year, it is wrong; because in the count which may be called a true calendar they count three hundred and sixty-five days, and once every four years they counted three hundred and sixty-six days with a feast which for this reason they observed every four years.

As to what he saith, that in this calendar there is no idolatry, it is a very great lie. For it is no calendar but a soothsaying device in which are contained a great deal of idolatry, many superstitions, and many invocations to the demons, tacitly and openly, as is shown in all of this preceding Fourth Book. So that the treatise aforementioned, which that member of a religious Order wrote, containeth no truth but rather very pernicious error and falsehood.

The treatise by that member of a religious Order proceedeth.

The Indians who well understood the secrets of these wheels and calendar showed and explained them to but few, because through their knowledge they gained their livelihood and were held in esteem and considered wise and intelligent. Nevertheless, almost all adult Indians knew and were informed about the year, as to both the number and house in which they were. But of the names of the days and weeks, and many other secrets and counts which they possessed, only those masters who worked with them attained knowledge.

Now, in order to understand the count which these natives had, in order to know how they kept a time-count by means of the wheels and figures here recorded, rules are given. These are written below.

Refutation of the above.

It is already said that the calendar is different from this count and hath nothing in common with it. The calendar dealeth with the months of the whole year, the days of the whole year, the weeks of the

dias, y de necesidad se avia de acabar ciento y cinco dias, antes de nuestro año: y ansi no podia començar con el nuestro año, si no algunas y muy raro:

en lo que dize que los indios se composiero desta cuenta, se mostraron philosophos naturales, es falsissimo: porque esta cuenta, no le lleuan por njnguna orden natural: porque fue invencion del demonjo, y arte de adiujnacion,

en lo que dize que faltaron en el bixesto es falso, porque en la cuenta que se llama, calendario verdadero, cuentan trescientos y sesenta y cinco dias, y cada quatro años, contauan trecientos, y sesenta y seis dias en fiesta, que para esto hazian de quatro en quatro años.

En lo que dize que en este calendario no ay cosa de idolatria, es falsissima mẽtira: porque no es calendario, sino arte adiujnatoria, donde se contienen, muchas cosas de idolatria, y muchas supersticiones, y muchas invocaciones de los demonjos, tacita, y espressamente, como parece en todo este quarto libro precediente: de manera que ninguna verdad contiene aquel tratado arriba puesto: que aquel religioso escriujo, mas antes cõtiene falsedad y mentira muy pernjciosa.

Siguese adelante en el tratado de aquel religioso.

Los indios, que bien entendian los secretos destas ruedas, y calendario, no los enseñauan, nj descubrian, sino a muy pocos, porque por ello ganauan de comer, y eran estimados, y tenjdos por hombres sabios, y entendidos, empero sabian casi todos los indios adultos y tenjan noticia del año, ansi del numero como de la casa en que andauan: mas de los nombres de los dias, y semanas, y otros muchos secretos, y cuentas que tenjan: solos aquellos maestros compotistas, lo alcançauanla de saber.

Agora para entender la cuenta, que estos naturales tenjan, y para saber, como contauan los tiempos: por las ruedas, y figuras aquj escritas: se ponen reglas, que son las infra escritas.

Confutacion de lo arriba dicho.

Ya esta dicho, que el calendario es distincto desta cuenta, y no tiene nada que ver con ella. Y el calendario tracta de los meses de todo el año, y de los dias de todo el año, y de las semanas de todo el año, y de las

whole year, and the fixed feasts of the whole year. All the priests and servants of the idols knew it, as well as many of the populace, because it is a simple matter which toucheth all. But the count of the soothsaying art, which he wrongly calleth a calendar, is a particular kind of count, because its purpose was established to foretell circumstances and events to befall those born under each sign or character. This count only the soothsayers and those who had the skill to learn it, knew; because it containeth many difficulties and obscurities. Those who knew this count they called *tonalpouhque;* they esteemed and honored them greatly. They considered them to be prophets and knowers of future things. Hence they depended upon them for many things, as in days of old the sons of Israel depended upon the prophets.

This [author] saith that the months are twenty in a year. This is not true, for there are only eighteen. Likewise he saith that the weeks are of thirteen days, and this is not true, for they are of only five days, so that there are four weeks or rather five-day periods in a month. The thirteen days which he wrongly calleth a week are only the number of days in which each of the twenty characters in this soothsaying art reigned, as is made clear in the preceding Fourth Book, which dealeth with this soothsaying art.

The chart and [explanation of] the manner of counting used by the soothsayers for this art, now follow.

To the reader.

This chart[3] before the friendly reader is the count of the characters or signs with which we have dealt in this Fourth Book. It proceedeth in this order. First are placed twenty characters, and by them their names; and after them are placed the days over which they reign, in numerical notation; and it beginneth one, two, three, etc. The character by or facing the number one reigneth over those thirteen days [beginning with it], and the counting is started from above to below. Reaching thirteen, one then returneth to the number one, and the character before which that number one standeth, reigneth during the thirteen following days. And so with all the remaining numbers and characters. So each one of the characters cometh to reign for thirteen days, and the number of all of these days is two hundred and sixty. From there it returneth again to the beginning.

fiestas fixas de todo el año: sabianle todos los satrapas, y todos los mjnjstros de los idolos, y mucha de la otra gente popular, porque es cosa facil, y toca a todos. Empero la cuenta de la arte adiujnatoria, a la qual falsamente llama calendario, es cuenta por si, porque su fin, se endereza a adiujnar las condiciones, y sucessos de los que nacen en cada signo, o caracter; esta cuenta sabianla solamēte los adiujnos, y los que tenian abilidad, para deprenderla porque contiene muchas dificultades, y obscuridades: y a estos que sabiā esta cuenta, llamauanlos Tonalpouhque y tenjanlos en mucho y honrauanlos mucho: tenjanlos como prophetas, y sabidores de las cosas futuras, y ansi acudian a ellos, en muchas cosas, como antiguamente los hijos de Israel, acudian a los prophetas,

dize este; que los meses, son viente en vn año, y no es verdad, porque no son mas de deziocho: dize ansimjsmo que las semanas, son de treze dias, y no es verdad: porque no son mas de a cinco dias, y ansi son quatro semanas o por mejor dezir qujntanas en vn mes: los treze dias, a que falsamente llama semana, no son, sino el numero de dias, que reynaua cada vno de los veinte caracteres, desta arte adiujnatoria, como esta claro, en el quarto libro precedente, que tracta desta arte adiujnatoria.

Siguese la tabla y manera de contar que tenjan los adiujnos en esta arte.

Al lector.

Esta tabla, que esta frontera Amigo lector, es la cuenta de los caracteres, o signos de que en este quarto libro auemos tractado, la qual procede por esta orden, que primeramente se ponen viente caracteres, y junto a ellos sus nombres, y despues dellos se ponen los dias, en que reinan por cifras del alguarismo: y comjença, vno, dos, tres, &c. El caracter donde esta junto el vno o frontero del, es el que reina aquellos treze dias, y comjençase a contar desde arriba hazia abaxo: y llegando a treze luego buelue a vno, y el caracter en frente de qujen esta aquel vno, es el que reina los treze dias que se siguen: y ansi de todos los demas numeros y caracteres. De manera, que cada vn caracter viene a reinar treze dias, y el numero de todos estos dias son dozientos y sesenta, y de alli buelue otra vez al principio.

3. See Plate 102.

Also at the opening of this count is placed the manner of counting the years, because these two counts are linked or matched.

Here followeth the reckoning of all the time-counts which these natives had.

The longest time-count which they reckoned was up to one hundred and four years. And this count they called a century.

Half of this count, fifty-two years, they called a bundle of years. This period of years they had reckoned from times past; it is not known when it began. But they considered it well established and a matter of belief that the world would come to an end at the conclusion of one of these bundles of years. They had a prophecy or oracle that at that time the movement of the heavens would cease, and they took as a sign [of this] the movement of the Pleiades. On the night of this feast, which they called Toximmolpilia [the Binding of the Years], it so befell that the Pleiades were at the zenith at midnight, with respect to the horizon in Mexico. On this night they made new fire, and before they made it, they extinguished all the fires in all the provinces, towns, and houses in all of this New Spain. And they went in a great and solemn procession. All of the priests and servants of the temple departed from here, the Temple of Mexico, during the first quarter of the night, and went to the summit of that mountain near Itztapalapan which they call Uixachtecatl. They reached the summit at midnight, or almost, where stood a great pyramid built for that ceremony. Having reached there, they looked at the Pleiades to see if they were at the zenith, and if they were not, they waited until they were. And when they saw that now they passed the zenith, they knew that the movement of the heavens had not ceased and that the end of the world was not then, but that they would have another fifty-two years, assured that the world would not come to an end.

At this hour a great multitude of people was on the mountains surrounding this province of Mexico — Texcoco, Xochimilco, and Quauhtitlan — waiting to see the new fire, which was a signal that the world would continue. And when the priests made the fire, with great ceremony, upon the pyramid on that mountain, then it was seen from all the surrounding

Tambien en el principio desta cuenta se pone la manera de contar de los años, porque estas dos cuentas andã vinculadas o pareadas.

La cuenta de todos los tiempos, que tenjan estos naturales, es la que se sigue.

La mayor cuenta de tiempo, que contauan era hasta ciento y quatro años, y a esta cuenta llamauan vn siglo,

a la mitad desta cuẽta, que son cincuenta y dos años llamauan vna gavilla de años, este tiempo de años, trayanla ab antiquo contados, no se sabe quando començo: pero tenjan por muy aueriguado, y como de fe, que el mũdo se auja de acabar en el fin de vna destas gabillas de años: y tenjan prenostico o oraculo, que entonce avia de cesar el moujmjento de los cielos, y tomauan por señal al moujmjento de las cabrillas: la noche desta fiesta, que ellos llamauan Toximmolpilia: de tal manera caya que las cabrillas, estauan en medio del cielo: a la media noche, en respecto deste orizonte mexicano. En esta noche sacauan fuego nueuo, y primero que los sacassen, apagauan todo el fuego, en todas las proujncias, pueblos, y casas de toda esta nueua españa: y iban con gran procession, y solemnidad. Todos los satrapas, y mjnjstros del templo: partian daquj del templo de mexico, a prima noche: y iban hasta la cumbre de aquel cerro, que esta cabe Itztapalapan: que ellos llaman Vixachtecatl, y llegauan a la cumbre a la media noche, o casi, donde estaua vn solemne cu, edificado para aquella cerimonja. Llegados alli, mjrauan a las cabrillas; si estauan en el medio, y si no estauan esperauan hasta que llegassen. Y quando vian, que ya passauan del medio, entendian que el moujmjento del cielo no cesaua, y que no era alli el fin del mundo, sino que avian de tener otros cincuenta y dos años, seguros, que no se acabaria el mundo.

En esta hora estauan en los cerros circunstantes que cercan a toda esta proujncia de mexico, Tezcucu, y Suchimjlco y quauhtitlan, gran cantidad de gente, esperando a uer el fuego nueuo; que era señal, que el mundo iba adelante, y como sacauan el fuego, los satrapas, con gran cerimonja, en el cu de aquel cerro: luego se parecia, en todo lo circunstante de los cerros:

mountains. Those who were there watching then raised a cry which rose to the heavens with joy that the world was not ending and that they had another fifty-two years assured.

The last ceremony of new fire which they held was in the year 1507. They held it with full solemnity, because the Spaniards had not come to this land. In the year 1559 ended the next bundle of years, which they call Toximmolpilia. On this occasion they held no public ceremony, because the Spaniards and members of the religious Orders were now in this land. So that this year, 1576, is the fifteenth of the current bundle of years.

When they made the new fire and held this ceremony, they renewed their covenant with the devil to serve him, and they renovated all the statues of the devil which they had in his house, and all the ornaments for his service, and those of their houses. And they rejoiced greatly to know that now they held the world to be secure and that it would not come to an end for fifty-two years. It is clear that this device of counting years was an invention of the devil to make them renew the covenant which they made with him every fifty-two years — [the devil] terrifying them with [the threat of] the end of the world and making them think that he lengthened the time and favored them thereby, letting the world move on.

Besides this they held, every eight years, a fast on bread and water, for eight days; and at its conclusion they celebrated a feast in which they held a solemn dance by various personages, in which they said that they revealed what would come to pass or what fortune they merited; and they called it Atamalqualiztli.

They observed another feast every four years, in honor of the fire [god], during which they pierced the ears of all the boys and girls; and they called it Pillauanaliztli. And during this feast it is likely, and there are conjectures, that they held their leapyear, reckoning six [days] of Nemontemi.

The remaining time-count is of the year, which they divided into eighteen months, to each of which they assigned twenty days. And each of these months was dedicated to one god, or to two, and during it they held their feast. Each of these months they divided into five-day periods, and held the fairs on the last day of these five in one town, and five days later in another, and another five days later in

y los que estauan alli a la mjra, leuantauan luego vn alarido que le ponjan en el cielo de alegria que el mundo no se acabaua y que tenjan otros cincuenta y dos años por ciertos.

La vltima solemnjdad, que hizieron deste fuego nueuo: fue el año de mill y qujnjentos, y siete: hizieronle, con toda solemnjdad, porque no avian venjdo los españoles, a esta tierra: el año de mjll y qujnjẽtos y cincuenta y nueue, se acabo la otra gabilla de años: que ellos llaman Toximmolpilia. En esta, no hizieron solemnjdad publica: porque ya los españoles, y religiosos estauan en esta tierra. De manera que este año de mjll y qujnjentos y setenta y seis, anda en quinze años, de la gabilla de años que corre.

Quando sacauan fuego nueuo, y hazian esta solemnjdad, renouauan el pacto que tenjan con el demonjo de servjrle: y renouauan todas las estatuas del demonjo, que en su casa tenjan, y todas las alhajas de su serujcio, y las de sus casas: y hazian grandes alegrias, por saber, que ya tenjan el mundo seguro, que no se acabaria por cincuenta y dos años. Claramente consta, que este artificio de contar, fue invencion del diablo, para hazerlos renouar el pacto que con el tenjan de cincuenta, en cincuenta y dos años: y amedrẽtandolos con la fin del mundo, y haziendolos entender, que el alargaua el tiempo y les hazian merced del passando el mundo adelãte.

Demas desta cuenta tenjan que de ocho en ocho años, hazian vn ayuno de pan y agua, por espacio de ocho dias, y hazian al cabo, vna fiesta donde hazian solemne areito de diuersos personajes; donde dezian, que descubrian ventura o que la merecian, y llamauanla Atamalcualiztli.

Otra fiesta hazian, de quatro en quatro años, a honrra del fuego, donde agujerauan las orejas a todos los njños, y njñas, y la llamauan pillauanaliztli. Y en esta fiesta es verisimjle, y ay conjecturas que haziã su bisexto, contando seis de nemontemj.

La otra cuenta del tiempo, es de vn año: el qual repartian en deziocho meses, y a cada mes le dauan veinte dias: y cada vno destos meses, era dedicado a vno, o a dos dioses: y hazian en el sus fiestas, cada vno destos meses, le repartian de cinco in cinco dias, y hazian las ferias el vltimo dia, destos cinco, en vn pueblo: y dende a cinco dias en otro, y dende a otros cinco dias en otro. De manera que el quarto qujn-

[still] another [town]. So that the fourth period of five days was the feast of the god who was honored in the following month. The five days in addition to the three hundred and sixty of the complete year they regarded as idle and unlucky, and so did not take account of them for any purpose. But they kept track of all the days and all the months of the year, and of all the five-day periods of the year, which are four in each month.

These natives had another count which followeth neither the year-count, nor the months, nor the five-day periods, which may wrongly be called weeks. This count hath twenty characters, as is represented in the chart behind this page.[4] To each one of these characters they assigned thirteen days, during which one of these characters reigned. Thus each one reigned thirteen days, and the round which these characters with their days made, is of two hundred and sixty days. This round includeth one hundred and five days less than a year. The count was used to foretell the circumstances and events of life which those born [on given day signs] would have. It is a difficult count, full of error, and with no foundation of natural astrology. For the art of judiciary astrology, common among us, is founded upon natural astrology, which is in the signs and planets of the heavens and in their courses and aspects. But this art of soothsaying followeth, or is founded upon, some characters and numbers in which no natural foundation existeth, but [are] only an artifice made by the devil himself. Nor is it possible that any man could have made or invented this art. For it hath no foundation in any science nor in any natural order. Rather it appeareth to be a thing of fraud and deceit than rational or ingenious. I say it was fraud and deceit in order to dazzle and derange people of low capacity and little understanding. Notwithstanding, this art of soothsaying, or rather, diabolical fraud or deceit, was highly regarded; and those who knew and practised it were also greatly honored and esteemed. For they told of things to come, and were regarded as truthful by the populace, although they spoke no truth except by accident and mistake. This art followeth neither years, nor months, nor weeks, nor five-year periods nor olympiads, as some, in their dreams, have said and erroneously affirmed.

tanario, era la fiesta del dios que se celebraua en el mes que se seguja: los cinco dias que son mas de los trezientos y sesenta de todo el año, tenjanlos por valdios, y haziagos: y ansi no hazian cuenta dellos para njnguna cosa. Pero cuenta tenjan con todos los dias del año, y con todos los meses del año, y con todas las qujntanas del año, que son quatro en cada mes.

Otra cuenta tenjan, estos naturales que nj sigue la cuenta del año, nj de los meses, nj de las qujntanas, que impropriamente se pueden dezir semanas. Esta cuenta, tiene viente caracteres, como esta pintado en la tabla, que esta detras desta hoja: a cada vno destos caracteres, atribuyan treze dias: en las quales reinaua uno destos caracteres: de manera que cada vno reinaua treze dias, y el circulo que estos caracteres con sus dias hazian, son dozientos y sesenta dias: el qual circulo, tiene ciento y cinco dias menos, que vn año. Esta cuenta se vsaua para adiujnar las condiciones, y successos de la vida, que tendrian los que naciessen. Es cuenta delicada, y muy mentirosa, y sin njngun fundamento de astrologia natural. Porque el arte de la astrologia judiciaria, que entre nosotros se vsa, tiene fundamento en la astrologia natural, que es en los signos, y planetas del cielo, y en los cursus y aspectos dellos. Pero esta arte adiujnatoria siguese o fundase en vnos caracteres, y numeros, en que njngun fundamento natural ay, sino solamente artificio fabricado, por el mesmo diablo, nj es posible que njngun hombre fabricasse, nj inventasse esta arte; porque no tiene fundamento, en njnguna sciencia, nj en njnguna razon natural: mas parece cosa de embuste y embaimjento, que no cosa razonal, nj artificiosa. Digo que fue embuste y embaimjento, para encandilar, y desatinar a gente de poca capazidad, y de poco entendimjento. No obstante esto, era tenjda en mucho, esta arte adiujnatoria o mas propriamente hablando embuste o embaimjento diabolico: y tambien los que la sabian, y vsauan erã muy hõrrados y tenjdos: porque dezian las cosas por venjr, y del vulgo eran tenjdos por verdaderos, aunque njnguna verdad dezian sino acaso, y por ierro. Esta arte, nj sigue años, nj meses, nj semanas, nj lustros, nj olimpiadas, como algunos soñando dixeron, y afirmaron falsamẽte.

4. See Plates 103 and 104.

Because the foregoing chart of the soothsaying art is difficult to understand and to reckon by, I have provided the following chart, because it is clearer and the count is easier and in conformity with the way they counted. And let no one think that this chart is a calendar; because, as is said, it is only a soothsaying device. The calendar of these natives is found at the beginning of the Second Book, and it is very easily understood because of the letters of the alphabet which it hath. On one side are counted their months, which are of twenty days each. And on the other side are counted our months, which are of thirty days, one more or less. And since this count is so given, it is easy to know, of their feasts, in which of our months they fell, and on which day of each month. The other count, which is of the years, is placed in the Seventh Book of this history. There it may be seen, if it please Our Lord that it be published.

Porque la tabla precedente del arte adiuinatoria esta difficultuosa de entender, y de contar: puse esta tabla que se sigue, porque esta muy mas clara y la cuenta muy mas facil, y conforme a como ellos contauan. Y no piense nadie, que esta tabla es Kalendario porque como dicho es, no es sino arte adiuinatoria. El Kalendario destos naturales se pone en el principio del segundo libro esta muy claro de entender, porque las letras del a. b. c. que tiene: de vna parte, se cuentan los meses suyos, que son de veynte en veynte dias. Y de la otra parte, se cuentan los nuestros meses: que son de a treynta dias, vno mas o menos. Y por estar esta cuenta desta manera, facil cosa es saber sus fiestas, en que mes de los nuestros cayan: y a quantos dias de cada mes. La otra cuenta que es de los años, se pone en el septimo libro desta historia: alli se podra ver, si plugujere a nuestro señor, que salga a luz.

BOOK FIVE -- THE OMENS

Libro quinto, que trata de
los agueros, y prenosticos: que
estos naturales, toma-
uan: de algunas a
ues, animales,
y sauandixas,
para adiuj
nar las co
sas futu
ras.

De los Agueros

FIFTH BOOK, IN WHICH ARE TOLD THE OMENS IN WHICH THE MEXICANS BELIEVED.

IC MACUJLLI AMUXTLI, VNCAN MOTENEOA: IN TETZAUJTL CATCA, IN QUJTETZAMMATIA IN IEHOANTIN MEXICA.

First Chapter. Here are related the omens in which they believed when, at night, someone heard some wild animal cry out, or when it seemed as if some old woman wept; and also what the readers of the day signs said, they who were called wise ones.

Ic ce capitulo, vncan mitoa, in tetzaujtl in qujtetzammatia: in iquac ioaltica, aca quicaquja: in chocaica itla tequanj, in anoce, iuhquj aca ilama chocaia: auh iequene, in tlejn qujtoaia, tonalpouhque: in mjtovaia tlamatinjme catca.

In olden times, when false gods were still being worshipped, thus said some of the old men, the ancient people, when we yet were concerned with nothing else, when we believed these things to be true, when still in our land we spoke of that which the departed ones testified to us — our ancestors who are no more. They told us of all these things which they knew to be omens, and knew as evil, the portents they heeded, which all considered portentous; the things which they thought ominous.[1]

In ie vecauh, in oc tlateotoco: in juh quitoa, cequjntin veuetque, veuetlaca: in oc titixcavitoque, in oc titomattoque, in oc totlalpan tiqujtoaia: in aiaaque technelotoque: in aiaque totlah onoque. Yzqujtlamantli, y, in qujtetzammatia, in quitetzaujtiaia, in tetzaujtl ipan quimatia in netetzaujloia, in tlatetzaujaia.

First is this: when anyone heard that a wild animal cried out — that a wild beast howled at him like one who blew a shell trumpet, and the mountains answered him. It wailed; [a sound] issued from its mouth as if a poor old woman wept. On this, they said, now he would perish in war, or die — he would die of a sickness.[2] Or now he would meet some kind of mischance. Perhaps he would be sold [into bondage] — he would incur a penalty; or he would have some of his children sold — he would bring the penalties and visit his sins upon them.[3] Misery would come upon his house, his fireside, and his hearth. Disaster would repeatedly appear in his house.[4]

Jnic centlamantli, iehoatl, in iquac aca quicaquia: in tequanj choca, tequanj ipan choca: in juhquj tecciztli qujpitza: tepetl qujnanqujlia: tehcuiooa, tlaoalanja: iuhqujn ilamapul choca. Ynjn, qujtovaia ie iaomjqujz: anoço ie mjqujz, tlalmiqujz: anoço, ie itla commonamjctiz, icnoiotl: aço monamacaz, motlanamjctiz: anoço ipilhoan ceme qujnmonamaqujliz, qujntlanamjctiz: qujntlatlaculnamjctiz, icnoiotl calaqujz, in jnextitlan, in jtlecujllan: atl neneciz in jchan.

1. Cf. Angel María Garibay K.: "Paralipómenos de Sahagún," *Tlalocan*, I, 4 (1944), p. 308.

2. Cf. Rémi Siméon: *Dictionnaire de la langue nahuatl ou mexicaine* (Paris: Imprimerie Nationale, 1885), *tlallomiqui*, to die a slave's death. Below (Chapter 12, n. 2), Sahagún translates *tlalmiqui* as to die of a sickness.

3. Leonhard Schultze Jena: *Wahrsagerei, Himmelskunde und Kalender der alten Azteken* (Stuttgart: W. Kohlhammer, 1950), p. 5: *"man werde sie austauschen, werde an ihnen sich schadlos halten."*

4. The corresponding Spanish text refers to *desventura*.

When it so befell him, because of it he went to see the reader of the day signs, [who] then encouraged and greeted him. He said to him:

"Thou art unfortunate, O slave, O servant, O lad, O youth, O chieftain! In truth thou seekest and askest encouragement. For so hast thou come that thou mightest come to see thy reflection,[5] to use the sacred book for thyself. Behold what thou hast merited; it is not gentle and good, not righteous and not fitting to one of good standing. For so said the ancients as they left us. For they have made fall [upon us] the digging stick and tump line of poverty. But on the other hand, enough! Perchance thou hast been negligent. Perchance already, tomorrow or the day after, he by whom we live will be wroth or require appeasement. Await the command. For here it is depicted in the book of days, which we have guarded for the commoners. Shall I, perchance, in truth, frighten and terrify thee? For the master our lord hath wished this upon thee. By no means hath the beast become as man.[6] Unfortunate art thou; for at such a time, truly, wert thou born. For so was thy day sign not a time of peace. But this hath indeed been verified: perchance thou mayest do honor to whatever may be thy deserts.[7] Take courage; be not sad, and use all thy force; be above the hardness of thy heart, thy tears and grief. For take care [lest] in vain I deck thee with flags and paper streamers, cure thee, and surround thee with medicines. Perform penances; forthwith and quickly prepare the papers. Thy blood offerings shall be made. Buy for thyself everything — paper, incense, rubber, etc. When [we have done] this, and we know that the day is here upon which we shall make offerings to Tlalxictentica, who is arising, thou shalt here return. Here I shall use my own hands; I shall arrange and place in order all that is needed. Everywhere will be standing our paper streamers, our blood offerings. For I, myself, shall go to burn them in thy home. I shall go to do it with my own hands."

Just so did they who believed in omens and were affected by them. Etc.

Yn jq̃c oiuh ipan muchiuh, y: njman ic iauh, qujttaz in tonalpouhquj: vmpa quellaquaoa, qujtlapaloa: qujlvia:

Timotolinja xole, xolotze, telpuchtle, tiacave: ca nel tictemoa, tiqujtlanj, in mellaquaoaloca: ca ic otiualla, in timotezcaujco, in timamuxvico: xicchie, in tlein oticmomaceuj: ca amo iuijan qualli: amo tlacaiectli, amo tlacaçemelle: ca iuh conjtotiuj, in techcauhtiuj, in vevetque: ca ujctli, mecapalli, icnoiotl, qujtemouja: ioan anoce, ie ixqujch: aço titlatlatziujti, aço ie muztla, viptla, moçomaz, monenequjz, in jpalnemoanj: ma xicmotlatolchieli, ca iuh ma chiotica, in tonalamapan: in vncan tictlapielia, in cujtlapilli, atlapalli: cujx çan nel njmjtzihiçaviz, njmjtzmamauhtiz? ca mopan oqujnec, in tlacatl totecujo: camo motlacaiocoia, in tequanj: timotolinja, ca nel iuhcan timotlacatili: ca iuh ca motonal, in amo tlacacemellecan. Auh injn, ca oneltico: aço ie tocommaujçoz, in quenamj momaceval: ma ximellaquaoa, ma titlaocux, ixqujch motlapal: oc motepitziollo, oc mochoqujz, motlaocul ipan xonie. Ca izca, ça oc nen ic njmjtzpantia, njmjtzteteuhtia, ic njmjtzpatia, ic njmjtzpaiaoalochtia: xitlamaceoa, ma iciuhca oniecauhtiuetzi, in amatzintli: in monextlaoal, onmuchioaz: xoconmococouj, in jzqujtlamantli in amatl: in copalli in olli &c. Iquac, yn, ticmattiuj: izca tonalli, in jpan tictlamacazque, tlalxictentica: in meujltitica, tioalmoujcaz: nican njcnomaujz, njccencaoaz, njctlatlamantiliz, in jxqujch monequjz: in jzqujcan icaz, toteteuh, tonextlaoal: ca nehoatl, nonoma njctlatitiuh, in mochan: njcnomaujtiuh.

Ivin, in qujchioaia, motetzaujanj, motetzauj. etc.

5. *Ibid.*: *"veniste a ver el espejo donde esta la declaracion de lo q̃ viste."*

6. *Ibid.*: *"no ay q̃ culpar al anjmal, porque el no sabe lo q̃ se haze, porq̃ caresce de entendimiento de rrazõ."*

7. *Ibid.*: *"agora averificarse en ti, la maldad del signo en q̃ naciste."*

8. *Ibid.*: *"vẽdras tal dia, que es oportuno para hazer la offrẽda q̃ es menester al señor dios fuego."* Tlalxictentica: identical with the fire god Xiuhtecutli; cf. Bernardino de Sahagún: *Historia general de las cosas de Nueva España* (Angel María Garibay K., ed.; México: Editorial Porrúa, S. A., 1956; hereafter referred to as Garibay ed.), IX, 3. Cf. Vol. I, p. 9, for reference system.

Second Chapter, in which is related the evil omen which they regarded in two ways: so it was when they heard that the white hooded hawk[1] cried out; and what the merchants did when somewhere on the road such befell them; perhaps it cried out at them.

Ic ome capitulo, vncan mjtoa: in tetzaujtl catca, in çan necoc tlachiaia: in juhquj catca, in jquac qujcaquja, in tzatzia oactli: ioan in tlein qujchioaia, puchteca in jquac cana iuhquj vtlica, in jnpan muchioaia in anoço inpan tzatzia.

Likewise they considered it an omen of evil when the white hooded hawk screeched at someone. As they said, it spoke in two [ways],[2] sometimes good and sometimes bad.

When it displayed good, then they heard its words which it said as it screamed: "A good time! A good time!" When this was the case, none were frightened; the travelers were in no way terrified by it. Rather, they rejoiced. It was as if their hearts were gladdened, because perhaps they would come upon something pleasing; perchance in something they would be favored; they would attain something beneficial.

But when they heard that it laughed too long, in a high pitch, — as if its bosom and side tightened; or as if it screamed swollen with joy, [then], as if they were sick and frozen, none spoke aloud. They went with heads hanging, with necks loose. No longer [was there] control. Because of this they felt that perhaps something woeful would now betide them; they would come upon something perilous. Either some one of them would die; or sickness would come or somewhere they would be cut off. This befell them when, perhaps, [they were] somewhere among the mountains, in a gorge, in the midst of the desert,[3] in the middle of the woods, in a thicket, within and among the trees. And if it were merchants, vanguard merchants, wayfarers, whom it befell that at them the white hooded hawk laughed, they said that perhaps now they should come upon something, or their goods would be carried away by the water, .or some evil men, thieves

No ioan, qujtetzammatia: in jq̃c aca ipan veuetzca, oactli: in juh conjtoa, vme vitz qujtoa: in quenman qualli, quenman amo qualli.

In jq̃c qualli qujnextia, ic qujcaquj in jtlatol injc vevetzca qujtoa: ieccan, ieccan, in jquac, yn, amo netemmacho: atle ic momauhtia, in nenenque: çan ie papaquj: iuhqujn acovetzi in iniollo: ipampa, aço itla qualtzin, in jpan ie oniazque: aço itla ipan mopovatiuj: itla qualli, qujcnopilujzque.

Auh in ie oqujcacque, in juhquj ommjmjctoc, ic vetzca, tlatlapitzaoa: in juhquj, ixillan, ijomotlan, onquaquauhti: in juhquj, mocacanaoa, paquj, vevetzca: iuhqujn ontlanavi, iuhqujn ocevetzi, aocac naoati: ça tlatoliuj, ça tlaquechpiliuj, aiocmo tenaoatili: ic qujmatia, aço itla ovi, inpan ie ommuchioaz: itla ouj, ie conmonamjctizque: anoço ceme aca ie mjqujz: aço ie vitz cocoliztli, anoço cana inpan, ie oalmotzaquaz. In jnpan muchioa, yn, aço cana tepetzalan, atlauhitic, ixtlaoatl itic, quauhnepantla, quauhiooacatla, quauhitic, quaujtl itic: auh intla puchteca, oztomeca, nenemjnj: iuhquj inpan omochiuh, in jnpan ovevetzcac oactli: qujtoaia. Aço, ie itla, commonamjctizque: aço ie ontlaatoctizque: anoço ie acame, tlaveliloque, inmac ie ommaqujzque, ichtecque, tetlacujcujlique, tetlatlaçaltique, tetlanamoelique, inmac ie ontlatlaçazque, qujntlacujcujlizque, qujntlacencujlizque, qujntlatlaçaltizque, qujntlanamoelizque: anoço cana ceme, ie onquauhtenue-

1. Cf. Eduard Seler: *Collected Works* (J. Eric S. Thompson and Francis G. Richardson, eds.; Cambridge: Carnegie Institution of Washington, 1939), Vol. IV, p. 48; he comments that the bird was thought an evil omen to traveling merchants.

2. Probably idiomatic. More literally, *vme vitz qujtoa* could be rendered "in two ways came what it said."

3. *Quauhnepantla.* Alonso de Molina, in *Vocabulario de la lengua mexicana* (Julio Platzmann, ed.; Leipzig: B. G. Teubner, 1880), translates the term as either woods or desert.

who had escaped from their hands, who pilfered, plundered, and robbed, would now wrest goods from their hands, and plunder, strip, sack, and rob them. Or somewhere, some of them might now faint and collapse, throw themselves to the ground. Or they would be eaten by wild animals — the fare of brutes; they would become the game of wild beasts. Or somewhere they would be encircled by, and encounter, war.

When this was so, he who was leader, who went commissioned leader, who proceeded as principal there along the road, then began to encourage them. He greeted his younger brethren with tears, his charges who were being taught. Along the way he instructed them and said to them:

"Be of good cheer, O my sons, O my younger brothers. Of what profit is it that we are afflicted? Let no one be sad or heavy of heart. In truth for this we came: we came to die; so went our hearts heavy and foreboding. Thus we went from and left our homes and the houses of others:[4] our aunts, our uncles, our nephews, our elder sisters. For this reason they shed tears for us; they poured out upon us their weeping, their sorrow, that perhaps here, somewhere, on the desert, on the plains, in the gorge, in the forest, in various places will lie scattered our bones and our hair; in many places our blood, our redness, will spread, poured out and slippery. For in truth this hath been our reward. Let no one feel womanish in heart. Yield completely to death; pray to our lord. Let none think of or brood over [our condition]; for only later shall we know of whatsoever things[5] we may strike against. Then, in the end, we may weep for ourselves.

"For truly, this is how we come giving honor[6] and luster to our lords, the merchants who lead, raising them to glory and lifting high their heads. Ere now they have gone knowing and marveling at such things. We are not then the first to discover and behold what will befall us. Strengthen your hearts, O my sons!"

And if somewhere night fell, they gathered, joined, crowded, and assembled themselves somewhere at the foot of a tree or the opening of a gorge,

tzizque, ie onvetzizque, ie ommomaiaujzque: noce, ie ontequancoalozque, tequãtlaqualtin, tequanjme intlaqualhoan, ie ommuchioazque: anoçe, cana inpan ie oalmotzaquaz iaoiotl: ie conmonamjctizque.

In jquac yn, in aqujn tachcauh, in tachcauhchiuhtiuh, in tachcauh icatiuh vtlipan, vncan peoa, in qujmelaquaoa, in qujnchoqujztlapaloa, iteiccaoan, itlahoapavalvan: in vtli ipan qujmixtlamachtia, qujmjlvia.

Ximellaquauacan, nopilhoane, noteiccaoane, quennel titotolinja: macaiac tlaocuja, nentlamati in jiollo, ca nel ic tioallaque, in timjqujco: ca iuh oalietia, iuh qujoalmattia in toiollo: injc ticoalalcaujque, tiquallalotique in tonca, in teca: in tauj, in totla, in tomach, in toueltiuh: ca ie injc techchoqujli, injc topan qujpixo, in ichoqujz, in jtlaocul: aço cana njcan, ixtlahoatl, atlauhtli itic, quavitl itic, cecemmantoz in tomjo: in totzon, nonoqujuhtoz, aalacatoz in tezço, in totlapallo: ca nel otomaceoaltic, ma caiac qujcioatlamachti in ijollo: xicmotlaquammacacan in mjqujztli, xicmotlatlauhtilican in totecujo: ma caiac tle itic qujnemjti, qujlnamjquj: ma ça qujn jc ticmatizque, in çaço tle itech titotzotzonativi: vncan ic cemmaian, tontochochoqujlizque:

ca nel iehoatl injc tiquinteiotico, tiqujmjtauhcaiotico, tiqujntonaleoaco, tiqujntzonteconacocujco intotechiuhcaoan, in puchteca, in jiaque: ca ieeppa iuh quimattivi, iuh qujmaujçotiuj, camo qujn tehoan iancujcan ie toconnextizque, ie toconjttazque, in tlein topan muchioaz: ximellaquaoacan, nopilhoane.

Auh intla cana oimpan ioac, cana quaujtl itzintlan, anoço atlauhcamac, ommololoa, onmocemololoa, ommotepeuhtitlalia, monechicoa, qujcujtlalpia, quj-

4. Probably *tonca* and *teca* are to read *tocal* and *tecal*. In Bernardino de Sahagún, "Memoriales en 3 columnas," *Historia de las cosas de Nueva España* (Francisco del Paso y Troncoso, ed.; Madrid: Hauser y Menet, 1906), Vol. VII, p. 390, the phrase is *yn toca, yn teca.* The corresponding Spanish text reads: *"quando partimos de nuestras casas."*

5. "Memoriales en 3 columnas," p. 391, after *in çaço tle,* inserts *tictonamictitiui, in çaço tle.*

6. In *loc. cit.*, it is *tiquĩtenyotico.*

and bound and tied, fastened together, and placed on the ground, all their staves, which represented their god Yiacatecutli. Here, before him, they did penances, bled themselves, cut their ears, and drew straws through them; so they only yielded to whatsoever might befall them. But no one worried or speculated whether it might befall them as the white hooded hawk had foreboded to them.

And perhaps they quite escaped, [or] perchance nothing happened to them who were then terrified when the time of their fright had occurred. If nothing befell them, their hearts were therefore again a little lifted; they raised their heads and revived their spirits; for their fates were so established that fear should no longer be with them.

But the fearful ones, the younger brothers who were not of firm fortune, not of rugged day signs, when they learned of [the omen], went fearing it. No longer were they happy; they talked no more — no longer did they speak aloud; nowhere were their hearts content. Things only worsened as they traveled; they only went engraving on their minds whatever they imagined. No longer with calm, but vainly, did they a little way follow the land; rather, they thought that perchance soon they would somewhere come upon what in truth meant their omen which had occurred and by which they had been frightened.

It hath already been said, nevertheless, that no one knew whether, indeed, it would be verified, or would not be so. For its words were understood, since it spoke in two [ways], to be good and evil.

cencujtlalpia, qujcemjlpia, qujcemmana in jntopil, in jpan qujxeoaia in inteouh: Yiacatecutli. Vncan ixpan tlamaceoa, mjço, monacaztequj, tlacoqujxtia, ça qujmocemmacatoque, in tlein inpan, ie ommuchioaz: auh aocac ontlamati, aocac itlamatia, intla iuhquj inpan muchioa, in juhquj ic oqujntetzauj oactli.

Auh anoçe çan maqujça, acaço tle inpan muchioa: in vncan in nemauhtiaia, in jnmaujzcujian omochiuhca. Intla catle inpan omochiuh, ic oc ceppa achitzin, oalmoiolizcalia: oalaquetza onmoquaahaiouja: ic ommotonallalilia: injc intech oacca maujztli:

auh in mauhcatlaca teteiccaoa, in amo tonalchicaoaque, in amo tonallapaliuj: ça ie in qujmattiuj, in qujmamattiuj: aocmo paquj, aocmo tlatoa, aocmo naoati, aoccan auja in jiollo: ça tlanauhtiuj, in nenemj, ça imjtic tlacujcujlotiuj, in tleinmach qujlnamiquj: aiocmo iujian, in oc nen achi qujtoca tlalli: ça ie in qujmati, aço qujn cana in ie commonamjctizque, in tlein vel qujtoznequj, intetzauh omuchiuh: injc omotetzaujque.

Ie omjto, tel aiac qujmati, in aço vel neltiz: in acanoçomo, ca itlatol itech mocaquj: injc ome vitz qujtoa, qualli ioan amo qualli.

Third Chapter, in which is told the omen taken as a portent when at night they heard as if someone shot iron arrows into something or as if he chopped wood; this they called the night axe.

Likewise there was an omen which was taken as and considered portentous; its name was the night axe. When it made itself heard, it was well into the night,[1] when none spoke aloud.

When the priests went forth to do penances and to lay down fir branches at their places of doing penance on mountain tops, wheresoever they all went, then it was heard that it resounded like someone chopping and splitting wood. It rang out for a great distance; much did it frighten the people. It made them faint and swoon with fear. This night axe, so we are told — it was said that it took the form of Tezcatlipoca, to make sport and fun of people.

They said that he who looked upon it, one who was bold and wise, and not given to fright, of strong spirit,[2] could then hurl himself at it. He seized it and would no more give up, in order to see it. He would call to it as to a person and, indeed, hang on to it — force himself on it — as he pursued it. He followed at its back and forced it on; because thus he could catch it and see what manner of omen his was. Thus do they say, that whosoever would catch it when he saw it could with difficulty approach it; yet he pursued it and made it go everywhere; everywhere he came up to it.

When he tired it, somewhere on the road he awaited it without fear. And when now he saw it, he beheld it like a man without a head — a headless one, with neck severed at the nape, and with chest framework and belly broken open. Thus they said it was thought that that which was heard was his [split] chest framework when its halves met [like] a mouth continually opening and closing, with a sucking sound.[3]

Ic ei capitulo, vncan moteneoa: in tetzaujtl catca, in tetzammachoia: in jquac iooaltica qujcaquja, in juhquj aca, tlatepuzmjuja: in juhquj quauhxeloaia, in qujtoaia, ioaltepuztli.

No ioan, tetzaujtl catca, netetzaujloia, tetzammachoia: in jtoca ioaltepuztli. Iquac caqujztia, in ouellallimjctimotecac: in aocac naoati.

In ontlamaceoato, in onacxoiatlalito tlamacazque: in jntlamaceoaian tepeticpac, in çaço campa ic, onuja, injc mocaquja, injc caquiztia, iuhqujn aca, tlaxeloa, quauhxeloa: cenca veca caqujzti, cenca temamauhti, teiolmjcti, teçotlauh. Inin, ioaltepuztli, iuh mjtoa, qujlmach iehoatl, ipan mjxeoaia, in tezcatlipuca: injc teca mocacaiaoaia, teca maujltiaia,

qujtoa. In aqujn qujttaia, in mjhiujntia, in jiollo qujmati, in amo momauhtianj, in tonallapaliuj, vel ic momotla: qujmomaca, aiocmo qujcaoa, injc vel qujttaz, qujtlacanotzaz, vel itech mopiloa, itech motlapaltilia, injc qujtoca: qujteputztoca, qujtlalochtoca, ipampa injc vel caciz: qujttaz, in quenamj itetzauh: in juh conjtoa, in aqujn vel cacia, in qujttaia: aiaxcan in vel itech pachiuj: oc qujtotoca, noujã qujnemjtia: noujan caaxitia.

Iquac in oqujciammjcti, cana otlica qujoalmuchieltia: auh in ie qujtta in ie qujtzticac, iuhqujn tlacatl quechcotonquj, quechcotoctic, quechtepultic: ioan elchiqujuhtlapanquj, ellapanquj: in juh conjtoa: qujlmach iehoatl, in caqujzti, ielchiqujuh: iuhqujn ommonamjquj onmocacamapiquj, ommopipiquj, onchachaquanj.

1. Corresponding Spanish text: *"al primer sueño de la noche: quando todos duermen profundamente."*

2. *Ibid.*: *"algun hombre animoso y esforçado y exercitado en la guerra."*

3. *Ibid.*: *"el pecho tenjale abierto: y tenja cada parte como vna portezilla, que se abrian, y se cerrauan, iuntandose en el medio: y al cerrar, dezian: que hazian aquellos golpes, que se oyan lexos."* See Pl. 2.

And of this [apparition] he to whom it appeared, whether priest or bold one, or reckless warrior, when he had succeeded in reaching and seeing it, then saw his heart. He seized it; he clutched it and took it tightly in his fist; he tore it out. So he demanded what it would give, grant, or award him — perhaps riches, perhaps the taking of captives, perhaps valor; or poverty — perhaps the hoe or the tump line. So was it said that all which it thus awarded him became his gift.[4]

And if it spoke to him, it said: "O our friend, O humming bird, O warrior. What dost thou say to me? What wilt thou have of me? Unhand me, and I shall give thee what thou wishest." At once did it then address him, calling him by his name as a man — whatever was his name — and his name as a nobleman.

And the vassal to whom it had appeared said to it: "I shall not let thee go, for I have taken thee."

Then it said to him: "Behold one thorn; I give it to thee. Leave me alone."

The brave-hearted one liked this not;[5] he thought it not well. At last he left it if it gave him three or four thorns. Thus these showed and made evident that he went skillfully to war, not going forth in vain.[6] As many [captives] would he take as it showed and gave him thorns. Thus he then received as reward all earthly happiness and contentment — flowers, tobacco, riches; capes, lip pendants, head bands.

And also it was said, and so was the common opinion and report, that whosoever could not make it talk, immediately tore and ripped out its heart. He who had cut out its heart fled from it and ran away. He buried it somewhere: he wrapped it up thoroughly and tightly, and later, when it had dawned, he looked at it, and then it showed him whether [his fortune were] good and propitious. When he saw a soft, white feather, or thorns — perchance one, or two — then it appeared that his lot would be good. But if it were not good, he saw a piece of charcoal or a rag. Thus it indicated that his reward had become only poverty and misery.

And whosoever was not of strong spirit, who was not well based — of poor foundations — the coward,

Auh ie iehoatl, in, yn aqujn oqujmottiti: in aço tlamacazquj, in anoço çan mihiujntia in jaotlaueliloc: in jquac in ouel cacic, in ouel qujttac, njman ie qujmottilia in jiollo: qujcujtiuetzi, qujtlalochana, qujmotzoltzitzquja, qujcotonilia: ic qujtlaitlanjlia, in tlein qujmacaz, in tlen qujnemactiz, in tlein qujmaceoaltiz: aço necujltonolli, aço tlamaliztli, aço oqujchiotl: anoço netolinjliztli, aço victli, aço mecapalli: iuh mjtoa, ca much ie qujtemaceoaltiaia, itenamac muchioaia.

Auh intla ie qujnotza, qujluja: Tocnjuhtze, vitzitle, iaotle: tle tinechiluja, tle tinechnequjlia, xinechcaoa: njmjtzmacaz in tlein ticnequj: vel njman ic tenotzaia, ic qujtlacatocaiotiaia, in aqujn tlein itoca, in jpiltoca.

Auh qujluja in maceoalli, in oqujmottiti: amo njmjtzcaoaz, ca onjmjtzan.

Ic vncan qujluja, izca ce vitztli: njmjtzmaca, xinechcaoa:

amo qujcelia, amo qujuelitta, in jollochicaoac: qujnjquac quicaoa, intla eei, anoço ie nauj, qujmaca vitztli: ic qujnextia, qujnezcaiotia, ca tlamatiuh in iavc, amo nenqujcaz: izquj caciz in oqujtenevili, in oqujmacac vitztli: ic much vncan, qujmaceoaltia in tlalticpac paqujliztli, neiollaliliztli: in xuchitl, in jietl, in netlamachtilli: in tilmatli, in tençacatl, in tlalpilonj.

Auh yoã mjtoa, iuhca in nenonotzalli, in tlatlatolli: in aqujn amo qujtlatlatoltia, çan vel njman qujcotonjlia, qujtlatzcotonjlia in ijollo: ixpampa iehoa, motlaloa in oqujcotonjli yiollo: cana qujtlatia, vel qujqujqujmjloa, qujtepitzilacatzoa: qujnjquac in otlathujc qujttac, in qujteittitia, intla qualli, intla iectli: in conjtta: iztac ivitl in molontica, anoço vitztli, aço çe, anoço vme, ic qujnextia ca qualli, in jmaceoal: omochiuh. Auh intlacamo qualli, in conjtta: tecolli, anoço tzotzomatli, ic qujnextia, in çan icnoiotl, netolinjliztli, oqujmaceoalti.

Auh in aqujn, amo cenca tonallapaliuj, in amo itzin, amo itzitzin, in mauhcatlacatl: amo can vel

4. "Memoriales en 3 columnas" has *itenemac.*

5. *Qujcelia*: either *qu-icelia* or *qui-celia* may be read. Cf. Molina, *op. cit.*

6. *Nenquicaz*: the tilde is omitted in the Nahuatl text.

could nowhere seize [the specter]. He only heard it, and, giving up the chase, left it in terror. He could not pursue it; he was exhausted, vexed; deadened was his body; he only went flattened on the ground; he could walk no more. So he knew that the night axe was an omen to him, only making sport and fun of him. Perchance sickness or death, or misery, slavery, and sin, [the specter] gave him when it came upon him.

cana, çanijo qujcaquj, çan icampa ontlacuecuetlaxoa, ontlacuecuechcaoa: amo vel qujtoca, çan onciammjquj, onmociauhcanequj, mjmjquj in jnacaio, ça vtlica chachapantiuh, aiocmo vel nenemj: ic qujmati in çan oqujtetzauj ioaltepuztli, çan ica onmocacaiauh, ica ommaujlti: aço cocoliztli, mjqujliztli: anoço icnoiotl, tlacujutl, tlatlaculli, in oqujmacac: injc oqujmotlac.

Fourth Chapter, in which is told the omen taken as a portent when the horned owl[1] hooted.

Ic nauj capitulo, vncan mjtoa: in tetzaujtl injc motetzaujaia, in jquac teculutl chocaia.

Likewise all took it as an omen and an augury, and it was considered a portent, when the horned owl hooted, when perchance on someone's roof terrace or on his roof top, or up in his tree, it was hooting when they heard it, and it was saying, "Tecolo-o-o! Tecolo-o-o!"[2] In this wise it sounded when it hooted.

No yoan netetzaujloia, tlatetzaujaia, tetzammachoia, in teculutl choca: in jquac tla aca ytlapantenco, anoço ixacalticpac, iquauhticpac chocatica: in qujcaquj qujtotica: Tecolo, o, o, tecolo o o, yvin in caqujzti, in choca.

They said that when it was heard, it signified death or sickness; it was an omen of death. He who heard it would perhaps die, or beg, or be slothful; he would die of sickness or in war; or one of his sons would die; or his slave would flee. Perhaps now his house would be destroyed, his land would shrink; water would continually appear; weeds would cover at the gateway or the courtyard; the walls would lie crumbled, in ruins — lie devastated. There all would answer the calls of nature — would urinate and defecate — and rubbish would be cast. Salts would lie evaporated; the earth would lie smoldering.

Qujtoa in jquac in cacoia, qujnextia mjqujztli: cocoliztli, mjqujztetzaujtl: in aqujn oqujcac aço ie mjqujz: aço tlaciujti, aço tlatlatziujti tlalmjqujz, anoço iaomjqujz, anoce aca ce ipiltzin ie mjquiz, anoço itlacauh ie choloz, aço ie tlalpoliujz in jchan, tlalli canaoaz, atl neneciz, acaoatimanjz in qujiaoatl, in jthoalli, tepantli xixitintoz, tlaujujtontoz, tlaueuelontoz, vncan nexixaloz, neaxixaloz, nemanaujloz, tlaçollaxoz, tequjxq'tl coxontoz, tlalli ipotocatoz:

Then it would be said, so that all might marvel: "Once, in this place, here, was the house of one who came commanding reverence. Here came a householder enjoying fame;[3] there was always honor, and [the house] was swept clean. At least the rubbish was cast aside somewhere. And none might urinate on his walls, [or] he would chide him.

iquac itoloz injc tlamaujçoloz: ie iuhcan ocatca in, ichan in vncan ontlamamauhtico: in vncan onmoteiotico chane: muchipa otlamavizmamanca, otlatetzcaliuhtimanca: ma cel cana ce tlaçolli ovetztoca: auh in jcaltech aiac vel omaxixaia, teaoaia:

"But now in his very place only the walls remain standing."[4]

auh yn axcan ie ça iuhcan, ça tepantli ieoatoc.

---

1. *Teculutl.* According to Seler, *op. cit.*, Vol. I, Pt. 3, p. 14, it is a horned owl or eagle owl. In Vol. IV, p. 48, he refers to it as a large owl "associated with darkness, night, and characters influential at night." Francisco F. Santamaría, in *Diccionario general de americanismos* (Méjico: Editorial Pedro Robredo, 1942), Vol. III, p. 147, identifies it with the *lechuza* (see, however, Chapter 5, n. 1, *infra*).

2. Garibay, *op. cit.*, p. 309, n. 6, referring to the superstition, *"Cuando el tecolote canta, el indio muere,"* translates *"Tecolo-o-o"* as *"Perjudica a alguno."* He identifies the bird as *Buho virginianus* L. (*buho de Anáhuac*).

3. Corresponding Spanish text: *"En este lugar biujo vna persona de mucha estima, y veneracion, y curiosidad."*

4. In *ibid.*, this is added: *"En este caso: el que oya este canto, del buho: luego acudia al que declaraua estos agueros: para que le dixesse, lo que auja de hazer."*

Fifth Chapter, in which is told what was the omen of the screech owl.[1]

Likewise all held and regarded the screech owl[2] as an omen, when it screeched from the front of someone's roof terrace, and went screaming.

They said: so, therefore, they thought that now someone would die; now some of the householders would die; now some would sicken. And if now twice or thrice it passed screeching, in the very same place, the front of the roof terrace or upon the house, so much were they frightened and filled with dread, that verily they believed that because of this, [misfortune] would not miss its mark — that in truth it would come to pass as the screech owl screeched at them.

Likewise, if someone were already sick when it let out a scream at him, they said that now he would not issue forth; now we would take our leave of him.[3]

For they said this: it was thought that this screech owl was the messenger, the envoy, of Mictlan tecutli and of Mictecaciuatl. It knew the land of the dead. Hence [the gods of the underworld] named it "seasoned warrior"; because it was the one who called and summoned people for Mictlan tecutli and Mictecaciuatl.

And when they heard it screech and rasp its claws,[4] then the men chid it and said to it: "Go quietly, O knave, thou with the big eyes sunk deep! Thou hast lain with thy mother!" And the women said to it, and thus chid it: "Vanish quietly, O sodomite! Hast thou perchance made a hole in the hair, with which I may drink [in the land of the dead]?[5] For not until then shall I go!"

When thus they had chidden it, it was thought that thus all were made secure. Thus they hindered, reversed, and headed off its warning, so that what he screeched at them would not befall them.

Ic macujlli capitulo, vncan mjtoa: in tetzaujtl catca, in jtechpa chiquatli.

No yoan netetzaujloia, tetzaujttoia, in chiquatli: anoço chichtli yn jquac aca, itlapanjxquac tzatzi: tzatzitiqujça,

in qujtoa: cuel, ic qujneltocaia, ca ie aca mjqujz: ic ceme mjqujzque in chaneque: ie ceme cocolizcujzque. Auh intla ie oppa, ie expa tzatzitiqujça: in çan ie vncan, in tlapanjxquac, anoço in calipan, ic cenca momauhtia, motemmati: vel ic qujneltocaia, ca amo çan tlaneoa: ca vel neltiz, injc inpan otzatzic chiquatli.

No ioan, intla ie aca mococoa, in jpan tzatzitiqujça, qujtoaia ca aiocmo qujçaz: ca ticcaoazque.

Ipampa iuh qujtoaia, qujlmach, in iehoatl chiquatli: intitlan, intlaioal, in mjctlan tecutli: yoan mjctecacioatl: ommat in mjctlan, ic qujtocaiotiaia, iaotequjoa: ipampa ca inteancauh, intenotzcauh, in mjctlan tecutli: ioan mjctecacioatl.

Auh in jquac, qujcaquja tzatzi: ioan in mozticacalatza njman conaoa, conjluja in toqujch: ma xitlamattiuh nocne, tixtecocoiocpul: monan ticieco. Auh in cihoa conjluja, injc caoa: ma xitlamatpolotiuh, cujlonpul: cuix oticcoionj in tzontli ic natlitiaz: ca iamo cuel in njiaz.

Injc iuh conaoa in, qujlmach iuhqujn ic onepatilo, ic queleltia, ic qujlochtia, ic qujiacatzacuilia, in itenotzaliz: injc amo inpan neltiz, ic qujntzatzilia.

---

1. Seler, *op. cit.*, Vol. IV, p. 52, says that the *chiquatli* is a smaller owl, the screech owl. Santamaría, *op. cit.*, Vol. I, p. 484, says of *chicuate* that it is *"nombre vulgar de un ave de la clase de los bubónidos, llamada también* lechuza llanera *y* chicuatotol (Speotyto cunicularia hypogaea *Ridgw.*)."

2. *Chiquatli* and *chichtli* are interchangeable terms. See corresponding Spanish text and Molina, *op. cit.*

3. Corresponding Spanish text: *"luego le pronosticauan la muerte."*

4. *Ibid.*: *"escaruaua con las uñas."*

5. *Ibid.*: *"con que tengo de beuer alla en el infierno."*

Sixth Chapter, in which is told what the omen was, so that they took it as a portent, when someone saw a weasel which crossed in front of him.

Likewise all regarded the weasel[1] as an omen when it entered someone's house or else he came upon it on the road and it crossed over in front of him and appeared before him.

They said that now perhaps he would meet an affliction; perchance something would spring upon him. He would not arrive where he planned to go. Perhaps he would fall into the hands of some men who would slay him; or now words would be raised against him. Maybe now someone would make a declaration about him, adding lies and inventing things about him.[2]

And when it was seen, all shuddered with fright, were terror-struck, stunned; their flesh crept.[3] — We became numbed and quivered; our hair stood on end; we panicked. It brought one woe and affliction.

And thus, in this manner, was it marked: with a large, varicolored, yellowish belly. And when it spoke, it squealed, as if one whistled through one's fingers. "Tocuileua," "Tocuilechua."[4] And also "seasoned warrior" did they name it.

Ic chiquacen capitulo, vncan mjtoa: in tetzaujtl catca, injc motetzaujaia: in jquac aca qujttaia, coçamatl in teixpan tlaujltequja.

No ioan netetzaujloia in coçamatl, anoço coçatli: in jquac aca ichan calaquja: anoço vtlica, cana qujnamjquj: qujiacaujltequj, ixpan tlaxtlapaloa:

qujtoaia, aço ie itla conmonamjctiz tetolinj: aço ie itla ipan oncholoz, amo vel iaz in campa iaznequj: aço acame inmac vetzitiuh, qujmjctizque: anoço ie tlatolli, itech oneoaz: aço ie aca, tlatolli coneoaltiz: contlatollaqujliz, contlatolchichiujliz.

Auh in jquac itto, netlacmauhtilo: necujtiuecho, cecepoca, cuecueioca, in tenacaio, ticecepoca, ticuecueioca, tiquacecepoca, titocujtivetzi: tetequjpachoa, teiollitlacoa.

Auh in juhquj, ic muchichiuh: yxtecujcujlpul coztic: auh injc tlatoa pipitzca, iuhqujn mapipitzoa: tocujleoa tocujlechoa: no iaotequjoa qujtocaiotiaia.

1. *Coçamatl* and *coçatli* are interchangeable terms; see Molina, *op. cit., cuçatli.*

2. Corresponding Spanish text: *"le aujan de leuantar algũ testimonio."*

3. *Ibid.*: *"se les espeluzauan los cabellos, algunos se ponjan jertos, o pasmados."*

4. Jena, *op. cit.*, p. 384, suggests that these terms may be the title of a ruler of the dead, like the rank and princely name *tocuillecatl.* See, however, Andrés de Olmos: *Grammaire de la langue nahuatl ou mexicaine* (Paris: Imprimerie Nationale, 1875), p. 235.

Seventh Chapter, in which is told the omen so taken as a portent concerning the rabbit when they saw that now it entered one's house.

Likewise all regarded as an omen the rabbit when it entered someone's house. The field workers, the people of the maize fields, said that now his house would be laid waste. Or else now someone would flee [from it]: he would follow the trail of the rabbit, or of the deer. Now he would be a rabbit or a deer; he would turn into a rabbit or a deer.[1]

Thus was marked the rabbit — with very long ears,[2] a blunt, very blunt snout, a white breast, and very much shortened tail.

Ic chicome capitulo, vncan mjtoa: in tetzaujtl injc motetzauja, in jtechpa tochin: in jquac qujttaia in je vncalaquj ichan.

No ioan, netetzaujloia in tochin: in jquac aca ichan calaquja, qujtoa in mjllaca, in mjlpan tlaca: ie tlalpoliujz in jchan. Anoço ie aca choloz, ie contocaz in tochtli, in maçatl ivuj: ie tochtiz, ie maçatiz, ie motochtiliz, ie momaçatiliz.

Injc muchichiuh tochin, nacazpapatlactic, tentipontic, tenteteponic, eliztac: ioan çan cujtlapiltetepontic.

1. Cf. Molina, *op. cit.* (*tochtilia*): *"hazerse conejo, o hazerse bestia, o tornarse bruto el hombre."*

2. If from *patlaua,* to lengthen; an alternative is *papatlaca,* to quiver.

Eighth Chapter, in which is told the omen which all took as a portent when they saw the chafer.[1]

Ic chicuei capitulo, vncan mjtoa; in tetzaujtl, injc motetzaujaia: in jquac qujttaia pinaujztli.

Likewise all regarded as an omen the chafer, [which was] like a bright, brilliant red spider.

No ioan, netetzaujloia in pinaujztli: iuhqujn tocatl tlatlauhquj, tlatlactic.

When it entered someone's house, and he saw it, or he intercepted it on the road, they said: "Now cometh sickness"; or, "Now we will meet some [evil]." Perhaps now someone would chide him — something would shame him.

In jquac aca, ichan calaquj, in qujtta: anoço vtlica qujiacanamjquj, qujtoa ie vitz cocoliztli, anoço ie itla conmonamjctiz: aço ie aca conaoaz, itla ic conpinauhtiz:

And when it was seen in one's house, he who saw it forthwith seized it. He traced lines on the ground in the four directions: he made marks on the ground which he caused to take the form of a cross. And in the middle, at its center, he placed [the chafer] and there spat upon it.[2]

auh in jquac, tla oittoc techan: in aqujn oqujttac: njman ic conana, nauhcampa qujtlallacujlhvia, qujtlalxochilia: iuhqujn cruz qujquechilia: auh nepantla yiolloco contlalia, vncan onchicha:

Thereupon he exhorted it; he said to it: "Wherefore didst thou come? Let me see, [that] I may hasten to marvel at it!"[3] Then he placed himself facing and looked toward the direction in which it would proceed.

njman ie ic qujtlatoltia, qujluja. Tlen jc otivalla, tla njqujtta, tlacuele nocommaujço: njman ic qujtztimotlalia, qujtztica in campa ie itztiaz.

If now it went northward, thus he who looked knew that soon he was to die. But if it did not go toward there, thereby he knew that perchance it meant something [else] perhaps of no great consequence.[4]

Intla ie vmpa itztiuh, mjctlampa: ic qujmati ca ie mjqujz, in oqujmottiti: auh intlacamo vmpa itztiuh, ic qujmati, aço çan itla in qujtoznequj, acaçomo cenca veixtica:

He who was shown the omen said: "Let it do [what it will]; let the little insect be aspersed! Shall we none the less be involved with it? Shall we none the less go with it? Later let us know what it meaneth."[5] Then he seized it and left it at a crossroads.

qujtoaia in motetzauj, tla qujioculi, tla motelchioa, in ioioliton: cujx çan ie toconmattiezque? cujx çan ie ipan toiezque? ma ça qujn jc ticmatizque in tlein, qujtoznequj. Niman ic conana: homaxac concaoa.

And some only threaded it on a hair and hung it up. If at dawn they saw that it no longer was there,

Auh in aca çan contzonuja, aco compilova: intla otlathvic aocac qujtta: ic cenca vel qujtetzammati.

1. Seler, *op. cit.*, Vol. V, p. 4, calls it a kind of chafer which the Mexicans considered an evil omen (citing Batres); he connects it with the *tzitzitzime*. Molina, *op. cit.*, defines it as *"cierto escarauajo q̃ teniã por aguero."* Garibay, *op. cit.*, p. 310, n. 10, defines it as *Cotinis motabilis, Strategus julianus*, or the like.

2. Corresponding Spanish text: *"hazian dos rayas en cruz en el suelo, y ponjanla en medio dellas y escupiala."*

3. *Ibid.*: *"A que as venjdo, qujero ver a que as venjdo."*

4. *Ibid.*: *"algun otro infortunjo de poca importancia."*

5. *Ibid.*: *"anda vete donde qujsieres, no se me da nada de ti, e de andar pensando por uentura en lo que qujsieres dezir, ello se parecera ante de mucho, no me curo de ti."*

they were then filled with much dread. But if it dawned and it hung at this very same place, they were consoled thereby. Little did they think of it; as nothing did they esteem it. And when they placed it in the midst of spittle or wine, they said it was made drunk by it. And also it was stated that sometimes it spoke in two [ways]: it also boded good. Perhaps something fortunate would be one's reward.

Auh intla çan ipã otlatvic, in çan ie vncan pilcac, ic moiollalia: amo cenca qujueimati, atle ipan conjtta. Auh injc contlalia tlanepantla, chichitl, anoço vctli: mjtoa ic contlaoantia: ioan no mjtoa, in quenman ome vitz qujtoa: no qualli qujnextia, aço itla qualli temacehoal muchioa

Ninth Chapter, in which is related the omen which they regarded as a portent when an animal of strong stench, called a skunk,[1] now entered one's home or else sprayed and loosed an odor.

Likewise all regarded as an omen the skunk when it entered someone's home or there bore its young. They said: "Now the householder will die"; because, so they said, its abode, its dwelling place, was by no means among houses, in one's home. Maize fields, meadows, maguey and cactus fields [were] its dwelling places and abodes.

Also, they supposed that it was the likeness of the demon Tezcatlipoca. And when it loosed an odor, when it loosed a foul odor at one, they said: "Tezcatlipoca breaketh wind."

And if someone tried to capture or chase it, thus it mocked and gibed him: it raised and lifted high its tail, and then, if it drew quite near one, it forthwith loosed its stench at him. Like one sprinkling, its spray appeared and was seen; like a rainbow it arose. And it penetrated one; its evil stench entered into one. With difficulty did it abandon him. So one's cape dropped — was cast aside, thrown away. [Its stench] was spread all over the area; it extended all over the region. It reached everywhere, and spread on people. So did its stink sicken one and molest one's nose.

And they said that when it arrived, when it was smelled, one should not spit. It was believed that if one spat, his hair would whiten; it would flare brightly. Hence they severely warned the children not to spit. When its stench was smelled, they only covered their mouths.

Ic chicunauj capitulo, vncan mjtoa: in tetzaujtl in qujmotetzaujaia, in jquac centetl iolquj, in cenca hijac, in jtoca Epatl: in jquac ie oncalaquj ichan, auh anoço in jquac moxixa: mjexi.

No ioan in epatl, netetzaujloia: in jquac aca ichan calaquj, anoço vncan mopilhoatia: qujtoa, ie mjqujz in chane: ipampa iuh qujtovaia, ca amo inentla, amo inemja in calla, in techan: ca mjlpan, çacatla, memetla, nonopalla, in jnemjia, in jqujçaia.

No ipan qujmatia, ca ixiptla in tlacateculotl, tezcatlipuca: auh in jquac mjexi, in teiexi, qujtoaia: omjex in tezcatlipuca.

Auh intla aca canaznequj, in ace qujtoca: çan ic qujqueloa, ic ica mocaiaoa: cenca qujquetza, cacoquetza in jcujtlapil: auh qujnjquac, intla ie uel itech onaci: njman ic qujualiexi, iuhqujn aca tlaalpichia, vel neci, vel itto, in jiel: iuhqujn aiauhcoçamalotl, ic moquetza: auh vel temaoa, tetechaquj in ijel, aiaxcan tecaoa: ic vetzi, ic tlaxo, ic tlaçalo in tetilma: vel centlalli momana, centlalli manj: nouijan aci, tepan moteca, injc yiac, injc tetlaelti: teiacaxolocho.

Auh qujtoa, in jquac in eco, mjnecuj, auel onchicha: qujlmach intla aca onchichaz, quaztaliujz, comonjz: ic cenca qujntlacaoaltia, in tepilhoã: injc amo onchichazque: in jquac ineco yel: çan onmotempachoa.

1. Seler, *op. cit.*, Vol. IV, p. 20.

Tenth Chapter, in which is related the omen, by which a portent was drawn, of ants or frogs, and mice.

Likewise ants, whether red or black, were regarded as an omen. When in someone's house they swarmed, they formed an ant hill, they indicated persecution. They said, when they were seen, "Perhaps one of our persecutors is come to bury something to our disadvantage." So was it said, so was it known that what the persecutor buried to people's disadvantage turned into ants when time had passed. What they buried, all of it, they attributed to the persecutor, the one who wished one dead, the one who hoped that one would die, the one who desired one to die, the great adversary of the people; the inhuman ones, demons, the so-called destroyers of people. These buried and placed the ants.

When they swarmed in someone's house, thus they boded and required[3] his death. He who was envious, hoped, wished, and desired that one might die, that one might perish. So he caused anger; he tormented, troubled, affronted, and afflicted;[4] and he rendered no aid.

In the same manner all such [men] bore and determined an ominous death. The persecutor perchance placed house frogs[5] somewhere in an opening of the wall or in the roof of the house. When they spoke, they croaked, and continued croaking.

So also the ominous mice, perhaps [as reported in] tales,[6] all these, the inhuman people, the persecutors, placed and buried. When they spoke, so were they heard; so did they sound. Much and everywhere did they squeak; they squeaked continuously.

Ic matlactli capitulo, vncan mjtoa: in tetzaujtl injc motetzaujaia, in jntechpa azcame, anoço cuecueia: ioan in qujqujmjchtin.

No ioan, netetzaujloia in azcame, in tlatlauhque, anoço tliltique: in jquac aca, ichan molonj, moputza: qujnextiaia in tecocoliliztli: qujtoaia in jquac oittoque, aço aca totecocolicauh itla otechtoqujlico: iuh mjtoa, iuh nemacho in tlein qujtetoqujlia, tecocolianj: iehoan in mocuepa azcame, iquac in ie vecaoa, tlein oqujtocaque: muchi iehoan intech tlamj in tecocolianj, in temjqujtlanjnj, in temjqujztemachique, in temjqujztemachianj, in teveijecoanj, in atlaca in tlatlacateculo: in moteneoa, tepoloanj iehoã qujntoca, qujntlalia in azcame.

In jquac aca ichan molonj, ic qujtetzauja, ic qujtlanja in jmjqujz: in aqujn tlacocoa, connectia, connequjlia, connequjltia: in macuele mjquj, in macuel ompopoliuj: injc tlaqualanja, injc tlaiolqujxtia, injc tlaamana, injc teiollo ixco icac, injc tlatequjpachoa, injc atetloc monequj.

Ça ie no iuhquj, muchiuhquj: qujcenujca, qujcemjtoa in mjqujztetzaujtl. In iehoatl calcujatl, aço cana tepancamac: calquac in qujntlalia tecocolianj: cotaloa, cotalotica injc tlatoa.

No iuhquj in tetzauhqujmjchin, anoço tetlaquechililli. Pl' chililti: muchi iehoan qujntlaliaia, qujntetoqujliaia, in atlaca, in tecocolianj: injc caco, injc mocaquj: vel pipitzca, pipipitzca, pipitzcaticate, injc tlatoa.

---

1. Corresponding Spanish text: *"aujan de tener persecusion los de aquella casa de parte de algun maliuolo, o imbidioso."*

2. *Muchi iehoan*: "Memoriales en 3 columnas" reads *muchipa.*

3. Jena, *op. cit.*, p. 23, translates this passage thus: *"Entsprechend wie die Übelwollenden einen (nur ein Stück Wegs) verfolgen, so ziehen auch sie, die Ameisen, sich wieder zurück. Wenn nun das, um dessentwillen jene ihn verfolgt haben, verjährt, so beenden mit diesen (der wieder verschwindenden Ameisen) auch die Übelwollenden für immer ihr Treiben."*

4. "Memoriales en 3 columnas," p. 397, has *quitlama* for *qujtlanja.*

5. *Tetlaquechililli. Pl' chililti*: probably an accidentally inserted grammatical note.

6. The corresponding Spanish text adds at the end of the chapter: *"En todos estos agueros, yuan a consoltar a los agureros: que lo declarauan, y dauan remedio contra ellos."*

Eleventh Chapter, in which is told the omen from which a portent was drawn when, at night, they saw the towering men, the giants.[1]

Likewise all regarded as an omen the towering man[2] when it was seen as an apparition at night. It was said: "But all this is the disguise, the transformation, of the demon Tezcatlipoca, with all of which he maketh sport of men."

When it was thus visible to someone, he thereby held it as an omen that he would either die in war or be carried off. But one who was very bold,[3] strong of heart or spirit, would not more let [it] go. He seized it firmly in his hands and hung on to it. He demanded thorns of it, thus seeking valor and the taking of captives.[4]

And it was said that one who was of simple mind, neither prudent nor determined, when he saw it only spat or hurled dung at it. But in nothing at all would it benefit him; it only cursed him with some misery, afflicted him, smote and brought disaster on him thereby, and visited him with the digging stick and the tump line.

And [when] he who was only a coward saw an apparition, in no way did he banish his fears. Indeed, he fainted and swooned away; he no longer had saliva—the roof of his mouth was all dry; his mouth was parched. His mouth stuck fast, no longer moist. Not now was his mouth wet. With caution he withdrew, leaving its presence. He no longer wished to look at it. He fled in terror, feeling, thinking that someone would now snatch him away. In some manner he went to reach his home and rushed inside it, bursting in through its door, coming in on all fours and throwing himself with outspread arms upon those who slept.

Ic matlactli oce capitulo, vncan moteneoa in tetzaujtl: injc motetzaujaia: in jquac iooaltica, qujmjttaia tlacaujaque, qujnameti.

No yoan, netetzaujloia in tlacaujiac: in jquac iovaltica moteittitia, mjtoa: çan ie muche inaoal, inecuepaliz in tlacateculotl tezcatlipuca, much ic teca mocaiaoa:

in jquac aca iuh qujmottitia, ic qujtetzauja in aço ie iaomjqujz, aço ie vicoz. Auh in aqujn vel mjhivintia, in jollotlapaliuj, in tonalchicavac, aiocmo qujcaoa, qujteteuhtzitzquja, itech mopiloa: qujtlanjlia in vitztli, injc qujtemolia oqujchiotl, in tlamaliztli.

Auh mjtoa in aqujn ahqujmamatcaoa, in amo iolizmatquj, in amo nenonotzale: in jquac oqujttac çan conchicha, anoço cujtlatl ic contepachoa: auh amo tle ic qujcnelia, çan no qujtelchioa, itla netolinjliztli ic qujteopoa, ic qujmotla, ic qujueipoloa, aço victli, mecapalli qujttitia.

Auh in aqujn, çan vel mauhcatlacatl qujmottitia: njman amo coniecoa, in jtemamauhtiliz: vel çotlaoa, iolmjquj, aocmo chiche: vel icopac tlaoaquj, icamac tlapoliuj, icamac tlaçaçalia: aocmo tlapalti, aocmo tlapaltia in jcamac: çan tlamach contlalcavia, ixpampa ieoa: aocmo qujoalittaznequj, momauhcatlaloa: in juh momati, ie omma aca ie qujcujtiuetziz: in oquenteltzin acito ichan, motlaloticalaquj, qujpetlaticalaquj in jtlatzacujl: tepan manenenticalaquj: tepan mamaçouhtiuetzi, in vncan cochioa.

1. See Pl. 5. The corresponding Spanish text translates the terms as *estantiguas*. Santamaría, *op. cit.*, Vol. II, p. 551, has the following notation: *"QUINAMETZIN. m. pl. Los quinames; primitivos pobladores del Anáhuac, anteriores a los aztecas, a los cuales la leyenda asigna talla de gigantes y que ocuparon las riberas del Atoyac, en Puebla, principalmente."*

2. Garibay, *op. cit.*, pp. 310-311, n. 13: *"El 'hombre largo' (tlacahueyac), a lo que parece, era una fantasma que se alargaba hacia el cielo, como los* coleletin, *o diosecillos de los remolinos."*

3. Corresponding Spanish text: *"algun soldado valiente, y esforçado."*

4. *Ibid.*: *"que auja de captiuar en la guerra tantos captiuos, quantas espinas le diesse."*

Twelfth Chapter, in which is related what was another omen, whose name was "bundle of ashes." [1]

Ic matlactli omome capitulo, vncan mjtoa: in oc centlamantli tetzaujtl catca: in jtoca catca: tlacanexqujmilli.

Likewise there was an omen, which was a portent to them, the "bundle of ashes." Thus was it said: "Indeed, all this is the disguise, the reappearance, the apparition of Tezcatlipoca."

When it was seen, it only went rolling, groaning, and billowing. He who saw it then held it as an omen that he would die, either in war or of some sickness;[2] or that something evil would meet and fall upon him.

Whoever was not strong and sturdy of heart, who was just a coward, if it appeared to him, only fled and ran from its presence. Then it frightened and terrified him, lest soon he die or something evil should come upon him, etc.

But he who was sturdy of heart, one who was renowned as intrepid in war, then prepared, arrayed, and bedight himself. Then he thus took counsel with himself: at night he would hunt the wizard who walks everywhere. He went in pursuit of him — on all the wide ways where he dwelt at night. He went seeking it, that perchance somewhere it would appear to him; that he might demand from it his reward, his gift — thorns.

And if now one appeared before him like this one, he sought it out and seized it; he grasped it firmly in his hands, and clung to it. Not now did he let it go; he tortured it. He said to it: "Who art thou, O rogue? Speak to me! Fail not to speak! For I have taken thee, and I shall not let thee go." For a long time he persisted in torturing it.

When it spoke to and answered him, if now he vexed it, when, perhaps, it was about to dawn and morning to break, it said to him: "Loose me now! Thou harmest me! Whatsoever thy heart wisheth, I shall give thee. What shall I give thee?" It said: "Take it. I give thee a thorn."

"I will not have it; I will not take it!"

No yoan, tetzaujtl catca, tetetzaujaia: in tlacanexqujmjlli, iuh mjtoa: çan ie muchi ieh inaoal, inecuepaliz, inenextiliz in tezcatlipuca:

in jquac ittoia, çan momjmjlotiuh, qujqujnacatiuh, tehtentiuh. In aqujn qujttaia, ic qujtetzanuja, in ie mjqujz: aço iavc, anoço çan tlalmjqujz: anoce ytla, amo qualli ie qujmonamjctiz, ipan vetziz.

In aqujn amo iollochicaoac, in amo iollatlapaliuj, in çan mauhcatlacatl, intla oqujmottiti: çan ixpampa iehoa, motlaloa: vncan qujtonalcaoaltia, qujhiçavia: injc yciuhca mjqujz, anoço itla amo qualli qujmonamjctiz. etc.

Auh in aqujn, vel iollotlapaliuj: in moteneoa: iaotlaueliloc, ic momanja, ic muchichioa, ic mocencaoa: njman iuh qujmolhuja, in iooaltica, naoaltetemoz, novijan nenemj: qujtotocatinemj, in jzquj vchpantli, iooalnenemj, qujtetemotinemj, in aço cana itla qujmottitiz: injc qujtlanjliz itenemac, iteicneliliz vitztli.

Auh intla ie oqujmottiti in juhquj y, qujtetemoa: qujcujtiuetzi, qujteteuhtzitzquja, itech mopiloa: aocmo qujcaoa qujtlatoltia, qujluja: ac tehoatl jn nocne? xinechnotza, amommaca titlatoz: ca onjmjtzan, amo njmjtzcaoaz: vecauhtica qujnemjtia, in qujtlatoltia:

iquac qujnotza, qujnanqujlia intla ie caamana: in ace ipan tlathviznequj, in ace qujtlathujltia, qujlvia: xinechcaoa ie tinechitlacoa, tlein qujnequj moiollo: njmjtzmacaz, tlein tinechmacaz: qujluja, yzca njmjtzmaca, ce vitztli:

amo njcia, amo njccelia

1. Cf. Garibay, *op. cit.*, p. 311, n. 14. The corresponding Spanish text describes them as *vnas fantasmas: que nj tienen pies, ni cabeça: las quales andan rodando por el suelo, y dando gemidos, como enfermo.*"

2. *Ibid.*: "*morir . . . en breue de su enfermedad.*"

"What shall I do?" It offered him two, three, four [thorns].

Verily, not for them did he loose it. Later, when it gratified and satisfied him, it now said: "I give thee all prosperity. Thou shalt be honored on earth." Then he released it;[3] for in truth he had realized what his heart sought — for which he had lived sighing and in discontent, etc.

tle njcchioaz, vme, Ey, nauj qujmaca:

ça nel amo ic qujcaoa: qujnjquac in oqujiolpachiujti, in oqujiolpachiuhcaioti in ie qujluja: muchi njmjtzmaca in necujltonolli, titlamaviçoz in tlalticpac: yquac qujcoa: ca nel oconjttac in qujtemoa ijollo, injc oelciciuhtinenca, onentlamattinenca. Etc.

3. *Qujcoa: quicaua* is meant.

Thirteenth Chapter, in which are told the rest of the omens which showed themselves at night.

Likewise all took as an omen [what] appeared before them called "hunched shoulder," or "little maize basket." In Acolhuacan it was called "little squashed one." [1] Thus were they named.

They said that they showed themselves to men only at the latrines, the dung heaps. If someone wished to urinate, and went forth quite alone at night, when, perhaps, the moon shone or it was dark, then they appeared to him. All this now only revealed to him an omen of death. He to whom it appeared thus took it as a portent that now he would die, or something would now befall him. But if he did not so do, it only terrified him.

And thus did it look — like a little girl, indeed, quite small; a very little girl, not a bit tall — only small like a sandal, a little cooking pot; a squat dwarf, pressed down like dung. She had hair, much hair, [flowing] like a garment, a mantle of hair, hanging. Clear to her hips did her hair fall — her mantle of hair. And as she walked, she only went creeping on the surface of the ground, waddling.[2]

He to whom she appeared could not catch her. If, now, he pursued her, she only disappeared from before him; thus she only mocked him. Further off, apart, she appeared. He pursued her there, he who tried to catch her; she vanished away. So he only let her alone, in terror; she tired him out; he was defrauded.

Just so, the severed head also appeared to the people at night. To him to whom it appeared, it often made known [its presence] by suddenly springing at the calf of his leg. Or else he heard it behind him, coming rattling[3] as it took after him.

Ic matlactli omei capitulo, vncan moteneoa: yn oc cequj tetzavitl, in iooaltica monextiaia.

No yoan, netetzaujloia moteittitiaia: in jtoca cujtlapanton, anoço cintanaton: mjtoa in acolhoacan centlapachton: iuh tocaiotilo.

Qujtoa, çan vncan in neaxixaloian, in tlaçulpan moteittitiaia: intla ie aca axixmjquj, in çan icel ioaltica qujça: in aço metztona, anoço tlaiooa: iquac qujmottitia: çan ieh much ie qujnextiaia in mjqujztetzaujtl. In aqujn qujmottitia, ic qujtetzanvia in ace miqujz, anoço itla ipan ie muchioaz: auh yn acanoço tlei, çan conmamauhtia:

auh injc ittoia, iuhqujn civapiltontli, çan vel tepiton, civapiltepiton: amo achi quauhtic: çan cacapanton, chachapaton, tzapaton, cujtlapachton, tzonqueme, tzotzonqueme, tzotzoquenpile: vel icujtlacaxiuhian vetzi, in jtzon, in jtzonquen: auh injc nenemj çan tlalli ixco onotiuh, pepeiocatiuh,

amo vel cana in qujmottitia: intla ie qujtoca çan ixpan ompolivi, çan jc qujqueloa: iene cecnj, in valmonextia: vmpa qujtoca in canaznequj ompoliuhtiuh: çan iuh commauhcacaoa, conciauhcaoa, ommonenencoa.

Çan ie no iuhquj in tzontecomatl, no moteittitia in iooaltica: in aqujn qujmottitia, çan jc qujmachitia, amo inemachpan in jcotzco choloa: anoce icampa, concaquj chachalcativitz, in qujualtoca: ic ixpampa iehoa, icampa chachalcatiuh in qujtoca.

1. Corresponding Spanish text: *"vna muger pequeña enana."* Cf. also Sahagún (Garibay ed.), Vol. IV, p. 326: *"'El enanillo.' Ser fantástico que era agüero." Cuitlapanton* is *caquilla* (*ibid.*, p. 332).

2. Corresponding Spanish text: *"vna muger pequeña enana . . . que tenja los cabellos largos: hasta la cinta, y su andar, era como vna anadeando."*

3. Cf. *ibid.* In Molina, *op. cit.*, however, *chachalca* is to scold. On *chachalaca,* see Horacio Carochi: *Arte de la lengua mexicana* (México: Imprenta del Museo Nacional, 1892), p. 476.

So he fled from its presence; back of him it went rattling at him as it pursued him. And if he stood, if he stopped in alarm, it also sat, and remained rattling. And if he gathered courage to seize it quickly, it only mocked him for doing so. Far did it rise when it jumped; he could not catch it. Hence, in the same manner, he let it alone in his fear; from its presence he fled, exerting all force in order to run terrified to his home.

Auh intla moquetza, motilquetza, no motlalia chachalcatinemj: auh intla omoiollochichili, injc qujcujtiuetziz çan jc qujqueloa, ueca ieoa in choloa, amo uel cana: çan no iuh conmauhcacaoa: ixpampa ieoa: ixqujch qujtoctia, injc momauhcatlaloa ichan.

Just so the dead also appeared to people. They were in [funeral] wrappings, with head wrappings, and were groaning. If, somewhere, one appeared before one, it moaned at him. Only the valiant could venture toward it in order to seize it and cling to it. But then it only made sport of them: perhaps a clump of grass or a hard clod remained in their hands. Thus they quickly transformed themselves. So it was said that all this was only a disguise of Tezcatlipoca by which he mocked men. Etc.

Çan ie no iuhquj in mjcquj, no moteittitiaia: yilpitica, quaquailpitica, quiqujnacatica: in cana moteittitiaia; tequjqujnatza: çan iehoan in jollochicavaque, vel iujc motlapaloa in qujcujtiuetzi: itech mopiloa. Auh injc çan inca mocacaiaoa, aço tlachcujtl, anoço tlaquavac tetl in jmmac mocauhtiqujça: injc mocueptiuetzi: iuh mjtoa, ca çan muchi ieh, inaoal in tezcatlipuca injc teca mocacaiaoaia etc.

The omen of the linnet.[4]

The linnet is a bird like a woodpecker,[5] and far into the forest is its home. And when it cried out at someone, it was taken as an omen.[6] They said: "It is not a good time that we have come; for something will spring out on us."

Tetzaujtl itechpa chiqujmoli.

In chiqujmoli, ca centetl tototl, iuhqujn quauhchochopitli: auh veca quauhtla in jchan. Auh in iq̃c tepan tzatzia, netetzaujloia: qujtovaia, ca amo qualcan, in otioallaque: ca itla ipan ticholozque.

The omen of the coyote.

They said it was Tezcatlipoca. Often he disguised himself as a coyote; and this coyote often intercepted men on the road. And when he did this, then was heard: "This is by no means a good time for him who goeth; perhaps thieves or robbers are somewhere on the road, or something harmful will spring out at them."

Tetzaujtl itechpa in coiutl.

Qujtoaia, ca in tezcatlipuca: mjiecpa qujmonaoaltiaia in Coiutl: auh injn coiutl, mjiecpa teiaíacatzacujlia in vtlica. Auh in jquac iuh qujchioa y, njman ic mocaquj, ca amo qualcan in viloa: aço ichtecque, anoço tetlatlaçaltique, cana vtlica cate: anoço itla ipan chololoatiuh, in tecoco.

Here end the omens which the natives of New Spain took as portents.

Nican tzonqujça in tetzavitl; yn qujtetzammatia, njcan nueua españa tlaca.

4. Molina, *op. cit.*: *sirguerito paxaro;* Santamaría, *op. cit.*, Vol. I, p. 514 (*chiquimole*): *jilguerillo — especie de jilguero.* Sahagún (Garibay ed.), Vol. IV, p. 334: *"Ave canora, sumamente parlera. . . .* Dryobates scalaris bairdi."

5. *Quauhchochopitli*: Nardo Antonio Reccho, in *Rervm Medicarvm Novae Hispaniae Thesavrvs sev Plantarvm Animalivm Mineralivm Mexicanorvm Historia ex Francisci Hernandez* (Rome: Vitalis Mascardi, 1651), p. 33, appendix, heads Chap. XCIV, *"De Quauhchochopitli, seu Auicula ligna excauante,"* and writes: *"Auicula est, Mexicanae Coturnicis formà, & magnitudine, plumis nigris, aut pullis, lineis albis, transuersim discurrentibus distinctis; ventre, pectoréque, minij colore: lingua picorum more, quorum est species prolixa: viuit in frigidis, & arbores rostro saepiusculè petitas excauat."*

6. Corresponding Spanish text: *"las bozes del pito* [magpie]: *quando le oyan bozear en las montañas."*

APPENDIX

Apendiz del qujnto libro,
de las abusiones: que vsauan
estos naturales.

BEHOLD THE APPENDIX OF THE FIFTH BOOK. HERE ARE TOLD THE DIFFERENT THINGS WHICH GOD'S CREATURES, THE IDOLATERS, WRONGLY BELIEVED.

IZCATQUJ YANCA INJC MACUJLLI AMUXTLI: VNCAN MJTOA, YN JZQUJTLAMÃTLI ITECHPA CHICOTLAMATIA IN JTLACHIVALOAN DIOS, IN TLATEOTOCANJME.

First Chapter, which telleth of the white amaryllis.[1]

This kind of flower was thus called — white amaryllis (*omixochitl*). And also a kind of sickness — decaying of the genitals — was also called *omixochitl,* because indeed in some such manner as [the flower], so was [the member] scarified. And so did the ancients invent, and so deceive themselves. It was said of him upon whom this sickness, which they called *omixochitl,* settled, that it began thus: perhaps one had urinated or stepped upon it; or one had smelled it many times. It was as if it had thereby bewitched him. In such manner did they deceive themselves.

Injc ce capitulo, ytechpa tlatoa in omjxuchitl.

Injn centlamantli suchitl: iuh motocayotia in omjxuchitl. Auh no centlamantli cocoliztli, tlapalanaltiliztli: no motocayotia omixuchitl: iehica ca çan vel iee injc ca, injc tzitziqujltic: auh injc compjquj, in juh moztlacaviaia veuetque: qujlmach in aqujn ytech motlalia, injn cocoliztli, in motocayotia omjxuchitl: ic peoa, in aço ypan omaxix, anoço oipan moquetz: in anoço mjiecpa oqujnecu, iuhquj injc qujxoxa, in juh moztlacavia.

Second Chapter, which telleth of the poinsettia.[2]

This kind of flower [was] fragrant. And yet another kind of sickness of the genitals was called *cuetlaxochitl* (poinsettia). And this sickness was especially the lot of women — particularly their sickness; not of men. And of this ill it was said that thus did it begin — so were the ancients deceived: they had perchance stepped over it, or smelled it, or else sat upon it. Therefore it then cast a spell upon her; thus it befell her. And hence mothers restrained and scolded their daughters; they said to them: "Do not smell it; do not jump over this flower; [the sickness] will be settled upon you."

Injc vme capitulo, ytechpa tlatoa in cuetlaxuchitl.

Injn centlamantli suchitl, ineconj. Auh oc no centlamantli tlapalanaltiliztli, no motocayotia cuetlaxuchitl: auh ynjn cocoliztli, oc cenca inpan muchioa in cioa, oc cenca incocoliz: amo no yehoan in toqujchtin. Auh injn cocoliztli: qujlmach ic peoa, in iuh moztlacavia vevetque: in aço oqujcuencolhuj, in anoço oqujnecu, in anoce oipan motlali: ipampa in juhquj ic qujxoxa, ic itech motlalia. Auh ipãpa in tenanoan qujntlacavaltiaia, qujmauaya in jmjchpuchoan, qujmjlhujaya: macamo xiqujnecujcan, ma ypan ancholoti injn xuchitl, amotech momanaz.

1. *Omixochitl,* according to Santamaría, *op. cit.,* Vol. II, p. 354, is the same as *omequelite* (*Polyanthus tuberosa* L., *P. mexicana* Zucc., *P. gracilis* Link), a fragrant flower appearing in July and August, used as a febrifuge. Sahagún (Garibay ed.), Vol. IV, p. 347: *Polianthes tuberosa, P. mexicana.* Seler, *op. cit.,* Vol. II, Pt. 3-4, p. 89: "bone flower" — "a white flowering Amaryllidacee or Iridacee."

2. *Cuetlaxochitl.* Francisco Hernández: *Historia de las plantas de Nueva España* (México: Imprenta Universitaria, 1946), Vol. III, p. 958: *Euphorbia* (*poinsettia*) *pulcherrima* Willd. Paul C. Standley: "Trees and Shrubs of Mexico," *Contributions from the United States Herbarium,* Vol. 23 (Washington: Government Printing Office, 1923), Part 3, p. 600: *cuitla-xochitl,* used in a decoction for nursing women to increase lactation. Sahagún (Garibay ed.), Vol. IV, p. 331: *Euphorbia fastuosa.*

Third Chapter, which telleth of flowers artificially arranged.[3]

Flowers arranged with artifice: there were many kinds thus named, flowers artificially arranged—flower shields; flowers for clipped heads, or for shorn ones, or drums; or spreading [flowers]. As to these flowers the ancients were also deluded. They said: "It is not our right to smell in the midst—the center—of them; he alone, he who pervadeth all, Titlacauan, may smell that place. Our right is only to smell them there at the edges."

Fourth Chapter, which telleth of dried grains of maize.

As to dried grains of maize, in many ways were the women none the less deluded. First, when they cooked it or set it in ashes—behold their folly: when they would place it in the olla with ashes, first of all they breathed upon it. It was held that in this way it would not take fright; thus it would not fear the heat. It was said that thus they mitigated the heat.

Second, they deceived themselves in this way: if they saw or came upon dried grains of maize lying scattered on the ground, then they quickly gathered them up. They said: "Our sustenance suffereth: it lieth weeping. If we should not gather it up, it would accuse us before our lord. It would say: 'O our lord, this vassal picked me not up when I lay scattered upon the ground. Punish him!' Or perhaps we should starve."

Fifth Chapter, which telleth of stepping over one.

As to stepping over one, the natives also [were] deluded. When some child lay stretched out across one's path, if someone stepped over him, then they chid him who passed over him, saying to him: "Why dost thou step over him?"

It was said that thereby the child would grow no more; he would be only small. And in order to cure him, so that [this] might not befall the child, once again he stepped back over him.[4] Thus was it remedied.

Injc ey capitulo, itechpa tlatoa, in suchitl yn ye tlatlalilli.

Suchitl ie tlatlalilli: ca mjiec tlamantli injc motocaiotia in suchitl tlatlalilli, chimalsuchitl, quateçonsuchitl, quachic, vevetl, moiauac: In jtechpa yn suchitl, no motlapololtiaya in vevetque, qujtoaia: ca amo tonemac in tlanepantla, in jnepantla tiqujnecujzque ca çan iceltzin vel vncan motlanecujltia in tloque naoaque, in titlacaoan: çanijo tonemac, in vncan titlanecujzque in jtenco.

Injc navi capitulo, itechpa tlatoa in tlaulli.

In jtechpa in tlaulli: mjiec tlamantli oc noma, ic motlapololtia in cioa. Injc centlamantli: in jquac qujcuxitia, in anoço qujnexquetza: izcatquj in jnnetlapololtiliz, in jquac ie contemazque in nexcomjc: oc achtopa conahaiovia, qujlmach ic amo momauhtiz, ic amo motonalmauhtiz: qujlmach ic contonallalilia.

Injc vntlamantli, injc muztlacavia: intla oqujttaque, in anoço oypan qujçato tlaulli chachaiauatoc tlalpan: njman conpepentiuetzi, qujtoa: motolinja in tonacaiutl, mochochoqujlitoc: ca intlacamo ticpepenazque, ca techteixpanujz in jxpantzinco totecujo: ca qujmolhujliz. Totecujoe, injn maceoalli: ca amo nechpepen, in jquac tlalpan njcenmantoca: ma xicmotlatzacujltili: auh anoce timaianazque.

Injc macujlli capitulo, itechpa tlatoa in tecuencholhujliztli.

In jtechpa tecuencholhujliztli: no centlamantli innetlapololtiliz in njcan tlaca: in jquac tla aca melavatoc piltontli, necujliuhtoc: intla aca oconcuencholhuj, njman caoa in aqujn otecuencholhuj, qujlhuja. Tle ipampa in ticcuencholhuja:

qujlmach ic ayocmo manaz in piltontli, ça ixqujchton iez: auh injc compatiaia, injc amo ipan muchioaz piltontli, oc ceppa qujoalpancholhuja: ic vmpatia.

3. *Suchitl yn ye tlatlalilli.* Corresponding Spanish text: *"las flores, que se componen de muchas flores."*

4. *Qujoalpancholhuja.* Corresponding Spanish text: *"eran menester tornar a passar sobre el, por la parte contraria."*

Sixth Chapter, which telleth of drinking.[5]

As to drinking, there, also was a delusion of the ancients, somewhat like the account of stepping over one.

And in this wise was the account of it: when, perchance, one drank; if one yet a small child drank first, and afterwards one drank who was a little older, already grown, then [the elder] restrained and took the water from the small child. He said to him: "Why dost thou wish to drink first? Thou wilt not grow large, but remain small. Now let thy elder brother drink, for he is already bigger." [6]

Injc chiquacen capitulo, ytechpa tlatoa in atliliztli.

In jtechpa atliliztli: no vncatca inneztlacaviliz in vevetque: çan ie achi no iuhquj in jtlatlatollo in tecuencholhujliztli.

Auh ivin in, ca itlatlatollo: in jquac tla ie atli, in tle ie achto atli oc piltontli: auh intla çatepan atli in ie achi tachcauh, in ie quauhtic: njman qujtlacaoaltia, qujcujlia in atl in piltontli, qujlhuja: tle ipampa in achto tatliznequj, amo tiquauhtiez, çan ye tixqujchtontiez: ma oc ie conj in motiachcauh, achic ca ie quauhtic.

Seventh Chapter, which telleth of him who dipped into the cooking pot.

Of this there was also a delusion of the natives, known especially of the men. And in this wise was it known: when, perhaps, men ate, and one only dipped into the cooking pot — not into a sauce dish — then also the mothers and fathers restrained him. They said to him: "Do not dip into the cooking pot; there [in war] thou wilt leave thy captives. If thou goest to war, none wilt thou seize; no one will become thy captive."

Injc chicome capitulo, ytechpa tlatoa: in aqujn xocco ontlapaloa.

In jtechpa in: no vncatca innetlapololtiliz, in njcan tlaca: oc cenca intechpa mocaquj in toqujchtin. Auh ivin in mocaquj: in jquac intla tlaqua toqujchti: auh çan xocco, in ontlapalotica, amo molcaxic: njman no qujtlacaoaltia in tenanoan, in tetaoan, qujlhvia: macamo xocco xontlatlapalo, vncan tiqujmoncaoa in momalhoan: intla tiaz iavc, aiac ticaciz, aiac momal muchioaz.

Eighth Chapter, which telleth of tamales stuck [to the cooking pot].

Concerning tamales stuck [to the cooking pot] as another deception of the natives, it was said that the men and women would not eat them. It was stated that if the men were to eat them, when they would shoot arrows in warfare, the arrow which was shot would not find its mark. Or perchance therefore they might die, or one's wife would with difficulty bear children.

And just so was it as to a woman. If she were to eat tamales which had stuck [to the cooking pot], she could not bear children. Her child would only adhere to and thus die in her womb. Therefore the mothers sternly forbade them to eat tamales which had stuck [to the cooking pot].

Injc chicuei capitulo, ytechpa tlatoa in jxqujuhquj tamalli.

In jtechpa in jxqujuhquj tamalli: oc no centlamantli inneztlacaviliz in njcan tlaca, qujlmach amo vel qujquazque, in oqujchtin, ioan cioa: qujlmach intla qujquazque toqujchti, amo axcan in qujçaz mjtl, injc qujmjnazque iauc: auh anoçe ic mjqujz, yoan aiaxcan tlacachioaz in jnamic.

Auh çan ie no yuhquj in jtechpa cioatl: intla qujquaz ixqujuhquj tamalli, amo vellacachioaz: çan itech ixqujviz in jconeuh, ic mjqujz in ijti: ipampa cenca qujtecaoaltiaia in tenanoan, injc amo moquaz, in jxqujuhquj tamalli.

5. Corresponding Spanish text: *"qujere dezir, beuer el menor, ante del mayor."*

6. *Ibid.*: *"si beujan dos hermanos. Si el menor beuja primero, deziale: el mayor: no beuas primero, que yo: porque si beues primero, no creceras: mas quedarte ás, como estas agora."* See also Carochi, *op. cit.*, p. 526: *"Achic, es adverbio, con que se muestra . . . que ai differencia entre vna persona, o cosa, y otra."*

Ninth Chapter, which telleth of the umbilical cord.[7]

The time of cutting the umbilical cord of small children was also [one of] their delusions. If it were the umbilical cord of a boy, they buried it far away. The brave warriors hung it on themselves and bore it with them into battle.[8] And if the father were skilled in war, he left it; he buried it there, in the midst of the battle ground. It was said that [the child] would be skilled in war, if he grew.

And if it were the umbilical cord of a girl, they only buried it at the edge of the hearth. It was said that this was because her abode was only the house; only and alone she took charge of drink and food, dwelling by the grinding stone. For this reason only in the house did they bury her umbilical cord.

Injc chicunavi capitulo, ytechpa tlatoa in toxic.

In jquac qujnxictequja pipiltotonti: no oncatca innetlapololtiliz. Intla oqujchtli ixic, veca in contocaia: vmpan iauc, tetech conpiloaia, qujtqujia in tiacaoan: auh intla iavc matinj teta, iehoatl concaoaia: vmpa contocaia in iaunepantla, qujlmach: iavc matinj yez intla veijaz.

Auh intla cioapiltontli ixic: çan netlecujltenco in contocaia, qujlmach ipampa: yn çan cali ynentla, in çan ie ixqujch qujmocujtlavia atl, tlaqualli, metlatitlan nenemj: ipampa yn, çan calitic contocaia in jxic.

Tenth Chapter, which telleth of the pregnant woman.

Of the pregnant woman there also was a delusion of the natives. If a pregnant woman wished to go walking during the night,[9] then she placed a little ash in her bosom.[10] It was said that thereby she protected the child within her, in order that he should not meet [an apparition] somewhere. In this wise she took care of her child.

Injc matlactli capitulo, ytechpa tlatoa in otztli.

In jtechpa in otztli: no vncatca innetlapololtiliz in njcan tlaca: in otztli, intla iooaltica nenemjznequj: njman ixillan contlalia aqujton nextli, qujlmach ic qujpalevia in jtic ca piltontli: injc amo qujtenamjctiz cana, iuhqujn ic qujmalvitiuh yconeuh.

Eleventh Chapter, which telleth of the woman lately delivered.

Another thing the natives did in their folly. When they would visit one who had [just] borne a child, if they took their [own] children with them, they then quickly placed ashes on their temples, knees, and shins, and everywhere [did they place ashes]. And the woman who applied the ashes sat before the hearth. It was said, if they did not place ashes on the knees of the children, that when they walked, their knees, wrists, ankles, and foreheads would crackle.[11]

Injc matlactli oce capitulo, ytechpa tlatoa in cioatl, in qujnoallacachioa.

No centlamantli a imaqujmamatcaio maytia, in njcan tlaca: yn jquac tla qujtlapalozque mjxiuhquj, intla inpilhoan qujnvica: njman yciuhca qujnnextiuja incanaoacan, in jntlanquac, in jntlanjtzco, in ye izqujcan toçaçaliuhcan: âcan qujmocavia, novian: auh in tenexhuja tlecujlixquac motlalia, cioatl: qujlmach intlacamo qujntlanquanexvizque yn pipiltotonti: çan tlatlatzintinemjz in jntlanqua, in jnmaquechtlan, in jnxoquechtlan, yn jmjxquac.

7. Literally, "our navel." Eduard Seler, in *Einige Kapitel aus dem Geschichtswerk des Fray Bernardino de Sahagun aus dem Aztekischen übersetzt* (Caecilie Seler-Sachs, Walter Lehmann, and Walter Krickeberg, eds.; Stuttgart: Strecker und Schröder, 1927), pp. 314 ff., translates a comparable passage found in the *Academia de la Historia MS.*

8. Corresponding Spanish text: *"al lugar, donde se dauan las batallas."*

9. *Ibid., "andar de noche, sin ver estantiguas."*

10. *Ibid., "en el seno, o en la cintura iunto a la carne."*

11. *Ibid., "si esto no se hazia aquellas criaturas, quedarian mancas de las coyunturas: y . . . todas ellas, cruxirian: quando las mouiessen."*

Twelfth Chapter, which telleth of earthquakes.

When the earth quivered, a delusion of the natives was to be seen. When the earth quaked, then they quickly took their children by the neck and lifted them,[12] so that they might soon grow big — so that they might mature quickly. It was said that if they did not take them by the neck and lift them quickly, they would with difficulty wax larger. And they said that the earthquake would bear [the child] away if they did not grasp him by the neck and lift him. And they sprinkled water upon their faces.

And their houses, their square wooden beams, their food storage bins, their cooking pots, and indeed all their goods, everything, they sprinkled with water. And if they forgot something, they wrangled over it; it was said that the earthquake would take it away. And everyone raised a din and cried out while striking the hand to the lips in order to make known [the earthquake] to those who knew not of it.[13]

Injc matlactli vmome capitulo, ytechpa tlatoa yn tlallolinjliztli.

In jquac tlallolinj, centlamantli neci innetlapololtiliz in njcan tlaca: in jquac tlallolinj, njman iciuhca qujnquechaana in jnpilhoan, injc yciuhca quaquauhtiezque, injc yciuhca manazque: qujlmach intlacamo qujnquechaanazque iciuhca, ayaxcan quauhtiazque: yoan qujtoaia, qujvica in tlallolinjliztli, intlacamo qujquechaanazque, yoan qujmjxalpichiaia.

Auh yn jncal, in jntlaquetzal, in jncuezcon, in jnxuc, in ye ixqujch intlatquj, muchi catzelhuja: auh intla ytla oqujlcauhque, yc maoaia: qujlmach qujvica in tlallolinjliztli: yoan ixqujch tlacatl ycaoacaia, motenvitequja: yc qujnmachiltiaya, in amo qujmati.

Thirteenth Chapter, which telleth of the [three] hearth stones.

Concerning the [three] hearth stones there was also a delusion of the natives. When they saw someone kicking[14] the hearth stones, they restrained him from doing so. They said to him: "Do not kick the hearth stones. It will deaden thy feet when, perchance, thou goest to war." They said to him that now he would not be able to walk or run in time of battle. His feet would be numbed; quickly he would fall into the hands of their foes. Hence the natives restrained their youths, that this might not befall them.

Injc matlactli vmey capitulo, ytechpa tlatoa in tenamaztli.

In jtechpa in tenamaztli: no vncatca innetlapololtiliz, in njcan tlaca: in jquac in aca qujtta, in qujtilicçatica in tenamaztli: yc qujtlacaoaltiaia, qujlhujaia: macamo xictiliçatia in tenamaztli mitzjcximjmjctiz in jquac intla tiaz iavc, qujlhuja: aiocmo vel nenemjz, aiocmo vel motlaloz in iaupan: ça ycximjmjqujz, yciuhca ynmac vetziz in jniaovan: ynjc qujntlacaoaltiaia in jntelpuchoan, in njcan tlaca, injc amo yuh inpan muchioaz.

Fourteenth Chapter, which telleth of the tortilla doubled over on the griddle.

When a woman made tortillas, if her tortilla doubled over, there was also a delusion of theirs. She said: "Someone who now cometh hath kicked

Injc matlactli onnavi capitulo, ytechpa tlatoa in comalco mocuelpachoa tlaxcalli.

In jquac tlaxcaloa in cioa, intla ocuelpachiuh itlaxcal: no vncatca innetlapololtiliz, qujtoa: aqujn ie vitz oqujoaltilicçac: auh in anoce yoqujchvi, in ca-

12. *Qujquechaana*: literally, they took them by the neck. The corresponding Spanish text reads: *"tomauan a sus niños con ambas las manos, por cabe las sienes, y los leuantauan en alto."*

13. *Ibid.*: *"para que todos aduertiessen, que temblaua la tierra."*

14. *Qujtilicçatica*: literally, were kicking it (cf. *tilicça*, Molina, *op. cit.*); corresponding Spanish text: *"los que ponjan el pie sobre las trebedes, que son tres piedras."*

it over." Or if, perchance, her husband had gone somewhere distant, she said: "Now he cometh, for he hath kicked over my tortilla."

napa veca oya, qujtoaia: ca ye hujtz, ca qujoaltilicçac yn notlaxcal.

Fifteenth Chapter, which telleth of small children who licked the surface of the grinding stone.

When small children licked the surface of the grinding stone, the mothers chid and scolded their young ones for it, and restrained them from it, saying to them: "Do not lick the grinding stone; your teeth will thus quickly break and fall out." Because of this, they filled their small children with great fear, so that this would not befall them.

Injc caxtolli capitulo, ytechpa tlatoa yn pipiltotonti qujxpaloa metlatl.

In jquac pipiltotonti qujxpapaloa metlatl: yc teaoaia, yc qujmaoaia, yc qujntlacaoaltiaia in tenanoan yn jnpilhoan, qujmjlhujaia: macamo xicpapalocan in metlatl, yc iciuhca cocotoniz, yciuhca vevetziz in amotlan. Ipampa yn, cenca qujmjmacaxiltiaia in pipiltotonti: injc amo iuh ynpan muchioaz.

Sixteenth Chapter, which telleth of him who leaned against a square pillar.

When they saw one who leaned against a square pillar, there also was folly of the natives;[15] they chid him for it, and restrained him from doing so; they prevented their children from doing it. They said to them: "Do not lean against the pillar; it is a liar." Thus did they speak: "It giveth one lies; it is like unto one who lieth." [With] this, they terrified the children lest such might befall them and they tell lies.

Injc caxtolli oce capitulo, ytechpa tlatoa: yn aqujn itech motlazticac tlaquetzalli.

In jquac aca qujttaia, in jtech motlazticac tlaquetzalli: no vncatca innetlapololtiliz, in njcan tla: yc teaoaia, ic tetlacaoaltiaia, ic qujntlacaoaltiaia in ynpilhoan, qujmjlhujaia: macamo ytech ximotlaztica in tlaquetzalli, yhjztlacati: iuh qujtoaia: ca iehoatl qujtemaca in jztlacatiliztli, itech qujcuj: in aqujn ihiztlacati. Injn, cenca qujmjmacaxiltiaia in tepilhoan: injc amo iuh inpan muchioaz, ynjc amo yhiztlacatizque.

Seventeenth Chapter, which telleth of the maidens who ate standing.

In times past, when the natives saw their maidens eat standing, they also restrained them from it. They prevented their children from doing so. They said to them: "Eat not while thou art standing. Thou wilt marry far from here.—Who will follow thee?" It was said that it would befall one that she would marry in a distant place; she would be taken somewhere far away, not in her own city where she lived.

Injc caxtolli omome capitulo, ytechpa tlatoa yn jchpupuchti in çan moquequetztimanj tlaqua.

In ie vecauh in njcan tlaca: in jquac in qujmjttaia in jmjchpuchoan ỹ çan moquequetztimanj tlaqua: no yc tetlacaoaltiaia, ic qujntlacaoaltiaia in jnpilhoan, qujmjlhujaia: macamo ximoquetztica in titlaqua, veca timocchotiz, ac mjtzicxitocaz: qujlmach iehoatl ipan muchioaia, in veca moqujchvatia, in cana veca vico: in amo yaltepeuh ipan nemj.

Eighteenth Chapter, which telleth how maize cobs were burned.

When one had just given birth to a child, she who, residing there, had given birth should not then burn maize cobs. It was said that if there [maize cobs]

Injc caxtolli omey capitulo, ytechpa tlatoa: in quenjn motlatia olotl.

In jquac aca mjxivia, avel vncan qujtlatiaia in olotl: in vncan onoc mjxiuhquj, qujl intla vncan tlatlaz: yc ichchichitinjz in piltontli. Auh intla ça

15. *In njcan tla*: read *tlaca*.

were to be burned, because of it the child's face would be pock-marked.[16] And if maize cobs were to burn there, first she passed and carried them before the child's face,[17] so that such would not befall him — so that his face would not be pock-marked.

vncan tlatlaz in olotl: achtopa ijxco conqujqujxtilia, ijxco convivica in piltontli: injc amo iuh ipan muchioaz, injc amo ichichitinjz.

Nineteenth Chapter, which telleth of the woman with child.

Injc caxtolli onnavi capitulo, ytechpa tlatoa: yn cioatl otztli.

The woman with child might not look at one whom they had hanged, because, it was said, when she gave birth, the child would come forth with a cord of flesh wrapped about his neck. Wherefore in times past they frightened pregnant women from doing so.

In cioatl otztli, amo vel qujttaz in aqujn ie qujpiloa: yehica, qujlmach in jquac mjxiviz, nacatica oalquechmecaiotiaz in piltontli. Ipampa yn, ic qujmjmacaxiltiaia in ie vecauh in ootzti.

Likewise, when a woman was with child during an eclipse of the sun or moon, she might might not look at it. It was said that if she saw it, her child would be harelipped. But in order to forestall this, the woman with child placed an obsidian knife in her bosom; it was said that thereby her child would not be harelipped.

No yoan yn jquac otztli cioatl, in jquac qualo tonatiuh, anoço metztli: amo vel qujttaia, qujlmach intla qujttaz: tenquatic iez in jconeuh. Auh injc qujpaleviaia otztli: ytztli ixillan contecaia, qujl ic amo tenquaiviz in piltontli.

Neither might she chew asphalt,[18] it was stated, lest the child be harmed in suckling[19] when he was born. And she could not walk about at night; it was felt that her child would be one who cried much. Likewise men might not walk about by night; perhaps they would come upon a ghost; perhaps the child would suffer a sickness of the heart. And so that this would not happen, the woman with child placed a pebble, or ashes from the hearth, or wormwood,[20] in her bosom. And the men [carried] a pebble, or tobacco [on the chest]; for it was said that also, at that time, [the child] might acquire what they called a swelling.[21]

Amono vel qujquaquaz in chapuputli, qujl ic amo motentzoponjz in piltontli: in jquac otlacat. Yoan amo vel iooal nenemiz, qujl cenca chocanj iez in jconeuh: no iuhquj in toqujchtin: amono vel iooal nenemjz, anoçe itla qujmonamjctiz, aço mjmjqujz. Auh injc amo iuh ipan muchiooaz otztli: xaltetl, anoço tleconextli ixillan qujtema, anoço iztauhiatl. Auh in toqujchtin xaltetl, anoço picietl: iehica qujl no vncan qujcuj, in qujtoa: aiomama.

16. Corresponding Spanish text: *"la cara del niño, que auja nascido: seria pecosa o hoyosa."*

17. *Ibid.*: *"tocauanlos primero en la cara del njño, lleuandolas por encima: sin tocar en la carne."*

18. *Chapuputli*: *"especie de asfalto; betún de Judea. . . . Los indios le usaban antiguamente como masticatorio"* (*chapapote* — Santamaría, *op. cit.*, Vol. I, p. 468). The corresponding Spanish text has *"aquel betun, que llamã tzictli."* On the relationship between *tzictli* and *chapopotli*, see Sahagún (Garibay ed.), X, 24, 18 and 27; and also Vol. IV, pp. 333, 366, for definitions.

19. Corresponding Spanish text: *"aconteceria aquello, que llaman motentzoponiz, que mueren dello, las criaturas rezien nacidas: y causasse de que quando mama la criatura, si su madre de presto la saca la teta, de la boca, lastimasse en el paladar: y luego queda mortal."* Cf. also Sahagún (Garibay ed.), Vol. IV, p. 344; and Bernardino de Sahagún: *Historia general de las cosas de Nueva España* (Carlos María Bustamante, ed.; México: Alejandro Valdés, 1829), Vol. II: "motentzoponiz (hoy mozezuelo) *o sea embarazo en la respiracion, que mueren de ello las criaturas recien nacidas."*

20. *Iztauhiatl*: *"vnos pocos de aiensos"* (corresponding Spanish text); *estafiate* (*Artemisia mexicana* Willd.) — *"las hojas despiden fuerte olor aromático y tienen sabor amargo. Úsase como antihelmíntico poderoso"* (Santamaría, *op. cit.*, Vol. I, p. 626).

21. Cf. Sahagún (Garibay ed.), Vol. IV, p. 324.

And when the swelling appeared, upon his back was as it were a small, blue bump. Or [he might catch] inflammation of the groin.[22] And when the inflammation of the groin appeared, the child cried every night; and on the groin and armpits were formed small, round or long [welts of] flesh. And in order to cure it, they cut them off and removed the little [welts] of flesh.

Auh injc neci aiomama, ycujtlapan ca, iuhqujn posatontli, iuhqujn texotic: anoçe cuetzpaliciviztli. Injc neci cuetzpalicivi piltontli: ceceiooal in choca, yoan yquexilco, yciacac motlatlalia nacatotonti, ololtòtonti, melactotonti. Auh injc pati: qujxoxotla, qujqujqujxtia in nacatotonti.

And as for the pregnant woman: before her child had been formed as a being, they restrained [any of] them, when the moon arose, from looking up at it. They said to them: "Do not look at the moon! Your children will suffer sickness of the heart, or else will be harelipped!"

Ioan in otztli: in jquac aiamo vel tlacatl motlalia in jconeuh, qujntlacaoaltiaia, in jquac oalmomana metztli: injc amo conacopaittazque, qujmjlhujaia: macamo xoconjttacan in metztli, mjmjqujz, anoçe tenquaiviz in amoconeuh.

Twentieth Chapter, which telleth of the monkey's hand.

Injc cempoalli capitulo, ytechpa tlatoa: in oçomatli ymacpal.

The merchants sought and cherished greatly a monkey's hand when they trafficked and sold goods anywhere. There they spread it out. It was said that thereby goods quickly were disposed of and soon all which they sold was bought. It was stated: "That which bringeth this about is the monkey's hand"—so foolish were they.

In oçomatli imacpal: in puchteca cenca qujtemoaia, qujmopialtiaia: in jquac in campa tiamjquja, in tlanamacaia: vncan qujtecaia, qujlmach ic iciuhca aquj, iciuhca muchi coalo in tlein qujnamaca: qujl iehoatl iuh qujchioa in oçomatli yma: ynjc motlapoloitia.

Also of the sellers of mantles—when nowhere was disposed of that which they sold, when no one bought either mantles, or shifts or skirts—it was said: "They make them eat chilis that the goods may be disposed of." And thus did they do it. When they returned to their homes, they said: "Our goods are nowhere disposed of. Give them chilis to eat." Then in their midst they placed perhaps two or three chilis. It was averred that thereby the goods were disposed of. When they so did this, they said that they had made [their mantles] eat chilis.

No iehoantin in tilmanamacaque: in jquac acan aquj in qujnamaca, in aiac qujcoa: in aço tilmatli, in anoço cueitl, anoço vipilli, qujlmach: qujchilquaqualtia, injc aquj. Auh injc qujchioaia: in jquac oalvia inchan, qujtoaia: acan oac in totiamjc: ma xoconchilquaqualtican: njman ic ijtic contema, aço vme, anoço Ey in chilli: qujlmach ic aquja, injc iuh qujchioaia in, ic qujtoa: qujchilquaqualtia.

Twenty-first Chapter, which telleth of the pestle and the griddle.

Injc cempoalli oce capitulo, itechpa tlatoa in texolotl, yoan comalli.

When one who played *patolli*[23] placed his pestle, and his griddle, and his grinding stone upside down in his home, and hung his pestle somewhere in a corner, it was said that thereby the householder would not lose, but only win.

In jquac aqujn patoaia, in jchan, in jtexolouh, ioan in jcomal, ioan in jmetl: ixtlapach qujmanaia: auh in texolotl cana xomolco qujpiloaia; qujlmach: ic amo qujtlanizque in chane, çan ie tlatlanjz.

22. Corresponding Spanish text: *"otra enfermedad, que llaman cuetzpaliciviztli, o con lobanillos en las ingles."* Note also *Codex Ríos* (*Il manoscritto messicano Vaticano 3738 detto il Codice Rios* [Rome: Stabilimento Danesi, 1900], p. 54).

23. The corresponding Spanish text refers to *pelota,* which is an error.

And [concerning] this pestle: when they caught, trapped mice,[24] they cast the pestle out the doorway. It was thought that if it were in the house, they could not be caught; it was said that it would warn them.[25]

Yoan in iehoatl texolotl: in jquac qujmaci, in qujnmôvia qujqujmjchtin: in texolotl qujiaoac qujoallaça, qujlmach: intla çan cali iez: amo vel macizque in qujqujmjchti, qujlmach çan qujmonjoatica.

Twenty-second Chapter, which telleth of mice.

Injc cempoalli omome capitulo, intechpa tlatoa in qujqujmjchti.

They said, in times past, that it was thought that mice knew well him who had a paramour, whether a young man or a woman. In order for it to be evident, the mouse made a hole in a large basket, or gnawed the edges of gourd dishes or bowls. Likewise, if men, or a woman, were married, he made holes in their mats, or the men's mantles. In the same way, he gnawed through a woman's shift or skirt. And everywhere the mouse made holes. It was said that thereby he made known that one's spouse had committed adultery.

Qujtoaia in ie vecauh, qujlmach in qujqujmjchti vel qujmati, in aqujn momemecatia: in aço telpuchtli, anoço cioatl. Injc neci in qujmjchin qujcoionja in chiqujvitl, anoço tecomatl, anoço xicalli qujtenquaquaia. No iuhque intla namjque toqujchtin, anoço cioatl: yn jnpetl, anoço yn jtilma toqujchtin qujcoionjaia: çã no iuhqujn cioatl, yn jcue, anoço yn jvipil qujcoionja: yoan noujan tlacocoionja in qujmjchin, qujl ic qujnezcaiotia: ca oqujtlaxin yn jnamjc.

Twenty-third Chapter, which telleth of turkey hens.

Injc cempoalli omey capitulo, intechpa tlatoa in totolme.

Turkey hens: when they were brooding, one who wore sandals might not go in among them. Especially when the chicks were about to break [the shells], it was said that [the hens] sat paralyzed. [The chicks] could not break [the shells, and] some would die. But some, when they hatched, it was thought, would only be paralyzed, those which were there in the shells. And it was said that in order that this might not happen, they placed old sandals among them when [the hens] brooded.

In totolme: in jquac tlapachoa, amo vel inpan calaquj in mocactia: oc cenca yquac in ie tlapanjzque totolti, qujlmach ic mocototztlalia: amo vel tlapanjzque, cequjntin ic mjquj: auh in cequjntin yn jquac tlacati qujl çan cocototzpipil, in vncan cate in cacalloc. Auh qujl injc amo iuh muchioazque yn, cacçolli intlan qujtema in tlapachoa.

Twenty-fourth Chapter, which telleth of turkey chicks.[26]

Injc cempoalli onnavi capitulo, intechpa tlatoa yn totolconentoton.

And when turkey chicks hatched, one might not enter among them who had a paramour, whether woman or man, or those who were married. When perchance the spouse [of one of them] had committed adultery, if he were to go in among [the chicks], they said: "He killeth them through filth."

Auh in jquac otlacatque in totolconentoton: avel inpan calaquj in momecatianj, in aço cioatl, in anoço toqujchtin, in anoço namjqueque: in jquac in aço oqujtlaxin inamjc, intla inpan ocalac, qujtoa: qujntlaçolmjctia.

24. *Ibid.*: *"quando armauan ratones en casa."*

25. *Ibid.*: *"no caerian los ratones: porque el maiadero, los aujsaria: para que no cayessen."*

26. *Totolconentoton*: read *totolconetoton.*

And when it appeared that indeed all the chicks fell upon their backs so that they died,[27] upon this they said: "They died of filth; perchance someone came to go in among them; or looked upon them; or indeed it was the householder who slew them by filth." Because of this, they believed, indeed all the turkeys had fallen upon their backs so that they died.

Auh injc neci çan muchintin aaquetztiuj injc mjquj totolpipil, ic qujtoa: ca tlaçolmjquj: aço aca inpan ocalaqujco, anoço oqujmjttac, anoço aca vel chane in oqujntlaçolmjcti: ic qujmatia, in çan muchin aaquetztivi totolme, injc mjquj.

It was said that also the same befell those who were married. If perchance somewhere one's spouse, whether woman or man, fell into adultery, they then believed that those which had fallen upon their backs or stumbled over, indeed accused him.

Qujl no iuh inpan muchioa in namjqueque: in aço cana qujtlaxima inamjc, in aço cioatl, anoço toqujchtin: injc qujmati, çan qujpiqui in aaquetztivetzi, anoce cana motlavitequj.

Twenty-fifth Chapter, which telleth of her who wove with yarn.

Injc cempoalli ommacujlli capitulo, ytechpa tlatoa: in icpatl qujqujti.

When [a woman] wove with yarn perhaps a mantle, or a shift, or a skirt, which came out awry, unevenly disposed, with crooked edges, they said and it was thought that the weaver of the mantle or shift was not generous. Just like a crooked seam, perverse [would she be]; not generous.[28]

In jcpatl, in aço tilmatli, anoço vipilli, anoço cueitl: in jquac qujqujti in chicopatilivi, in chicoviaqujxtiuh, in tennecujliuhtiuh, qujtoaia: qujlmach amo tlacaiollo yn tilmaoa, yn vipilli: çan cueciuhquj, çan tlatlaveliloc: amo tlacaiollo.

Twenty-sixth Chapter, which telleth of hail.

Injc cempoalli on chiquacen capitulo, ytechpa tlatoa in tecivitl.

When it rained, and much hail fell, one who there [had] his maize, chili, bean, or chía field scattered ashes from the hearth out of the entrance into the courtyard. It was said that thus his maize field would not be hailed out; it was thought that thus the hail would disappear.

In jquac qujavi, in cenca tecivi: in aqujn vnca imjl, anoço ychilcuen, anoço yiecuen, ychian: tleconextli qujiaoac qujoaltepeoa, itvalco: qujlmach yc amo teciviloz in jmjl, qujl ic poliui in tecivitl.

Twenty-seventh Chapter, which telleth of sorcerers.

Injc cempoalli on chicome capitulo, yntechpa tlatoa in tlatlavipuchti.

At night walked demons — perchance wizards and sorcerers — where they harmed one in one's home. When the householders saw them, when perhaps some [demon] so [would] harm them, they then placed an obsidian knife in water, behind the door, or in the courtyard. They laid it down at night. They said and it was believed that there the demons and sorcerers would look at their reflections when they would harm one, or there would be death, or sickness would come upon the people.

In iooaltica nemj tlatlacateculo: aço nanaoalti, tlavipuchtin in canjn ontepoloa in techan: in oqujmjttaque in aço itla ic qujnpoloa in chaneque: njman atlan conteca ytztli puertatitlan, anoço itoalco qujmana in iooaltica, qujtoaia: qujlmach vncan onmotezcavia in tlatlacateculo, yn tlavipuchtin in tepoloa: aço mjcoaz, anoce cocoliztli tepan muchioaz.

27. Corresponding Spanish text: *"los pollos se cayan muertos, las patas arriba: y esto, llaman tlaçolmjqui."*

28. Corresponding Spanish text: *"se parecia, en que la tela, se paraua bizcornada." Cuecueço,* in Siméon, *op. cit.,* is to make a false seam.

At once they fled; nevermore would they come to harm one when they had seen the obsidian knife resting in the water.

Ic njman choloa, aiocmo ceppa tepolotivi: in jquac oqujttaque itztli, atlan onoc.

Twenty-eighth Chapter, which telleth of the gnawed leavings of a mouse.

Injc cempoalli on chicuei capitulo, ytechpa tlatoa in qujmjchin ytentlacaoal.

Whatsoever a mouse had gnawed none might eat. It was said that he who ate what a mouse had left would be falsely accused. For it was said that the mouse came to steal it; he came to eat it in stealth. Wherefore no one might eat gnawed leavings of a mouse. Likewise it was said of it that he who ate the gnawed leavings of a mouse would be accused falsely of some sort of story or of that which might be missing.[29]

In qujmjchin in çaço tlein qujqua: aiac vel qujqualiaia, qujlmach in aqujn qujqualia yn q'caoa qujmjchin, itech tlatlamjz, ca mjtoa: oqujchtequjco in qujmjchin, oqujchtacaqua. Ipampa y, in aiac vel qujqualiaia in itentlacaoal qujmjchin. No yuh ipan mjtoz: in aqujn qujqua itentlacaoal qujmjchin, itech tlatlamjz, in çaço tlein tlatolli, anoço in tlein poliviz.

Twenty-ninth Chapter, which telleth of nails.

Injc cempoalli on chicunavi capitulo, ytechpa tlatoa in jztitl.

It was said that, when nails were pared, they cast them into the water. It was thought that this was because the water dog[30] would make good [nails] grow out — not broken; they would be sound. For when it drew someone into the water, [the water-dog] tore away his nails and eyes.

Qujlmach in tozti, in jquac motetequja, atlan contepeoaia, qujlmach ipampa: in iehoatl avitzotl, qualli qujxoaltiz: amo papatzaoaz, qualli yez. Ipampa: in jquac aqujn qujlaqujaia, qujqujxtiliaia in jzti, ioan ixtelolo.

Thirtieth Chapter, which telleth of sneezing.

Injc cempoalli ommatlactli capitulo, ytechpa tlatoa in acucholiztli.

When someone sneezed, they said, in times past: "Someone speaketh of me; someone saith well of me." Or they said: "Someone speaketh ill of me." Or they said: "Some people discuss me." It was thought that they made it evident, and knew, when they sneezed, that someone far away mentioned them.

In jquac aca acuchoa, qujtoaia in ie vecauh: aqujn nechitoa, aqujn nechteneoa: anoce qujtoaia: aqujn nêchicoitoa, anoçe qujtoa: aqujque in noca mononotza. Qujl iehoatl qujnezcaiotiaia, iehoatl ic qujmatia: in jquac acuchoa, in aca canapa veca qujnteneoa.

Thirty-first Chapter, which telleth of small children.

Injc cempoalli ommatlactli oce capitulo, ỹtechpa tlatoa in pipiltotonti.

When small children still lay in the cradle and something was eaten or drunk,[31] first they placed it upon [their] foreheads.[32] It was said that in this way [the child] would not hiccough or be afflicted by what he ate or drank.

In iehoantin in pipiltotonti: in jquac yn oc coçolco onoque: in jquac tlaqualo, anoço itla mjz, achto ijxquac contlaliaia, qujlmach ic amo tzitzicunoz, amo motolinjz in tlein moqua, anoço mj.

29. Corresponding Spanish text: *"de hurto, o de adulterio, o de otra cosa."*

30. *Avitzotl*: Seler, in *Collected Works*, Vol. IV, 2. 21, refers to it as a spectral water animal or sprite "which drew men down into the water and ate off the nails and hair of intoxicated men" (citing Sahagún, XI, cap. 4, § 2, and V, App., cap. 29). Santamaría, *op. cit.*, Vol. I, p. 66 (*ahuizote*), calls it *nutria o perro del agua* (Lutra felina).

31. Corresponding Spanish text: *"quando comjan, o beujan en presencia de algun njño."*

32. *Ibid.*: *"en la boca."*

Thirty-second Chapter, which telleth of green stalks of maize.

Of green stalks of maize, it was said that no one should chew them at night. One who chewed them at night, it was said, would thereby have toothache.[33] Whosoever had toothache had done this: he had chewed green stalks of maize at night. But if one were to chew a little, first he heated it in the fire. It was said that in this way nothing would befall him.

Injc cempoalli ommatlactli omome capitulo, ytechpa tlatoa in ooatl —

In iehoatl ooatl: qujlmach aiac vel iooaltica qujquaquaz: in aqujn iooaltica qujquaquaz, qujlmach ic tlanqualoz: iehoatl iuh qujchioa in aqujn tlanqualo: in iooaltica oqujquaqua ooatl. Auh intlaca qujquaquaz tepiton: achtopa qujtotonja tleco, qujl ic amo iuh ipan muchioaz.

Thirty-third Chapter, which telleth of creaking roof beams.

When during the day, or at night, the roof beams creaked, like the snapping of sticks, or, indeed, the roof beam itself broke, they said and it was thought that it indicated that perhaps the householder would die; or he would be sick, or else his children and kin living there in his house.

Injc cempoalli ommatlacomey capitulo, itechpa tlatoa: in calquavitl nanatzca.

In jquac cemjlhujtl, anoço iooaltica in tlatlatzca, in juhquj popoztequj: anoce vel poztequj in calquavitl, qujtoaia: qujl iehoatl qujnezcaiotia in aço ie mjqujz in chane, anoce ie mococoz, anoce ypilhoan, anoce yoajulque in vel vncã nemj ichan.

Thirty-fourth Chapter, which telleth of grinding stones.

The grinding stone was an omen of evil to the natives, when someone was grinding there, and it broke. Thus it appeared, it was said, that she who ground would die; or else the householder, or[34] their children, or some of their household would die.

Injc cempoalli ommatlactli onnavi capitulo, ytechpa tlatoa in metlatl.

In iehoatl metlatl, qujmotetzaujaia in njcan tlaca: in jquac aca vncan teztoc in oalpuztequj: ic necia: qujlmach ie mjqujz in otecia, anoce iehoatl in chane, anoco inpilhoan, anoce ceme mjqujzque in jnchantlaca.

Thirty-fifth Chapter, which telleth of drilling a new fire in the house.

When someone made himself a house, when he drilled a new fire for it, he assembled all the old men, and before them he drew the new fire. If quickly he made a fire — if it did not take long — they said and it was believed that the householder who had erected the house would rejoice and be content. But if with difficulty the fire fell, it was said that thus the old men saw that the householder would not be happy and content.

Injc cempoalli on caxtolli capitulo, ytechpa tlatoa yn calmamaliliztli.

In jquac aqujn mocaltiaia: in jquac calmamali, muchintin quĵcentlalia in vevetque, imjxpan in tlequauhtlaçaia. Intla iciuhca qujtlaça, in amo vecauhtica, qujtoa: qujlmach mopaqujltitiez, vellamattiez in chane: in omocalti. Auh intlacaiaxcan vetzi in tletl, qujlmach ic qujttaia in vevetque: amo pactiez, amo vellamattiez in chane.

---

33. Cf. Molina, *op. cit.*: *"tener neguijon, o gusano en los dientes y muelas."*

34. *Anoco.* The cedilla is omitted in the MS.

Thirty-sixth Chapter, which telleth of the sweat house.

Although the sweat house were very hot, where all bathed, if one known as a twin went there, then he would dispel the steam and destroy [the heat], however hot the sweat house were — even if he went to stand only at the doorway; even more so if he were to bathe among [the others]. But thus could he remedy it; it was said that four times he himself cast potsherds on the ground and sprinkled them with water. It was thought that thus he would not dispel the heat. It would be even hotter.

And when two were born who were called twins, it was said that wherever something was dyed, when [someone] dyed rabbit fur, they might not enter there. If they were to enter there, it was said, they would cast a spell over it; they would blow the colors off. It would come out badly — it would become multicolored, especially [if the dye were] chili red. But thus was it remedied: [the dyer] made him taste the dye water. It was said that in this way the rabbit fur would not be damaged.

Likewise, neither might those known as twins enter where tamales were cooking; because, it was said, if they came in there, they would also bewitch the tamales and the cooking pot. They would not cook, though [left there] all day. The tamales would each one cook only on one side. And in order to remedy it, so that it would not thus happen, when perhaps they went to enter, they placed the cooking pot on the fire. And if by chance the tamales were placed in the pot in [their] presence, they made them lay one [of them] in place. It was said that thus the tamales would not be harmed.

Injc cempoalli on castolli oce capitulo, ytechpa tlatoa: in temazcalli.

In temazcalli, in vncan netemalo: intlanel cenca totonquj, intla vmpa iaz, in moteneoa cocoa: njmã qujpouhtitlaça, qujpoloa injc cenca totonquj ocatca in temazcalli: intlanel çan qujiaoac onmoquetzatiuh: oc cenca intla tehoan motemaz. Auh injc patiz qujl nappa in vel inoma contlaçaz, in conatequjz tapalcatl: qujl ic amo qujpoloz, injc totonquj: çan oc cenca totonquj iez.

Ioan in vmẽtin tlacati, in mjtoa cocoa, qujlmach in canjn tlapalo, in qujpa tochomjtl: amo vel vmpa calaquj: yntla vmpa calaqujz, qujlmach qujxoxa, qujpitza in tlapalli: amo qualli in qujça, çan mocujcujcujloa: oc cenca yehoatl in chichiltic. Auh injc pati, achi contlapaloltia in tlapalatl: qujl ic amo ytlacaviz in tochomjtl.

No yoan in iehoantin in mjtoa cocoa, in canjn mopaoaci tamalli: amono vel vmpa calaquj: iehica qujlmach intla vmpa calaqujzque, no qujxoxa in tamalli, yoan in comjtl: amo vel ycuci, intlanel cemjlhujtl: çan chichicoycuciz in tamalli. Auh injc pati, injc amo iuh muchioaz: in jquac tla ocalaqujto, contlatiz in comjtl. Auh intlanoçe ijxpan mocontema tamalli, centetl ipan contlalilia: qujl ic amo ytlacaviz in tamalli.

Thirty-seventh Chapter, which telleth of the time when the teeth of small children dropped.

When the teeth of small children dropped out, the mothers cast them into a mouse-hole, or they said to their children: "Place it in the mouse-hole." For it was said that if they were not to do this, the small child's teeth could not grow; he would remain quite toothless.

* * *

Injc cempoalli on castolli omome capitulo, itechpa tlatoa: in jquac vetzi intlan pipiltotonti.

In jquac vetzi intlan pipiltotonti: yn tenanoan itlacoiocco contlaça in qujmjchin, anoçe inpilhoan, qujmjlhuja: ytlacoiocco xictlali in qujmjchin: iehica qujl intlacamo iuh qujchioazque, amo vel ixoaz in jtlan piltontli: çan tlancotoctic iez.

* * *

These superstitions harm the Faith, and therefore it is well to recognize them. Only these few have

Estas abusiones, enpecen a la fe: y por esso, conujene sabellas, y predicar, contra ellas. Anse puesto,

been recorded, though there are many more. But diligent preachers and confessors should seek them out, in order to understand them in confessions and to preach against them; for they are like a mange which sickeneth the Faith.

estas pocas: aunque ay otras muchas, mas los diligentes predicadores, y confessores, busquenlas, para entenderlas, en las confessiones: y para predicar, contra ellas: porque son como vna sarna, que enferma a la fe.